LEARNING FROM THE LIVED EXPERIENCES OF GRADUATE STUDENT WRITERS

LEARNING FROM THE LIVED EXPERIENCES OF GRADUATE STUDENT WRITERS

EDITED BY
SHANNON MADDEN
MICHELE EODICE
KIRSTEN T. EDWARDS
ALEXANDRIA LOCKETT

UTAH STATE UNIVERSITY PRESS
Logan

© 2020 by University Press of Colorado

Published by Utah State University Press
An imprint of University Press of Colorado
245 Century Circle, Suite 202
Louisville, Colorado 80027

All rights reserved

 The University Press of Colorado is a proud member of the Association of University Presses.

The University Press of Colorado is a cooperative publishing enterprise supported, in part, by Adams State University, Colorado State University, Fort Lewis College, Metropolitan State University of Denver, University of Colorado, University of Northern Colorado, Utah State University, and Western State Colorado University.

ISBN: 978-1-60732-957-2 (paperback)
ISBN: 978-1-60732-958-9 (ebook)
DOI: https://doi.org/10.7330/9781607329589

Library of Congress Cataloging-in-Publication Data

Names: Madden, Shannon, editor. | Eodice, Michele, 1957– editor. | Edwards, Kirsten T., editor. | Lockett, Alexandria, 1983– editor.
Title: Learning from the lived experiences of graduate student writers / edited by Shannon Madden, Michele Eodice, Kirsten T. Edwards, Alexandria Lockett.
Description: Logan : Utah State University Press, [2019] | Includes bibliographical references and index.
Identifiers: LCCN 2019055979 (print) | LCCN 2019055980 (ebook) | ISBN 9781607329572 (paperback) | ISBN 9781607329589 (ebook)
Subjects: LCSH: Academic writing.
Classification: LCC P301.5.A27 L43 2019 (print) | LCC P301.5.A27 (ebook) | DDC 808.06/6378—dc23
LC record available at https://lccn.loc.gov/2019055979
LC ebook record available at https://lccn.loc.gov/2019055980

The University Press of Colorado gratefully acknowledges the generous support of the University of Oklahoma Writing Center and Office of the Vice President for Research toward the publication of this book.

Cover illustrations, clockwise from top left: © Efetova Anna/Shutterstock; © CARACOLLA/Shutterstock; © Color Symphony/Shutterstock; © Liliya Kulianionak/Shutterstock.

Dedicated to the memory of Destiny Guerrero

CONTENTS

Acknowledgments ix

Introduction: Valuing Lived Experiences and Community Mentorship
Shannon Madden 3

PART 1: VOICES

1. The Trauma of Graduate Education: Graduate Writers Countering Epistemic Injustice and Reclaiming Epistemic Rights
Beth Godbee 35

2. Incidents in the Life of Kirsten T. Edwards: A Personal Examination of the Academic In-Between Space
Kirsten T. Edwards 52

3. Voices from the Hill: HBCUs and the Graduate Student Experience
Richard Sévère and Maurice Wilson 73

4. Race, Retention, Language, and Literacy: The Hidden Curriculum of the Writing Center
Wonderful Faison and Anna K. (Willow) Treviño 92

5. Paying It Forward by Looking Back: Six HBCU Professionals Reflect on Their Mentoring Experiences as Black Women in Academia
Karen Keaton Jackson, Hope Jackson, Kendra L. Mitchell, Pamela Strong Simmons, Cecilia D. Shelton, and LaKela Atkinson 108

PART 2: BRIDGES AND BORDERS

6. Graduate Writing in Communities: Critical Notes on Access and Success
Alexandria Lockett 125

7. *Mi Testimonio*: Crossing Borders in the Academy
Amanda E. Cuellar 131

PART 3: APPROACHES

8 "I Cut Off My Hand and Gave It to You, and You Gave It Back to Me with Three Fingers": The Disembodiment of Indigenous Writers and Writers of Color in U.S. Doctoral Programs
Jasmine Kar Tang and Noro Andriamanalina 139

9 Research Writing as an Adaptive Challenge: A Study with Implications for Supervisory Feedback Practices
Daniel V. Bommarito 156

10 From Avoidance to Action: Helping Dissertation Writers Manage Procrastination
Lisa Russell-Pinson and Haadi Jafarian 174

11 Dissertation Boot Camps: Developing Self-Efficacy and Building Community
Rachael Cayley 198

12 Not Just Nuts and Bolts: Building a Peer Review Framework for Academic Socialization
Anne Zanzucchi and Amy Fenstermaker 218

13 Playing with Theory in Graduate Writing Groups
Rochelle Rodrigo and Julia Romberger 242

14 Planning, Implementing, and Evaluating a Campus-Wide Graduate Writing Initiative at an Urban Midwestern University
Jennifer Friend, Jennifer Salvo, Michelle M. Paquette, and Elizabeth Brown 257

An After(Word) on the Future of Higher Education
Kirsten T. Edwards 278

About the Contibutors 283
Index 289

ACKNOWLEDGMENTS

With gratitude, the editors would like to thank all the graduate student writers with whom we have worked and who are the motivation for the work and for this collection. We have learned so much from working with the amazing scholars in this book; we are grateful to the authors for participating in this project and for sharing their stories and studies. By extension we also want to thank the research participants and the writers whose experiences are represented in this volume. We appreciate the labor and mentoring provided by the three anonymous reviewers who offered extensive feedback in several rounds on the works collected here. Many thanks to Steven Alvarez, Asao Inoue, Al Harahap, and Sarah Summers, who were an important part of the first phase of this project. Finally, we are grateful for Michael Spooner, Rachael Levay, Kami Day, and the editorial team at Utah State University Press for their support and labor in bringing this work to an audience.

LEARNING FROM THE LIVED EXPERIENCES OF GRADUATE STUDENT WRITERS

Introduction
VALUING LIVED EXPERIENCES AND COMMUNITY MENTORSHIP

Shannon Madden

It is important to remember that negative interactions with peers as well as in the community surrounding campus will also shape [students'] college experiences. Their words testify to the truth of the burden imposed on minoritized students. . . . It is a weight no student should be made to carry. Listen to their voices.

—Mary Jo Hinsdale

To say that racial justice is peripheral to [professional academic] work would ignore the realities faced by student writers. We need to listen to and learn from—and with—the voices and epistemologies of historically underrepresented communities.

—Jasmine Kar Tang and Noro Andriamanalina

The standard for whites to show their compassion & humanity is so low in comp-rhet that it's literally them learning to listen to PoC [people of color] while PoC have to constantly work to prove their humanity, have compassion for & accept the apologies of whites who are STILL learning.

—Anna K. (Willow) Treviño

Higher education probably will never listen. It was founded on a commitment to not listen.

—Kirsten T. Edwards

INTRODUCTION

I was in the audience at a faculty development workshop when Dr. Bryan Dewsbury, a renowned expert on inclusive practices in STEM education, encountered this question during his guest presentation: *"How many students are we talking about, really?"* Dewsbury was presenting data that showed how students of color were experiencing substantially larger rates of attrition in core courses like chemistry and biology, known informally to students as the "weed-out" courses that prevent the underprepared from entering the upper-division coursework of their desired major. The statistics showed that roughly 50 percent of all U.S.-born students of color enrolled in these courses were receiving Ds or Fs or not completing. A few slides later in the presentation, Dewsbury noted that students of color comprised roughly 8 percent of the enrollment totals of those courses overall. At this point, a senior faculty member in the audience interrupted. "How many students are we talking about, really?," he said loudly. "You were saying half, but if you're only talking about 8 percent of students overall, 4 percent doesn't amount to much. You're really only talking about a handful of students." We were only a few minutes into the presentation and nowhere near the Q&A. Several in the audience turned to look at the man who spoke. I shifted in my chair. Dewsbury took a beat and then answered with astonishing calm and grace, "It may only be a handful of students. But what are the pathways to inclusion for those students? How can we help all of our students complete the course successfully rather than simply allowing them to fail out?"

The faculty member's question—*How many students are we talking about, really?*—prompts reflection on a range of deeper issues relevant to graduate education. In particular, it should make us ask ourselves, How many students must be involved, how many people must be affected by something before we think that *something* is impactful? Important to assess? Meaningful to the trajectory of individual lives? Essential to consider as we design spaces, courses, policies, and programming for students? As is well documented, attrition rates for graduate students overall have been hovering around 50 percent for three decades or more (Bowen and Rudenstein 1992; Casanave 2016; Council of Graduate Schools 2008; Golde 2005; Lovitts 2001). Among those who leave their graduate programs, students from historically marginalized groups are statistically more likely to suffer from attrition or prolonged time to degree (Bell 2011; Council of Graduate Schools 2008; National Center for Education Statistics 2012; Sowell, Allum, and Okahana 2015). A 2017 report by the Council of Graduate Schools (CGS) shows that in recent years, the number of earned doctorates by Black students as well as students of Latinx origin were the highest they have been in the last decade (Okahana 2017). However, the percentages of those students among doctoral students overall have continued to stagnate (Okahana 2017). Hispanic/Latinx students earn 7 percent of doctoral degrees; Black and African American students represent 6.5 percent of earned doctorates.

Less than 1 percent of all earned doctorates go to Indigenous or Native American-identified students (Okahana 2017).

These numbers suggest that even when institutions or individuals are doing better, graduate education writ large still has a long way to go toward becoming inclusive. In a sense, the question *How many students are we talking about?* is already operating in myriad ways when it comes to change in higher education. When faculty and administrators ask how much effort or money should be put toward a particular policy, program, or initiative—whether it will "move the needle"—they restate the question *How many students are we talking about?* in different terms. How many students can we impact with this program, and is that number big enough to justify whatever it will cost us in labor, time, effort, or attention? How many students are enough to matter? The faculty member who interjected his question during Dewsbury's presentation, a cisgender white man with stereotypical disheveled gray hair and dressed-down attire, has probably never had to wonder whether his experiences are being considered in programmatic decisions or his needs accounted for in educational practice. If a problem does not seem to impact everyone or even the majority of students, there is a tendency to minimize its importance. If white administrators and faculty do not have access to that experience themselves because it does not reflect their own background or it does not align with the ways we experienced graduate education—as I may not as a cisgender white woman—we may not even recognize it is happening. That is called *privilege*. The question *How many students?* absolves white administrators and faculty from prioritizing the needs and experiences of marginalized students. *There aren't that many here, so we don't have to worry about them, right?*

Of course, many factors overlap and coalesce to produce problems of attrition, noncompletion, and lack of diversity in our graduate programs. This collection strives not to be reductive of these multiple factors but to highlight how these issues play out from the perspective of lived experience—from the perspective of the graduate students who are impacted. Paying attention to and learning from graduate students' lived experiences, this collection asserts, is essential to identifying pathways to inclusion and to creating institutional structures that welcome graduate students from historically marginalized groups to contribute new knowledges, epistemologies, and innovative research studies to their disciplines. Doing so requires, first, that we recognize students as holders and creators of knowledge (Delgado Bernal 2002). Toward that end, *Learning from the Lived Experiences of Graduate Student Writers* bridges graduate students' voices and narratives of their lived experiences with recommendations for responsive and critical models for mentoring, teaching, and working with graduate student writers. The chapters offer testimony, experiential data, qualitative scholarship, and critical reflections that attest to how inclusion, discrimination, community, and identity function in the various rhetorical and educational contexts graduate student writers encounter.

As the title of the collection implies, listening to students' stories and seeking to understand their experiences is a forceful theme throughout the book. Narrative has been an important mode of inquiry for scholars in many disciplines and for many communities. In a special issue of the *Journal of Educational Research* on narrative inquiry, Petra Munro Hendry (2009) makes the point that in the West, narrative is typically construed as the opposite of science, but Hendry wants us to reconceptualize inquiry beyond a binary framework that privileges science and empiricism. As she notes, new ways of making, representing, and communicating knowledges are necessary if we are to innovate research and push the boundaries of our understandings (77). Critical race and writing theorists such as Keith Gilyard (1991), Victor Villanueva (2006), Jacqueline Jones Royster and Gesa Kirsch (2012), Elaine Richardson (2003), Candace Epps-Robertson (2016), Aja Martinez (2016), and Jamila Kareem (2018) remind us of the importance of narratives and storytelling to reveal insights and illuminate nuanced issues in more depth and complexity (see also Clandinin 2000). In addition to data-supported studies, authors in this collection use narratives of their own experiences and the voices of their research participants to illustrate circumstances within academe that impact graduate writers but that may not be immediately evident on the surface or easily quantifiable through statistical and empirical evidence. Moreover, as Candace Epps-Robertson (2016) notes, "Personal stories are a means for underrepresented groups to push against master narratives that often silence the experiences of those who are othered." The powerful narratives in this collection demonstrate the rhetorical force of testimony[1] and highlight critical issues from the perspective of lived experience—from the perspective of the individuals and groups impacted. In stories of lived experience, we can see critical issues in context (van Manen 1990). John Dewey (1938) noted that education is interactive, relational, and experiential, and the experience of education from the student's perspective is what we need to know more about and pay more attention to (Eodice, Geller, and Lerner 2016). One way to do that, as this collection shows and as Linda Tuhiwai Smith (1999), Mary Jo Hinsdale (2015), and Jasmine Kar Tang and Noro Andriamanalina (2016) remind us, is through honoring their voices and learning from their experiences.

While the charge to listen to and learn from students' experiences may seem to emphasize the personal and individual, this collection persistently foregrounds the systemic nature of the issues that impact graduate student writers as well. The majority of graduate education in the U.S. context takes place in predominantly white institutions (PWIs) that are founded on—and continue to enact—a long history of cultural exclusion and eradication (Dancy, Edwards, and Davis 2018). Historians of education have pointed out that the establishment of U.S. educational institutions was intertwined with colonial settler imperialism (Churchill 2004; Dancy, Edwards, and Davis 2018; Wilder 2013; Wright and Tierney 1991). Many U.S. universities, including some considered today to be the most elite campuses in the country (e.g., Harvard, Princeton, Yale), included in their early university mission statements explicit objectives to "civilize" and colonize Indigenous peoples (Churchill 2004; Dancy, Edwards, and Davis 2018; Wright and Tierney 1991). Native students' hair was cut and their traditional clothing was traded out for uniforms, and they received severe physical punishments for speaking Indigenous languages in these schools (Wright and Tierney 1991). Ward Churchill (2004) explores how this educational system amounted to cultural genocide. When nondominant cultural practices, languages, and epistemologies were not punished and erased, they were ignored and dismissed; Smith (1999) outlines the processes through which Eurocentric knowledge systems have come to occupy an unchallenged and colonizing position of cultural superiority in Western educational institutions. Hinsdale (2015) extends Smith's ideas to consider how entrenched practices of cultural eradication continue to impact students from historically marginalized groups in the academy (30–31). As she puts it, "Mentoring can be one means of assimilating a student into the academic status quo" by reproducing the logic of white supremacy in mentoring models, instead of using mentorship interactions to enable students to innovate and transform knowledge, study the questions that interest them, and bring their full identity to bear on the academic context (33).

The work of deconstructing white supremacist practices in higher education is more important than ever given our current political moment. In the United States, Black and brown people and children are routinely killed by police officers (*Michael Brown, Philando Castile, Stephon Clark, Terence Crutcher, Eric Garner, Tamir Rice, Magdiel Sanchez, Joey Santos, Walter Scott*) or die while in custody of the state (*Tanisha Anderson, Sandra Bland, Freddie Gray, Jameek Lowery, Natasha McKenna, Jeffrey Pendleton, Derek Williams*). These violences extend and infect university contexts; on college campuses, white students and parents have called the cops to report

Black and brown students who are eating lunch (*Oumou Kanoute*), sleeping in their dormitory building (*Lolade Siyonbola*), and participating in a campus tour as prospective students (*Lloyd Skanahwati Gray, Thomas Kanewakeron Gray*). At the University of Maryland, the athletics staff showed so little care for the health of football player Jordan McNair that he died of a heat stroke during training. While these incidents may not seem directly related to historical patterns of cultural exclusion, T. Elon Dancy, Kirsten T. Edwards, and James Earl Davis (2018) trace the treatment of Black and brown people in early U.S. universities to our current context in the United States. They, like Denise Baszile (2006), point out that academia mirrors these violences in a different way. In particular, they note that a settler colonialist paradigm is still evident today in, for instance, differentiated labor expectations for academics of color and the ways universities still capitalize on (and profit from) Black and brown bodies as property (Dancy, Edwards, and Davis 184). The broader U.S. political context that is hostile to and oppressive of communities and individuals of color reverberates to interactions between students of color and the academic institutions in which they participate (Hinsdale 2015; Kynard 2015; Tang and Andriamanalina 2016). In this way, the question *How many students are we talking about?* is not only a provocation for us to reconsider our educational practices. The question also reveals a pervasive belief rooted in this broader pattern of dismissal, exclusion, and exploitation that graduate deans, faculty, and support service providers must acknowledge and actively dismantle. It is the explicit expression of the multitude ways Black and brown people are treated as disposable—as if they are "nobody"—in the U.S. nation-state (Hill 2016). The question shows us, once again, the consistent and intentional disregard for Black and brown lives. Valuing students from historically oppressed groups requires understanding and honoring their voices and experiences.

WHERE WE HAVE BEEN

While the research on graduate students' experiences has recently expanded, historically, conversations about graduate education have focused on strategies for helping students adapt to disciplinary communities of practice as they develop from novices to emerging experts. Over the past several decades, researchers have begun to investigate the conditions that lead graduate students to succeed—or not—in their academic disciplines. Within this burgeoning body of scholarship, interest in graduate students as writers has grown in a number of key areas. Early studies highlighted faculty mentorship and the multifaceted ways graduate students get apprenticed as they develop facility in disciplinary communication practices (Belcher 1994; Liu 2011; Myles and Cheng 2003; Schunk and Zimmerman 1998; Simpson and Matsuda 2008). This research prompted further inquiry into the needs and experiences of multilingual graduate students, who came to be recognized as a population with particular learning needs that require additional consideration and specialized attention (Matsuda 1998; Morita 2004; Seloni 2014).

Yet scholars also recognized that disciplinary communication practices are an acquired language even for English-fluent students (Casanave 2014; Curry 2016; Hyland 2004). As Christine Casanave puts it, "Academic discourse is a 'second' language to everyone, full of terminology (necessary), jargon (needless and pretentious), formal turns of phrases, and unfamiliar research methods, theories, and philosophical stances" (23). In this light, students undertaking advanced writing in graduate school must learn to enact the specialized discursive performances through which disciplinary knowledge is made (Curry 2016). However, the processes through which students are meant to gather information about disciplinary communication practices are typically left tacit and invisible (Kittle-Autry and Carter 2015; Swales 1996, 2004; Starke-Meyerring et al. 2011). In other words, when faculty assume too much about students' capabilities coming into their graduate programs, they communicate too little about the discursive practices that matter in particular disciplinary spaces. The challenge for pedagogies and support services for graduate writers, then, is to socialize and enculturate graduate students to academic communities of practice (Casanave and Li 2008; Curry 2016; Dressen-Hammouda 2008; Lave and Wenger 1991; Paré, Starke-Meyerring, and McAlpine 2011). Doing so would presumably make visible the language practices as well as the social expectations that orient graduate students as the emerging scholars of their fields.

WHERE WE ARE NOW

Recently the availability of approaches to working with graduate students as writers has expanded. The establishment of the Consortium on Graduate Communication as an official professional organization created a necessary opportunity to bring scholars from several fields together to share research and practical strategies for supporting graduate writers in a range of contexts. Several collections offer program models and data-supported strategies for working with graduate student writers, including Cecile Badenhorst and Cally Guerin's (2016) *Research Literacies and Writing Pedagogies for Masters and Doctoral Writers*,

Michelle Campbell and Vicki Kennell's (2018) faculty guide *Working with Graduate Student Writers*, Steve Simpson, Nigel Caplan, Michelle Cox, and Talinn Phillips's (2016) *Supporting Graduate Student Writers*, Susan Lawrence and Terry Zawacki's (2019) *Re/Writing the Center*, and special issues of *Across the Disciplines* (Brooks-Gillies, Garcia, Kim, Manthey, and Smith 2015) and the *Journal of Second Language Writing* (Starfield and Paltridge 2019). These volumes offer necessary interventions into institutional practice and perspectives on communication pedagogy for graduate student writers across disciplines. Despite these shifts in understanding and the rich literature on graduate communication development as a lifelong process of enculturation, the experiences of U.S.-born graduate students from historically marginalized groups have been underexamined, and voices of students from these groups have not been centered in the conversation. These voices would offer needed responses—and challenges—to the normative functions of academic enculturation. Significantly, similar patterns of oppression exist across academic rank for both graduate students and faculty—a parallel that indexes an underlying systemic issue.

Stories of how discrimination is woven throughout the experiences of faculty of color, with dis/abilities, on the LGBTQ+ spectrum, and from historically marginalized groups are documented in Gabriella Gutierrez y Muhs, Yolanda Niemann, Carmen González, and Angela Harris's collection *Presumed Incompetent* (2012), Patricia Matthew's edited volume *Written/Unwritten* (2016), and Eric Grollman's blog *Conditionally Accepted*, among other places. Graduate students and faculty of color report similar experiences of microaggressions (DeCuir-Gunby and Gunby 2016; Gomez 2015; Sue 2010), tokenism and pressure to perform acceptable forms of cultural identity (Alvarez, Brito, Salazar, and Aguilar 2016; Burrows 2016; Green 2016; Holling, Fu, and Bubar 2012; Niemann 2012), being made to feel unwelcome (Allen 2012), and being "presumed incompetent" (Allen 2012; Burrows 2016; Martinez 2016). In the introduction to her edited collection about the experiences of faculty of color on the tenure track, Matthew (2016) notes that while in many cases the oppression is not explicit, overt, or intentional, there is nonetheless a distinct "interrelationship of race, meritocracy, and institutionalized discrimination" (8). Jay Dolmage's (2017) *Academic Ableism* and Abigail Stewart and Virginia Valian's (2018) *An Inclusive Academy* likewise examine how inequities play out in hiring, tenure, and promotion practices for academics from historically marginalized groups, which form a pipeline of oppression experiences that contribute significantly to faculty attrition (Garvey and Rankin 2018). The conversation about graduate students as writers must grapple with the fact of structural academic racism if we are to address the problems of attrition, underrepresentation, and negative and traumatic experiences for graduate students from historically oppressed groups.

The entanglement of meritocracy with structural discrimination—what Edwards in chapter 2, drawing from critical race theory, calls the "myth of meritocracy"—is poignantly visible at the graduate level, where students' ability to perform unspoken and "occluded" genre conventions (Swales 1994, 2004) in such high-stakes writing situations as the dissertation is viewed as evidence of their disciplinary acumen and intellectual capability. Many scholars have noted how pedagogical gaps and obscured academic communication practices enact a "survival-of-the-fittest" mentality that impacts scholarly productivity and learning development for graduate student and faculty writers (Aitchison et al. 2012; Boice 1990; Geller 2013; Tarabochia and Madden 2018). In the context of research writing, discrimination is intertwined with writing assessment (Inoue 2015); assumptions about "rigor" and "fitness" hide the implicit epistemic and ideological judgments behind them. When a white faculty member asks a Black student if they are an athlete, it may be an obvious microaggression. Yet telling a Black graduate student that their research interests do not fit in the field or that their voice does not sound like it belongs in an academic journal hides discriminatory value statements behind a façade of intellectual neutrality and ideological objectivity. To be told your Black body does not belong in the "white space" (Anderson 2015) of the academy may be offensive and painful; to be told your writing does not fit—connected as writing is to your identity, the issues and questions you care about, and the way you express yourself—is more insidious and harder to challenge.

Marginalized students' reports of their writing and mentoring experiences should urge us to consider how writing pedagogies at the graduate level reinscribe hegemonic perspectives and reinforce what Asao Inoue (2015, 2016, 2019) calls a "white racial habitus." In Inoue's words, "A dominant white discourse . . . operates in all of our judgments on writing" (2016, 97). Importantly, the conversation about how best to help students succeed raises questions about how "success" gets defined—success for what community and on whose terms. Graduate communication experts need to learn *from students* how to support them in accomplishing their own goals they set for themselves that reflect their identities and communities. Only then will we be able to support student writer-researchers in doing work that matters to them, in taking risks that push the boundaries of knowledge and move disciplines forward.

In response to these exigencies and how they materialize in writing center work with and by graduate students, Michele Eodice and I coedited a special collection of *Praxis: A Writing Center Journal* in 2016 that focused on graduate writers' lived experiences, especially those of writers from historically marginalized groups. For that collection, we asked scholars of color, scholars with disabilities, and multilingual scholars to share their stories about writing as graduate students in predominantly white, predominantly abled universities—spaces that have historically been and continue to be exclusionary and oppressive of individuals situated outside those identities. In an effort to describe and ultimately disrupt the ways graduate programs erect barriers to access for students from underrepresented groups, authors offered critical reflections, theoretical discussions, methods for nondominant and nonnormative mentorship, new models for graduate writing communities, and frameworks that indicate a need for reconsidering graduate writing center work.

The *Praxis* special issue, which included the work of thirty authors, brought to light what is missing from much of the literature on graduate support and professionalization—direct engagement with the lived experience of writing as a graduate student. The *Praxis* articles provide testimony from scholars of color about being disrespected, talked down to, and "presumed incompetent" by faculty mentors, writing center consultants, and professional colleagues (Burrows 2016; Green 2016; Martinez 2016; Smith-Campbell and Littles 2016). The articles demonstrate that linguistic difference is (still) framed as deficit in the academy (Cirillo-McCarthy, Del Russo, and Leahy 2016; Green 2016), despite extensive research on how hegemony functions through literacy education and how Standard American English has been used as a gatekeeping mechanism throughout the history of writing instruction in the United States (see for instance Farr, Seloni, and Song 2009; Greenfield and Rowan 2011; Inoue 2015; Matsuda 2006; Rafoth 2015; Villanueva 2006; Young 2007; Young, Young-Rivera, and Lovejoy 2013). Contributors to the *Praxis* collection document how others' perceptions of their embodied identities impact their lived experiences as marginalized students in PWIs. As Cedric Burrows (2016) notes, African American students are compelled to perform acceptable versions of Blackness or cultural identity within the PWI, they are treated as if they should appreciate white benevolence for "being allowed into their institutions," and they are expected to recognize themselves and their identity as an intrusion into [white] university spaces. Moreover, they are considered to represent their entire race; Black students are treated as if they are multiple iterations of the same person or identity rather than individuals. Burrows describes these factors together as a "Black tax" that compounds the difficulty of the graduate student experience, which is already challenging and isolating (Cotterall 2013).

In these and other ways, *Praxis* issue 14.1 made evident the multiple ways students/scholars from historically marginalized groups are disproportionately impacted by disenfranchising institutional discourses and structures that compel particular kinds of performances, as well as the need for paying attention to their voices and narratives. For instance, feelings of isolation and imposter syndrome are sometimes dismissed as commonplaces of the graduate experience, as something all graduate students go through at some point. Yet for minoritized students, imposter syndrome can be amplified by the belief, which gets communicated to them implicitly and explicitly, that they are token "diversity additions" in their graduate programs (Alvarez et al. 2016; Burrows 2016; Green 2016; Martinez 2016) rather than valued for contributing to the educational and experiential richness that accrues in environments that not only welcome but foster cultural difference. The authors speak to the difficulty of engaging the high stakes genres of graduate school in educational environments that do not support student communities, that are selective about which students they groom, and that communicate to students from marginalized groups that they do not belong in the PWI, in their discipline, or in academe.

As *Learning from the Lived Experiences of Graduate Student Writers* shows, what gets ignored in discussions of programs and interventions is epistemic injustice—in which difference becomes a barrier in the mind of the institution and the advisor, in which a student's way of knowing is discounted or dismissed, and in which the reasons for attrition reside within the student's body. Miranda Fricker (2007, 1) defines epistemic injustice as unwillingness to grant another person the right to their own knowledges and ways of knowing (see also Godbee 2017). For instance, listening to someone and automatically disbelieving what they say is a form of epistemic injustice. Epistemic injustice can take many forms ranging from mild skepticism to actively believing what a person says is incorrect, irrelevant, or untrustworthy; often epistemic injustice is rooted in prejudiced beliefs. In May 2018 at Yale University, a white woman called the police when she saw a Black graduate student, Lolade Siyonbola, napping in the dormitory common area—and then the police questioned whether Siyonbola had the right to be there even when she showed them her key to the building and her student ID. That is epistemic injustice. The 2012 volume *Presumed Incompetent* (Gutiérrez y Muhs, Niemann, González, and Harris) lays out various forms of epistemic injustice as they relate to women of color in higher education. As chapters in *Presumed Incompetent* as well as the works in this collection show, the insidious presumption that scholars who inhabit nonwhite, dis/abled, or LGBTQ+ bodies do not "belong" in the academy is still pervasive and gets communicated to students in myriad ways. Beth Godbee (2017) elaborates Fricker's work on intellectual courage in the context of student writers' rights to their own language(s). Particularly because writing at the graduate level and making an original contribution to the scholarship requires boldness and confidence, it is essential to consider how we can affirm graduate writers and support them in taking scholarly risks that push the boundaries of our knowledge forward (see also Godbee, chap. 1 of this collection). We can start to do so when we stop denying them the rights to their own ways of knowing.

The charge to acknowledge and challenge epistemic injustice for graduate student writers highlights a central tension of mentoring practice. As Griffin Keedy and Amy Vidali (2016) note, mentors' assumptions about the writing process always and inevitably influence how they mentor student writers—how we think about and approach writing ourselves influences how we communicate what writing is and how it functions as a process to student writers we advise and student teachers we train. In this way, assumptions about writing become both normative and normalizing for individual mentors, institutionally and disciplinarily. The systematic way writing mentorship can circumscribe writers and their writing materialized as particular challenges for us as editors during the process of editing the *Praxis* collection, as well as this book. For both collections, we invited articles across a range of genres and explicitly sought pieces that exceed the boundaries of traditional "academic" writing. However, as we encountered writing that challenged the discourse norms of our field's mainstream publications, we often found ourselves struggling to provide feedback that was constructive without being regulatory. Part of the challenge was an audience-based one; audiences encountering an explicitly academic venue such as a scholarly journal or book collection expect adherence to certain conventions, we reasoned. Yet we also wanted to make space in both collections for opportunities and insights outside the boundaries of traditional academic writing. So our problem in providing feedback to authors who challenge (white/Western) academic conventions was how to help writers orient the audiences without colonizing their own writerly voices and discourses. This problem seems to us to be the perennial one for writing instructors and has particular relevance for working with graduate writers—How can we as writing mentors encourage, foster, and value a range of discursive possibilities within a system that explicitly values only a limited set of linguistic expressions? Our experience led us to rethink mentoring as one of the commonplaces of working with students.

Significantly, the *Praxis* special issue offered many avenues and approaches toward inclusion and empowerment—not by bestowing empowerment upon marginalized students as if it belonged to white faculty and was available to give away but by creating the conditions through which such students could activate their agency, do the work they care about, and ultimately teach their teachers (and their disciplines). Graduate students testified to empowering themselves through writing co-mentoring communities and self-sponsored coalitions (Alvarez et al. 2016), as well as informal affinity groups (Bell and Hewerdine 2016). Scholars described using their graduate-level writing projects to connect to their identities in a meaningful way while contributing new research knowledge and transforming disciplinary understandings. (Epps-Robertson 2016; Green 2016). Charmaine Smith-Campbell and Steven Littles (2016) advocated and modeled a Freirean "pedagogy of love" approach—an approach to working with students rooted in justice, respect, collaboration, and transformative dialogue.

Yet the collection also showed there is much work still to be done if we are to make programs and institutions—and graduate education writ large—inclusive. Inoue (2015, 2016, 2019) claims forcefully that a white racial habitus infuses the teaching of writing across contexts. The work for faculty advisors, writing centers, intensive English programs, and those who support graduate students' professional development is to recognize and honor writers' identities and lived experiences. We also must check and challenge the complex and intricate ways white racial privilege, whiteliness, and Standard American English determine writing pedagogies, expectations, and standards at the graduate level (Inoue 2016, 94). We must move beyond accountability toward pedagogies, program models, and research methods that are "answerable" (Patel 2015) to the lives of the writers we seek to support. While the academy has typically characterized mentoring efforts, honoring identity, and building community as separate categories of support, the revision offered in *Learning from the Lived Experiences of Graduate Student Writers* calls for integration. We see a trend in questioning the value of mentoring as a solution to the need for engaging and enculturating students (see Hinsdale 2015). Familiar mentoring models, whether destined relationships or designed by program initiatives, may be lacking in vision. Can we even name the downstream goal of our mentoring, or are we simply going through the motions? What if our mentoring methods had a trickle down effect?

WHAT WE NEED NEXT

Perhaps it is time to reconsider our mentoring practices. The traditional model of apprenticeship through which graduate students learn to perform research by carrying out faculty study designs serves an important function in graduate training—and yet it is a colonized model. If students are expected to serve as temporary employees or interns who perfunctorily execute faculty lab work or continue (without challenging) the research legacies of their field's best-known scholars, knowledge advances will be ever more incremental. As becomes clear, knowledge innovations will require new research methods and patterns of communication (Hendry 2009; Tardy 2016); as such, they will also require new mentoring models. Hinsdale (2015) writes, "Mentoring [students who are positioned as] outsiders calls for an open, responsive approach to students—one that welcomes not only their bodies and social experiences, but also the knowledge[s] they bring and the questions they wish to research" (xiv). This approach is critical to enacting support for graduate writers—it is not enough to increase graduate enrollments for students of color and assume doing so will fix the white supremacy problem in higher education. We must recognize how certain ways of knowing are privileged in the academy over others and consider what impact that privileging has on writers from marginalized identity groups, as well as the future of knowledge across fields. When we are not critical about how university language practices enact and sustain structural and epistemic privilege, we risk communicating to students who occupy nondominant identities and perspectives that their unique ways of knowing and forms of expertise are invalid. Further, we risk stifling innovation—and graduate students are supposed to be contributing new knowledge to their disciplines; their work is meant to offer the next "big idea."

We imagine dissertations developed within a more "expansive frame" (Engle, Lam, Meyer, and Nix 2012) could lead to remarkable outcomes. For example, as a doctoral student at Clemson University, A. D. Carson created a mixtape as part of his dissertation, "Owning My Masters: The Rhetoric of Rhymes and Revolutions" (2017). As found in *The Meaningful Writing Project* (Eodice, Geller, and Lerner 2016), assignments designed with an expansive frame invited students to make a personal connection (to interests, passions, people, and topics) while imagining their future selves. If we can bring an expansive frame to our work with graduate student writers, we might begin to open a space for student agency and empowerment. If we can resist (simply) attempting enculturation to the university, we can then see ways to challenge the structures that colonize knowers/learners and do more to reverse epistemic injustices

(Aitchison and Mobray 2013; Bosanquet and Cahir 2016; French 2016; Fricker 2007; Peterson 2007; Welch 2002). Not only would we offer more opportunities for students to engage multiple facets of their ways of knowing, we could acknowledge that the process of writing a dissertation is part of this whole being and becoming, especially if it is set within an expansive frame (Engle et al. 2012) that allows for more creative and imaginative work tied to the researcher identity.

The focus on identity points back to community. Supporting graduate students in confirming and establishing researcher identit(ies) points back to the contexts that support or inhibit these processes. The process of connecting with identity happens in dialogue with others, in the exchange of ideas, and in building context for one's own perspectives and experiences. For this reason, *Learning from the Lived Experiences of Graduate Student Writers* challenges graduate educators to leverage mentoring as a community investment. As Phillips (2016) puts it, the goal of our programs and pedagogies should be to produce teams of better writers, communities of better writers—not to produce better writers in isolation. Agnes Bosanquet and Jayde Cahir (2016) tell us that intentional and intensive attention to researcher identity, when "developed in conjunction with the support of scholarly community, can act as a buffer against negative experiences" (141). Godbee and Julia Novotny (2013) show how feminist co-mentoring enables writers to make stronger claims and more confidently assert their positions, and Godbee (2018) explores how multiple mentoring structures "can disperse the concentrated power associated with a single supervisor [and] can help [writers] with reclaiming personal power and becoming empowered to stand tall in one's research and professional identity." Jeanette Alarcón and Silvia Bettez (2017) call for nonhierarchical peer mentoring, the development of partnerships and coalitions, and valuing "community cultural wealth" as efforts departments can begin (25). Michelle Maher and Brett Say (2016) advocate for multiple mentors, cochaired committees, and more coauthoring in the process of earning a doctorate. Further, they suggest programs begin to "require doctoral supervisors to create and actively maintain a collaborative intellectual culture within their own department" (291). Carmen Kynard (2017) explores how mentors who shared racial identifications provided her as a Black woman academic with "a framework for surviving hostile environments based on the cultural memory and history of my own people." As she puts it, inclusion for Black scholars at PWIs is not (only) a question of making clear the implicit rules of the academy, "it's about centering Black thought and Black life in people's lives at the academy."

Our sense is that most research recommendations and institutional fixes tend to ask faculty to be more "accountable" in the process of advising graduate student writers. We propose that mentoring models centered on the concept of accountability shift to the concept of *answerability* (Patel 2015). As Leigh Patel (2015) describes it, "Answerability includes aspects of being responsible, accountable, and part of an exchange. It is a concept that can help to maintain the coming-into-being with being in-conversation-with" (73). She advocates answerability to learning, to knowledge, and to context. The chapters in this collection are a timely contribution to this movement. Answerability requires centering marginalized voices and the lives of marginalized peoples in the academy (Kynard 2017). The authors here provide lenses for rethinking and refracting our work with graduate student writers and offer insights about areas of the graduate writing experience such as mentoring, identity, and community that challenge the easy assumption that the potential for success or failure resides entirely in the individual student. In this way, we hope this collection will inspire our audience to think beyond pedagogies and practices that seek to acclimate or enculturate the individual graduate student to university cultures. Rather, our goal should be to privilege incomes—the concerns, experiences, knowledges, and goals students bring to the academy—over outcomes (Guerra 2008). We must do more to recognize the sites at which institutions of higher education are systematically excluding and oppressing students from underrepresented groups and create the conditions that will enable all students to do the work they care about and that is needed for the future.

The movement to recast mentoring as a community endeavor expands possibilities for graduate students to develop and gain confidence in their new identities. At the University of Michigan, a group of graduate students in the sciences created MiSci Writers, a student-led organization that offers communication support for other students (MiSciWriters). Students at the University of North Carolina Nutrition Research Institute founded a student-led group that provides professional development opportunities for students and postdoctoral researchers (Catalyst Group). This kind of grassroots, student-led support structure has potential to decolonize mentoring and also to offer a space where student writers can create community while developing their scholarly and professional identities. Doctoral students are at work on problem solving for our futures, and they are, through their writing, helping us imagine the next thing. Constraining students to standard genres and language forms leaves little room for innovation, especially for students from culturally or linguistically minoritized communities.

What is needed next, as this collection shows, is attention to students' lived experiences and an understanding of the conditions that promote students' flourishing and development—*on their own terms*. By focusing on the responsibility we have as educators to fostering our students' growth, this collection seeks to challenge the narrow ways success is defined and modeled in graduate education and to consider how institutional racism functions within and throughout graduate programs in the United States, infusing trauma into students' experiences. In this way, the collection proposes a "pedagogy of love" approach (Smith-Campbell and Littles 2016). A pedagogy of love is rooted in epistemic justice (Smith-Campbell and Littles 2016) and in this way is "answerable" to students (Patel 2016). Work with graduate student writers should be grounded in pedagogical love in order to foster students' engagement with their disciplines and enable them to innovate their fields. Helping students develop their own intellectual and writerly identities, rather than forcing them to fit existing or traditional beliefs about who they should be or recreating students in our own image, should be our mission. This collection aims to shed light on paths toward that goal.

WHAT WE CAN LEARN FROM GRADUATE STUDENT WRITERS' LIVED EXPERIENCES

This collection offers narratives of graduate students' experiences as writers in order to provide a complex and nuanced picture of what graduate education is like in its lived reality. The stories offered here challenge universities and individuals to pay attention to students' voices. We imagine that the problems highlighted in this collection are already felt by many in their local contexts and that people may want an easy fix. *Learning from the Lived Experiences of Graduate Student Writers* does not offer a manual for how to fix the problems of graduate student attrition, prolonged time to degree, and oppression in your university. Instead, we offer a framework for how to think about these problems. The chapters offered here seek to reorient perceptions of what the actual problem is; rather than lumping marginalized students together as people who are going to struggle and who may not finish, we must acknowledge who they are as individuals and honor their identities, which is something universities have historically and intentionally worked not to do. We must reorient ourselves to the question of how students from historically oppressed groups should be supported—and recognize the reparations they are owed (Dancy, Edwards, and Davis 2018). Researchers and institutions, this collection shows, must pay careful attention to students' experiences and needs if we are to enact scholarship, programming, pedagogies, and institutional practices responsive to the lived realities of the writers we hope to support.

Part 1: Voices offers theoretical frameworks, narratives, and voices of students' experiences in graduate education. Beth Godbee (chap. 1) advances the central concept this collection advocates and performs: *epistemic justice*. Through her study of writers' talk around their writing processes, Godbee explores the traumatic impact of graduate education on scholars from minoritized groups and shows how feminist co-mentoring communities can be inclusive sites where students counter epistemic injustices and heal epistemic trauma. Godbee challenges administrators and educators to ask themselves of every policy, program, and interaction whether it affirms graduate writers' rights. Kirsten T. Edwards's award-winning article—written while she was a graduate student—uses narrative inquiry to explore how academics of color are positioned as "dislocated insiders" in PWI spaces (chap. 2). By "crystallizing" individual perspectives from different positions on a spectrum of privilege, Edwards analyzes how minoritized individuals occupy an "in-between" positionality within antagonistic university environments hostile to their very presence. Her analysis hearkens to Sara Ahmed's point, which was posted on October 24, 2017, on her blog *Feminist Killjoys*, that marginalized individuals are burdened with adapting themselves to existing oppressive structures rather than the onus being on the institution to change itself to become more inclusive.

Several chapters show what PWIs could learn from the ways community is modeled and enacted at minority-serving institutions (MSIs). Although researchers have begun to address academic/institutional belongingness for students from historically marginalized groups and the implications of belongingness for motivation and retention (see e.g., Gray 2017; Gray, Hope, and Matthews 2018; Ostrove, Stewart, and Curtin 2011; Solorzáno 1998; Strayhorn 2012), research is limited on how belonging materializes as a writing issue in graduate students' academic experiences such that communication support reinforces epistemologically oppressive paradigms of who or what "belongs" in graduate education. The theme of belonging is important in the work of Richard Sévère and Maurice Wilson (chap. 3), who reflect on their experiences in the transition from undergraduate education in historically Black colleges/universities (HBCUs) to graduate school in a PWI. Their narratives highlight the competing burdens placed upon students from marginalized groups in the PWI of representativeness for their race/group on the one hand and the need to reject their culture in order to be accepted in the ivory (white) tower on the other. Sévère and Wilson note that writing center spaces and writing groups provided them with access to supportive cohorts and enabled a sense of belonging in otherwise unwelcoming conditions. Extending these ideas, Wonderful Faison and Anna K. (Willow) Treviño (chap. 4) offer a composite narrative of their parallel and distinct searches for hospitable spaces within the PWI as women of color. The details of their stories suggest how racist and classist assumptions are built into the material environment and pedagogies of the writing center, as well as how the peer-to-peer writing and language work that takes place in writing centers can enable student agency and "brave(r) spaces." Karen Keaton Jackson, Hope Jackson, Kendra L. Mitchell, Pamela Strong Simmons, Cecilia D. Shelton, and LaKela Atkinson (chap. 5) offer an edited discussion performance piece through which they reflect on their experiences mentoring and being mentored by other women of color in HBCUs. The authors share aspects of mentoring in HBCUs and communities of color that may be absent in PWI mentoring and emphasize the value and liberatory function of informal mentoring groups among scholars of shared racial identifications. Taken together, the analyses and stories in part 1 reveal how universities can do more to foster inclusion and community for students from minoritized groups. By listening to their voices, we can see "through the eyes of the one who is living it or telling it" (Edwards 2009, 119). These perspectives show how essential it is to create welcoming spaces that make space for graduate student writers to activate their agency and that enable their sense of belongingness.

As the chapters in part 1 show, researchers and practitioners must grapple with students' lived experiences in the academy; these experiences construct and circumscribe their graduate-level writing, and students' experiences and perspectives should be central to our research and work with them. In Part 2: Bridges and Borders, Alexandria Lockett and Amanda E. Cuellar connect the frameworks and voices presented in part 1 of the collection to the data-supported approaches offered in part 3. Lockett (chap. 6) identifies key themes of the experiences in part 1, such as isolation, minoritization, and the persistent gatekeeping culture of graduate education that suggest that the question of how to support or motivate students must be reframed to consider "the scope of community necessary for ensuring graduate students' ability to strengthen their writing." Writing struggle, Lockett notes, "is also often a consequence of racism and linguistic imperialism—interrelated forces that reduce motivation as a traumatic effect." Cuellar's reflection (chap. 7) echoes Lockett's challenge to recognize how hegemonic conceptions of what graduate-level writing is materialize in students' experiences. Cuellar gathers several impressions that together make her wonder what "the conscious and unconscious expectations that inform professors' reactions to (or constructions of) [her] Otherness" are. Cuellar weaves metaphors of the border and border crossing with memories from graduate school to explain how as a Chicana woman at a PWI she felt discouraged by vague faculty feedback and a lack of connection with other writers. Cuellar reminds us that although the idea of a "natural academic writing voice" gets tossed around casually in a range of graduate education contexts, *academic voice* is a highly artificial white and Western construction that is not natural at all.[2]

While scholars have long since advocated the use of peer learning, these chapters provide evidence to support the integration of mentoring, community, and identity that is needed next. Jasmine Kar Tang and Noro Andriamanalina (chap. 8) present results from qualitative interviews with doctoral student writers of color and from Indigenous communities. They show that two common forms of feedback faculty give to these writers—praise and of shame—reflect "liberal multiculturalist ideologies that subsume or individualize racial/ethnic difference." As Tang and Andriamanalina show, two seemingly opposed forms of writing commentary (praise and shame) can equally be "whitely exercise[s] of racial privilege by white advisors." Mentoring around the dissertation writing process, then, becomes "another heightened site at which racism and racialization can surface in the lives of people of color." Daniel V. Bommarito (chap. 9) examines the impact of mentoring feedback on students' research writing processes in his study of two multilingual doctoral students working with a faculty advisor/supervisor.[3] Although the challenges students have in performing the conventions of graduate-level writing are often treated in institutional practice as technical problems, problems for which routinized solutions already exist, Bommarito shows graduate writing is better understood as being what Linda Flower describes as an "adaptive challenge"—a challenge that requires transformation in order to address it—that is too complex to solve within existing frameworks. This important distinction makes clear that "exhorting writers to perform a writing-related task does not necessarily induce acquisition the way we might expect were these technical problems"—they cannot be solved with an easy recipe or formulaic solution. Mentoring models must shift in response; writing at the graduate level has a psychosocial dimension and is not a simple matter of command of Standard Academic/American English. In that vein, Lisa Russell-Pinson and Haadi Jafarian (chap. 10) explore how writing a dissertation is wrapped up in the broader emotional situations students are positioned in; they show that procrastination on writing (among other struggles) can result from other causal factors such as unhealthy advisory relationships, financial difficulties, systemic barriers, and (fictional) idealized standards for what writers do and how they behave to which graduate students hold themselves. Drawing from composite narratives and extensive experience working with graduate student writers, they explore the role of emotional factors such as stress and anguish in the writing process and demonstrate that multiple emotional complications that often stem from relational issues with advisors can materialize as writing procrastination; their chapter proposes an integration of writing and emotional support services.

As becomes clear, graduate-level programming must create more opportunities for community building and collaboration. Several of the chapters in part 3 connect new frameworks for supporting students in building self-efficacy and resilient coalitions through community mentoring models. Rachael Cayley (chap. 11) answers the call from Steve Simpson (2016) to gather evidence on the effectiveness of supports that have become commonplaces of working with graduate writers. Cayley provides qualitative data to show writing facilitation provided in a dissertation completion camp setting builds students' self-efficacy as writers and their sense of belongingness. Particularly by sharing their writing experiences in peer interactions, graduate students in "boot" camps integrate community experiences in their own writing practice; sharing experiences empowers them to counter "persistent notions of individualized success and failure in graduate school." Amy Fenstermaker and Anne Zanzucchi (chap. 12) likewise examine the systematic use of peer-with-peer mentoring methods in their discussion of a nonhierarchical mentoring framework that goes beyond nuts-and-bolts advice toward holistic and inclusive support. Shelley Rodrigo and Julia Romberger (chap. 13) propose a playful "sandbox" course for supporting students in engaging with theory and developing interdisciplinary research methods. Using a digital Lego application, timelines, and theory trees, students reorganize conceptual knowledge through a community of practice approach to incorporating theory and methodology in their research writing. Finally, Jennifer Friend, Jennifer Salvo, Michelle M. Paquette, and Elizabeth Brown (chap. 14) provide needs assessments and results that informed a university-wide graduate writing initiative to address students' writing concerns. Their efforts demonstrated tangible early outcomes while they created campus networks and garnered support that enabled them to "build momentum, relationships, and credibility" as their program developed. Taken together, these chapters advance a variety of approaches to support practices that foster inclusive communities, that are answerable to students' identities, and that honor the lived experiences of graduate students as writers.

Learning from the Lived Experiences of Graduate Student Writers resists a tidy ending and an easy solution. We do not offer a program model, a writing rubric, or a budget amount for the number of resources needed to improve the situation. We advocate creating opportunities for graduate students to do the work they care about and bring their voices to the conversation. In her after(word), Kirsten T. Edwards reminds us that students from historically oppressed groups deserve reparations. Although students' voices, experiences, and needs should be driving programming in all aspects of higher education, Edwards worries that "higher education probably will never listen. It was founded on a commitment to not listen." She goes on:

> Despite its dominant narrative as an engine of social equality, [higher education] continues to participate in social reproduction. It is fundamentally rooted in a system of winners and losers. Nevertheless, instead of feeling defeated by this reality, it compels me to question, "What magic will minoritized graduate writers produce in response to this bleak present and unknown future?" What kinds of educational futures will they imagine if we diligently create spaces and strategies committed to their freedom?

My coeditors and I hope readers will join us in appreciating the voices included here; we hope these voices influence readers to design programs and initiatives *committed to students' freedom*. With Victor Villanueva, we believe strongly that—like teaching and mentoring—"editorial work is about supporting unheard voices, expanding the types of knowledge, the types of writing, which impact our understanding" (Selfe, Villanueva, and Parks 2017, 3). Educators must stop replicating white-privileging structures and then apologizing for not doing enough to hear and respond to what marginalized voices are saying. As Neisha-Anne Green (2018) has said, white people committed to dismantling privilege in higher education must stop being (or proclaiming to be) "allies" who remain quiet and passive when injustices are happening. White people must be accomplices—the critical difference being that "accomplices support and help through word and deed"; they "actively demonstrate allyship" (29). It has never been enough—and at this moment in U.S. political history it is not only insufficient but is damaging—"to *quietly* help and support" in a passive and only-when-convenient way (29; emphasis added). The reflections in this collection challenge us all to do the work every day, to consider more expansive ways of framing success, to challenge entrenched practices that may limit the potential for students to become what academe has always defined as a scholar—someone who makes new knowledge and contributes their own original voice.

ACKNOWLEDGMENTS

Many thanks to Michele Eodice; working with you over the years shaped how I do the work and who I want to be. Heartfelt thanks to my other collaborators and the communities that sustained me through the process of putting this collection together, especially Sandra L. Tarabochia, Ryan Omizo, Clarissa J. Walker, and Amanda Cuellar. Conversations with all of them infused this work. I am very grateful for the opportunities and community available to me in the Consortium on Graduate Communication; thanks in particular to Steve Simpson, Michelle Cox, Talinn Phillips, Nigel Caplan, Lindsey Ives, Shyam Sharma, Angelo Pitillo, Lisa Russell-Pinson, the CGC Executive Board, and Dan Bommarito for their support and collaborations. Many thanks to the students I have worked with and from whom I learn so much, including Shenita Denson, Bernard "BJ" Durham, Erin Elliot, Iwinosa Idahor, Stella Jackman-Ryan, Ashish Kapoor, Whitney McCoy, Ayana Sadler, Valeria Soto Márquez, Bethany Van Scooter, and Matthew Warren. Thanks to Anna Sicari, Melvin "Jai" Jackson, and Zach Beare for their support and collaboration. Working with our other two editors, Kirsten T. Edwards and Alexandria Lockett, enriched my experience greatly. Finally, thanks to the three anonymous reviewers of this collection for their critical feedback and thoughtful commentary, and to Michael Spooner, Rachael Levay, and Utah State University Press for helping us bring this project into being.

NOTES

1. Thank you to Clarissa J. Walker for the phrase "the rhetorical force of testimony."
2. Thanks to Michelle Cox for making this point about voice during her panel discussion at the Conference on College Composition and Communication in 2018.
3. *Supervisor, advisor,* and sometimes *chair* are used interchangeably throughout this collection to refer to faculty who mentor students' dissertations and thesis projects.

REFERENCES

Aitchison, Claire, and Susan Mowbray. 2013. "Doctoral Women: Managing Emotions, Managing Doctoral Studies." *Teaching in Higher Education* 18 (8): 859–870.

Aitchison, Claire, Janice Catterall, Pauline Ross, and Shelley Burgin. 2012. "'Tough Love and Tears': Learning Doctoral Writing in the Sciences." *Higher Education Research and Development* 31 (4): 435–447.

Alarcón, Jeannette D., and Silvia Bettez. "Feeling Brown in the Academy: Decolonizing Mentoring through a Disidentification 'Muxerista' Approach." *Equity and Excellence in Education* 50 (1): 25–40.

Allen, Brenda J. 2012. Introduction to *Presumed Incompetent: Intersections of Race and Class for Women in Academia*, edited by Gabriella Gutiérrez y Muhs, Yolanda Flores Niemann, Carmen G. González, and Angela P. Harris, 1–19. Logan: Utah State University Press.

Alvarez, Nancy, Francia N. Brito, Cristina Salazar, and Karina Aguilar. 2016. "Agency, Liberation, and Intersectionality among Latina Scholars: Narratives from a Cross-Institutional Writing Collective." *Praxis: A Writing Center Journal* 14 (1): 9–14.

Anderson, Elijah. 2015. "The White Space." *Sociology of Race and Ethnicity* 1 (1): 10–21.

Badenhorst, Cecile, and Cally Guerin, eds. 2016. *Research Literacies and Writing Pedagogies for Masters and Doctoral Writers*. Leiden: Brill.

Belcher, Diane. 1994. "The Apprenticeship Approach to Advanced Academic Literacy: Graduate Students and their Mentors." *English for Specific Purposes* 13 (1): 23–34.

Bell, Katrina, and Jennifer Hewerdine. "Creating a Community of Learners: Affinity Groups and Informal Graduate Writing Support." *Praxis* 14 (1): 50–55.

Bell, Nathan E. 2011. *Data Sources: Graduate Students with Disabilities*. Washington, DC: Council of Graduate Schools.

Boice, Robert. 1990. *Professors as Writers: A Self-Help Guide to Productive Writing*. Stillwater, OK: New Forums.

Bosanquet, Agnes, and Jayde Cahir. "'What Feelings Didn't I Experience!': Affect and Identity in PhD Writing." In *Research Literacies and Writing Pedagogies for Masters and Doctoral Writers*, edited by Cecile Badenhorst and Cally Guerin, 132–148. Leiden: Brill.

Bowen, William, and Neil Rudenstein. 1992. *In Pursuit of the Ph.D.* Princeton, NJ: Princeton University Press.

Brooks-Gillies, Marilee, Elena G. Garcia, Soo Hyon Kim, Katie Manthey, and Trixie G. Smith, eds. 2015. "Graduate Writing Across the Disciplines." Special issue, *Across the Disciplines* 12. https://wac.colostate.edu/atd/special/graduate/.

Burrows, Cedric D. 2016. "Writing While Black: The Black Tax on African American Graduate Writers." *Praxis: A Writing Center Journal* 14 (1): 15–20.

Campbell, Michelle M., and Vicki R. Kennell. 2018. *Working with Graduate Student Writers*. https://owl.purdue.edu/writinglab/faculty/documents/Writing_Lab_Faculty_Guide_Summer_%202018.pdf.

Carson, A. D. 2017. "Owning My Masters: The Rhetorics of Rhymes and Revolutions." Master's thesis, Clemson University.

Casanave, Christine Pearson. 2014. *Before the Dissertation: A Textual Mentor for Doctoral Students at Early Stages of a Research Project*. Ann Arbor: University of Michigan Press.

Casanave, Christine Pearson. 2016. "What Advisors Need to Know about the Invisible 'Real-Life' Struggles of Doctoral Dissertation Writers." In *Supporting Graduate Student Writers: Research, Curriculum, and Program Design*, edited by Steve Simpson, Nigel A. Caplan, Michelle Cox, and Talinn Phillips, 97–116. Ann Arbor: University of Michigan Press.

Casanave, Christine Pearson, and Xiaoming Li, eds. 2008. *Learning the Literacy Practices of Graduate School: Insiders' Reflections on Academic Enculturation*. Ann Arbor: University of Michigan Press. https://transforming-science.com/catalyst/.

Churchill, Ward. 2004. *Kill the Indian, Save the Man: The Genocidal Impact of American Indian Residential Schools*. San Francisco: City Lights Books.

Cirillo-McCarthy, Erica, Celeste Del Russo, and Elizabeth Leahy. 2016. "'We Don't Do That Here': Calling Out Deficit Discourses in the Writing Center to Reframe Multilingual Graduate Support." *Praxis: A Writing Center Journal* 14 (1): 62–71.

Clandinin, Jean. 2000. *Narrative Inquiry: Experience and Story in Qualitative Research.* San Francisco: Wiley and Sons.

Cotterall, Sara. 2013. "More Than Just a Brain: Emotions and the Doctoral Experience." *Higher Education Research and Development* 32 (2): 174–187.

Council of Graduate Schools. 2008. *Ph.D. Completion Project.* Washington, DC: Council of Graduate Schools.

Curry, Mary Jane. 2016. "More Than Language: Graduate Student Writing as 'Disciplinary Becoming.'" In *Supporting Graduate Student Writers: Research, Curriculum, and Program Design*, edited by Steve Simpson, Nigel A. Caplan, Michelle Cox, and Talinn Phillips, 78–96. Ann Arbor: University of Michigan Press.

Dancy, T. Elon, Kirsten T. Edwards, and James Earl Davis. 2018. "Historically White Universities and Plantation Politics: Anti-Blackness and Higher Education in the Black Lives Matter Era." *Urban Education* 53 (2): 176–195.

DeCuir-Gunby, Jessica T., and Norris W. Gunby Jr. 2016. "Racial Microaggressions in the Workplace: A Critical Race Analysis of the Experiences of African American Educators." *Urban Education* 51 (4): 390–414.

Delgado Bernal, Dolores. 2002. "Critical Race Theory, Latino Critical Theory, and Critical Raced-Gendered Epistemologies: Recognizing Students of Color as Holders and Creators of Knowledge." *Qualitative Inquiry* 8 (1): 105–126.

Dewey, John. (1938) 1959. *Experience and Education.* New York: Macmillan.

Dolmage, Jay Timothy. 2017. *Academic Ableism: Disability and Higher Education.* Ann Arbor: University of Michigan Press.

Dressen-Hammouda, Dacia. 2008. "From Novice to Disciplinary Expert: Disciplinary Identity and Genre Mastery." *English for Specific Purposes* 27 (2): 233–252.

Edwards, Kirsten T. 2009. "Incidents in the Life of Kirsten T. Edwards: A Personal Examination of the Academic In-Between Space." *Journal of Curriculum Theorizing* 26 (1): 113–128.

Engle, Randi A., Diane P. Lam, Xenia S. Meyer, and Sarah E. Nix. 2012. "How Does Expansive Framing Promote Transfer? Several Proposed Explanations and a Research Agenda for Investigating Them." *Educational Psychologist* 47 (3): 215–231.

Eodice, Michele, Anne Ellen Geller, and Neal Lerner. 2016. *The Meaningful Writing Project: Learning, Teaching, and Writing in Higher Education.* Logan: Utah State University Press.

Epps-Robertson, Candace. 2016. "Writing with Your Family at the Kitchen Table: Balancing Home and Academic Communities." *Praxis: A Writing Center Journal* 14 (1): 43–49.

Farr, Marcia, Lisya Seloni, and Juyoung Song, eds. 2009. *Ethnolinguistic Diversity and Education: Language, Literacy, and Culture.* New York: Routledge.

French, Amanda. 2016. "Exploring Post/Graduate Academic Writing Practices, Research Literacies and Writing Identities." In *Research Literacies and Writing Pedagogies for Masters and Doctoral Writers*, edited by Cecile Badenhorst and Cally Guerin, 113–131. Leiden: Brill.

Fricker, Miranda. 2007. *Epistemic Injustice: Power and the Ethics of Knowing.* Oxford: Oxford University Press.

Garvey, Jason C., and Susan Rankin. 2018. "The Influence of Campus Climate and Urbanization on Queer-Spectrum and Trans-Spectrum Faculty Intent to Leave." *Journal of Diversity in Higher Education* 11 (1): 67–81.

Geller, Anne Ellen. 2013. Introduction to *Working with Faculty Writers*, edited by Anne Ellen Geller and Michele Eodice, 1–18. Logan: Utah State University Press.

Gilyard, Keith. 1991. *Voices of the Self: A Study of Language Competence.* Detroit, MI: Wayne State University Press.

Godbee, Beth. 2018. "The Trauma of Graduate Education." *Inside Higher Ed.* https://www.insidehighered.com/advice/2018/07/09/how-trauma-affects-grad-students-their-career-search-opinion.

Godbee, Beth. 2017. "Writing Up: How Assertions of Epistemic Rights Counter Epistemic Injustice." *College English* 79 (6): 593–618.

Godbee, Beth, and Julia C. Novotny. 2013. "Asserting the Write to Belong: Feminist Co-Mentoring among Graduate Student Women." *Feminist Teacher* 23 (3): 177–195.

Golde, Chris. 2005. "The Role of the Department and Discipline in Doctoral Student Attrition: Lessons from Four Departments." *Journal of Higher Education* 76 (6): 669–700.

Gomez, Jennifer M. 2015. "Microaggressions and the Enduring Mental Health Disparity: Black Americans at Risk for Institutional Betrayal." *Journal of Black Psychology* 41 (2): 121–143.

Gray, DeLeon L. 2017. "Is Psychological Membership in the Classroom a Function of Standing Out While Fitting In?: Implications for Achievement Motivation and Emotions." *Journal of School Psychology* 61: 103–121.

Gray, DeLeon L., Elan C. Hope, and Jamaal S. Matthews. 2018. "Black and Belonging at School: A Case for Interpersonal, Instructional, and Institutional Opportunity Structures." *Educational Psychologist* 53 (2): 97–113.

Green, Neisha-Anne S. 2016. "The Re-Education of Neisha-Anne S Green: A Close Look at the Damaging Effects of 'A Standard Approach,' the Benefits of Code-Meshing, and the Role Allies Play in This Work." *Praxis: A Writing Center Journal* 14 (1): 72–82.

Green, Neisha-Anne S. 2018. "Moving beyond Alright: And the Emotional Toll of This, My Life Matters Too, in the Writing Center Work." *Writing Center Journal* 37 (1): 15–34.

Greenfield, Laura, and Karen Rowan, eds. 2011. *Writing Centers and the New Racism: A Call for Sustainable Dialogue and Change*. Logan: Utah State University Press.

Guerra, Juan. 2008. "Cultivating Transcultural Citizenship: A Writing across Communities Model." *Language Arts* 85 (4) 296–304.

Gutiérrez y Muhs, Gabriella, Yolanda F. Niemann, Carmen G. González, and Angela P. Harris, eds. 2012. *Presumed Incompetent: The Intersections of Race and Class for Women in Academia*. Logan: Utah State University Press.

Hendry, Petra Munro. 2009. "Narrative as Inquiry." *Journal of Educational Research* 103 (2): 72–80.

Hill, Marc Lamont. 2016. *Nobody: Casualties of America's War on the Vulnerable, from Ferguson to Flint and Beyond*. New York: Atria Books.

Hinsdale, Mary Jo. 2015. *Mutuality, Mystery, and Mentorship in Higher Education*. Rotterdam: Sense.

Holling, Michelle A., May C. Fu, and Roe Bubar. 2012. "Dis/Jointed Appointments: Solidarity Amidst Inequity, Tokenism, and Marginalization." In *Presumed Incompetent: The Intersections of Race and Class for Women in Academia*, edited by Gabriella Gutiérrez y Muhs, Yolanda F. Niemann, Carmen G. González, and Angela P. Harris, 250–265. Logan: Utah State University Press.

Hyland, Ken. 2004. *Genre and Second Language Writing*. Ann Arbor: University of Michigan Press.

Inoue, Asao B. 2015. *Antiracist Writing Assessment Ecologies: Teaching and Assessing Writing for a Socially Just Future*. Fort Collins, CO: WAC Clearinghouse and Parlor.

Inoue, Asao B. 2016. "Afterword: Narratives That Determine Writers and Social Justice Writing Center Work." *Praxis: A Writing Center Journal* 14 (1): 94–99.

Inoue, Asao B. 2019. *Labor-Based Grading Contracts: Building Equity and Inclusion in the Compassionate Writing Classroom*. Fort Collins, CO: WAC Clearinghouse.

Kareem, Jamila M. 2018. "Transitioning Counter-Stories: Black Student Accounts of Transitioning to College Writing." *Journal of College Literacy and Learning* 44: 15–35.

Keedy, Griffin, and Amy Vidali. 2016. "Productive Chaos: Disability, Advising, and the Writing Process." *Praxis: A Writing Center Journal* 14 (1): 21–26.

Kittle-Autry, Meagan, and Michael Carter. 2015. "Unblocking Occluded Genres in Graduate Writing: Thesis and Dissertation Support Services at North Carolina State University." *Composition Forum* 31.

Kynard, Carmen. 2015. "Teaching While Black: Witnessing and Countering Disciplinary Whiteness, Racial Violence, and University Race-Management." *Literacy in Composition Studies* 3 (1): 1–20.

Kynard, Carmen. 2017. "Black Language Matters: Black Languaging/Black Mentoring of Young Black Faculty." http://carmenkynard.org/black-mentoring/.

Lave, Jean, and Etienne Wenger. 1991. *Situated Learning: Legitimate Peripheral Participation*. Cambridge: Cambridge University Press.

Lawrence, Susan, and Terry Myers Zawacki. 2019. *Re/Writing the Center: Approaches to Supporting Graduate Students in the Writing Center*. Logan: Utah State University Press.

Liu, Lu. 2011. "An International Graduate Student's ESL Learning Experience beyond the Classroom." *TESL Canada Journal* 29 (1): 77–92.

Lovitts, Barbara E. 2011. *Leaving the Ivory Tower: The Causes and Consequences of Departure from Doctoral Study*. Lanham, MD: Rowman and Littlefield.

Madden, Shannon, and Michele Eodice, eds. 2016. "Access and Equity in Graduate Writing Support." Special issue, *Praxis: A Writing Center Journal* 14 (1).

Maher, Michelle A., and Brett H. Say. 2016. "Doctoral Supervisors as Learners and Teachers of Disciplinary Writing." In *Research Literacies and Writing Pedagogies for Masters and Doctoral Writers*, edited by Cecile Badenhorst and Cally Guerin, 277–294. Leiden: Brill.

Martinez, Aja Y. 2016. "Alejandra Writes a Book: A Critical Race Counterstory about Writing, Identity, and Being Chicanx in the Academy." *Praxis: A Writing Center Journal* 14 (1): 54–61.

Matsuda, Paul K. 1998. "Situating ESL Writing in a Cross-Disciplinary Context." *Written Communication* 15 (1): 99–121.

Matsuda, Paul K. 2006. "The Myth of Linguistic Homogeneity in U.S. College Composition." *College English* 68 (6): 637–651.

Matthew, Patricia A., ed. 2016. *Written/Unwritten: Diversity and the Hidden Truths of Tenure*. Chapel Hill: University of North Carolina Press.

MiSci Writers. "Our Mission." https://misciwriters.com/about/.

Morita, Naoko. 2004. "Negotiating Participation and Identity in Second Language Academic Communities." *TESOL Quarterly* 38 (4): 573–603.

Myles, Johanne, and Liying Cheng. 2003. "The Social and Cultural Life of Non-Native English Speaking International Graduate Students at a Canadian University." *Journal of English for Academic Purposes* 2 (3): 247–263.

National Council for Education Statistics. 2012. "Fast Facts: Degrees Conferred by Sex and Race." https://nces.ed.gov/fastfacts/display.asp?id=72.

Niemann, Yolanda Flores. 2012. "Lessons from the Experiences of Women of Color Working in Academia." In *Presumed Incompetent: Intersections of Race and Class for Women in Academia*, edited by Gabriella Gutiérrez y Muhs, Yolanda F. Niemann, Carmen G. González, and Angela P. Harris, 446–499. Logan: Utah State University Press.

North Carolina Research Campus Catalyst Research Group. n.d. "North Carolina Research Campus Catalyst Group." https://transforming-science.com/catalyst/.

Okahana, Hironao. 2017. "Data Sources: A Quick Look into the Latest Survey of Earned Doctorates Data." Council of Graduate Schools. http://cgsnet.org/data-sources-quick-look-latest-survey-earned-doctorates-data-0.

Ostrove, Joan M., Abigail J. Stewart, and Nicola L. Curtin. 2011. "Social Class and Belonging: Implications for Graduate Students' Career Aspirations." *Journal of Higher Education* 82 (6): 748–774.

Paré, Anthony, Doreen Starke-Meyerring, and Lynn McAlpine. 2011. "Knowledge and Identity Work in the Supervision of Doctoral Student Writing." In *Writing in Knowledge*

Societies, edited by Doreen Starke-Meyerring, Anthony Paré, Natasha Artemeva, Miriam Horne, and Larissa Yousoubova. Fort Collins, CO: WAC Clearinghouse and Parlor.

Patel, Leigh. 2015. *Decolonizing Educational Research: From Ownership to Answerability*. New York: Routledge.

Peterson, Eva Bendix. 2007. "Negotiating Academicity: Postgraduate Research Supervision as Category Boundary Work." *Studies in Higher Education* 32 (4): 475–487.

Phillips, Talinn. 2016. "Building Our Field of Dreams: Programs for Graduate Writing Support." Keynote, Summer Institute of the Consortium on Graduate Communication, New Haven, CT.

Rafoth, Ben. 2015. *Multilingual Writers and Writing Centers*. Logan: Utah State University Press.

Richardson, Elaine. 2003. *African American Literacies*. London: Routledge.

Royster, Jacqueline Jones, and Gesa Kirsch. 2012. *Feminist Rhetorical Practices: New Horizons for Rhetoric, Composition, and Literacy Studies*. Carbondale: Southern Illinois University Press.

Schunk, Dale H., and Barry J. Zimmerman, eds. 1998. *Self-Regulated Learning: From Teaching to Self-Reflective Practice*. New York: Guilford.

Selfe, Cynthia, Victor Villanueva, and Steve Parks. 2017. "Generating the Field: The Role of Editors in Disciplinary Formation." *Composition Forum* 35. https://compositionforum.com/issue/35/parks-selfe-villanueva-interview.php.

Seloni, Lisya. 2014. "'I'm an Artist and a Scholar Who Is Trying to Find a Middle Point': A Textographic Analysis of a Colombian Art Historian's Thesis Writing." *Journal of Second Language Writing* 25 (1): 79–99.

Simpson, Steve. 2016. "Introduction: New Frontiers in Graduate Writing Support and Program Design." In *Supporting Graduate Student Writers: Research, Curriculum, Program Design*, edited by Steve Simpson, Nigel Caplan, Michelle Cox, and Talinn Phillips, 1–20. Ann Arbor: University of Michigan Press.

Simpson, Steve, Nigel Caplan, Michelle Cox, and Talinn Phillips, eds. 2016. *Supporting Graduate Student Writers: Research, Curriculum, Program Design*. Ann Arbor: University of Michigan Press.

Simpson, Steve, and Paul Kei Matsuda. 2008. "Mentoring as a Long-term Relationship: Situated Learning in a Doctoral Program." In *Learning the Literacy Practices of Graduate School: Insiders' Reflections on Academic Enculturation*, edited by Christine Pearson Casanave and Xioming Li, 90–104. Ann Arbor: University of Michigan Press.

Smith-Campbell, Charmaine J., and Steven Littles. 2016. "Freire's Pedagogy of Love and a Ph.D. Student's Experience." *Praxis: A Writing Center Journal* 14 (1): 34–42.

Smith, Linda Tuhiwai. 1999. *Decolonizing Methodologies: Research and Indigenous Peoples*. London: Zed Books Limited.

Solorzáno, Daniel G. 1998. "Critical Race Theory, Race and Gender Microaggressions, and the Experience of Chicana and Chicano Scholars." *International Journal of Qualitative Studies in Education* 11 (10): 121–136.

Sowell, Robert, Jeff Allum, and Hironao Okahana. 2015. *Doctoral Initiative on Minority Attrition and Completion*. Washington, DC: Council of Graduate Schools.

Starfield, Sue and Brian Paltridge, eds. 2019. "Thesis and Dissertation Writing in a Second Language: Context, Identity, Genre." Special issue, *Journal of Second Language Writing* 43.

Starke-Meyerring, Doreen, Anthony Paré, Natasha Artemeva, Miriam Horne, and Larissa Yousoubova, eds. 2011. *Writing in Knowledge Societies*. Fort Collins, CO: WAC Clearinghouse and Parlor.

Strayhorn, Terrell L. 2012. *College Students' Sense of Belonging: A Key to Educational Success for All Students*. New York: Routledge.

Stewart, Abigail J., and Virginia Valian. 2018. *An Inclusive Academy: Achieving Diversity and Excellence*. Cambridge: MIT Press.

Sue, Derald Wing. 2010. *Microaggressions in Everyday Life: Race, Gender, and Sexual Orientation.* Hoboken, NJ: Wiley and Sons.

Swales, John. 1996. "Occluded Genres in the Academy: The Case of the Submission Letter." In *Academic Writing: Intercultural and Textual Issues,* edited by Eija Ventola and Anna Mauranen. Amsterdam: John Benjamins.

Swales, John M. 2004. *Research Genres: Explorations and Applications.* Cambridge: Cambridge University Press.

Tang, Jasmine Kar, and Noro Andriamanalina. 2016. "'Rhonda Left Early to Go to Black Lives Matter': Programmatic Support for Graduate Writers of Color." *WPA: Writing Program Administration* 39 (2): 10–16.

Tardy, Christine M. 2016. *Beyond Convention: Genre Innovation in Academic Writing.* Ann Arbor: University of Michigan Press.

Tarabochia, Sandra, and Shannon Madden. 2018. "In Transition: Researching the Writing Development of Doctoral Students and Faculty." *Writing and Pedagogy* 10 (3): 423–452.

van Manen, Max. 1990. *Researching Lived Experience.* London: Althouse.

Villanueva, Victor. 2006. "Blind: Talking about the New Racism." *Writing Center Journal* 26 (1): 3–19.

Welch, Nancy. 2002. "Other Than Oedipus: Sideshadowing Tales of Dissertation Authority." In *The Dissertation and the Discipline: Reinventing Composition Studies,* edited by Nancy Welch, Catherine G. Latterell, Cindy Moore, and Sheila Carter-Tod, 34–44. Portsmouth, NH: Boynton/Cook.

Wilder, Craig Steven. 2013. *Ebony and Ivy: Race, Slavery, and the Troubled History of America's Universities.* New York: Bloomsbury.

Wright, Bobby, and William G. Tierney. 1991. "American Indians in Higher Education: A History of Cultural Conflict." *Change* 23 (2): 11–18.

Young, Vershawn Ashanti. 2007. *Your Average Nigga: Performing Race, Literacy, and Masculinity.* Detroit, MI: Wayne State University Press.

Young, Vershawn Ashanti, Rusty Barrett, Y'Shanda Young-Rivera, and Kim Brian Lovejoy. 2013. *Other People's English: Code-Meshing, Code-Switching, and African-American Literacy.* New York: Teachers College Press.

PART 1

Voices

1
THE TRAUMA OF GRADUATE EDUCATION
Graduate Writers Countering Epistemic Injustice and Reclaiming Epistemic Rights

Beth Godbee

> *When there's no name for a problem, you can't see a problem. When you can't see a problem, you can't solve it.*
> —Kimberlé Crenshaw

INTRODUCTION

During my graduate education, I began an empirical study of collaborative writing talk, or one-with-one writing conferences, seeking to identify the power and potential of this talk. I experienced a sense of "transformation" as both a writer and tutor in one-with-one conferences (Godbee 2012), and I noted that many scholars in writing studies similarly attributed extracurricular writing talk as having transformative potential (e.g., Denny 2010; Gere 1994; Heller 1997; Whitney 2008). These initial observations led me to videotape conferences and interview writers and educators involved in ongoing partnerships, in both campus and community writing centers. From this study emerged several focus populations, among them graduate student women, as their work of "asserting the right to belong" in academia emerged as particularly poignant (Godbee and Novotny 2014).

Graduate writers are expected to produce particularly complex and high-stakes writing, from first publications and original research to CVs and other job search materials. They also navigate complex asymmetrical power relations when working with faculty advisors, committee members, employers, and disciplinary colleagues. At the same time, graduate writers are working to create space for themselves and their research projects, commitments, and contributions within higher education. The challenges abound but also emerge differently and with different

DOI: 10.7330/9781607329589.c001

consequences depending on how graduate writers are (institutionally + historically + socially + culturally) positioned. Listening to participants, I heard a chorus of struggles—and downright trauma—associated with graduate education. In articulating what was helpful in making it through the trauma, participants emphasized the importance of writing conferences as essential "therapy"—that is, academic or writing therapy. Without exception, *every* graduate writer in my study used the words "therapy" or "healing" to describe the psychological and emotional benefits of their collaborative writing partnerships.

From these starting points, I describe in this chapter the trauma of graduate education, particularly for people marginalized within academia. In addition to facing everyday microaggressions (e.g., Gomez, Khurshid, Freitag, and Lachuk 2011; Sue 2010), many graduate writers experience epistemic injustice, or harm in their capacity as knowers (e.g., Alcoff 1999; Fricker 2007). Rather than presenting an empirical study, I use stories from research and experience to build our collective linguistic resources for talking about the trauma of graduate education, the problem of epistemic injustice, and the potential of epistemic rights. To do so, the chapter is organized into three sections: (1) defining epistemic injustice; (2) countering epistemic injustice, affirming epistemic rights; and (3) valuing feminist co-mentoring. After defining epistemic injustice, I call for educators to affirm writers' epistemic rights, or the rights to knowledge, experience, and earned expertise. And I highlight cases of graduate student women of color who collaboratively affirm and assert their epistemic rights—work that illustrates why feminist co-mentoring matters in graduate education.[1]

IDENTIFYING TRAUMA AND INJUSTICE IN GRADUATE EDUCATION

The literature on graduate writing and writers includes attention to writing groups (e.g., Aitchison 2009; Aitchison and Guerin 2014); to providing support for graduate writers across disciplines (e.g., Brooks-Gillies, Garcia, Kim, Manthey, and Smith 2015; Lawrence and Zawacki 2016); and to the experiences of and need to support faculty writers (e.g., Boice 1990; Geller and Eodice 2013). Cross-disciplinary literature also addresses the need for various types of mentoring: not only mentoring by faculty members and dissertation advisors (e.g., Eble and Gaillet 2008; Wiltshire 1998) but especially peer or co-mentoring with and among graduate students (e.g., Goeke, Klein, Garcia-Reid, Birnbaum, Brown, and Degennaro 2011; McGuire and Reger 2003; Patton 2009). Together, this literature suggests the importance of ongoing and structured feedback from multiple in-field and out-of-field, expert and non-expert readers. It draws our attention to the need for support structures like writing groups and one-with-one conferences, as well as the value of the support colleagues and friends provide as mentors.

What has been under-addressed in this literature is the need to counter the trauma associated with graduate education, a trauma Black queer feminist sociologist Eric Anthony Grollman addresses in his blog *Write Where It Hurts*. In a March 16, 2016 post, "Recovering from Graduate School: Rewriting the Trauma Narrative," Grollman argues that to recover from graduate school, it is important to "rewrite the trauma narrative." For Grollman, this rewriting involves "writ[ing] down every challenging, offensive, and potentially traumatizing event or condition" that can be remembered; naming these experiences *as trauma*—that is, identifying "just how traumatizing graduate school was"; and then rewriting the narrative to include moments of "pushing back," "defining [your] career for [your]self," or "defying mainstream expectations." Such rewriting is a process of recasting and reclaiming agency within graduate education and of healing from the trauma. And trauma itself is more widespread than typically realized, as illustrated by the related special issue of *Praxis* on graduate writers and equity (see, e.g., Cedric Burrows's "Writing While Black: The Black Tax on African-American Graduate Writers" [2016] and Neisha-Anne Green's "The Re-Education of Neisha-Anne Green: A Close Look at the Damaging Effects of 'A Standard Approach,' the Benefits of Code-Meshing, and the Role Allies Play in This Work" [2016]).

To explain the trauma of graduate education, we might look to the edited collection *Presumed Incompetent* (Gutiérrez y Muhs, Niemann, González, and Harris 2012), which provides a framework and the language for interpreting the many compounding experiences that lead graduate students and faculty women of color—and those of us with marginalized identities—to experience our worth as diminished within higher education. As editors Angela P. Harris and Carmen G. González (2012) explain in their introduction, the same systemic inequities, pervasive biases, and daily microaggressions that are part of the world around us permeate higher education. And inequities and injustices are further amplified because "the culture of academia is distinctly white, heterosexual, and middle- and upper-middle-class. Those who differ from this norm find themselves, to a greater or lesser degree, 'presumed incompetent' by students, colleagues, and administrators" (3). This experience is widespread and saturated within campus climates, faculty-student relationships, and social hierarchies in academia. It represents both individual and collective experience, and it thrives in current challenges facing higher education, including corporatization of universities, shifts in academic labor toward non-tenure-track and part-time positions, and the treatment of education as commodity and students as consumers (5–6). Yet, despite its widespread and insidious nature, the condition of being "presumed incompetent" often goes unnamed, making it more easily internalized by those who are marginalized and written off by those with privilege and power.

To illustrate, Brenda J. Allen (2012) describes the impact of the book and its title—*Presumed Incompetent*—on a colleague, a Black woman faculty member, who responded, "'That was exactly my experience in grad school. . . . You just don't know what I went through . . . I can't believe how much this still hurts'" (17). By all measures, this colleague was thriving in higher education, having passed her dissertation "with flying colors," having earned a tenure-track position and then tenure and promotion, and having succeeded at both her home institution and within her profession. Yet, the experience of being "presumed incompetent" marked her experience along this journey and still brought much hurt—much trauma (Grollman 2016)—related to "feeling unwelcome" and facing ongoing "strife" and "struggles" within the work (Allen 2012, 17). What this colleague relates, Allen says, reflects the reports of "countless other women of color graduate students and faculty members who have shared stories similar to this young woman's" (17). And it certainly reflects the experiences shared with me by graduate writers in my own qualitative study.

I begin with these stories of trauma and of being presumed incompetent because they represent the injustice that is part and parcel of graduate education for *many* graduate writers, particularly for people who don't match the "mythical norm." As Audre Lorde (1984) explains, "In america, this norm is usually defined as white, thin, male, young, heterosexual, christian, and financially secure" (116). And this norm defines what is valued and expected within academia to such a high degree that the connections are often implicit, if not hidden, from view. For instance, the valuing of rationality and "value-free science" connects with masculinity and the Western intellectual tradition (Harris and González 2012, 4–5). In turn, "rigorous" or "objective" research gets prioritized in ways that value not only mythical-norm people but also the epistemologies (ways of knowing, being, and acting) associated with the norm. Concomitantly, preferences for the mythical norm carry over into teaching so that white, male instructors are strongly favored—by men and women, white people and people of color alike (6).

The unconscious bias that leads to the favoring of mythical-norm research/researchers and mythical-norm teaching/teachers further influences hiring practices, committee reviews, and systems of tenure and promotion. In these high-stakes contexts, "unconscious bias triggers greater scrutiny of the presumptively incompetent applicants of color while the flaws of white male applicants [or thesis or dissertation writers] are minimized or disregarded" (Harris and González 2012, 8). Such differential valuing means graduate writers who are marginalized face what philosopher Miranda Fricker (2007) refers to as an "identity-prejudicial credibility deficit," or "epistemic deficit," meaning that structural prejudice operates on the hearer's part to give the speaker less credibility (17). This deficit is in opposition to an epistemic or credibility excess that benefits people with privilege and institutional power who are readily listened to/for based on their mythical-norm identities. When graduate writers are presumed to be incompetent, they face not only epistemic deficit but also are further disadvantaged/differentiated from those who have an inflated or excess credibility. The result, Fricker terms, is "epistemic injustice," or "a wrong done to someone specifically in their capacity as a knower" (1).

I turn next to considering the manifestation of two forms of epistemic injustice within graduate education and a range of primary and secondary harms that result from this injustice. Such a discussion, I hope, helps us name and identify what many graduate writers face, as well as helps us imagine and make interventions toward countering this deep injustice.

DEFINING EPISTEMIC INJUSTICE

The work of higher education is work within the knowledge economy, and as such, it involves dealing in—reading, responding to, challenging, and contributing—knowledge. Such work is inherently epistemological, involving ways of knowing, making meaning, experiencing, and articulating (i.e., writing) the world. And such work is not value neutral but instead value laden, with particular ways of knowing valued over others (see, e.g., Deloria 1970; Yosso 2005). This context matters for graduate writers who must navigate their own and others' epistemic agency, entitlement, and rights. Among the many philosophers interested in these matters, Fricker provides in-depth analysis in her 2007 book *Epistemic Injustice* in which she explores the associations among power, prejudice, and the ethics of knowing. Fricker identifies two types of epistemic injustice: (1) testimonial injustice and (2) hermeneutical injustice. Both these types, I maintain, relate to graduate writers, particularly writers who don't fit the mythical norm and are presumed incompetent within academia.

First, "testimonial injustice" refers to epistemic deficit or the experience of being "perceived incompetent," as it "occurs when prejudice causes a hearer to give a deflated level of credibility to a speaker's word" (Fricker 2007, 1). It occurs whenever prejudice (often implicit and unconscious) leads a hearer/reader to give less credibility to a speaker/writer than otherwise would be given (4). Fricker offers the example of police officers and juries not believing Black defendants, witnesses, and others *because* they are Black. Testimonial injustice can also be seen in situations like the Flint water crisis: though community members knew and reported a number of problems with their tap water, their knowledge was downplayed, if not disbelieved. It was not until professors, physicians, and researchers became involved and verified lead contamination that the media took notice and a state of emergency was declared (see Lurie [2016] for a timeline). Testimonial injustice wrongs people in their capacity to share experiences, give information, and construct new knowledge.

Within academia, we might think of stories like the one Linda Martin Alcoff (1999) relates of an untenured Chicana philosophy professor who suffered undermining complaints from a white male teaching assistant (TA). Not until a senior white professor suffered the same sort of complaints did colleagues support the untenured professor. Fricker uses this example to explain double testimonial injustice, or the problem of not being believed about not being believed. In this case, a first testimonial injustice occurred when the TA undermined the faculty member's teaching, and a second testimonial injustice arose when departmental colleagues failed to believe her reports about the undermining. This double testimonial injustice deeply impacted the untenured faculty member "as a giver of knowledge" (Fricker 48), and we can infer similar impacts on graduate writers, who also occupy positions of institutional instability and vulnerability. As Burrows (2016) writes about "the Black tax," Black graduate writers are often called into question: we find evidence in his own account of being questioned by a white tutor in the writing center. Put simply, testimonial injustice undermines one's credibility and related confidence, achievements, sense of self-worth, and even personhood.

Second, though often working in conjunction with testimonial injustice, "hermeneutical injustice" manifests "at a prior stage, when a gap in collective interpretive resources puts someone at an unfair disadvantage when it comes to making sense of their social experiences" (Fricker 2007, 1).

Whereas the experience of being perceived incompetent represents testimonial injustice, the creation of the term *perceived incompetent* helps correct the hermeneutical injustice of having this experience unnamed and largely unknown. Fricker shows that, historically, naming and defining concepts like sexual harassment and postpartum depression have helped correct for "hermeneutical inequality" (162). When these critical concepts were named, new understandings "awakened hitherto dormant resources for social meaning that brought clarity, cognitive confidence, and increased communicative facility" (148). Such naming counters epistemic marginalization and can open channels—from collective consciousness raising to the pursuit of economic or legal recourse—for challenging injustice.

Again, turning to academia, I think of a story of my own. In my graduate program, students were regularly taking a year or more to move from the prelim defense (earning ABD status) to dissertation proposal defense (initiating data collection), so a new guideline was created, indicating that the proposal defense should take place within six months of prelims. Despite the new guideline, I struggled after prelims with exhaustion, mental depletion, and shaken confidence (from a year-long experience I am making sense of to this day *as trauma*). With concerted effort, I defended my dissertation proposal nine months after prelims, all the while feeling I was behind schedule and therefore falling short. It was not until some months later when talking with a friend in social work (a graduate program across campus) that I learned the term "the lost year." In social work, this phrase names the recovery time needed following prelims. The term itself enables a supportive environment in which graduate students prioritize self-care, and faculty expect students to move slowly through this stage in their graduate careers. When I learned of the term, I experienced enormous relief and a feeling that I wasn't alone. The very concept of the lost year allowed me to rewrite the narrative of my progression from prelims to proposal defense: instead of falling behind, I had actually moved ahead in *under* a year! While not challenging the "more, faster, better" philosophy of the knowledge economy (e.g., Bauerlein and Jeffery 2011), this revision allowed me to redefine myself as successful and to regain confidence. The naming of this experience was liberatory in the way that countering injustice (in this case, arising through institutional power that limits the voices and experiences of graduate writers) can be.

Both testimonial and hermeneutical injustice occur within graduate education and impact graduate writers—and notably some more than others. Fricker (2007) traces numerous *primary and secondary harms* of epistemic injustice for those who experience it, those who contribute to it, and the communities in which we all live. While epistemic injustice hurts everyone and influences even large domains like the economy (e.g., when a smaller pool of collective resources and contributors limits new ideas, inventions, and their related economic gain), it also does direct, dehumanizing harm to those who experience it. In addition to the primary harm of being wronged in one's capacity as a knower, secondary harms "can cut deep" and "tend to ramify in a person's life" (49). Harms are both wider reaching and deeper than we might expect. When a person is insulted, undermined, or otherwise wronged, they also face exclusion and marginalization: in higher education, this exclusion and marginalization can be felt within one's home institution, disciplinary community, or both.

While avoiding "Oppression Olympics" (Martínez 1993), it is important to note that histories of injustice mean marginalized peoples, particularly Black, Indigenous, and people of color (BIPOC), face deeper and more persistent epistemic injustice than those who experience power, privilege, and epistemic excess associated with the mythical norm. Though graduate writers as a group are vulnerable because of student status and are often writing to those institutionally positioned with *power over* them, student status alone does not add up to "persistent and systematic" (Fricker 2007, 54) epistemic injustice. Like other microaggressions, when epistemic injustice compounds—doubling, tripling, and adding up to a serious, ongoing case of injustice—it impacts most directly and deeply graduate writers who are marginalized within academia. When epistemic injustice is persistent and systematic, it cuts down a person based on their social identity (race, class, gender, and other intersecting identities), so it cuts down human dignity, respect, and even personhood. Hence, Fricker describes these deep cuts as a "double assault on one's personhood" (54). It is no wonder Grollman (2016) names the cumulative effect of such everyday microaggressions as *trauma*.

Moreover, repeated epistemic injury can erode intellectual courage, or the ability to take a stand for one's own convictions (Fricker 2007, 49–50). Intellectual courage is an important virtue and one I see particularly aligned with what is expected of graduate writers. Much of our writing in academia involves making and defending claims. Even when we offer original research findings, we present this knowledge by situating our ideas—and, truly, ourselves—within disciplinary frameworks, epistemological practices, and others' scholarship. These rhetorical actions require intellectual courage, as do other communicative actions like seeking feedback from thesis and dissertation directors, speaking with in-field colleagues, sending manuscripts for review, and promoting one's self through CVs and job-search materials. Epistemic injustice, therefore, impacts the core of and perhaps all of one's graduate education. Think of how difficult it is to "speak with authority" when "a history of injustices gnaws away at a person's intellectual confidence" (Fricker 2007, 50)—this intellectual courage being an essential ingredient of success in higher education.

COUNTERING EPISTEMIC INJUSTICE, AFFIRMING EPISTEMIC RIGHTS

Given this picture of epistemic injustice in graduate education, how do we respond? Though the answers certainly depend on one's institutional power, intersectional identities, and social positioning, answers must involve valuing and affirming writers' epistemic rights. Drawing from sociolinguistic research (e.g., Goffman 2016; Heritage and Raymond 2005; Raymond and Heritage 2006), I define *epistemic rights* as rights to knowledge, experience, or earned expertise. Recognition of epistemic rights suggests the importance of a broader repertoire of *writers' rights*, which would include rights researchers in composition, rhetoric, and literacy studies have long advocated. These include linguistic rights (e.g., Perryman-Clark, Kirkland, and Jackson 2015; Smitherman and Villanueva 2003; Conference on College Composition and Communication 1974); human rights (e.g., Diab 2016; Lyon and Olson 2014); and intellectual property rights (e.g., Lunsford, Fishman, and Liew 2013). This language of rights (of which epistemic rights are an important type) could help us understand how writers are hurt when they—or their language or knowledge—are undermined, devalued, or written off. Further, the language of rights calls on us all (and educators and administrators especially) to value, affirm, and uphold writers' rights and to correct the injustice that manifests when rights are denied. In the case of epistemic rights, this call means we all (and educators and administrators especially) have responsibility to affirm writers' rights to know, relate, report, claim, and act based on knowledge, experience, and earned expertise.

My ongoing research (Godbee 2017) sheds light on moments when educators affirm and when writers assert their epistemic rights. I show how affirmations and assertions of epistemic rights can work to counter epistemic injustice, particularly when writers are supported in "writing up" (akin to speaking up) to audiences with greater institutional power and more implicit right to speak. And through "writing up," writers are positioned to "upgrade" their epistemic rights—that is, to assert authority in writing in ways that challenge the identity-prejudicial credibility deficit associated with testimonial injustice. Conversation analytic renderings of collaborative composing depict how writers—many of whom are graduate students—"write up" to thesis and dissertation committees, potential employers, and other audiences who are institutionally positioned with *power over* the writer.

As an illustration, one case focuses on two Black graduate student women working within a predominantly white university like the authors of *Presumed Incompetent* (Gutiérrez y Muhs et al. 2012). Together, the tutor Traci and writer Ella B. (pseudonyms) build solidarity that allows Ella B. to compose a strong critique, asserting her right to enter and alter academic discourse. Specifically, Ella B. writes about popular representations of Black women, identifying a larger "damaged discourse" that has been shaped from the outside by unrealistic expectations. In making this analysis, Ella B. engages in self-representation, defining her own experiences through insights gained through original, historiographic research. She critiques the damaged discourse she identifies having experienced herself, and she engages in the very practice she finds reclaims agency: that of Black women writing their own stories.

As a tutor, Traci supports this work by endorsing (verbally and nonverbally) both Ella B.'s claims and her act of asserting herself within higher education. For example, in one interaction, Traci moves her hand like a pen, showing that Ella B.'s idea deserves to be written, recorded, and remembered. Another time, when Ella B. arrives at a strong claim after several minutes of struggling to find the words, Traci says, "That's right! Let 'em know," while holding her fist in the air, a sign of strength and Black power. These gestures (and many others) serve as affirmations for Ella B.'s work. They embody the experience of having another person involved—another person validating, appreciating, and encouraging one's writing, especially when it is likely to be met with resistance. In this and other cases, we see graduate student women of color navigating a largely closed community, which tests, if not undermines, their credibility. And the work of countering epistemic injustice arises in relationship—in the educator affirming and the writer (re)claiming epistemic rights.

Another example appears in the article "Asserting the Right to Belong: Feminist Co-Mentoring Among Graduate Student Women," in which Julia Novotny and I share the case of Charisse and Andrea. The tutor Charisse (a Black woman) and writer Andrea (Chicana) devote weekly writing conferences to talking through the theoretical framework of Andrea's dissertation proposal in education. This talking involves relating, reliving, and processing past educational experiences—that is, using the feminist/womanist epistemological practice of storytelling (Collins 2003) to make meaning and clarify the central concerns of Andrea's dissertation. Andrea shares her insights as a former classroom teacher, and Charisse positions herself largely as a listener, scribe, and recipient of Andrea's research. In doing so, Charisse assumes the stance of *power with*, or a relational approach of providing mutually empowering/mobilizing support. We describe this relational stance of *power with* as "feminist co-mentoring" for its potential "to redress structural inequities and to restructure power relations" (Godbee and Novotny 2014, 180).

Novotny and I analyze a span of nine minutes of Charisse and Andrea's talk in which "we see Andrea move from a place of hedging, slumping, and what appears to be uncertainty to a place of strongly asserting her argument based on her expertise not only as a researcher, but especially as a former classroom teacher" (Godbee and Novotny 2014, 184). Like Traci, Charisse signals *power with* both verbally and nonverbally, even clicking her teeth as an embodied and affirming response to show when an idea has truly clicked. Charisse validates Andrea's experience as an important source of information and validates storytelling as a valuable form of meaning making. As Andrea shares her teaching experience, she asserts her expertise. In asserting her expertise, she also (re) claims her epistemic rights—again, working to counter epistemic injustice that undermines her expertise as an experienced teacher. (I hope interested readers will read the article for a fuller analysis.)

When undergraduate researcher Natalie DeCheck wrote about Andrea and Charisse in her article "The Power of Common Interest in Motivating Writers: A Case Study" (2012), she described Charisse as having a "deep curiosity" about Andrea's work and a "passion" for education herself. DeCheck shows how an educator's "interest in the writer's work can improve the writer's motivation" (30), and she makes this case by describing Andrea and Charisse's rich relationship, which motivated them both to write, to meet in writing conferences, and to stay focused on their graduate studies. Though Andrea had visited the writing center twice before, it was not until she was paired with Charisse that she began to schedule regular, weekly meetings. Charisse indicates in an interview that it mattered to her that she and Andrea shared experiences as women of color, interests in Black and Chicana feminism, and commitments to equity in education. DeCheck finds that these points of common ground motivated Andrea as a graduate writer.

Like other participants in my study, both sets of tutoring partners—Ella B. and Traci and Andrea and Charisse—form what I would characterize as a mutually supportive relationship of feminist co-mentoring. First, they share challenges they've faced in graduate education, processing epistemic injustice through a sort of therapy to counter trauma. Second, though they are positioned as colleagues (hence, the *co* in feminist co-mentoring), the tutors act as responsible educators by affirming the writers' epistemic rights—encouraging Ella B. and Andrea to write based on their experience and expertise. Third, by working in ongoing writing partnerships, they all are strengthened by having another person involved in writing—someone affirming and also modeling how to (re)claim rights. Together, these pieces indicate the importance of supportive writing relationships, mentoring, and people standing-in-solidarity toward countering epistemic injustice, affirming epistemic rights.

Case studies of feminist co-mentoring highlight that many graduate writers are successfully navigating the rocky terrain of graduate education, especially when working in partnership with other graduate writers. When asked by a colleague how faculty mentors can support graduate writers in this work, I realize we need to employ the epistemic resources we see graduate student women of color employing. These are hermeneutic resources, or those that help us *name* the problem of epistemic injustice, a problem many/most of us must confront within ourselves. We can begin by asking questions like the following:

- Which writers do we imagine as more competent? Which do we presume incompetent?
- What actions do we take when we see presumed incompetence or other sorts of epistemic injustice playing out on campuses or in our disciplines—in courses, defenses, reviews, publications, conferences, committee meetings, and so forth?
- What sorts of knowledge (e.g., empirical data, references to published scholarship, historiography, lived experience, storytelling) do we value *and devalue*? And why?
- How do we support writers who face epistemic injustice and other forms of trauma in graduate education? Do we validate the existence of trauma, or do we invalidate and deny this lived experience? Are we aware of trauma when we see it?
- Can we articulate a full set of writers' rights? How do we affirm epistemic, linguistic, cultural, and other rights? How do we respond when we see these rights denied?

You can imagine how questions such as these will proliferate if we are to engage in ongoing, self-reflexive inquiry aimed at changing ourselves and our institutions. To invest in countering epistemic injustice, we must invest *both* in seeing the problem for ourselves *and* envisioning more just relations, relations like those we see among the graduate student women of color who affirm their individual and collective epistemic rights.

As I hope is apparent throughout this chapter, the work of countering epistemic injustice begins with countering the hermeneutical injustice that obfuscates naming, identifying, and understanding the trauma of graduate education. As Kimberlé Crenshaw (2016) says in her TEDWomen talk (the epigraph at this chapter's opening): "When there's no name for a problem, you can't see a problem. When you can't see a problem, you can't solve it." Therefore, I hope we all—writers, tutors, faculty advisors, mentors, writing program administrators, and leaders in higher education—invest in seeing the problem of epistemic injustice. Once we name epistemic injustice as a true and significant problem to reckon with, how can we possibly stand silent or still, continuing graduate education as it currently is?

VALUING FEMINIST CO-MENTORING

Once we see the trauma of graduate education, we must ask, like Grollman (2016), how to resee/rewrite it. How do we intervene in educational trauma and epistemic injustice? How do we enact graduate education that upholds and honors *all* writers' rights? For Grollman, rewriting trauma involves (1) "pushing back," (2) "defining my career for myself," and (3) "defying mainstream expectations." When educators affirm and graduate writers assert their epistemic rights, they are engaged in this important rewriting work. I find much to appreciate—and to learn from and to replicate—in the cases of graduate student women of color engaged in feminist co-mentoring. When writers affirm their epistemic rights, they simultaneously counter epistemic injustice, shaking up/off the assumption of presumed incompetence and challenging others to see them (and their writing) differently. These acts of resilience and resistance make use of and also build "community cultural wealth," which Tara J. Yosso (2005) explicates as multiple strengths of Communities of Color.

When educators assume the relational and feminist co-mentoring stance of *power with*, possibilities for reseeing/rewriting emerge (Godbee and Novotny 2014). *First, graduate writers* can acknowledge and tap into the six types of community cultural wealth Yosso identifies: aspirational, linguistic, familial, social, navigational, and resistance capital. Cultivating and making use of these strengths make it possible for writers to recover from cumulative moments of trauma in graduate education. *Second, educators* (tutors, instructors, faculty advisors, mentors, and others) can rethink the strengths and contributions of graduate writers, breaking biases associated with inequitable epistemic excess and deficit. In addition to engaging in self-reflexive inquiry and ongoing question asking, educators can invest more in affirming writers' epistemic rights—not only by working directly with graduate writers (through mentoring, one-with-one writing conferences, and written feedback) but also by advocating with faculty colleagues and changing the culture within programs, departments, and universities. *Third, program administrators and leaders* can value writers' epistemic and *many* rights in all aspects of leadership, including recruitment, hiring, and retention; mission statements and programmatic materials; curricular decision-making and designs; staff education and professional development; budgeting, salaries, and financial matters; and ongoing research agendas. For all decisions, no matter how small, administrators can ask: Does this decision stand in solidarity with graduate writers? Does this decision affirm writers' rights?

As these questions indicate, we must envision institutional change. For relational work to be more than piecemeal—more than Andrea luckily finding Charisse on her third (and likely last) try with the writing center—feminist co-mentoring must be studied, supported, and truly valued. We all—and especially educators and writing program administrators—can do more to learn about and create institutional structures that support this important work. These structures might range "from giving individuals 'credit' for the time involved in relational work to rethinking systems of credit that get in the way of more meaningful mentoring" (Godbee and Novotny 2014, 191–192). These structures could include writing groups/conferences led by and for graduate writers of color, as well as professional development for educators to learn more about epistemic injustice and epistemic rights. Additionally, these structures could readily involve writing programs in advocacy with faculty who mentor graduate writers and in collaboration with graduate programs/schools.

Certainly, a number of relational and institutional responses are needed for those of us in higher education to begin intervening in the epistemic injustice represented in the phrase *presumed incompetent*. But intervene we must. We must interrupt the many harms that result from persistent and systematic epistemic injustice. I ask that we consider seriously the implications of epistemic rights as part of a broader repertoire of writers' rights. And I ask that we look to our writing programs for making institutional change. The more we create conditions for graduate writers to engage in feminist co-mentoring, the more we envision and enact meaningful, mutually supportive relations. Such a relational approach is needed for supporting graduate writers who are actively countering epistemic injustice and reclaiming epistemic rights.

ACKNOWLEDGMENTS

With gratitude, I would like to thank the participants of this study, who trusted me (a white woman) with their stories—no small matter; the collection's editors and reviewers; and colleagues who have read and engaged critically with this work, especially Rasha Diab, Cedric Burrows, Bonnie Williams, Julia Novotny, and Jonathan D'Andries. This research has been supported by the Josephine de Karmen Fellowship and Marquette University's Center for Peacemaking. It continues to shake and shape me as I see how much more unlearning—lifelong healing and repair work—is needed to redress many wrongs.

NOTE

1. Through primarily theoretical, this chapter weaves together cross-disciplinary literature with insights gained through IRB-approved qualitative research (protocol SE-2009-0013 at the University of Wisconsin–Madison and HR-2544 at Marquette University).

REFERENCES

Aitchison, Claire. 2009. "Writing Groups for Doctoral Education." *Studies in Higher Education* 34 (8): 905–916.

Aitchison, Claire, and Cally Guerin, eds. 2014. *Writing Groups for Doctoral Education and Beyond*. New York: Routledge.

Alcoff, Linda Martin. 1999. "On Judging Epistemic Credibility: Is Social Identity Relevant?" *Philosophic Exchange* 29 (1): 1–22.

Allen, Brenda J. 2012. Introduction to Part 1 of *Presumed Incompetent: The Intersections of Race and Class for Women in Academia*, edited by Gabriella Gutiérrez y Muhs, Yolanda Flores Niemann, Carmen G. González, and Angela P. Harris. Logan: Utah State University Press.

Bauerlein, Monika, and Clara Jeffery. 2011. "All Work and No Pay: The Great Speedup." *Mother Jones*, July/August. http://www.motherjones.com/politics/2011/06/speed-up-american-workers-long-hours.

Boice, Robert. 1990. *Professors as Writers: A Self-Help Guide to Productive Writing*. Stillwater, OK: New Forums.

Brooks-Gillies, Marilee, Elena G. Garcia, Soo Hyon Kim, Katie Manthey, and Trixie G. Smith, eds. 2015. "Graduate Writing Across the Disciplines." Special issue, *Across the Disciplines* 12. http://wac.colostate.edu/atd/graduate_wac/index.cfm.

Burrows, Cedric D. 2016. "Writing While Black: The Black Tax on African-American Graduate Writers." *Praxis: A Writing Center Journal* 14 (1): 15–20.

Collins, Patricia Hill. 2003. "Toward an Afrocentric Feminist Epistemology." *Turning Points in Qualitative Research*, edited by Yvonna S. Lincoln and Norman K. Denzin, 47–70. Walnut Creek, CA: Rowman & Littlefield.

Conference on College Composition and Composition. 1974. "Students' Right to Their Own Language." 1974. Updated 2006.

Crenshaw, Kimberlé. 2016. "The Urgency of Intersectionality." TEDWomen video, 18:42. https://www.ted.com/talks/kimberle_crenshaw_the_urgency_of_intersectionality.

DeCheck, Natalie. 2012. "The Power of Common Interest in Motivating Writers: A Case Study." *Writing Center Journal* 32 (1): 28–38.

Deloria, Vine Jr. 1970. *We Talk, You Listen: New Tribes, New Turf*. New York: Macmillan.

Denny, Harry C. 2010. *Facing the Center: Toward an Identity Politics of One-to-One Mentoring*. Logan: Utah State University Press.

Diab, Rasha. 2016. *Shades of Ṣulḥ: The Rhetorics of Arab-Islamic Reconciliation*. Pittsburgh: University of Pittsburgh Press.

Eble, Michelle F., and Lynée Lewis Gaillet, eds. 2008. *Stories of Mentoring: Theory and Praxis*. West Lafayette, IN: Parlor.

Fricker, Miranda. 2007. *Epistemic Injustice: Power and the Ethics of Knowing*. New York: Oxford University Press.

Geller, Anne Ellen, and Michele Eodice, eds. 2013. *Working with Faculty Writers*. Logan: Utah State University Press.

Gere, Anne Ruggles. 1994. "Kitchen Tables and Rented Rooms: The Extracurriculum of Composition." *College Composition and Communication* 45 (1): 75–92.

Godbee, Beth. 2012. "Toward Explaining the Transformative Power of Talk about, around, and for Writing." *Research in the Teaching of English* 47 (2): 171–197.

Godbee, Beth. 2017. "Writing Up: How Assertions of Epistemic Rights Counter Epistemic Injustice." *College English* 79 (6): 593–618.

Godbee, Beth, and Julia Novotny. 2014. "Asserting the Right to Belong: Feminist Co-Mentoring among Graduate Student Women." *Feminist Teacher* 23 (3): 177–195.

Goeke, Jennifer, Emily J. Klein, Pauline Garcia-Reid, Amanda S. Birnbaum, Tiffany L. Brown, and Donna Degennaro. 2011. "Deepening Roots: Building a Task-Centered Peer Mentoring Community." *Feminist Formations* 23 (1): 212–234.

Goffman, Erving. 1971. *Relations in Public: Microstudies of the Public Order*. New York: Harper & Row.

Gomez, Mary Louise, Ayesha Khurshid, Mel B. Freitag, and Amy Johnson Lachuk. 2011. "Microaggressions in Graduate Students' Lives: How They Are Encountered and Their Consequences." *Teaching & Teacher Education* 27 (8): 1189–1199.

Green, Neisha-Anne. 2016. "The Re-Education of Neisha-Anne Green: A Close Look at the Damaging Effects of 'A Standard Approach,' the Benefits of Code-Meshing, and the Role Allies Play in This Work." *Praxis: A Writing Center Journal* 14 (1): 72–82.

Grollman, Eric Anthony. 2016. "Recovering from Graduate School: Rewriting the Trauma Narrative." *Write Where It Hurts* (blog). March 16. http://www.writewhereithurts.net/recovering-from-graduate-school-rewriting-the-trauma-narrative/.

Gutiérrez y Muhs, Gabriella, Yolanda Flores Niemann, Carmen G. González, and Angela P. Harris, eds. 2012. *Presumed Incompetent: The Intersections of Race and Class for Women in Academia*. Logan: Utah State University Press.

Harris, Angela P., and Carmen G. González. 2012. Introduction to *Presumed Incompetent: The Intersections of Race and Class for Women in Academia*, edited by Gabriella Gutiérrez y Muhs, Yolanda Flores Niemann, Carmen G. González, and Angela P. Harris. Logan: Utah State University Press.

Heller, Caroline E. 1997. *Until We Are Strong Together: Women Writers in the Tenderloin*. New York: Teachers College Press.

Heritage, John, and Geoffrey Raymond. 2005. "The Terms of Agreement: Indexing Epistemic Authority and Subordination in Assessment Sequences." *Social Psychology Quarterly* 68 (1): 15–38.

Lawrence, Susan, and Terry Zawacki. 2016. "Supporting Graduate Student Thesis and Dissertation Writers in a Writing Center." Special issue, *Writing Lab Newsletter* 40 (5–6).

Lorde, Audre. 1984. "Age, Race, Class, and Sex: Women Redefining Difference." *Sister Outsider: Essays and Speeches*, 114–123. Freedom, CA: Crossing.

Lunsford, Andrea A., Jenn Fishman, and Warren M. Liew. 2013. "College Writing, Identification, and the Production of Intellectual Property: Voices from the Stanford Study of Writing." *College English* 75 (5): 470–492.

Lurie, Julia. 2016. "A Toxic Timeline of Flint's Water Fiasco." *Mother Jones*, January 26. http://www.motherjones.com/environment/2016/01/flint-lead-water-crisis-timeline.

Lyon, Arabella, and Lester C. Olson. 2014. *Human Rights Rhetoric: Traditions of Testifying and Witnessing*. New York: Routledge.

Martínez, Elizabeth. 1993. "Beyond Black/White: The Racisms of Our Times." *Social Justice* 20 (1–2): 22–34.

McGuire, Gail M., and Jo Reger. 2003. "Feminist Co-Mentoring: A Model for Academic Professional Development." *NWSA Journal* 15 (1): 54–72.

Patton, Lori D. 2009. "My Sister's Keeper: A Qualitative Examination of Mentoring Experiences among African American Women in Graduate and Professional Schools." *Journal of Higher Education* 80 (5): 510–537.

Perryman-Clark, Staci, David E. Kirkland, and Austin Jackson, eds. 2015. *Students' Right to Their Own Language: A Critical Sourcebook*. Boston: Bedford/St. Martin's.

Raymond, Geoffrey, and John Heritage. 2006. "The Epistemics of Social Relations: Owning Grandchildren." *Language in Society* 35 (5): 677–704.

Smitherman, Geneva, and Victor Villanueva, eds. 2003. *Language Diversity in the Classroom: From Intention to Practice*. Carbondale: Southern Illinois University Press.

Sue, Derald Wing. 2010. *Microaggressions in Everyday Life: Race, Gender, and Sexual Orientation*. Hoboken, NJ: Wiley & Sons.

Whitney, Anne. 2008. "Teacher Transformation in the National Writing Project." *Research in the Teaching of English* 43 (2): 144–187.

Wiltshire, Susan Ford. 1998. *Athena's Disguises: Mentors in Everyday Life*. Louisville, KY: Westminster John Knox Press.

Yosso, Tara J. 2005. "Whose Culture Has Capital? A Critical Race Theory Discussion of Community Cultural Wealth." *Race, Ethnicity, and Education* 8 (1): 69–91.

2
INCIDENTS IN THE LIFE OF KIRSTEN T. EDWARDS
A Personal Examination of the Academic In-Between Space

Kirsten T. Edwards

Reader, be assured this narrative is no fiction. I am aware that some of my adventures may seem incredible; but they are, nevertheless, strictly true. I have not exaggerated the wrongs inflicted by slavery; on the contrary my descriptions fall short of the facts. . . . I had not motive for secrecy on my own account, but I deemed it kind and considerate towards others to pursue this course.

—Harriet Jacobs

INTRODUCTION

January 20, 2009 11:43 pm

Well I had another "White Boy" experience at work today. Actually I had several "White Boy" experiences today. It truly is a rarity for me to have an advising appointment with a White male student (and sometimes White female) that's not antagonistic, or competitive, or where he's simply respectful. I don't know what it is! I'm thinking to myself, "If I'm going to visit with my academic advisor or any university official, heck any human being, I'm going to try to have a positive, respectful interaction." But noooo, this is obviously too much to ask. It's almost as if they're incapable of seeing me as an equal individual. I mean they are utterly oblivious. What did Peggy McIntosh (2008) say, "carefully taught"? I think I'm really starting to get it now. These students really have been taught by everything around them, everything that makes them who they are, that they are superior. That they don't have to have respect for anyone they deem unworthy. Sometimes I get the distinct feeling that they feel like they are paying for their "university experience" and therefore they reserve the right to view me as just another part of the "product." Like I'm some sort of a servant, or dare I say slave, as opposed to a university professional. It really is frustrating. It's like I try not to get all prideful, but heck I have a master's degree, I'm a grown woman, I'm educated, I'm smart, and most important, I have the information they need to make it through the university and ultimately graduate. But they apparently see me as some sort of Aunt Jemima servant, whose only goal in life is to wait on them hand and foot. Like obviously they are of superior intelligence, better in every way, and there's no advice I could give to them that would be of any use. And all I need to do is meet their demands and my purpose will have been served . . .

Recently, I read a narrative piece by theorist Denise Taliaferro Baszile (2006). In the text she describes a concept she terms the "ontoepistemological in-between," the place where she does not quite belong. When I read the text, I felt a light bulb turn on. There was an immediate understanding, communication, bonding between me and the author (or the concept). Although Baszile was describing her experiences as a Black, female, junior faculty member at a predominately white institution (PWI), I knew instantly what she was talking about. I felt it. I did not simply theoretically understand the concept. I just knew! Maybe it was the place I was in as a Black, woman, doctoral student and professional employee. Maybe it was the intersection of the professional and academic. Or maybe, as I feared to admit the most, it was years of navigating White, male spaces in my educational and professional career. It was years of "feeling" like I was not "doing" what I was supposed to be doing. I was not functioning as I was expected to function; as if I was occupying the "wrong" space; as if something just did not fit right. But for whatever reason, I knew and I wanted to know more.

In addition, I wanted to know how others experienced this space. My experiences are individual and personal and are limited in their scope. By listening to the stories of other "in-betweeners," I hoped to gain a fuller appreciation for this academic navigation (Richardson and St. Pierre 2000). Therefore, I decided to have a conversation with three other academic "in-betweeners" who occupy different socially constructed spaces. I am interested in how other members of academia who do not fit neatly into these ideological boxes negotiate the treacherous waters of the academy. What do we do when our race or gender or ideologies do not coincide with the original design, with the underlying/ historic values of the institution? (Anderson 1988; Solomon 1985; Thelin 2004). And what do our navigational practices and understandings tell us about higher education today? As well, I made another decision to embark on this journey of discovery with postcolonial discourse and narrative inquiry lenses. I believe the historical significance of colonization and postcolonization, as well as the value of telling stories or counternarratives, will significantly aid in the development of this "in-between" concept. And so I begin.

COLONIZATION/POSTCOLONIZATION

As a formerly colonized nation, the United States has a legacy of exclusion and oppression, especially within established institutions such as higher education (Anderson 1988; Solomon 1985; Thelin 2004). We, like many other parts of the world, have been "discovered" and subsequently conquered by a European power. We have a history of forced labor and genocide. Our past is filled with laws, rules, and policies meant to excessively privilege one group by systematically oppressing others (Memmi 1965). However, what establishes us as a postcolonial nation are events such as the Revolutionary and Civil Wars, the Civil and Women's Rights Movements, the Civil Rights Act of 1964, Brown vs. Board of Education 1954, affirmative action, and so forth. We have laws in place now that supposedly confirm to us that "all men (and women) are created equal," that we all have the right to "life, liberty, and the pursuit of property." And these laws apparently overturn previous institutional establishments to the contrary. Yet, are these edicts of equality materializing in our everyday lived experiences? Has legislation been successful in eradicating the North American colony? Or is the length of their reach limited to black and white, pen and paper?

US higher education serves as a significant starting point to begin this investigation of presumed decolonization. As one of the first incorporated institutions in the colonial state, higher education was marked with the DNA of the colony (Thelin 2004). Its explicit function was to operate within and for the new colonial entity. Not only was it created to educate the male offspring of the colonizers—the next generation of the privileged—it also aided in teaching these colonial students what it meant to be the controlling class. In the same instance, as the sons of the colonizers were away preparing to control, the daughters were staying home to domesticate and reproduce (Palmieri 1987; Solomon 1985). In addition, the Black and Red bodies of the colonial space, the "officially" colonized, were introduced to yet another institution that would facilitate their servitude, marginalization, and subsequent dehumanization. So even in its inclusions and exclusions, higher education—as with all colonial institutions—was reinforcing the demands of the colony. It was modeling for the colonial peoples, male and female, Black, White, and Red, the expectations of the colonial state. While Native Americans were "invited" to attend and adopt the ways of Europeans in their newly created Halls of Erudition; while White women were made to stay home and reproduce the "Republican Motherhood" and later provided an alternative education that was separate and unequal; while Black slaves worked in the kitchens and on the grounds of the institution, or their young Masters carried them to college as personal servants, the whole design reflected the requirements of the new colony (Anderson 1988; Churchill 2004; Palmieri 1987; Solomon 1985; Thelin 2004).

Higher education was only a cell—albeit a potentially important cell—in the body of the colonial state. It was one microcosmic replica of the larger North American colony. And because of its static nature, higher education has miraculously maintained much of its colonial DNA for over three centuries (Thelin 2004). As John R. Thelin (2004) argues, there remained a constant calling, or need to maintain a connection, to colonial roots by many of the oldest higher education institutions, such as Harvard and William and Mary, well into the late twentieth century. In reality, much of what we as a nation consider the "collegiate experience" is a simulacrum of the colonial university. As Thelin (2004) reminds us in the introduction of his comprehensive text *A History of American Higher Education*, "[Higher education's] deep roots in the American past have given it an unusual mixture of perspective, confidence, and *continuity of purpose*" (xiii; italics added). Well what exactly was that purpose? According to Barbara Miller Solomon (1985), author of *In the Company of Educated Women*, that purpose was to educate future "ministers, lawyers, doctors, and *men of affairs*" (2; italics added), to provide a "mark of distinction [for the] *potential leaders* [of the new colony] (2)." Those "potential leaders" and "men of affairs" were definitely not female, nor were they non-White. We see in these two simple passages that the early purpose of colonial higher education was to create clearly delineated classes and functions for different groups of people. And we also see that in many ways, US higher education has not deviated from its original purpose. One example is the ranking of higher education institutions today. While the presence of different "types" of institutions for the "common man and woman" may lead us to believe that we as a nation are providing educational opportunities for a broader spectrum of individuals, the most prestigious institutions are still reserved for the formation of the "colonial elite" (Thelin 2004, 25). And the other "types" are perceived as adapted models of normal schools for the training of the twenty-first-century middle class (Anderson 1988). The prestigious universities not only produce the bourgeois class, they also continue the maintenance of the proletariat by preserving classist divides that are cut along sexist and racists lines (Memmi 1965).

This preservation of divides leads me back to my original topic of inquiry. Who are the "academic in-betweeners?" In my opinion, bearing in mind different socially constructed identities created in a colonial state, these individuals navigate spaces among privilege, oppression, and discomfort within the academy. While some of us do occupy the space of the bourgeois colonized, as philosopher Albert Memmi argues (1965), an intermediary class of slightly privileged colonized peoples, this is not the extent of our in-between experience. The "beauty" of the in-between space is that it has the ability to physically and metaphysically embody the professional, academic, and ideological position of both the colonizer and the colonized simultaneously, not simply that we enact colonizer and colonized behavior (Freire 1970). I will attempt to bring some grounding to this concept by way of my own lived experience. I, as a Black, female, administrator, and scholar, do not simply function to my White male student as a class above the poor, useless servants and maintenance/facility workers he encounters daily. By virtue of my professional position in the institution, I also function as a personal authority to him. Therefore, in the same epistemological space, I represent to my student both a higher ranking colonizer and a subhuman colonized. Where the challenges of the in-between space surface is when the colonizer within my White male student sees in me a physically marked colonized individual and desires to demote said colonized or bourgeois colonized to my intended space.

Therefore, the core of my argument is not simply that universities are racist and sexist spaces (which they are) but that they still function and subsequently resurrect ideologies based on a colonial model. So, unlike Patricia Hill Collins (1998), I do not classify academic in-betweeners as necessarily "outsiders-within" US higher education. Alternatively, I may describe us as "dislocated insiders." We are supposed to be here. A colony cannot exist without both the colonizer and the colonized (and, I may argue, the bourgeois colonized). However, the nuance of the academic in-between space is that we also serve as reminders, testifiers, or potentially the "conscious" of the remaining educational colony (DuBois 1903). The experiences of the in-betweener, the experience of the in-between space, says loud and clear, "Something ain't right!" When our "colonizing agent" students look into our faces confused, disgusted, confrontational, it is not because we should not be here. It is because we should not stand there. The slave should definitely be in the house, just in the kitchen, or the washroom, or on the grounds. Not in the family room, or the den, or the classroom, or the administrative office. And alternatively, the White "master" and "mistress" should want to remain blissfully unaware of the daily trials of life in the slave quarters. They should be committed to the continuation of the (post)colonial system, invested in the reproduction of injustice.

Therefore, I ask, based on my own lived experiences as well as the lived experiences of my three gracious participants, Has forty-five years, or one generation, after the Civil Rights Act, not been long enough to forget that White is supposed to be supreme, that male is the leader, that Black is designed for labor, that people of color are subhuman, that White is the producer of knowledge (Anderson 1988; Asher 2002; Memmi 1965; Rodney 1972; Watkins 2001)? And if you are asking the same questions, what happens when Black is the holder of knowledge, when Asian is the leader, when female refuses to simply reproduce subordination, when White is challenging inequality and oppression, when male chooses to follow those leading the revolution? What happens when individuals occupy a space of academic "mixed-class," as I like to call it, when their position within the academy communicates one class but their physical markers identify them as affiliated with an entirely different class group in a colonial system? How do these "colonial contradictions" navigate this formerly colonized space?

Now before I further investigate this in-between concept, I would like to say that I do not mean to ignore the many advances in equality we have made as an institution and nation. It is clear I, as a Black woman, have access to resources my predecessors did not. I have the privilege to spend my days discussing theory, epistemology, and ontological experiences. I own the roof over my head. I am a professional with an advanced degree. Honestly, the list of my privileges goes on and on. I would be "carefully taught not to recognize" as Peggy McIntosh (2008, 62) might say, if I did not acknowledge the privileged space I occupy. But what is the extent of this privilege? And why is it still a privilege? If I embrace the myth of meritocracy, then I should believe that this privilege is no privilege at all but the product of hard work and dedication. And the reason others occupy more or less "comfortable" positions is again a product of their individual effort and innate abilities. However, this is hard for me to believe. For example, the fact that the proportion of ethnic minorities that live in poverty, are unable to access healthcare, and are provided substandard educational resources far exceeds the proportion of Whites seems less a product of individual commitment and ability and more a product of systemic inequality (Lui, Robles, Leondar-Wright, Brewer, and Adamson 2006).

While "growing up" in the academy, I am attempting to actively resist the subtle and lethal poison of the oppressor (Freire 1970). Influenced by the self-reflexive theories of Frantz Fanon (1967) and Paolo Freire (1970), I ask myself, "How can I gather enough of the poison to dissect it, investigate it, then reject it and infuse my own cultural understandings in a way that works toward social justice within the academy?" While continually preoccupied with the work of equity, I struggle to remind myself that my own cultural understandings cannot "heal" the problem of colonization (Fanon 1967). It can only begin the work of dismantling the issue. Deconstruction of an unjust system is one thing. Reconstruction of a just system is another. Therefore, in light of the complexities associated with the postcolonial state of US higher education, through this paper I have only attempted to begin the work of deconstructing the inequitable in-between space within the institution. However, my hope is that this small beginning will eventually inspire myself and others to continue and complete the work of deconstruction and ultimately begin the work of reconstructing an equitable educational institution.

Furthermore, socially just deconstruction is further complicated by the continued efforts of the established institution. As university administrators/colonizers work to create a "home" space for White and male students within the academy, it becomes less and less of a home for the "Other" (hooks 1994). If "Other" students are to be successful (or succeed according to the standards of the established regime), they must adapt to the sovereignty of the colonizer (Memmi 1965). This means allowing parts of their authenticity to shrink to gain facility with the language of the colonizer (Collins 1990; Lawrence 1995). Therefore, it becomes a struggle for these "colonial contradictions" within the academy like myself who have submitted to the process of academic colonization, the academic in-betweeners, to then represent ourselves in nonstereotypical, emancipatory ways (hooks 1994; Memmi 1965). We must choose to navigate the academy in an extremely thoughtful manner if we hope to work towards socially just practices within this not-home space (hooks 1991). This is not to say that I seek to provide through these stories solutions for the unjust, academic in-between, not-home space. As mentioned before, the goal of this paper is to aid in deconstruction, not to begin reconstruction. However, through an examination of and subsequent summation of these narratives, we can begin to ascertain a more robust understanding of the academic in-between experience and, therefore, become better equipped to think about tangible possibilities for future solutions.

I recognize that my conception of navigation is biased towards socially just ends and that submitting to the oppressive, White-supremacist, patriarchal, heterosexist, capitalist hegemonic understandings of academia to attain the rewards of that system such as money, prestige, promotion, acceptance, albeit contaminated (selling out), is a navigational tool as well. However, through this paper I will focus on the navigational practices of those who are like minded, those individuals who choose to acknowledge the antagonistic nature of the academy, those who refuse to accept the values of the colonizer as sovereign and choose instead not to ignore the indoctrination of the academy. With that being said, I continue to recognize the oppressor within myself (Freire 1970). I am privileged. My conceptions of social justice are flawed. I am part of an academic elite. The very fact that I am spending hours writing a paper on colonization within the academy proves that I am far removed from much of the struggle for equity and social justice on the larger scale. Indeed, my conceptions of the postcolonial binaries are informed by this privileged position. However, I press on. I choose to use this place of not belonging as a starting point but remain intent on maintaining a space of critique within my own academic discourse.

NARRATIVE INQUIRY

March 27, 2008 5:16 pm

Today I met with my boss to do sort of an informal performance evaluation. Anyway, the evaluation was going well. She had a lot of good things to say about me. I was actually quite surprised! But then she said something not so "positive." She said maybe I should start calling myself "Ms. Edwards" or "Ms. Kirsten" with the students to make the relationship more formal. I told her how I like to keep it informal so the students—especially the minority students—will feel comfortable coming to see me. It can be so difficult for them to make it at a PWI. I want them to know there's someone here to support them that they can talk to. She said she understood, but she thinks sometimes the students (code for White students) don't see me as an authority figure because "I look so young." So when I tell them something, they go behind me and ask her if what I said was correct. What?!!! I couldn't believe what I was hearing. She said maybe if I had them address me with a title, they would see me as more of an authority figure.

Obviously she doesn't see the real issue. I reminded her that my coworker Kendall lets the students call her by her first name and they (White students) never question her authority. In fact, they love her and worship the ground she walks on precisely because of her informality. And furthermore, Kendall was the one who trained me because she, my boss, wanted me to be trained by the more "student-friendly" advisor as opposed to the other advisor who demands that students call her Ms. Tessle. The students hate Ms. Tessle! Now, all of a sudden I need the students to address me as Ms. Edwards? Why can't she see what's really happening here? The only difference between me and Kendall is Kendall's White and I'm Black. We both have master's degrees and are current doc students, we're around the same age, and our advising styles are pretty much the same because, again, SHE TRAINED ME! You know, sometimes I wish people would just listen . . . I wish they would just hear me . . . I wish they understood. It seems like you have to shove it in their faces before they get it. And even when you do, you're viewed as "angry," "radical," or my favorite, "overreacting." Oh well, I guess it doesn't matter, nobody cares about my side of the story anyway. But damn it! I'm not about to change the way I interact with my students because of some racist kids! And although I realize that because of the racist environment I'm working in, there may be different requirements necessary for me to receive "some" of the same results (Hell, I'm not completely stupid!), I'll be damned if I just give in. The environment needs to change, not me! Shoot, if they don't respect me now, "Ms." definitely won't help . . .

Before I began this journey of researching the "in-between," I knew I wanted to tell my story. I wanted to be heard. But with no one to listen, I told myself. Journaling or keeping a diary had been a part of my life since I was a teenager. I have written the most during the most frustrating, confusing, difficult moments of my life. So it was comforting when other "elder" scholars of color encouraged me to document my most trying times as a doctoral student and future academic. I have been told on multiple occasions to use my experiences as fuel for my writing and to treasure the storms I weather in the in-between as gold nuggets refined in the fire. Consequently, while I was encouraged by scholars I highly respect to "write it down," it was natural and logical for me to begin the chronicle of my in-between experience. Journaling was the healing response to my feelings of silencing and being disregarded in the academy. Anytime I spoke out about how I was feeling, I was viewed as complaining or not being a team player. It was as if I was being told I needed to just get over it. There were things I wanted to "say"—things that were not in research journals, or quantitative analysis, or flagship agendas. These were issues that were not easily fixed or "leadership developed" out of the organization. These were simply reality, truth, my truth. And I wanted it to be heard. But how do you make sharing your journaling, being heard, telling your story, a research project? As I would soon discover, you do it through narrative inquiry! As Laurel

Richardson and Elizabeth Adams St. Pierre (2000, 965) remind us, "This new qualitative community could . . . reach beyond academia and teach all of us about social injustice and methods for alleviating it."

Narrative inquiry has offered me the opportunity to position my perspective as well as the perspectives of other "in-betweeners" (Chase 2005; Collins 1990; Moen 2006). Reality is now able to be viewed through the eyes of the one who is living it or telling it. The subject of the experience becomes the final authority of that experience. As Torill Moen (2006) states, "It is impossible to understand human mental functioning without considering how and where this occurs through growth" (58). Embedded in this quote is the idea of subjectivity and a unique lived experience. She goes on to say that there is "no static and everlasting truth. Instead there are *different subjective positions* from which we experience and interpret the world" (63; italics added). This means not only is my truth subjective, but the hegemonic "Truth" that is inscribed within academic discourse is subjective and open to interpretation. In addition, this method of research has allowed me to not only tell the stories of others navigating the institution but also weave my own development into the text (Miller 2005). By positioning our perspectives, I am in a small way attempting to centralize our experiences in the academic discourse, or better stated, penetrate the current hegemonic discourse about the university experience. I want to, as Charles R. Lawrence (1995) says, provide a "counter narrative." I would like my readers to listen and to (re)think how they view the higher education institution. And if they hear a disconnect, contemplate why Academic Truth (that is supposedly complete and, for all intents and purposes, Fact) does not coincide with our truth(s). In addition, I want to "crystallize" the in-between experience (Richardson and St. Pierre 2000). I want to view it from multiple angles, multiple sources. In so doing, I wish to provide a fuller, more substantial understanding of these experiences. I want to hear someone else. And then I want to ask, "How does their navigational practice further inform this very personal experience/concept." I am interested in seeing how other in-betweeners' experiences further develop this concept that came to me during my own individual struggle with(in) the academy. When writing about researching the autobiographies of early women teachers, Maria Tamboukou says,

> I have considered the author's disappearance as an immensely thrilling and exciting theme that has been radically reworked in the narratives revolving around the construction of female subjectivities. These autobiographical narratives, I have argued, have constructed a space "in the margins of hegemonic discourses" . . . for the female self in education

to emerge rather than disappear. This emergence however, has not constituted a unitary core self, but rather a matrix of subject positions for women "writing themselves" to inhabit, not in a permanent way, but rather temporarily, as points of departure for going elsewhere, becoming other. (Andrews, Squire, and Tamboukou 2008, 108)

Like Tamboukou, I am not seeking a "unitary core self" for the mixed-class, academic in-betweeners. I simply desire to create a space in this academy where alternative voices can be heard. I also want to give others the opportunity to be heard. I do not know if they want to be heard. But I know I want to be heard, so I am inviting them along on my quest. And honestly, I want to add validity to my experience (Richardson and St. Pierre 2000; Riessman 2008). I already know the isolation I had encountered when attempting to communicate my personal view of the university to the "powers that be." Alone, I feel like my narrative will be (has been) treated like the early publication of *Incidents in the Life of a Slave* Girl (Smith and Watson 2000). Upon release, it was immediately ridiculed as falsified information. Its validity and value were stripped away because it did not conform to the dominant culture's perceived "reality." I realize four narratives may not bring down the beast of hegemonic discourse. However, maybe they can be part of the process. With that being said, I do not fail to realize my agency in the presentation of these narratives. While I listen to the conversations I have had with my three colleagues, I acknowledge my own frames and ideologies. I know that my personal understandings can affect the way I interpret their words (Andrews, Squire, and Tamboukou 2008). I am listening to these narratives at a specific point in my own human development, which has a profound impact on what I see in the data. As narrative researcher Molly Andrews states, "All of us bring to our research knowledge which we have acquired through our life's experiences, and indeed how we make sense of what we observe and hear is very much influenced by that framework of understanding" (Andrews, Squire, and Tamboukou 2008, 86). In addition, during a lecture given by Janet L. Miller (2009), she reminded us as budding researchers that themes do not "emerge." We as researchers identify themes based on our own understandings and beliefs. I know that I am particularly vulnerable to "identifying" specific themes in this project because it is so close to me. The subject of this paper is not some abstract phenomenon that I researched in a textbook. The in-between is my everyday lived experience. It is who I am. I cannot deny my personal investment. However, despite my reservations, I choose to continue. The work is far too important for me to ignore. I have a responsibility as a scholar to add to the body of knowledge within my scholarship community (Riessman 2008). Therefore, I am committed to identifying myself throughout this work to add transparency and authenticity (Miller 2005). As well, I have made every effort to be as honest in my description and interpretation of the narratives as possible. While I work with these conversations, I remind myself to be a reflexive researcher (Denzin and Lincoln 2000). As I interpret the words of my colleagues, I am also deconstructing my own understanding of those words. I am working to allow our voices to be heard and not to hear my voice in their words. It has been a difficult task but a necessary one if I am to work as a narrative researcher. I also understand that this is a worthwhile labor of love (hooks 2003). Therefore, I press forward, hoping to produce scholarship that is meaningful, authentic, transparent, and socially just.

VOICES

For this project I have selected three individuals I have identified as academic in-betweeners. Because of different socially constructed identities, these individuals navigate spaces between privilege, oppression, and discomfort within the academy. In no way do I assume that among the four of us, we represent the totality of the in-between experience. Rather, I expect our shared stories will begin the process of crystallizing that experience (Richardson and St. Pierre 2000). These stories thus provide different angles to refract light onto this "in-betweenness." Hopefully these multiple points of view will help us gain a fuller appreciation for the "in-between space" and a greater understanding of the nature of the postcolonial academy.

Professor Martin: The Familiar Guest

I interviewed Professor Martin[1] on February 23, 2009, at 12:25 p.m. He is a Black assistant professor at a large research university in the South. His academic experience has been varied. As he mentioned in the beginning of our conversation, his participation in several different types of institutions, from a small historically Black college/university (HBCU), to a small PWI with less than a 1 percent Black population, to a large PWI with a very active Black community, has significantly informed the way he navigates the academic institution, or as he puts it, "White spaces." One of the first remarks he made was,

> One of the things I learned from my major professor, which in some ways I think is a compliment and on the other hand I feel is a put down . . . but

> I think really guides the way I think about the academy, as he put it so eloquently . . . he says I have a way of making White people feel comfortable. That framing of making White people feel comfortable means that you are clearly in a White dominated society. How do you navigate it? What insights go into it? How does your knowledge of White supremacy guide the way you move within the institution?

He went on to say,

> At a Black institution you gain a certain kind of grounding, and what that grounding looks like is you know that even though you're in an all-Black environment you understand that environment is functioning in a wider White society. So how do you get your sea legs when you're going out into a community that may not have the same kind of values?

Through my conversation with Professor Martin, I felt a very distinct navigational process. He was clear about his understanding that he was moving through a not-so-welcoming environment. He was also clear that to make it through this system, it would require every tool he had picked up along the way. He stated there has been "this kind of racial-sociocultural-political kind of lens that has guided the way I move in the institution."

Regardless of the fact that he had acquired all of the necessary credentials to participate fully in the academy, he still felt like a "guest." His physical markers still in many instances outweighed those credentials. He appeared to have an understanding that he did not belong here, or at least that the dominate culture did not feel he belonged here. He was not expected to occupy the space of "scholar" in the academy. However, the nature of his chosen profession and his desire to work for social justice in the academy required that he continue the navigational process. As he went on to say,

> I've been as welcomed [by the dominant culture in the institution] as they can be, but ultimately for the institution to really be welcoming to a man of color, there'd be so many things they would have to drastically change [which causes me to] feel familiar but I still feel like a guest in a lot of ways.

This statement personally resonated with me. As I move through the academic institution, I constantly feel like I am bumping against walls and structures that do not fit me, that were not designed with me in mind. I understood Professor Martin's constant struggle to figure out a way to move within and apart from the institution. The institution establishes clear expectations. Oftentimes, these expectations do not coincide with the experiences or the understandings fostered in communities of color. Many times these expectations stand as contradictions to the person of color. When speaking of his students' reaction to him as a Black professor, as the "knower" in the classroom he said,

> When the old White guy says "I don't know everything but let me tell you what I know," they listen. But when the Black teacher says "I don't know everything," they're like, "We know so quit making stuff up (laughter)." It's the honest to goodness truth. I had one student tell me after the fact that when they first met me they assumed I didn't know what I was talking about.

I definitely understand this experience. Oftentimes, the students I work with question my directives. They go over my head to my White supervisor to confirm the validity of my statements. It is as if my race automatically contradicts my position as knower. Apparently, there are some points of community within this navigational in-between process. However, how well does my experience connect when the racial dynamics are changed?

Jane: Tough Choices . . .

I interviewed Jane on March 2, 2009, at 4:45 p.m. Jane is a White, female, self-identified feminist, doctoral student. She has completed her coursework and is now working on her dissertation. She attends the same above-mentioned university. Her research interests include issues of diversity and leadership. Specifically, she wants to look at the motivating factors that encourage White leaders in the academy to serve as mentors or "allies" for Black students. As she mentioned, her own struggles with gender equity have informed her desire to participate in social justice research. However, these struggles were not the impetus for such work. It was her participation in a required Race and Gender course that sparked her interests. She stated,

> I had not thoughtfully taken it to the next step to say if I can recognize my experiences as a woman are a unique set of experiences and that there are still limitations and there are still . . . societal challenges related to being a woman, let me extrapolate that and say what kind of challenges might other kinds of people face. So I . . . use that phrase the "diversity Kool-aid" because I'm not naïve enough to think that everyone who's exposed to the ideas, to those kinds of readings and conversations that I had, I'm not naïve enough to think that everyone just through exposure would have the same kind of mindset.

When I listened to Jane's story, the impression I received, especially after having interviewed Professor Martin, was that Jane possessed a greater level of agency or choice in her navigational process. I believe this is significantly informed by Jane's race. As we talked, it seemed Jane's first real encounters with having to navigate the academy came after her experience in the Race and Gender class, when she chose to participate in social justice work. She went on to say,

> If I didn't want to think about it, I wouldn't have to. And I try to recognize that. . . . I've never had to worry about whether I was, am I going to be representing or are they going to think I'm the voice of the "Other" am I . . . even as a woman I work with a lot of women. So I never feel like I'm the female voice. But . . . I recognize that other people in the college, women, minorities, in different settings, that is a barrier for them that that they may feel that their opinions and their voices may really be ignored. May really be discounted. So um, I recognize that privilege that's associated with my Whiteness and I try not to take advantage of it.

Unlike Professor Martin, who seems to be forced to negotiate a place of not belonging, Jane has to make a conscious decision to recognize the privilege associated with her Whiteness. She has made a choice to occupy the in-between space, to drink the "diversity Kool-aid," because of her personal conviction to function as a socially just agent. As she stated, her Whiteness provides the privilege to choose.

> I would say being a White woman, a White anything interested in diversity at a school like this definitely qualifies as an in-between space. I would say . . . yes I think it is sometimes a struggle. But even to say that I think is very selfish because I have a choice to be in this struggle. And there are other in-between spaces that are much more uncomfortable, where people don't have a choice. They can't opt out of. So the reason that I choose to navigate this space is I feel like I have some moral imperative as a decent human being, as a Christian.

Jane continued with an example of how she can as a White body "opt out" of the in-between: "The ways that I struggle with are, well there are a couple of ways. So when I'm sharing my dissertation topic and you get the funny looks. So then the struggle is the next time somebody asks you, what kind of answer do you give? And do you just, 'Well I'm interested in . . .'"

Talking with Jane was extremely enlightening for me. Although she was a self-proclaimed feminist and was honest about her struggles in the academy as a woman, she seemed clear about having a place, a fit in the academy as a White person. She also seemed to understand that her Whiteness provided a definite privilege. She was honest about the reality that her navigation was a choice and that while she is choosing to struggle, she is alongside many who do not have the privilege of that same choice.

Li: Invisibility

As I worked through this idea of the academic in-between, I recognized the very clear Black/White binary I used to frame this space in. Because of the legacy of slavery, especially in the South, participants in the US institution of higher education tend to hold very distinct understandings of what it means to be Black and what it means to be White in the institution. However, what happens when you do not fit into either one of these boxes?

I sat down to have a conversation with Li on March 18, 2009, at 3:30 p.m. Li is a Chinese doctoral student. She is still in the coursework stage of her doctoral process. Li completed her undergraduate degree in China. She received her master's degree from a large PWI in the Midwest United States and is working on her doctorate at the same southern institution Jane attends and at which Professor Martin teaches.

When thinking through Li's navigational practices, I realized hers, of course, were quite different from both Professor Martin's and Jane's. Li does not possess the same privilege of having a place in the institution and choosing to negotiate an in-between space as Jane does. However, she does seem to negotiate the in-between space very differently than Professor Martin. While Professor Martin seems to experience a very visceral reaction to his presence as a "knower" in the academy, Li seems to experience more of an isolation or ignoring. She said,

> You write a paper and don't mind anybody else's business. It's like there's to me, as [an] outsider especially. Not a White person, I think it's . . . there's this sense of isolation. People . . . everybody does their own thing and it is understood that you do your own thing and don't mind anybody else's [business]. That's the part I learned. I had to somehow adjust.

I had the impression that her presence is responded to as an anomaly in the academy. Since the academy does not know what to do with her, it just rejects her, boxes her off. She went on to say, "I also feel that I'm waiting to do the 'adjust,' but obviously my surroundings doesn't really care. It doesn't want to do the adjustments towards me because . . . you get what I mean."

When she made that statement "you get what I mean," she looked at me knowingly, as if there was a shared understanding between the two of us as fellow in-betweeners negotiating an oppressive space. There was an acknowledgement that she did not belong and I did not belong as well. As she further developed this feeling of isolation, she explained how her accent affects her interactions with members of the university community. She said,

> First of all in America[n] society . . . it's [a] very strong sense of individualism and capitalism and everybody's so busy, so busy. And we don't have time for anything for anybody else especially "here comes Li." Especially during [the] beginning years. I myself speak English. I don't feel as comfortable as I should and I am conscious, very conscious, aware of my accents. I am afraid and concerned that because of my accents people will not understand me . . . I'm not saying that I'm not comfortable communicating with people. But when people see me, my existence and the way I speak, my accents, people respond to that even though I explain myself quite clearly. But they like they will for some people they will not even look at you when you're trying to tell them . . . something for some people the nice ones they will look at you like really trying hard. You can see it from their facial expression. They're trying to read hard your lips. I think . . . that's their effort. But I don't really think that's necessary, because I don't speak a weird language. There might be some accents, but it's not weird. It doesn't require that much effort.

Li is correct in saying it does not require that much effort. As we spoke I understood every word she said. Yes, she does speak with an accent, but her English is quite clear. But as she said, her "existence" is a contradiction in the academy. The immediate response she receives from university members is to assume that interactions with her will be laborious. They instinctively identify her as "Other" and subsequently as a "bother." When I asked her whether or not she thinks she fits in the academy she said,

> Do you think I fit? I don't care! After one year, two year, ten years, how much I can fit? How much I'm able to really fit myself with my surroundings? I think that's out of my control . . . I cannot say how exactly it will work out because as long as I try, as long as there's an interact[ion] with my surroundings, things will work. Whether they work out, work up, work down, I don't know. It will change. I believe in that so I don't really focus on do I fit. Do I fit? No, I don't think that's important.

The more I spoke with Li, the more I perceived that she had psychologically opted out of the system. She realized that she did not fit in the academy and that to experience some sense of belonging would require more effort than she was willing to expend. Therefore she made the choice to disengage. This disengagement seems like a direct response to the isolation she is already experiencing as a Chinese student.

In addition, my conversation with Li made me wonder why I do not choose to disengage. I wonder whether or not I have the choice to disengage. I believe my race, as a Black woman, informs my decision to actively struggle with(in) the academy. While there are some moments of isolation, I also feel moments of attack, when perceptions and ideologies of the Black woman in the academy stand in direct contrast to who I know myself to be as a scholar. Li's experiences definitely helped me to better understand my own experiences as well as this broad in-between space. I recognize that although her race forces her into the in-between space, it also provides/demands the opportunity/decision to disengage that space, to negotiate out. Li's Chinese identity categorizes her as "outsider" in this US institution of higher education, while my identity as Black places me in the position of subordinate, servant, "not" knower. Subsequently, these categories are attached to very specific dominant culture expectations about how we are to move within the academy. Professor Martin as a Black man should not be producing or providing knowledge; he should be taking orders from the knowledge producers. Jane as a White person should be providing and reproducing dominant forms of leadership and knowledge. Alternatively, Li as a Chinese woman should neither provide knowledge nor receive orders; she should simply not be there.

DECONSTRUCTIONS . . . AND BEGIN AGAIN THE WORK

In conclusion, I would like to say that I definitely do not have the answer for, the Truth about, the solution to, the academic in-between. However, I do believe I have had the opportunity to take a glimpse of this space through four very different lenses. These lenses have assisted me in recognizing that navigational tools come in many different packages. Whether they require constant use and multiple techniques gained through a lifetime of strategizing, or they are the everyday decision to choose to navigate, or they are the tool to use to navigate out and disengage when able, they are navigational tools nonetheless. Furthermore, the very existence of these tools reminds us that they are responses to an extremely robust and often overwhelmingly oppressive space. This space is real. It is not a figment of our imaginations. Every day we move through the academy, every time we have to employ a tool, we are reminded that we do not fit. We are forced to acknowledge that the colonial architects did not have us in mind when they established the requirements for functioning within this academy. It is also apparent that the legacy of colonization persists within this entity we call twenty-first-century US higher education. As well, the postcolonial gatekeepers are not making efforts to reverse its effects. At best, they are only making attempts to camouflage or minimize the recognition of said effects. Therefore, it becomes the responsibility of those in-betweeners, the dislocated insiders, those colonial contradictions, the mixed class, whether born into the in-between space or choosing to occupy it, to use their voices to begin the work.

I hope through this narrative project that we have not only identified the in-between space and provided some ontological grounding for this lived experience, but that we have as in-betweeners highlighted the nature of the academy. Our experiences in the in-between were not our own constructions but responses to an antagonistic environment, an environment that does not agree with our currently held positions, an academic environment. This is the nature of the academy. By highlighting this reality through providing a space for the voices or narratives of fellow in-betweeners to be heard, I hope to have done part of the deconstruction work. As I mentioned earlier, deconstruction of an unjust system is one thing, reconstruction is an entirely different work. However, I am confident that hearing the stories of those that contradict the hegemonic academic narrative is necessary in beginning the process of deconstruction (Richardson and St. Pierre 2000). As such, we should never minimize the preliminary work of deconstruction. While reconstruction may be some time away, deconstruction is immediately at hand. As with a building overcome by asbestos, while the ultimate goal may be to build a new habitable construction, the work cannot begin without first tearing down the old hazardous environment, attacking and destroying the poison within. We all as members of the academic community have a responsibility to attack inequity within the institution. However, that attack can be much more successful when it is strategic. If we have a clearer understanding of the chemical properties and effects of the poison, we can make better choices about our responses, our deconstruction. As is apparent, the academy still recognizes who is expected to occupy the space of Knower or Subordinate, and who does not have a space at all. And that recognition does not seem to be dissolving anytime soon. Unfortunately, through the voices heard in this project, we are reminded that if an individual does not conform to these demands because of their race, gender, and/or ideologies, they may ultimately find themselves negotiating the academic in-between, or the space where they don't quite belong. Nevertheless, deconstructing that space of not belonging through our voices can help us begin to see the promise of a true academic space of liberation.

NOTES

This essay was originally published in the *Journal of Curriculum Theorizing Review* volume 26, issue 1 (2010), and won the Bergamo Conference Distinguished Graduate Student Paper Award for that publication. Reprinted with permission.

1. All participants' names have been changed.

REFERENCES

Anderson, James D. 1988. *The Education of Blacks in the South, 1860–1935*. Chapel Hill, NC: University of North Carolina Press.

Andrews, Molly, Corinne Squire, and Maria Tamboukou. 2008. *Doing Narrative Research*. Thousand Oaks, CA: SAGE.

Asher, Nina. 2002. "(En)gendering a Hybrid Consciousness." *Journal of Curriculum Theorizing* 18 (4): 81–92.

Baszile, Denise. 2006. "In This Place Where I Don't Quite Belong: Claiming the Onto-Epistemological In-between." In *From Oppression to Grace: Women of Color and their Dilemmas Within the Academy*, edited by Theodorea Regina Berry and Nathalie D. Mizelle, 195–208. Sterling, VA: Stylus.

Chase, Susan. 2005. "Narrative Inquiry: Multiple Lenses, Approaches, Voices." In *Handbook of Qualitative Research*, 3rd ed., edited by Norman K. Denzin and Yvonna S. Lincoln, 651–679. Thousand Oaks, CA: SAGE.

Churchill, Ward. 2004. *Kill the Indian, Save the Man: The Genocidal Impact of American Indian Residential Schools*. San Francisco: City Lights Books.

Collins, Patricia Hill. 1990. *Black Feminist Thought: Knowledge, Consciousness, and the Politics of Empowerment*. Boston, MA: Unwin Hyman.

Collins, Patricia Hill. 1998. *Fighting Words: Black Women and the Search for Justice*. Minneapolis: University of Minnesota Press.

Denzin, Norman. K., and Yvonna S. Lincoln. 2000. "Introduction: The Discipline and Practice of Qualitative Research." In *Handbook of Qualitative Research*, 2nd ed., edited by Norman K. Denzin and Yvonna S. Lincoln, 1–28. Thousand Oaks, CA: SAGE.

Du Bois, W. E. B. 1903. *The Souls of Black Folk*. Chicago: A. C. McClurg.

Fanon, Frantz. 1967. *The Wretched of the Earth*. New York: Grove.

Freire, Paolo. 1970. *The Pedagogy of the Oppressed*. New York: Continuum.

hooks, bell. 1991. *Yearning: Race, Gender, and Cultural Politics*. Boston: South End.

hooks, bell. 1994. *Teaching to Transgress: Education as the Practice of Freedom*. New York: Routledge.

hooks, bell. 2003. *Rock My Soul: Black People and Self-Esteem*. New York: Atria Books.

Jacobs, Harriet. (1861) 2001. *Incidents in the Life of a Slave Girl*. New York: Dover Publications.

Lawrence, Charles R. 1995. "The Word and the River: Pedagogy as Scholarship as Struggle." In *Critical Race Theory: The Key Writings That Formed the Movement*, edited by Kimberlé Crenshaw, Neil Gotanda, Garry Peller, and Kendall Thomas, 336–351. New York: New Press.

Lui, Meizhu, Bárbara Robles, Betsy Leondar-Wright, Rose Brewer, and Rebecca Adamson. 2006. *The Color of Wealth: The Story Behind the U.S. Racial Wealth Divide*. New York: New Press.

McIntosh, Peggy. 2008. "White Privilege and Male Privilege: A Personal Account of Coming to See Correspondences through Work in Women's Studies." In *The Feminist Philosophy Reader*, edited by Alison Bailey and Chris Cuomo, 61–69. New York: McGraw-Hill.

Memmi, Albert. 1965. *The Colonizer and the Colonized*. New York: Orion.

Miller, Janet L. 2005. *Sounds of Silence Breaking: Women, Autobiography, Curriculum*. New York: Peter Lang.

Miller, Janet L. 2009. "Transnationality, Subjectivity, Representation: (Im)possibilities of Feminist Autobiographical Practices." Paper presented at the *Louisiana State University Women's and Gender Studies Conference*, Baton Rouge, LA, March 5.

Moen, Torill. 2006. "Reflections on the Narrative Research Approach." *International Journal of Qualitative Methods* 5 (4): 56–69.

Palmieri, Patricia A. 1987. "From Republican Motherhood to Race Suicide: Arguments on the Higher Education of Women in the United States, 1820–1920." In *Educating Men* and Women Together: Coeducation in a Changing World, edited by Carol Lasser, 49–64. Champaign: University of Illinois Press.

Richardson, Laurel, and Elizabeth St. Pierre. 2000. "Writing: A Method of Inquiry." In Handbook of Qualitative Research, 2nd ed., edited by Norman K. Denzin and Yvonna S. Lincoln, 959–978. Thousand Oaks, CA: SAGE.

Riessman, Cathy. 2008. Narrative Methods for the Human Sciences. Thousand Oaks, CA: SAGE.

Rodney, Walter. 1972. How Europe Underdeveloped Africa. London: Bogle-L'Ouverture.

Smith, Sidhonie, and Julia Watson. 2000. "Life Narrative: Definitions and Distinctions, and Autobiographical Subjects." In Reading Autobiography: A Guide for Interpreting Life Narratives, edited by Sidhonie Smith and Julia Watson, 1–48. Minneapolis: University of Minnesota Press.

Solomon, Barbara M. 1985. In the Company of Educated Women: A History of Women and Higher Education in America. New Haven, CT: Yale University Press.

Thelin, John R. 2004. A History of American Higher Education. Baltimore, MD: Johns Hopkins University Press.

Watkins, William H. 2001. The White Architects of Black Education: Ideology and Power in America, 1865–1954. New York: Teachers College Press.

3
VOICES FROM THE HILL
HBCUs and the Graduate Student Experience

Richard Sévère and Maurice Wilson

INTRODUCTION

The 2015 special issue of *Across the Disciplines* titled "Graduate Writing Across the Disciplines" focuses specifically on the experiences of graduate student writing, acknowledging and building on the work that has been done in the area of writing resources for graduate students (Brooks-Gillies, Garcia, Kim, Manthey, and Smith). Other collections such as Cecile Badenhorst and Cally Guerin's (2016) *Research Literacies and Writing Pedagogies for Masters and Doctoral Writers* and Steve Simpson, Nigel Caplan, Michelle Cox, and Talinn Phillips's (2016) *Supporting Graduate Student Writers: Research, Curriculum, and Program Design*, in addition to broader conversations in the fields of TESOL and applied linguistics, have also engaged in conversations about graduate student writing. Absent from those conversations, however, are the voices of underrepresented graduate students whose experiences with writing are aligned with personal, social, political, and historical challenges that impact both the process of writing and student success. The reflections presented in this essay are those of two men of color who attended the same historically Black college/university (HBCU) in the South and went on to earn graduate degrees in English at separate predominantly white institutions (PWIs). These voices reflect on their perceptions of academic discourse and preparedness in engaging in such discourse, as well as how the HBCU experience provided a foundation for navigating other academic communities. One reflection demonstrates the extent to which perceptions of alienation and isolation in the graduate learning experience emerge from a lack of understanding of the different socialization practices of academic and military institutional discourses, while the other focuses on the ways building a sense of community helps to foster confidence through inclusion and collaborative partnerships.

Together, both voices serve as a starting point for larger conversations regarding graduate student preparedness and success. Moreover, they bring special attention to the ways institutions can support underrepresented students seeking graduate degrees. Most important, while contributing to a collective voice that speaks to writing and the graduate student experience, the contrasting experiences provided in this essay are also intended to inspire students of color to reflect on their own personal journeys in their graduate programs. In addition to addressing graduate students, we aim to speak directly to a community of scholars who are often points of contact as both mentors and professionals charged with the grooming and professional development of emerging scholars. Specifically, we hope to make that community recognize that a deliberate effort must be made in order to address the lived experiences and needs of underrepresented graduate students.

OVERCOMING MY POSITIONALITY AS "CLUELESS" ACADEMIC *MAURICE WILSON*

The first time I was compelled to consider the extent to which "ignorance" was as much a factor of my learning as my "knowledge" was during my initial military assignment as a recent Army ROTC and HBCU graduate. I was assigned to a helicopter unit as a pilot and platoon leader when, during a developmental counseling session, I was queried repeatedly by my commanding officer about information outside the scope of my experience or knowledge. I felt that maintaining an image of a capable, competent, and decisive leader was expected, so I often stumbled to provide answers rather than say, "I don't know, sir." My commander, growing more impatient with my responses, referenced Yogi Berra and quipped, "Maurice, you don't know what you don't know." I did not immediately know what the commander meant or what he was trying to get me to consider, and I struggled with that quotation for years. It was only later I finally understood the commander was not calling me stupid (though he often referred to me and the other junior officers as such); he wanted me to appreciate that in spite of talent, skill, or knowledge, becoming an expert in any field or discipline did not mean merely discovering the answers to the problems or questions I would encounter but, more important, discovering the appropriate questions or problems to be solved. The commander certainly might have more clearly made his point had he also offered me Confucius's words "true wisdom is knowing what you don't know," but, again, as his aim was not primarily to teach but to train me through the tear-down-in-order-to-build-up model, Berra's words were apropos. I would only later appreciate how this teaching moment would be as befitting to my professionalization and socialization as an academic and composition scholar as it was to my development as an army officer and aviator. As a man of color, I particularly appreciate how I must negotiate the privilege inherent in the positions I hold as composition instructor and writing center fellow/consultant, as well as the subordination inherent in my status as graduate student and learner—a complex task, to be sure, that benefits my continued efforts to overcome what Gerald Graff (2003, 1) suggests as "cluelessness" for myself and the students I teach and tutor in composition classrooms and writing centers.

As I reflected upon my experiences within the writing spaces of my academic journey, I found myself constantly plagued by "imposter syndrome" (see Clance and Imes 1978) throughout my academic endeavors, thereby always needing to prove to myself that I was worthy, that I belonged, and that I deserved the opportunities I had. I was not surrounded by a "community" of individuals providing me the encouragement and support on a path that would inevitably guide me on a journey of higher education pursuit, nor did I have a model to follow or road map for how such a journey would happen. As a Black male from a working-class family (at times dependent upon government assistance/aid) on the near-west side of Chicago, I would not have the advantages of mentorship and support prior to my undergraduate endeavor. Most others around me were also working-class, welfare families whose concerns were tied to near-poverty social and economic conditions; going to college was not a matter of "where" but rather a condition akin to striking it rich by playing the lottery—possible, but not likely. My journey to academia, then, would be profoundly personal with respect to appreciating vulnerability, isolation, and self-doubt, as I internalized the inherent inadequacies and shortcomings of poverty's social, economic, and academic conditioning rather than realizing these factors for what they were: external and, by design, formative.

I did not have a strong vocabulary, or rather my vocabulary was limited to mimicking in my speech and writing the vernacular of Black English I heard in my daily interactions, assuming such to be the "standard" or "correct" modes of communicating. (As a composition scholar, I have, of course, long since appreciated the CCCC's 1974 resolution admonishing a "standard American dialect") (Conference on College Composition and Communication 1974). And as I did not encounter or engage a non-Black person until I was fifteen, I would not appreciate how my practice of "code-switching," notwithstanding its seeming benefit of inclusion, "force[d] [me] to view [my] language culture and identity as antithetical to the U.S. mainstream" (Young, Barrett, Young-Rivera, and Lovejoy 2014, 9). I wrongly bought into the concept of poverty as a determiner of outcome, and the state of ignorance as being directly accountable to my race—somehow I learned to see myself and others like me as poor, dumb, and destined always to be such. I had not yet encountered Betty Hart and Todd Risley's (2003) "Early Catastrophe," which explains how my "vocabulary resources in language and interaction styles" were "well established" by the time I was three years old and directly tied to my "parents in stature and activity levels" (7)—I was reared in a single-parent household. I would only later abandon this ridiculously flawed view of myself and work to change the same acquired system of values in the students of color I would tutor and teach, but not before contending with an overwhelming sense of being the "imposter," particularly in my graduate experience. Yet, while I was aware of the ever-widening gap plaguing my academic progress, I was not certain my deficiencies could be overcome and, more important, how to address and overcome them if they could be.

Out of financial necessity, I enlisted in the army after high school and, after fulfilling a five-year obligation and earning an Army ROTC scholarship, transitioned to an HBCU as a nontraditional student-veteran and English major. Enrolled in a first-year composition course, my challenge would be twofold: dealing with a profound lack of self-worth and an overwhelming sense of not belonging, even in a setting where most everyone else looked like me and came from social or economic backgrounds not dissimilar to my own, and learning the conventions of academic writing while appreciating that my "cluelessness," as Graff (2003) offers, is "a natural stage in the process of education" (1). As I did not yet understand how my uncertainty and fear emerged from the conditioning of a socioeconomic environment seemingly designed to perpetuate my feelings of self-doubt and inadequacy, I could not learn the "jargon and specialized terminology" appropriate for academic discourse or, more important, demystify the manner in which the academic experience "obscures the life of the mind" (2). In retrospect, however, it would have benefitted me (particularly in my graduate course pursuits) to seek out individuals with whom I could feel safe in sharing my weaknesses and form a community within which I could learn and engage the appropriate discourse.

If Lucille McCarthy (1987) is correct in her assertion that "*successful* students are those who can, in their interactions with teachers[,] determine what constitutes *appropriate texts* in each classroom: the content, structures, language, ways of thinking, and types of evidence required in that discipline and by that teacher" (233; emphasis mine), then academically I embodied the "stranger" trying to navigate the unfamiliar terrain of academia, particularly academic writing. My undergraduate professors at the HBCU were quite supportive and encouraging of me and my writing, and I rarely received negative or harsh teacher feedback on my writing. In fact, my instructors usually expressed to me (in written response and oral communication) that they found my ideas to be valuable, engaging, and thoughtful, and they often encouraged me to keep writing about my ideas. As a Black, working-class, male military veteran navigating the unfamiliar terrain of undergraduate coursework and culture, I needed the support and encouragement I found in the HBCU learning environment. However, frequent praise, coupled with the strong grades I earned, inadvertently taught me to see academic writing as merely the expression of my ideas, so I assumed a command of academic writing I did not have. It would not be until I was a graduate student in a master's program in Chicago that I was told just how weak I was in both my writing and understanding of academic discourse. In my first year as a graduate student, while enrolled in seminar aptly titled Language and Literacy, I received some humbling comments from the professor on a short written response about critical theory, which in no uncertain terms stated, "It's as if you have no idea what graduate writing is." I was quickly reminded of two things: writing at the graduate level would be unlike writing at the HBCU, and I would have to put aside the discourses of my home and the military to adopt, more quickly, the discourse of academia. In responding to my short written piece, the professor learned what I already knew—I was a weak academic. However, along with receiving these sobering, yet obvious, comments, I had hoped to receive some information to explain how I might address my academic weaknesses, or how to more appropriately integrate my ideas into academic speak and in such a way demonstrate my status more appropriately as an emerging scholar instead of just a weak academic, but my professor did not include such information. In other words, my professor missed an opportunity not only to teach but also to mentor and groom me (assuming he was interested in doing so) for the discourse community of which I was now a part.

My "cluelessness" would remain with me for much of my graduate student experience, and, being ignorant of how, as Graff (2003) suggests, "the mixed messages imbedded in the curriculum" involve a "paradoxical, double quality that [is] otherwise . . . confusing" (29), I continued to force the social and writing practices of certain arenas (military or academic) into contexts and conditions within which they did not belong or appropriately fit. Of course, I had considered myself prepared for the program given that the entirety of my undergraduate English work was limited to discussing and responding to various literary works, save for my first-year composition course and my work as a tutor in the university's writing lab. I assumed those same practices and writing habits would naturally transfer into my master's program work, but I could not have been more wrong. McCarthy (1987) cautions that "stranger[s] . . . who cannot [determine] what constitutes appropriate texts, for whatever reason—cultural, intellectual, motivational—are those who fail, deemed incompetent communicators in that particular setting" (233). My "cluelessness" meant I had not learned what James Britton, Tony Burgess, Nancy Martin, Alex McLeod, and Harold Rosen (1975) call the "rules of the game," which include many conventions and presuppositions not explicitly articulated for academic writing contexts (76). Nor had I learned to recognize what Graff (2003) elucidates as the ways academia "obscures" and "reinforces cluelessness" (1). Put another way, I had not learned the moves or rules, nor had I understood that the various arenas within which I operated were governed by specific sets of conventions, choosing instead to find my own way by mostly relying on tools I already possessed, no matter how inadequate they were for the conditions. In the supportive and nurturing HBCU setting, I was, as McCarthy (1987) suggests, "successful" insofar as my "interactions" with my professors garnered positive results, particularly strong grades. However (and in fairness to my graduate school professor), I failed to discover that the "texts" appropriate for my undergraduate writing, military writing, and my community were not appropriate for the contexts and academic rigors of writing as a graduate student. Early in the graduate experience, I had learned what it was I did not know: "appropriate" academic discourse.

In the army, I, like most soldiers, was often trained or taught new tasks in a common format: the instructor (sender) provides all necessary and relevant information to the learner (receiver) in a manner not unlike what Paolo Freire (1970) refers to as "an act of depositing, in which the students are the depositories and the teacher is the depositor" (72). I had twelve years of army acculturation and learning in this "banking" model, and I had tried to attempt a similar learning tactic in my graduate courses. Entering into graduate learning was not unlike my formative learning early in my military career. The drill instructors who were responsible for my integration and acculturation into the army mold hurled insults and threats and used other humiliating tactics to "build me up" by first "tearing me down," and while this teaching model was not ideal (and certainly not one I endorse), it was, most certainly, an effective means of indoctrination.[1] I began my master's program only three weeks after having returned from a combat tour in Afghanistan, prepared for what I anticipated to be an academic "boot camp" or indoctrination. In retrospect, I should have appreciated the experience as it more appropriately was: an immersion in academic culture. Notwithstanding the failing of my limited perspective, the transition and adjustment to academic life and the graduate learning experience would be no less daunting than my basic training learning experiences and other professional military encounters. The professors were collegial—they did not yell, scream or resort to humiliating tactics. However I was no less intimidated by my professors' authority, expertise, knowledge and, quite often, sheer presence. Plagued by this invalid fear, I made a number of ill-informed assumptions about the conditions of my graduate learning. First, I assumed my professors were not unlike my military instructors in that they would not invite me to have a conversation about my learning nor would they seek out the opportunity to aid me in my transition and acculturation into academic discourse. Next, I assumed that the "observe, listen, and learn" conditions of learning common to my army experiences would be effective in my graduate learning experiences. Last, I assumed my graduate school counterparts were not unlike my military counterparts; I saw them as competitors (rather than as peers) vying for the approval and favor of a superior or commander (in the case of the professor) whose written evaluation of my performance directly impacted my promotion and advancement potential. Ultimately, I chose not to reveal my inadequacies to my colleagues and professors due to an invalid fear and a misunderstanding of academic culture.

It would not be until a few years later, while assigned as an instructor of English at the United States Military Academy at West Point, that I would appreciate how the "invitation" to dialogue about ideas is inherently understood, always exists, and, in fact, is often expected among academics. I would learn in conversations with trusted colleagues around the water cooler or in the hallways between class sessions that others, too, shared feelings of inadequacy, isolation, and fear about the graduate learning experience. As a junior officer, I was often encouraged by my superiors to seek out trusted mentors who could aid and guide my development and growth, and as a more senior ranking officer, I often served as a mentor to junior officers and soldiers in their development. To be sure, I would have greatly benefited from the counsel and mentorship of a trusted colleague or professor, particularly in those early experiences as a graduate student.

A seemingly simple solution to overcoming my cluelessness about the expectations of academic rigor and professionalization would have been simply to ask for help from a trusted colleague or mentor. After graduating from the HBCU with a commission through the Army ROTC, I owed a six-year obligation of military service that I fully expected to fulfill and continue beyond, so further pursuit of advanced degrees in English seemed at odds with that obligation. Further, I would not have known what questions to ask or what information to seek about academic pursuits beyond the undergraduate level, particularly in that I struggled in some ways to find my academic footing while transitioning from military life to undergraduate academic life. It seemed that my commander's words would remain appropriate and befitting even outside my military endeavors, including my experiences as a writing tutor and instructor.

Notwithstanding my academic cluelessness, I was quite adept in my work as a tutor or consultant for composition students, particularly with students of color or other nontraditional students not unlike myself. Working with students at the HBCU writing lab, much of my work was helping students identify and improve errors of grammar, spelling, syntax, and, to a lesser degree, vocabulary. I was passionate about the work I was doing and the types of students I worked with, but I felt it was important to master the skills of composition and to be an expert on the rules of writing, so I studied handbooks and worked closely as a sort of protégé with my first-year composition instructor. Drawing upon my experiences in the Chicago public school system writing courses, as well as my work in my first-year composition course as an HBCU undergrad, I functioned as a writing tutor in much the same way, which is to say I privileged the current-traditional model of writing instruction. Then, helping others' literacy meant privileging a language value often associated with the white middle class and, sadly, too often privileged as the correct or standard mode of writing or speaking. Now, however, I work in my classrooms and writing center spaces to help students appreciate ways to balance traditional and progressive discourses in their writing and speech. Because, as McCarthy (1987) states, "all writing is context-dependent, and because successful writing requires the accurate assessment of and adaptation to the demands of particular writing situations" (233), my teaching practices and pedagogical philosophy include helping my students and tutees understand "the rules of the game" (Britton, Burgess, Martin, McLeod, and Rosen 1975, 76) and the baggage (social, economic, etc.) they bring to their writing as necessary, valuable, and, most important, valid.

Twenty years have passed since I began my journey as a scholar of English and an army officer at an HBCU. And like most HBCU grads, I am quite proud (and in retrospect, grateful) for having done so, more so because I matriculated from the first recipient of the *Time* magazine-Princeton Review's College Guide College of the Year award—a notable accomplishment for any institution of higher learning—HBCU or PWI. As a Black male navigating the cultural, political, social, and professional realms of the military and academe (two institutions that, I would only later discover, have a great deal in common), it is clear to me now how my experiences in the HBCU setting set the groundwork for my success in both these challenging and rewarding arenas.

FINDING COMMUNITY *RICHARD SÉVÈRE*

It took me twenty-four years to realize that as a man of color pursuing higher education, I was somewhat of an anomaly. Though the numbers of Black men earning degrees has risen slightly over the last decade, the figures remain alarmingly low compared to other cultural groups. Growing up in a Haitian household, I knew going to college was never in question, but rather my siblings and I dealt with deciding which institution to attend. I chose to attend an HBCU (historically Black college/university) partly because I had attended a predominantly Black high school in Miami, Florida, where going to an HBCU upon graduation was the norm among most students. I entered undergrad having already declared a major in English and French studies, although English was my third language and one hardly spoken in the home. I was not yet aware of the societal implications of literacy and language (the literacy myth)—I knew I liked reading from a young age, and thus studying English seemed a proper fit. Though I am reluctant to say the transition into college was seamless, it was not as terrifying for me as for most eighteen-year-olds leaving home for the first time. The move from high school to college was less daunting because I entered college already part of a community—a community of people who looked like me and shared similar passions, one that understood the importance of why people who looked like us needed to be successful and prepared to navigate a world in which we would need to prove our worth continuously to those who felt we did not belong. As I reflect, I am reminded of Christie Launius's (2009) "Brains versus Brawn," in which discussions of masculinity, class, race, and education intersect. In many ways, as for the men in that article, life at an HBCU meant we were part of a community where our professors served as mentors who reminded us, directly or otherwise, that education is inextricably linked to privilege, access, and power and is certainly a way to keep us on the margins of society.

Being at an HBCU where everyone looks the same—our very own safe space as put forth in the grand narrative of writing centers—taught us how to distinguish ourselves from each other in a positive way, what DeLeon Gray (2017) calls "standing out while fitting in." My time as an undergraduate student was spent learning from men and women of color who all had advanced degrees and were renowned scholars in their fields. Classroom environments were centered around a sense of communal learning, nurturance, safety, collaboration, and camaraderie all held together by a productive spirit of competition. It is within the auspices of this community setting that I decided to pursue graduate studies immediately after undergrad—I was motivated by and wanted to emulate those men and women who taught and mentored me.

Coming from an environment in which we were mentored and supported by our professors through most life decisions, including academic pursuits, I must admit I had no idea what going to graduate school meant and the amount of time and work I would need to invest. In many ways I was both spoiled by the HBCU experience and naïve to think such an approach would be consistent at all institutions. I do recall that prior to leaving to pursue a doctoral degree at a large research institution in the Midwest, I was warned that the environment and the people would be nothing like the South—quite an understatement to say the least.

Like most students entering a graduate program, I was particularly apprehensive about my academic abilities, giving credence to Margaret Salee, Ronald Hallett, and William Tierney's claim (2011) that "the expectation is that students already know how to write before they begin grad school" (66). I am also mindful of Harry C. Denny's (2005) notion that "schooling often assumes students possess intellectual capital for effective operation in its discourse communities" (46). In this case, I was "clueless" about a discourse community outside the HBCU. And certainly, while I thought I knew how to write, I recognized my writing up to that point was composed for a specific audience who intended on seeing me succeed. As such, comments on my writing were often very directive, demanding that I be clearer and more concise in my prose. I had become accustomed to the writing process from an undergraduate perspective but had no idea what writing at a graduate level truly meant in an unfamiliar environment with unfamiliar professors. Moreover, as someone coming from an HBCU, I not only needed to perform academic tasks, such as writing a dissertation and later securing a tenure-track position in order to infiltrate the "ivory tower," but I also a needed to retain my identity while being socially connected and accepted. After all, one of the most important things we are taught at an HBCU is to be proud of who we are—to be unapologetically Black. Again, Launius's (2009) interrogation of masculinity and education is worth noting while considering how, for some men of color, entrance into the "ivory tower" means undermining both their masculinity and culture. And thus, further complicating this new concept of graduate school was the fear of admitting to the shortfalls (my cluelessness) that are perhaps shared by many but that seem particularly damaging for students who look like me.

Coming into the graduate program, I was faced with the inescapable myth that graduate studies (especially at the dissertation stage) would be an isolating process that oftentimes has individuals questioning their intellectual capabilities. Marilee Brooks-Gillies, Elena Garcia, Soo Hyon Kim, Katie Manthey, and Trixie Smith (2015) make it a point to say that "graduate education is fraught with identity struggles and self-doubt, much of which centers around the ability to write effectively to meet the expectations of faculty mentors and the field at large." To build on Christine Casanave's (2016) notion of "invisible struggles," graduate students of color deal with an added identity struggle and self-doubt that may very well stem from the fact that they are in programs where very few people come from backgrounds similar to their own. Thus, having been accustomed to interacting with peers who looked like me and most often shared similar ideologies, being in an environment where this was not the case was isolating. For several years, I was the only Black male in my area of concentration and one of only two men of color in the graduate program—we would later have four during a six-year period. It is at this time it became clear I was indeed an anomaly. And thus being a "good," or even decent, writer was an added anxiety among many. I was burdened with the pressures of representing the so few who looked like me and, most important, burdened by the notion that failure would somehow confirm the stereotypes imposed onto a social group of which I was a part. More important, in the words of Cedric Burrows (2016), I was burdened by the Black tax: "the societal charges placed on African Americans in order to enter and participate in white spaces. At the heart of the Black tax is the notion that if African Americans work hard and rise above their situation without complaining about racism, they will gain privileges that whites already have." Because of this fear, I was not going to admit I struggled with academic discourse; such a confession would further socially and politically code my identity as a Black male. As Burrows notes, "When individuals represent an entire race, the stakes are incredibly high, and each person is levied a similarly high tax." Needless to say, writing was and is perpetually a high-stakes process riddled with inherent bias and subjectivity.

I recall submitting my first major writing assignment in graduate school after what I was certain were the hardest two weeks of my academic career—I earned a B minus. It is after earning this grade that I made up my mind I would be returning to Florida after the first semester. I had not constructed the narrative I would deliver to my family, former professors, and friends back home—the individuals who were so proud I was pursuing a PhD. Yet here I was about to fail after the first semester. I was the only one of my friends to pursue a terminal degree at the time and the first in my family to pursue a PhD—my siblings had pursued other, more lucrative, professional degrees. Nevertheless, as is the case most often when people of color beat the odds of the system intended to further marginalize them, I was not only representing myself but also my culture, family, the many people who supported me, and the many before me who had tried but did not succeed.

To use Denny's (2010) words, "People's access to education and literacy is charged with politics and carries the weight of wider historical relations, all of which impact on their sense of agency and facility with writing for particular discourse communities, most often the academic" (88). Denny's claims are especially relevant in the context of the Black male who navigates through the world of higher education in a state of isolation. In many instances, even if students of color are prepared for graduate writing, their self-efficacy is challenged by the pervasive fear of not succeeding or integrating into a community where, historically, linguistic and communication diversity are coded as inadequate and strongly discouraged—it is in the academic space that the "imposter syndrome" becomes most salient. I am also reminded here of Laura Greenfield's (2011) "The 'Standard English' Fairy Tale" in which she maintains that "Standard English necessarily creates a system of inequality in which many people of color are expected to be bidialectical or bilingual as a condition for being taken seriously as communicators, whereas privileged white people—regardless of their actual speech—*always already* speak a language of power" (43). Greenfield's observation is especially relevant for students coming from an HBCU environment, where we deal with our own sense of homogeny, which oftentimes includes linguistic similarities. After earning the grade I did on that first graduate assignment, I realized I would need to learn yet another language (keep in mind I was currently enrolled in a Middle

English Language course at the time) if I was to be successful in the graduate program. With the help of some graduate student colleagues I knew from class and the writing center, I was determined to never be in a position where I would need to craft a narrative to explain my failure in graduate school.

It was my time spent in the writing center as an undergraduate that led me to pursue tutoring in the writing center at my graduate institution, which in turn paved a path for creating a sense of community that aided me as a writer. For one, I was inspired to work in the writing center by my former writing center director in undergrad, who is man of color. His guidance during my undergraduate career was invaluable, and thus it seemed natural that I would seek an opportunity to work at the writing center at my graduate institution. I recall fondly my time spent in the center and did not truly consider then the level of professional development it would afford me at the graduate level. Our writing center at the HBCU was an extension of the classroom—it was not uncommon to see our professors spending time in the space, at times tutoring individuals or giving advice as needed. I must admit I have since learned that the global narratives regarding writing centers, their spaces and their missions, do not take into consideration the local narratives of the HBCU. As a graduate student, I was nostalgic for the "it takes a village" mentality—an atmosphere my HBCU's writing center provided. I needed an atmosphere where my unfamiliarity with academic discourse, my sense of cluelessness, would not be perceived as inadequacies of my race but as an opportunity to grow as a scholar.

For me, the overarching ideology of the writing center as a space where all individuals are welcomed drove my desire to seek a community among my peers. Although as a graduate tutor I was working with other writers to build their confidence, mine was at an all-time low. I realized I was, and in many ways continue to be, a very needy writer who prefers a more directive approach when it comes to my work. I sought the confirmation of skill and aptitude my professors in undergrad seemed to always provide. And while Jeff Brooks (1995) and his idea of minimalist tutoring loomed in my memory bank, I knew I was not that type of student or writer—I wanted to own my writing only when I felt it was worthy of ownership. I needed consistent feedback and affirmation that my work was worthy of my place in the program.

As a Black male, the fear of inadequacy was equally motivating and debilitating. For most, being in a graduate program is a time to learn and engage with academic discourse, so to disclose that one is unprepared to do so is admitting to certain shortcomings that can be socially or politically coded and interpreted. In other words, we run the risk of further marginalizing ourselves in admitting our weaknesses. To address these anxieties, I sought an opportunity to be a part of a writing group consisting of two other writers in the same field, all at the same stage in our program—inspired by the model of the writing center. Although the other students I worked with did not look like me, they provided a community of like-minded individuals with similar goals. We began working with one another early in our graduate school experience. I can distinctly recall Saturday mornings at our local coffee shop working on various assignments. Though our writing center did not offer any structured writing groups, two of us worked in the writing center and perhaps unconsciously recognized the value of collaborative learning as a pathway for our success. I realized that in order for our collaboration to truly be effective, I needed to allow myself to be vulnerable—even though I carried a fear of vulnerability with me most of my graduate school career. Our writing circle was not based on rivalry but rather a sense of respect and accountability. Weekly meetings were done over meals and dedicated to providing feedback on each other's chapters and/or other pieces of writing. Because there were only three of us, accountability was rather important. No one wanted to be the individual who did not have something written for the week, although if that were the case no one was made to feel guilty or inadequate. What was most beneficial from this collaboration was the mentorship and perspectives we provided one another, not just about writing but also about how to navigate a number of issues pertaining to life as a graduate student and beyond. From my experience, being a part of a writing community of peers not only proved essential for my success in completing the dissertation but also provided a sense of integration into the academic world that in turn built my confidence throughout the entire program.

There are numerous studies about the benefits of writing communities, dissertation/thesis writing groups, or other similar resources. As Sherri Gradin, Jennifer Pauley-Gose, and Candace Stewart (2006) make clear, "Writing groups can help students discover and fulfill the most important and most difficult purpose of their current academic project: becoming a colleague in one's field and emerging into the discourse community of the discipline with authority." Rachael Cayley in this collection demonstrates that dissertation boot camps help writers develop self-efficacy through their emphasis on building community among graduate student writers (see chap. 11). Ultimately, such efforts are not found at most institutions—as demonstrated by Beth Godbee and Julia Novotny's (2013) "Asserting the Right to Belong: Feminist

Co-Mentoring among Graduate Student Women" and Burrows's (2016) "Writing While Black: The Black Tax On African American Graduate Writers." However, the manner in which those groups are constructed is essential in providing support for individuals who also seek the identity and emotional support needed to be successful. Burrows (2016) is accurate in suggesting "that universities, writing programs, and writing centers create spaces for people of similar backgrounds, especially shared racial identifications, to work together." And while writing groups are especially useful and productive at the dissertation stage, peer mentorship (especially from individuals with different social backgrounds and early in the graduate program) can also prove beneficial. Certainly, I am informed by my own experiences as a Black male from an HBCU and a graduate tutor at the writing center, and theoretically by Brooks-Gillies et al. (2015) who claim "professionalization and support in graduate writing education needs to include identity and emotional support."

Though I am not suggesting writing groups will solve all the concerns underrepresented graduate writers face, especially in light of the dearth of perspectives dealing with minority-serving institutions and writers, they do, however, stand to be a local resource for such an audience. I fully recognize I make these statements from a position of privilege. I worked in writing center spaces and was familiar with writing center scholarship and ideology—not all graduate students have those opportunities and knowledge base. Because higher education and composition studies have taken a strong position in addressing social and political inequities, conversations about *how* to create and implement such spaces and resources for underrepresented students must now move into the implementation stages. Nancy Grimm (2011), in "Retheorizing Writing Center Work," offers this point:

> If writing centers understand their work . . . not as inducting individual students into a discourse community, but as places where the academic community actively recruits new members, welcomes creativity of those with multimemberships, and studies the reconciliation work that occurs on the boundaries of communities, then their scope of practice and their function within the university changes in significant ways. (91)

To build on Grimm's call to action, I argue that we take this charge not only in the context of writing centers. Rather, institutions as a whole can broaden the scope of their inclusive functions by providing further support for graduate writers, particularly those underrepresented students whose struggles with writing threaten their success in graduate programs. Ultimately, peer and faculty mentorship, writing groups, outreach, and ongoing professionalization opportunities are ways of being more deliberate and implementing resources that will aid graduate students in navigating various academic discourses.

CONCLUSION

Collectively, our voices and reflections are intended for multiple audiences. We start with the student of color (undergraduate and graduate) who is anxious about navigating a new academic discourse while trying to maintain a sense of identity in a community that may be socially and politically biased: to this student, we offer these reflections to articulate, first, unwavering support for pursuing graduate study and, second, to stress the importance of continuing on that path although it may seem stacked with insurmountable obstacles. Keep in mind that by the time one gets to a graduate program, whether it is directly from an undergraduate program or returning after a long absence, one is certain to feel underprepared or even "clueless"—such a feeling can be consistent across most groups of graduate students. Overcoming the pervasive sense of doubt and building confidence is integral in creating a path to success. One must be willing to embrace moments of vulnerability and find ways to share such moments with other colleagues and or mentors; more than likely they have a shared experience. Do not shy away from the idea of cluelessness but rather embrace it as a means of humbleness and desire to excel.

Seek out ways to build a community of like-minded individuals who can champion you and your work. Foster an environment of collaboration—within and beyond your specific discipline. The idea is to identify a group in which there is productive dialogue, meaningful and effective feedback, abounding trust, and a desire for success. Consider mentorship opportunities—seek a mentor and serve as a mentor. Mentorship provides another avenue to communicate any anxieties and generate the support needed to move students beyond such emotions. Moreover, serving in the role of mentor allows the opportunity to "pay it forward" (Jackson, Jackson, Mitchell, Simmons, Shelton, and Atkinson, chap. 5 in this volume), as well as ways to think through potential issues you may not have faced but many others have.

Our reflections are intended to also renew silenced conversations regarding graduate students, particular those from underrepresented institutions and backgrounds. As put forth by Anne Ellen Geller, Michele Eodice, Frankie Condon, Meg Carroll, and Elizabeth Boquet, citing John Tagg (2003), let us be reminded that "in order for leaders in the post-secondary context to instigate, promote, and effectively sustain institutional transformation, structural leaders must also be functional leaders who 'will use the authority of their offices to achieve the mission of institutional transformation'" (11). In this case, the idea of authority extends beyond writing faculty and practitioners to include administrators, faculty mentors, and other professionals who are in direct contact with graduate students. Outreach is especially key for the underrepresented student coming from an HBCU who may perhaps be hesitant in seeking out mentors and mentorship for the simple fact of deference or in many instances the students see professors and other individuals of authority as unapproachable and/or inaccessible. As individuals who are currently traversing the academic landscape, we offer these reflections to those who work with graduate students in an effort to demonstrate the need for meaningful mentorship that begins in the early stages of graduate programs and proves beneficial throughout.

ACKNOWLEDGMENTS

I want to thank my coauthor Maurice, who agreed to this collaboration amid a very busy time in his life. I am so grateful for that random phone interview that allowed for this "rattler" partnership.

RICHARD SÉVÈRE

I cannot thank my coauthor Richard enough for his gracious invitation to join him on this journey—this writing experience has been one of great reflection and discovery. Richard and I also wish to thank the editors, especially Shannon and Michele, for their vision, hard work, and insight into this profoundly meaningful collection. We are also grateful to the anonymous reviewers of our chapter whose comments and expertise greatly added to our finished work.

MAURICE WILSON

NOTE

1. As Melinda L. Pash posits in *In the Shadow of the Greatest Generation*, "Almost all literature on basic training emphasizes the primary function of tearing down the individual Boot and refashioning him or her into a soldier" (see Kindsvatter 2003, 27; Ozinger 1999, 58; US President's Commission 1955). "Report on Training," December 1955, 35, US President's Commission on Veterans' Pensions (Bradley Commission): Records, 1954–58, A69-22 and 79-6, Box 58, Dwight David Eisenhower Library (Hereafter Bradley Commission and DDE Library); Peter S. Kindsvatter, *American Soldiers: Ground Combat in the World Wars, Korea, and Vietnam* (Lawrence: University Press of Kansas, 2003), 27; and James R. Ozinger, *Altruism* (Westport, CT: Praeger, 1999), 58.

REFERENCES

Badenhorst, Cecile, and Cally Guerin, eds. 2016. *Research Literacies and Writing Pedagogies for Masters and Doctoral Writers*. Leiden: Brill.

Britton, James, Tony Burgess, Nancy Martin, Alex McLeod, Harold Rosen. 1975. *The Development of Writing Abilities*. London: Macmillan.

Brooks, Jeff. 1995. "Minimalist Tutoring: Making the Student Do All the Work." In *The St. Martin's Sourcebook for Writing Tutors*, edited by Christina Murphy and Steve Sherwood, 83–87. New York: St Martin's.

Brooks-Gillies, Marilee, Elena G. Garcia, Soo Hyon Kim, Katie Manthey, and Trixie Smith. 2015. "Graduate Writing Across the Disciplines, Introduction." In "Graduate Reading and Writing Across the Curriculum," edited by Marilee Brooks-Gillies, Elena G. Garcia, Soo Hyon Kim, Katie Manthey, and Trixie Smith. Special issue, *Across the Disciplines* 12. http://wac.colostate.edu/atd/graduate_wac/intro.cfm.

Burrows, Cedric D. 2016. "Writing While Black: The Black Tax on African American Graduate Writers." *Praxis: A Writing Center Journal* 14 (1): 15–20.

Casanave, Christine Pearson. 2016. "What Advisors Need to Know about the Invisible 'Real-Life' Struggles of Doctoral Dissertation Writers." In *Supporting Graduate Student Writers: Research, Curriculum, and Program Design*, edited by Steve Simpson, Nigel A. Caplan, Michelle Cox, and Talinn Phillips, 97–116. Ann Arbor: University of Michigan Press.

Clance, Pauline R., and Suzanne A. Imes. 1978. "The Imposter Phenomenon in High Achieving Women: Dynamics and Therapeutic Intervention." *Psychotherapy: Theory, Research and Practice* 15 (3): 241–247.

Conference on College Composition and Communication. 1974. "Students' Right to Their Own Language." *College Composition and Communication* 25 (3): 1–32.

Denny, Harry. 2005. "Queering the Writing Center." *Writing Center Journal* 25 (2): 39–62.

Denny, Harry. 2010. *Facing the Center: Toward an Identity Politics of One-To-One Mentoring*. Logan: Utah State University Press.

Freire, Paolo. 1970. *Pedagogy of the Oppressed*. New York: Continuum.

Geller, Anne Ellen, Michele Eodice, Frankie Condon, Meg Carroll, and Elizabeth Boquet. 2007. *Everyday Writing Center: A Community of Practice*. Logan: Utah State University Press.

Godbee, Beth, and Julia C. Novotny. 2013. "Asserting the Right to Belong: Feminist Co-Mentoring among Graduate Student Women." *Feminist Teacher* 23 (3): 177–195.

Gradin, Sherri, Jennifer Pauley-Gose, and Candace Stewart. 2006. "Disciplinary Differences, Rhetorical Resonances: Graduate Writing Groups Beyond the Humanities." *Praxis: A Writing Center Journal* 3 (2): 1–5.

Graff, Gerald. 2003. *Clueless in Academe: How Schooling Obscures the Life of the Mind*. New Haven, CT: Yale University Press.

Gray, DeLeon L. 2017. "Is Psychological Membership in the Classroom a Function of Standing Out While Fitting In?: Implications for Achievement Motivation and Emotions." *Journal of School Psychology* 61: 103–121.

Greenfield, Laura. 2011. "The 'Standard English' Fairy Tale: A Rhetorical Analysis of Racist Pedagogies and Commonplace Assumptions about Language Diversity." In *Writing Centers and the New Racism: A Call for Sustainable Dialogue and Change*, edited by Laura Greenfield and Karen Rowan, 33–60. Logan: Utah State University Press.

Grimm, Nancy M. 2011. "Retheorizing Writing Center Work to Transform a System of Advantage Based on Race." In *Writing Centers and the New Racism: A Call for Sustainable Dialogue and Change*, edited by Laura Greenfield and Karen Rowan, 75–100. Logan: Utah State University Press.

Hart, Betty, and Todd R. Risley. 2003. "The Early Catastrophe: The 30 Million Word Gap by Age 3." *American Educator* 21 (1): 4–9.

Kindsvatter, Peter S. 2003. *American Soldiers: Ground Combat in the World Wars, Korea, and Vietnam.* Lawrence: University Press of Kansas.
Launius, Christie. 2009. "Brains versus Brawn: Classed and Racialized Masculinity in Literacy Narratives by Rose, Rodriguez, Villanueva, and Gilyard." *College Composition and Communication* 61 (2): 283–309.
McCarthy, Lucille P. 1987. "A Stranger in Strange Lands: A College Student Writing across the Curriculum." *Research in the Teaching of English* 21 (3): 233.
James R. Ozinger. 1999. *Altruism.* Westport, CT: Praeger.
Pash, Melinda L. 2012. *In the Shadow of the Greatest Generation.* New York: New York University Press.
Sallee, Margaret, Ronald Hallett, and William Tierney. 2011. "Teaching Writing in Graduate School." *College Teaching* 59 (2): 66–72.
Simpson, Steve, Nigel Caplan, Michelle Cox, and Talinn Phillips, eds. 2016. *Supporting Graduate Student Writers: Research, Curriculum, Program Design.* Ann Arbor: University of Michigan Press.
Tagg, John. 2003. *The Learning Paradigm College.* Bolton, MA: Anker.
US President's Commission on Veterans' Pensions (Bradley Commission) Report on Training. 1955. Records, 1954–58, A69–22, 79–6. Box 58. Dwight David Eisenhower Library.
Young, Vershawn Ashanti, Rusty Barrett, Y'Shanda Young-Rivera, and Kim Brian Lovejoy. 2014. *Other People's English: Code-Meshing, Code-Switching, and African-American Literacy.* New York: Teachers College Press.

4
RACE, RETENTION, LANGUAGE, AND LITERACY
The Hidden Curriculum of the Writing Center

Wonderful Faison and Anna K. (Willow) Treviño

OUR STORIES ARE NOT ANECDOTES: WRITING AS ONE TO WRITE AS TWO

When we began the process of writing this piece we realized how troubled we were. My mama would say we were "troubled in our souls." Our souls, our bodies, our very selves were troubled by the gap (the disharmony) between what the vast majority of writing center (WC) literature purports the WC to be and do—a comfortable, inclusive, anti-institutional space where students work on their writing with peers—and what the WC often is and does: reproduce upper-middle-class white domestic comforts (Grimm 1999; Grutsch-McKinney 2013) that may often exclude those not from that class, race, or domestic space. Although WC scholars have begun to critique this common narrative of the WC as comfortable and anti-institutional, few critiques of the WC ideology or space have come from those people WC scholars argue may be unintentionally excluded from their space either through WC design or pedagogy: People of Color (POC) and, more specifically, Women of Color (WOC).

While we write this piece as one, we also write this piece as two. The reason we choose to write this piece in this way is so readers can discern our two different voices, two different styles, two different lenses, two distinct perspectives, two distinct languages and rhetorical practices that, though distinct, are not anecdotal. These stories are an attempt to begin to form an experiential preponderance of stories likely to accrue similar stories. Our work is an attempt to show that not all POC/WOC are the same. We are often collapsed into having the same struggle—seeing race or any oppression through the same lens. This is nothing more than myth. Our stories, our narrative, our critique is an attempt at a "bringing together." Bringing these differing lenses (Latina and Black lesbian)

DOI: 10.7330/9781607329589.c004

together to critique the discord between WC literature that positions the WC as anti-institutional and comfortable, and its practical application of that ideal, not only can better refine how WCs desire to position themselves but also may bring more pedagogical and practical ways writing centers can better align with that ideal.

MI CONFESIÓN

I must confess. I never imagined I would work for a writing center. My original understanding of writing centers and writing center work was formed by what I would now call an irresponsible, but perhaps well-meaning, first-year composition instructor. While I was a first-year student taking composition, he forced us to get our papers checked and validated. Upon submission, our papers needed to have, stapled to them, The Slip, which was signed by the tutor, who always checked the boxes of The Things We Worked On and sometimes left additional comments in the space provided. If the proof of the writing center visit was absent, a penalty would be reflected in our grades. He weaponized the writing center, and I hated having to go because the sessions mostly consisted of tutors telling me where I needed commas. Once, I had the courage to state that I did not know "where to put commas." The answer I received, of course, was no different than the same mumbo jumbo nonsense that had always been said to me: "where you pause or take a breath; between two independent clauses." I never understood why, after admitting I did not know where to put commas, the tutor would assume I could identify independent clauses in my own writing. Believe it or not, despite this major flaw of mine, I successfully completed all undergraduate writing assignments and even minored in English! Beyond my first year as an undergrad, I never returned for writing tutoring, but as is now obvious, I continued into graduate school.

I earned my BA and MA from a Hispanic serving institution[1] (HSI) in South Texas, where the students were predominately Mexican American, working-class, first-generation college students (~65%). While a master's student there, I learned about Paulo Freire, Ira Shor, and bell hooks. I also rebelled against teaching first-year curriculum from pre-1960s, which is still in place at too many institutions, good ol' EDNA.[2] This rebellion was mostly silent; I used my thesis to research and argue against current-traditional rhetoric, especially in the context of class issues. In the classes I was teaching, I mostly followed the not-so-wonderful curriculum, trying to find spaces to subvert untheoretical teaching: beginning college-level composition courses by introducing the anatomy of the essay—the five-paragraph theme—was not acceptable; justifying that the current curriculum is in place "because most students are not English majors" is no justification at all. The students deserved better.

I was twenty-two when I first stepped into the college classroom as a graduate teaching assistant, not much older than most of my students. I had more privilege because I held one degree and was on my way to completing my second, but in terms of socioeconomics and ethnicity, most of my students were not too different from me. While there most certainly were white middle-class conservative students, they were not the majority. As a new teacher with no training, my in-class experiences my first semester teaching were terrible. I felt uncomfortable, lacked confidence, so of course, some students did not respond well. Most of the students who didn't were white, middle-class women, but there were a few Mexican American men students who pushed back as well. With a bit more experience, age, and knowledge of composition theory and history, I grew in confidence and authority, and I learned that students were more responsive the more I shared my perspectives on teaching and writing with them—that is, why I did not agree with certain assignments, where and why I disagreed with the readings, why I was sneaking in readings, what rhetoric and composition meant to me, and so on. Teaching became a part of me and the way I saw the world.

After earning my master's degree, I started a PhD program at a midwestern university, where I am now working for the writing center. At this particular predominantly white institution (PWI), I first worked as a teaching assistant; my responsibilities included teaching two sections of first-year composition. The differences in attending and teaching at an HSI and a PWI were particularly jarring. Since I have lived in South Texas my entire adult life up to this point, it was the first time I felt like a minority. The students I was now responsible for were predominately white, middle class, and conservative. The program here has a legitimate writing program director in charge of creating and disseminating legitimate writing curricula, and yet, I enjoyed teaching even less. I tried to make sense of this struggle and decided it was a transition issue; I had not "acclimated to the campus and its culture" (Scott 2015, 288). I was failing to apply the keys to success I had introduced to my first-year seminar students the academic year before beginning my doctoral program. As the semester continued, I decided on one thing—I could not bear teaching at a PWI much longer.

Fate intervened that semester. There was an opportunity for me to become a writing tutor. I even met with the associate director. She seemed nice enough, and the tutor I interviewed regarding his experience at the writing center seemed sincere in his responses, but ultimately I could not pursue a position in the center. The uneducated but personal beliefs I held of the writing center—a site of hegemony, of Standard English, of product-centered and current-traditional rhetoric—focused on "the ways in which and the degree to which the academy echoes within the walls of the center" (Boquet 2002, 52). This made me hesitant and ultimately reject the possibility of working at the writing center during the second semester of my doctoral program.

I still had half of my first semester to go, and I struggled even more. I began to realize I was frequently moody, mostly angry. I began to cry on my drive to campus, during breaks and office hours when I was alone, and again when I stepped inside my apartment. The shift from attending and teaching in an HSI to a PWI took a hefty toll on me during my first year at the PWI. Mostly, I felt loss, an emptiness caused by the disconnect between my identity and my surroundings, as well as facing the reality of how much of myself, of my ties to family and heritage, I gave up to be here. I betrayed myself, and it disgusted me. My academic success and accomplishments began to taste more like failure. I also felt somewhat afraid and vulnerable as a woman of color teaching at a PWI. Struggling with teaching meant I was struggling with my values and goals, which represent aspects of my identity.

My heightened sense of struggle and identity, of Otherness, as an Other of the Other, as more American (in the white sense) than Mexican, complicated my new teaching experience, and slowly my passion for teaching composition, first year or otherwise, disappeared that first semester. The conflict of who I was, who I am, who I should be, and who I am told to be led me to believe that composition classes could never be more than sites of hegemony, sites for Standard English. I went from sneaking works by Freire and hooks into first-year composition and first-year seminar classes at an HSI—from attempting to theorize about and practice liberatory pedagogies, from thinking about class issues because such pedagogical theories and considerations matched who I was and who my students were (it made sense!)—to attempting to comprehend that I was now at a PWI, where the classrooms are comprised of seas of Apple Inc. products and where people have time to lie in hammocks or play frisbee in the grassy areas—literally things I had only seen in movies!

Despite the disconnect, I still tried to do the best I could for both my classes each semester, but it didn't help that discussions of literacy and writing in the curriculum centered on and validated white, middle-class people's typically positive relationships with and interpretations of the concepts. Nor did it help that the conversations of diversity and difference in the department solely centered on the Other students, not the experiences or struggles of (the single-digit number of) POC instructors.

When I reflect on my first year at a PWI, my in-class teaching experiences are notably absent. My reflection steers me to relive the feelings I attributed to what I felt was a colorblind curriculum the invalidation, that is, that the Grand Equalizer (colorblind ideology) boasts as kindness and respectfulness. Day in and day out, I played into the ideology. I performed whiteness (which to me meant to be emotionally absent from my teaching and learning so that people would not have to see my color) to the best of my ability for my students, peers, and professors, which I'll admit was not too hard considering I do not have a colored accent and my skin color, well, is light enough to make people wonder "what I am." "The more passing I can present myself, the less students will challenge me," I thought. My evaluations proved it to be true. The times when I said too much, when I was myself, were seen as inappropriate. But, it was damaging, you know, especially because I had previously attended and taught at a predominately Hispanic HSI in South Texas, where of course performance of whiteness was still expected to some degree, but the border culture allowed for more opportunity to, as Cindy Cruz (2001) states, "[migrate] between First and Third Worlds," and the students there seemed to appreciate it (660).

Time, painfully, went on. I began my second semester with the baggage and failure of acclimation during my first, still scheduled to teach two classes. Identity was a hot topic in one of my grad comp classes that semester. It was also the topic of most of my counseling sessions. My counselor was a Native man. He seemed to understand what is like to not be from a "legacy family" of the university, to not have parents who are pharmacists, lawyers, or any other middle-class occupation, to understand what it is to feel like a token minority at a PWI.

Fate intervened again, or perhaps, had mercy. The same position I had rejected at the writing center my first semester was still open. I met with the director that time. She also seemed nice enough. I was still hesitant, but as the desire to teach first-year composition had fled my body and taken along with it my perception of it as a space of possibility, I began to see the writing center as a more accepting space, a space where I "might amplify, even distort, the noise of the academy" (Boquet 2002, 53). Most important, I also began to believe that the writing center would not only give me a new space in terms of exploring writing theory and pedagogy, but that it could make room for me.

CONTEMPLANDO LAS FRONTERAS DE WRITING CENTERS

Reflecting on my narrative, I see how I have attributed my struggles at a PWI to identity, but it is equally important to note that it is also a story of space. More specifically a story of the relationship between the mind-heart, body, and space. When I look into a mirror, a phenotype (my body) reflects onto me an identity, and every day I live (at least) two stories: mine and the one projected onto me by the white gaze. Some days, I too am complicit and internalize the white gaze, which pierces, denies, and rips apart my Third Space consciousness (Licona 2005). I see, in the (dominant) eyes of others the reflection of me as they see me: a Hispanic, Mexican American, or Xicana and, hence, not someone with whom to engage.

The white gaze tells and expects me to be different (because I am not white). But not too different (because I am not white). Be myself (which is not white). But not the self (which is not white) that pushes against the status quo and makes whites, and therefore (nondominant) me, uncomfortable. It asks: Do you want to carry the weight of really being you, of having to own and reclaim your culture when Mexicans are "bringing drugs. They're bringing crime. They're rapists. And some [might be] good people" (Trump 2015), while simultaneously demanding that you carry it (because you are Mexican) AND leave it behind (because you are also American—and the U.S. kind)?

The weight(lessness) of the word *culture* (my mind-heart) depends on my self-description and identification, but my phenotype determines how the people in the world do or do not engage with me and I with them. My expression of the weight(lessness) of mi cultura también determina, o será mejor decir obstruye, la interacción. ¿Cómo me veo, cómo me oigo cuando hablo y escribo en mi lengua? Es más. ¿Cómo se siente? ¿Cómo sentirme? En mi casa y con mi familia no se siente raro. Ahorita, se siente rebelde. ¡Xicana!

Cultures and identities can be suppressed by spaces; rhetorical spaces can welcome some and push others out. But it is not always that simple. For example, while student retention efforts boast and claim to help college students succeed, many ableist, racist, classist, xenophobic, and/or sexist assumptions and institutional practices are embedded in student success initiatives under the guise of generosity or altruism, which are a direct cause of student Third Space herida (Anzaldúa 2012) hemorrhages. La justificación de esta herida dicen many in academia que es required acclimation to the campus and its culture. El cemento y los ladrillos tienen mucho más derecho de reclamar cultura.

Rhetorical spaces can welcome a person's certain culture and identity while also rejecting a person's other culture(s) and identities—the denial of the possibility of the Third Space and the severing of the Third Space into only two possibilities. The rhetorical spaces of PWIs are spaces of such violence for students who are not white, middle-class men because it is their cultures, identities, and even phenotypes that are embedded en los ladrillos y el cemento. Y es por eso que algo inanimate is considered to have a more valuable culture than minority students, faculty, and staff. Our funds of knowledge (Moll, Amanti, Neff, and Gonzalez 1992) are checks not cashed by the PWIs.

Originally, I saw writing centers as merely spaces that echoed such violence and saw the first-year composition classroom as a space that provided room for distorting those echoes because that was true for me at my HSI. Writing centers were certainly not spaces that I would consider safe(r). A change in place, moving from Texas to Oklahoma, did not immediately prompt me to renegotiate the relationship among my mind-heart, body, and space. The overwhelming noises found and echoed in a new space began to drown out the sound of my mind-heart, skewing my understanding of my own identity that I would hardly consider anywhere near complete or wholesome. The rhetorical spaces of the PWI—new department and first-year composition classes—amplified echoes of whiteness, which filtered me, the Other, out as distortion. One space's distortion, however, can be a good fit for another's melody.

Here I am now, a predominantly asexual, Mexican American, working-class, first-generation college student in a composition, rhetoric, and literacy PhD program at a PWI who has worked for a writing center for only eight months (during the time of the initial draft of this chapter). Currently, I am the only nonwhite graduate student in the comp-rhet concentration, and while I would argue that my department does not actively engage in retention efforts, it always automatically engages in retention for specific groups. Because white middle-class men and women are not racialized minorities in academia, and are largely the representative body of faculty members, retention efforts for such groups regarding identity development and expression are inherently embedded in institutional practices, admittedly more so for white, middle-class men. In other words, retention practices, or lack thereof, are "the default function . . . of center[ing] the experiences of dominant groups without naming it as such" (Rodriquez 2016, 66).

Despite the fact that I am the only Mexican American writing tutor, the writing center is considerably more diverse than my graduate program. Does this diversity make the writing center and/or this PWI a safe(r) space for me? No. One could argue it does the exact opposite. It provides a space where I can openly discuss the continual renegotiation of the relationship among my mind-heart, body, and space, and where I can also openly discuss resistance to and possible ways to subvert problematic discourses and practices of exclusion with not only the other tutors but with writers who also need my support beyond writing.

Think back, for example, to my first ever experience with writing centers. Remember my first-year composition instructor that required all his students to not only go to the writing center, but to get a slip to show as proof (or be penalized)? He's not the only one who engages in such practice nor has it ended. On more than one occasion, I have had writers express that their highest concern was grammar because that was the area their professors marked the most off their grades. I've had writers who were required to ask for my signature to show as proof of visiting the writing center. I've had writers tell me that if they had more than three grammar issues they'd fail their science papers. I've also had a writer express to me that her professor doesn't like the way she speaks and doesn't want her to write that way. I've had a writer talk to me about feeling harassed by her professor regarding a resumé assignment. I've had a writer open up to me about being targeted by a racist and discriminatory professor.

As a writing tutor, I listen.

As a writing tutor, I know.

It is a well-documented fact that student writing is reviewed in particular ways.[3] It is also a well-documented fact that grammar doesn't really mean one thing.[4] None of that is recent, like the abundant scholarship that exists that discusses the racist, sexist, and classist ideologies that inform the way a writer's work is viewed and the way writing is taught. Having good intentions or meaning well does not make up for untheorized, uncritical pedagogies; having good intentions or meaning well does not excuse the reproduction of racist, classist, sexist, or other oppressive ideologies. There is no substitute for informed, reflexive teaching.

As a writing tutor, I ask.

"What does your professor mean exactly when he/she/ze says 'grammar?'" "Have you received any specific feedback regarding your grammar?" "What did your professor mean when he/she/ze said _____ to you?" "How do you feel about your writing?" "Would you mind if I speak to either the associate director or director about this?"

As a writing tutor, I share.

"Grammar doesn't really mean anything. Typically, everyone means something different." "In terms of grammar, I didn't see anything too concerning, just the little things we talked about. I would recommend asking your professor to mark specific examples where he/she/ze sees grammatical mistakes." "I don't know what your professor means when he/she/ze said ____. That doesn't make any sense to me." "English is a difficult language. It's borrowed from so many others that a lot of the times, the rules contradict each other." "No. That doesn't sound okay to me. There's a website where you can report this incident." "If you would like to, I am sure the associate director or director would be happy to listen and/or help in more ways than I can."

Writing doesn't just happen between pen and paper or during the clicks of the keyboard. It grows out of the renegotiations among one's mind-heart, body, and space. It is evident in the sheer existence of my reflection that my writing center can be read as a brave(r) space. However, it does not merely exist as one. My writing center exists as a place of possibility for me, a place where I have decided to be brave, purposefully creating a braver space.

GUESS WHO'S COMING TO DINNER: THE WRITING CENTER AS HOME

As a Black, lesbian, working-class, disabled woman studying in and working at a PWI, I sought a space where I could feel "at home." A space where white shadows do not fall.[5] I was certain the practice of the writing center would match the "comfortable, iconoclastic places where all students go to get one-to-one tutoring with their writing" (Grutsch-McKinney 2013, 3). However, what I saw were aesthetics (sofas, refrigerators, coffee pots, plants, painted walls, etc.) all meant to serve those who inhabit the space the most: tutors and faculty. But aesthetics are never merely aesthetics.

Aesthetics are invested with ideas about not only who will populate a space but also what they will find both pleasing and comfortable. Within this imaginary, the dominant culture and its upper-middle-class, white ideologies are often hidden in, enacted on, and inscribed within WC pedagogies that function, by and large, on an autonomous model, which insists "that the dominant literacy is neutral, but . . . also uses markers of this literacy for political purposes, ranking and sorting people based on features of their texts . . . in an attempt to maintain their own conventions are superior" (Street quoted in Grimm 1999, 30). Even Bethany Davila (2006), who urges writing centers to become more accepting of students from diverse racial, ethnic, and cultural backgrounds, positing, "Writing centers need to be aware of the values and ideology inherent in academic discourses and to rewrite the writing center space as a place where students of all races are able to negotiate the difference between their discourses and those of the academy" (2), still suggests a type of assimilation that may be detrimental to students entering the WC from various ethnic, cultural, and racial backgrounds.

Working in a predominately white writing center at a predominately white institution in the Midwest, I constantly found myself asking, "What is this space?" When hearing other tutors complain about having to work with another international student that "couldn't speak English," or when overhearing other tutors dismiss or ignore the suggestions of more experienced tutors of color, I wondered, "What resistance is this?" This dismissiveness is a common practice by many white WC scholars, who often disregard stories of racism, particularly from their colleagues and students of color, in an attempt to label such racism as a misunderstanding. For example, I have had other white tutors question what knowledge I had to assume I could tell POC that their home language is not respected by the academy because the academy prefers them to write like a white man—linear, direct, point by point, and with as little narrative as possible.

I have also had many tutees assume (1) I am the receptionist or (2) that whatever coffee I just made must have been for them. When talking with other white tutors about this raced if not racist response to me, I was often called sensitive, given blank stares or a metaphorical wag of their fingers, suggesting I should drop the issue and move on. However, Harry Denny (2010) argues these responses exposed that these scholars did not recognize their "power—agency, authority, gumption—in such moves" (2). These power moves, I argue, are also reflected in the design of writing centers at both US universities and community colleges.

When working at another community college in the Midwest, I learned that many instructors had asked the provost why the WC had so many sofas? The provost's response to this question was telling: "They deserve nice things too." This response is embedded with—and, to some degree, unintentionally so—racist and classicist undertones. Often, race may/can be read through who one presumes has access to money, which would allow one to obtain/buy expensive furniture, appliances, and so forth. Therefore, following this logic, one can draw several assumptions from the provost's statement: (1) that whoever is served in the WC is somehow an Othered body. After all, who is the "they" of which the provost speaks?; (2) that whoever is served in the writing center does not have nice things; (3) that whoever is served in the writing center wants the same nice things as the director, tutor, and provost (in this case);

(4) that anyone served in the WC is working class/poor (the "they" who deserve these "nice" things).

These classed and raced assumptions are embedded in the provost's discourse. While both class and race are cultural and geographic—that is, working-class southern white people and northern white people are not the same people even though they may both be of the same economic class—similarly, the cultural differences can be the same, if not more burdensome, for working-class Blacks with regard to geography and the racial perils that come with being Black in America.

However, the provost's embedded assumptions lead one to ask, When the provost notes "they deserve nice things, too," who is the "they" of whom he speaks? Why does the provost assume "they" do not have nice things? Furthermore, why does the provost assume "they" deserve nice things and want the same nice things as the upper-middle-class provost with the upper-middle-class income? Because community colleges historically serve the working class and the poor, would it not be logical to assume that working-class and poor people may have different ideas of comfort and how a comfortable space may look?

I do not suggest a working-class space would be without its own issues. Class is also a cultural performance, and to make a working-class space would collapse those various performances and would fall on the same homogenizing discourses that lead to writing centers as home and/or comfortable—identities such as gender, class, race, and so forth are inseparable from the individual. As Anne Geller, Michele Eodice, Frankie Condon, Meg Carroll, and Beth Boquet (2007) posit, "These dominant images of people of color in the white imagination are operative inside the writing center and . . . these images can impact how tutors recognize, receive, and respect (or not) one another" (88). As such, it is logical to question the white imagination in the construction of the WC and whether or not POC were envisioned as inhabitants of that same space.

Some of the tutors of color (particularly those who identified as Black or of African descent) in the WC in which I work noticed and felt a similar discomfort of both institutional domination and oppression in this supposedly comfortable, anti-institutional space called the WC. While we worked in a PWI (predominately white institution), we were still at a loss at to why our WC employed and served few Black students/clients, and I was at a loss as to why our WC seemed to suffer from a severe case of Black flight in our tutors. In other words, why couldn't the WC retain the tutors of color it employed?

As an emerging WC scholar and researcher, my concerns grew as I listened to my fellow tutors of color openly wonder why there were so few graduate tutors of color on so few of the committees, especially those concerned with race, diversity, and multilingualism. I continuously wondered and questioned whether or not graduate tutors of color were less likely to serve in positions of power in the predominately white WC? Essentially, we, as tutors of color, often wondered, what mess had we gotten into? Who or what made the mess and who or what was supposed to clean it?

It is through this critiquing of the physical space of the WC as home, comfortable, and anti-institutional that I began to listen intently not only to the discourse of the tutors of color but also to the discourse of the tutors of color about this supposed comfortable space. In other words, I wanted to know how, or rather if, the WC space, that is meant to be read as home or homelike, may be embedded with dominant ideologies that could, under the right conditions, create a racialized space that can exclude POC from the WC. This exclusion, I argue, begins with the visual aesthetics: the aloe plants, soft lighting, pastel colors, earthy tones, and so forth one encounters in various writing centers across various PWIs.

Throughout the article we hoped to highlight that as WOC, Wonderful and I do not share the same voice nor lived experiences. However, there are points in which our lived experiences intersect. I, too, struggle with concepts of home, hospitality, comfort, and even work. As I grew up in poor neighborhoods, as a welfare kid, I didn't exactly live in homes that most middle-class individuals would consider comfortable, and this is not a judgment. I want to stress that feelings of familiarity, of knowing, and of being used to things are a part of what makes spaces feel comfortable and homelike, but I did not grow up in a home surrounded by white middle-class comforts. Las casas en que he vivido tenían paredes blancas, which more often than not had paint chipping away from them and drafty windows, and nothing that resembled a plant would be found inside, plastic or not. All the houses in which I lived were old, worn; they felt inhabited in a way that told me that my family was not the first nor only one to live there, and as we were migrant farm workers, we would not be the last. Thus, middle-class comforts do not immediately feel comforting to me. In particular, white middle-class spaces typically feel sterile and unused—almost too perfect to me.

AND MILES TO GO BEFORE WE SLEEP: DESIGNING A WAY FORWARD

Writing centers are more than method and site (Boquet 1999, 467). They are more spaces that perform or spaces that are read. Writing centers are contact zones.⁶ Writing centers tell stories. However, some of the stories the WC tells to POC are another type of story: a lie. These stories are the hidden assumptions that middle-class white domestic comforts are neutral and therefore desirable to POC, as well as people from lower classes. Accordingly, there is also the assumption that these bourgeoisie domestic comforts are desirable by POC who are, in fact, middle class. Thus, not only does WC design reflect the middle-class comforts of the dominant culture, it also dismisses the possible different cultural, racial, and ethnic middle-class comforts of POC, essentially rendering them invisible.

The WC's attempts at making itself a home by designing a space also shows a real disconnect from the body. A home is made a home through emotional labor and through acts of love, compassion, empathy. But we ask, where is the emotional labor of the WC design? How can one make a home when the people who inhabit it have moderate, at best, and low, at worst, emotional connection to one another? Home brings emotional connotations and how one makes a home is largely dependent on those emotional connections one has to home.

When I came to writing centers, I came seeking nothing more than a steady paycheck to get me through grad school. When Anna came to writing centers, as a doctoral student, she came seeking a workplace outside FYC. However, our years in the WC made the WC more than a place to work. It became a place of learning, a place of pedagogy, a place of praxis, a place of research. However, for me, it also became a place of racism (the constant inquiry about and workshops on how to fix Black-language writers), of isolation (being Black in a PWI WC leaves one feeling like a fly in buttermilk⁷), of anger (at white faces that turn away from me upon my entering the WC), of discontent and disillusionment.

These feelings of isolation and disillusionment working in the WC came from a lack of diverse representations of consultants and staff as well as a heavy leaning on Eurocentric art to convey inclusivity, that is, pictures of Madea, American Gothic, and so forth. It is not that these images never reflected inclusivity to us but that they represented the inclusivity of one particular raced body and its ideologies of inclusive iconography. We claim that writing centers can further their diversity missions by using images that are not nationalist, ethnocentric, or Eurocentric. Therefore, a concerted effort to learn how consultants and clients view WC images assists us in further diversifying the overall look/image of the WC in a PWI.

WHY WE STAY: POC IN THE WRITING CENTER

In terms of retention, our narrative exemplifies the lack of support we felt as both working-class first-year composition instructors and as graduate minority students in our departments. As sites of retention, to some degree our writing centers and our institutions have failed us—not through a lack of desire but through a significant blind spot over ideas of domestic comfort. However, we stay in this space because there is a concerted effort to respond to the needs of clients, consultants, faculty, and staff in the WC. There is a concerted effort to assist students from myriad cultures and races to understand not only academic discourse but also to understand how to situate their own discourse patterns within academic discourse. And while we failed to fully acclimate, as a raced body never acclimates to racial erasure or silencing, it is also clear we were actively resisting this acclimation. To not have done so would have erased vital parts of our identities.

This erasure can occur casually, just like racism, take the form, as it did in our cases, of a lack of support for active identity development and expression. But while this erasure occurs casually, blatantly, or subversively, we, as historically marginalized and oppressed bodies, through acts of resistance can expose this subtle erasure and make visible those voices and experiences from the margins. Systemic erasure may never be undone because as one actively resists erasure, the very act(s) of resistance only reconstitutes the very systemic erasure and oppression one wishes to undo. Essentially, by referencing the very ideas, discourses, and practice(s) of racism through acts of resistance, we effectively risk its reification.

However, we assert that not resisting racism, not publicly critiquing the ideologies of racism, not attempting to undo racial/racist discourses, and not decrying the systemic treacherous practices of racism makes it significantly more insidious. As such, we need to shift the way we orient to writing centers, so that WC research may begin to undo the hidden curriculum of the WC by (1) conducting research that focuses on the experiences of historically marginalized bodies working and receiving assistance/services in the WC, (2) valuing those experiences of POC within a cultural context, and (3) considering the experiences of POC both valid and measurable (Lindsay-Dennis 2015, 2). By placing these experiences at the forefront of WC research, theory, pedagogy, praxis, and design, we do not necessarily disrupt common educational and WC practices, but we expand and alter those practices by making the experiences of marginalized bodies operating in the writing center the standard by which we theorize, critique, research, and reenvision the writing center as a truly brave-er space.

ACKNOWLEDGMENTS

Dr. Wonderful would like to thank her coauthor Willow Trevino, as well as *The Peer Review*, for allowing us to republish this article. We would like to thank Frankie Condon and Michele Eodice for their encouragement and feedback throughout our drafting process, and an extra-special thanks to Michele Eodice for connecting the two of us.

NOTES

This essay was originally published in *The Peer Review* Volume 1, Issue 2 (2017). Reprinted with permission.

1. The US Department of Education (2016) defines an HSI as having "an enrollment of undergraduate full-time equivalent students that is at least 25 percent Hispanic students." Thus, an HSI can still be a PWI, but this was not the case for this institution.
2. See Robert Connors (1981) for more about the essay sequence based on teaching the modes of writing as independent of each other—and exposition, description, narrative, and argumentation.
3. See Joseph Williams (1981).
4. See Patrick Hartwell (1985).
5. See Nancy Grimm (1999).
6. Contact zones are "social spaces where cultures meet, clash, and grapple with each other, often in contexts of highly asymmetrical relations of power, such as colonialism, slavery, or their aftermaths as they are lived out in many parts of the world today" (Pratt 1991, 34).
7. James Baldwin, *Fly in the Buttermilk*.

REFERENCES

Anzaldúa, Gloria. 2012. *Borderlands/La Frontera*. 4th ed. San Francisco: Aunt Lute Books.

Baldwin, James. 1961. "Fly in the Buttermilk." In *James Baldwin: Collected Essays*, 187–196. New York: Penguin.

Boquet, Elizabeth H. 1999. "'Our Little Secret': A History of Writing Centers, Pre- to Post-Open Admissions." *College Composition and Communication* 50 (3): 463–482.

Boquet, Elizabeth H. 2002. *Noise from the Writing Center*. Logan: Utah State University Press.

Connors, Robert. 1981. "The Rise and Fall of the Modes of Discourse." *College Composition and Communication* 32 (4): 444–455.

Cruz, Cindy. 2001. "Toward an Epistemology of a Brown Body." *Qualitative Studies in Education* 14 (5): 657–669.

Davila, Bethany. 2006. "Rewriting Race in the Writing Center." *Writing Lab Newsletter* 31 (1): 1–6.

Denny, Harry C. 2010. "Facing Race and Ethnicity in the Writing Center." In *Facing the Center: Toward an Identity Politics of One-to-One Mentoring*, edited by Harry C. Denny, 32–57. Logan: Utah State University Press.

Geller, Anne Ellen, Michele Eodice, Frankie Condon, Meg Carroll, and Elizabeth H. Boquet. 2007. *The Everyday Writing Center: A Community of Practice*. Logan: Utah State University Press.

Grimm, Nancy. 1999. *Good Intentions: Writing Center Work for Postmodern Times*. Portsmouth, NH: Boynton/Cook.

Grutsch-McKinney, Jackie. 2013. *Peripheral Visions for Writing Centers.* Logan: Utah State University Press.

Hartwell, Patrick. 1985. "Grammar, Grammars, and the Teaching of Grammar." *College English* 47 (2): 105–127.

Licona, Adela C. 2005. "(B)orderlands' Rhetorics and Representations: The Transformative Potential of Feminist Third-Space Scholarship and Zines." *NWSA Journal* 17 (2): 104–129.

Lindsay-Dennis, LaShawnda. 2015. "Black Feminist-Womanist Research Paradigm: Toward a Culturally Relevant Research Model Focused on African American Girls." *Journal of Black Studies* 46 (5): 506–520.

Moll, Luis C., Cathy Amanti, Deborah Neff, and Norma Gonzalez. 1992. "Funds of Knowledge for Teaching: Using a Qualitative Approach to Connect Homes and Classrooms." *Theory into Practice* 31 (2): 132–141.

Pratt, Mary Louise. 1991. "Arts of the Contact Zone." *Profession*, 33–40.

Rodriguez, Tomika. 2016. "The Promise and Challenge of Leadership Development for Women of Color." In *Closing the Opportunity Gap: Identity-Conscious Strategies for Retention and Student Success*, edited by Vijay Pendakur, 62–79. Sterling, VA: Stylus.

Scott, Tony. 2015. "Writing Enacts and Creates Identities and Ideologies." In *Naming What We Know: Threshold Concepts of Writing Studies*, edited by Linda Adler-Kassner and Elizabeth Wardle, 48–50. Logan: Utah State University Press.

Street, Brian V. 1984. *Literacy in Theory and Practice.* Cambridge: Cambridge University Press.

Trump, Donald. 2015. "Here's Donald Trump's Presidential Announcement Speech." http://time.com/3923128/donald-trump-announcement-speech/.

Williams, Joseph M. 1981. "The Phenomenology of Error." *College Composition and Communication* 32 (2): 152–168.

5

PAYING IT FORWARD BY LOOKING BACK
Six HBCU Professionals Reflect on Their Mentoring Experiences as Black Women in Academia

Karen Keaton Jackson, Hope Jackson,
Kendra L. Mitchell, Pamela Strong Simmons,
Cecilia D. Shelton, and LaKela Atkinson

Research tells us we often learn best from those who look like us.
—Dr. Regina Dixon-Reeves

KAREN'S VERSION OF HOW THIS ALL GOT STARTED . . .

Regina Dixon-Reeves (2000) suggests that "looks like us" does not always equal gender or skin color, but it does imply that having a connection with someone leads to a positive learning environment. Initially, I was reluctant to write this chapter about providing adequate support—specifically mentoring—for graduate students of color; reluctant not because I did not want to contribute but because finding the time to complete yet another task on top of several others seemed nearly impossible! Then I thought about how this publishing opportunity for *me* could turn into a publishing opportunity for *we*, for the reality is that my perspective is only one of many. Thus, I created an electronic pseudo-roundtable discussion from a list of questions I sent to my coauthors via email. This document is—in a sense—a performance piece in that it captures the voices of multiple black female scholars.

While our writing center experiences are what brought us all together, the writing center itself is nothing more than a backdrop for this multidisciplinary conversation about the importance of mentoring African American women graduate students. I recognized that if I wrote this piece, I could invite some of my African American sister-scholar-friends (a term coined by my sister-scholar-friend Dr. Dawn Hicks Tafari) to share their ideas, too. Five colleagues responded to my call for this work:

Dr. Hope Jackson, former writing center director and current English instructor at North Carolina A&T State University; Dr. Kendra Mitchell, instructor at Florida A&M University and former Fulbright ETA/Guest Lecturer at the University of Pretoria–Groenkloof; Dr. Pamela Simmons, associate professor of English and director of the writing in the major program at Winston-Salem State University; Ms. Cecilia Shelton, former writing center director at St. Augustine's University and current PhD student at East Carolina University; and Ms. LaKela Atkinson, former professional writing consultant at North Carolina Central University and current PhD student at East Carolina University.

While we are excited about this work, it is important to note that several other female scholars of color have addressed the need for mentoring African American women in academia. The *Journal of Black Studies* dedicated a full issue in September 2003 to the role of race in the academy, and it featured an article, "Mentoring as a Precursor to Incorporation," by Regina Dixon-Reeves (2003, quoted in the epigraph to this chapter) in which she calls on professors of color to commit to mentoring. Other scholars such as Gloria Ladson-Billings (2005) and Cynthia Cole Robinson and Pauline Clardy (2010) engaged in studies that support mentoring of African American female scholars. The 2016 special issue of *Praxis: A Writing Center Journal* on "Access and Equity in Graduate Writing Support" (Madden and Eodice) also offers critical perspectives and mentoring strategies designed to create more inclusive inroads for graduate education.

As an academic of color, I see mentoring as a requirement because no one makes it alone, especially those of us who do not see many faces who resemble ours in the field. Thus even the inclusion of my colleagues in this article is a way for me to mentor, for I know we all benefit from having publications on our vitae. From this point forward, I am shifting the narrative voice from *I* to *we*, for this chapter is a collective effort on the part of us all, as we each wanted to add more theory and consult additional research in which to ground our experiences. All I did was gather together five of my phenomenal colleagues for an exchange. They did all the rest . . .

THE COLLECTIVE *WE*

While Karen was deliberately choosing participants currently or formerly employed at HBCUs, at some point she realized all of us possess HBCU undergraduate degrees. We don't know whether this realization was a subconscious one, but some scholarship suggests HBCUs reside at the helm of successful mentoring of African American students (Reddick 2006). As Ivory Toldson (2018) mentions, although HBCUs constitute only 3 percent of US colleges and universities, "they remain among the nation's top baccalaureate-origin institutions" for African American doctoral recipients (95; Fiegner and Proudfoot 2013). Similarly, an April 2010 MLA report entitled "Data on Humanities Doctorate Recipients and Faculty Members by Race and Ethnicity" (Modern Language Association 2010) showed that from 1997 to 2006, three of the top five institutions granting bachelor's degrees to those African Americans who went on to earn PhDs in the humanities were HBCUs—topping Stanford, the University of Pennsylvania, Brown, Georgetown, and Harvard (5). And the top bachelor's institution, Spelman College, is one of the smallest (if not the smallest) in terms of student population. And of the top twenty-one bachelor's institutions for those African Americans earning PhDs in the humanities during that same time period, seven were HBCUs, which totaled one-third of all students earning the PhD in the field (6).

We are confident our approach to mentoring our students and each other is a direct reflection of our HBCU experiences. While many Research 1 (R1) institutions focus on research first, teaching second, and mentoring third, HBCUs often invert this model. HBCUs emphasize all of these, but many argue teaching and mentoring tie for first while research resides right behind them. Consequently, teaching loads remain heavy and office hours are usually dominated by student visits instead of research or grading. Ida Jones (2008) describes this familial learning philosophy, in *loco parentis* (Latin for "the place of a parent"), as a sustained "fixture and curative within the collegiate experience for many African American students," which speaks to the multifarious implicit roles of HBCU faculty (55). In bell hooks's (1994) text *Teaching to Transgress*, even the title hints at the role of teaching—and by extension tutoring—to change. We concur. Teaching is more than lecturing; it is an almost nontraditional performance, as we share our experiences in our classrooms and offices. In turn, this sharing becomes "a catalyst," encouraging active participation in learning (11). With this reciprocity established, students become comfortable with us and share both their personal joy and pain through engaged pedagogy both in and outside the classroom. As such, the teaching transgresses geographical spaces; easily recognizable, the teaching and mentoring become synchronous.

Moreover, Richard Reddick (2006) indicates his "mentors [HBCU graduates] have absorbed the importance of community uplift," as well as "serving students' needs through psychosocial support and career advisors" (63). Karen said it best while once recalling a meeting with one of her students: "I [have] been a professor, writing tutor, health counselor/nurse, financial-aid counselor, and academic advisor all in one." Within the HBCU environment, extemporaneous teaching and mentoring techniques emerge, becoming more than theory: they are liberatory practice. While many might condemn the concept of theory as another dominant tool, hooks (1994) disagrees and suggests that "theory as intervention" can be used "as a way to challenge the status quo" (60). Therefore, the theory along with its practice suggests transformation for both students and us as faculty. We share, reflect, and grow together.

Critical race pedagogy (CRP) recognizes dominant narrative practices within education (Reddick 2006). Textbooks don't reflect the language, images, or lifestyles of our students. As such, we must be prepared to confront these painful realities with our students. Sometimes, our eyes meet with an unspoken "I feel you." Other times, students share their emotions about the injustices before them. Doing so not only engages CRP but also informs it with Patricia Hill Collins's (2008) Black feminist thought (BFT). While CRP emphasizes the recognition of the oppression, BFT invites an atmosphere that encourages sharing these painful experiences within a nurturing context. This pedagogy is what Karen means. All her described roles resonate with the role of nurturer and provider. hooks (1994) indicates her gratitude for the "women and men who dare to create theory from the location of pain and struggle," calling their work "liberatory" (74). By mentoring students utilizing an engaged pedagogy informed by both CRP and BFT, hooks (1994) offers liberatory education as one that "creates new visions" by challenging the status quo (12). While the aforementioned liberatory practices were essentially infused into our HBCU undergraduate experiences, at the graduate level we found that we craved those same transformative experiences, as well. That need for more culturally relevant experiences where we felt a sense of belonging and that our whole selves were being embraced still existed and aided in our success.

While many of our responses about the roles of mentors overlapped with much of mainstream mentoring scholarship, some distinct attributes were more consistently prominent amongst us as peers of color. Specifically present were (1) the emphasis on one's spiritual development (in addition to professional and personal growth); (2) the importance of informal mentors just as much as, if not more than, formal mentors; and (3) the unique advice given from African American female mentors about how to navigate the predominately white terrain of academia.

A brief review of literature shows a mentor is commonly defined as an "expert or senior person [who] voluntarily gives time to teach, support, and encourage another" (Santamaria quoted in Inzer and Crawford 2004, 31). Other researchers note that effective mentors inspire their protégés to be their best and that the mentors "facilitate the development of independence, self-confidence, job satisfaction, upward mobility, and decision-making/problem-solving skills" (Schrubbe 2004, 324). In short, most of the focus is on the professional development of the mentee, with some emphasis on personal growth. Yet, of the five persons contacted for this article, three of us explicitly noted that spiritual development also is important. Dr. Pamela Simmons feels

> mentors also help mentees set up progressive places for personal, spiritual, and educational progress.

Dr. Hope Jackson agrees.

> A mentor is an individual who provides personal, professional, and sometimes spiritual support usually to a younger, and sometimes less experienced mentee.

Perhaps it's not really a surprise that some African Americans view spirituality as critical to their success, for historically the Black church has been the cornerstone of our community, and traditionally, Black intellectuals often come from the church. In truth, the Black church is not only a cornerstone but also the earliest place for structured education for many. During Jim Crow, the Black intellectuals weren't only pastors but teachers, too. In fact, the Black church was a primary supporter of HBCUs when possible. Many private HBCUs were founded by Black religious denominations and are still connected to them today, such as St. Augustine's University (North Carolina), Livingstone College (North Carolina), Morehouse College (Georgia), and several others. A number of those schools maintain strong overtones of Black church rituals infused in their campus rituals. Additionally, many of us can certainly think of times while in our own graduate programs that we only survived another exam or completed another chapter because of personal faith and prayers—many of those prayers said alongside us and/or by our mentors.

The second area of mentoring that was distinctive amongst this collection of sister-scholar-friends versus the general literature on mentoring we reviewed was the difference between formal and informal mentors. While this difference is not explicitly discussed by any of us here, we have all implied that our formal mentors were encouraging yet more matter-of-fact and focused on our professional accomplishments, while our informal mentors were more in tune and concerned with our personal development, particularly with how we experienced the academy as women of color. More times than not, our formal mentors were White, as these were our thesis/dissertation directors or committee members. However, our Black mentors quite often were recruited informally. This leads into and is further explained by the last aspect of mentoring that is distinctive for graduate students of color, which is the difference between their White mentors and their mentors of color. Pamela explains:

> My initial mentor, a Caucasian woman, relied heavily on the computer to engage her thoughts. She was not familiar with HBCUs. However, she treated me like a graduate student. Dr. King, the African American mentor, gave wisdom and sound doctrine. Her family understands the power of service and mentoring ... [for] her sister was one of the four little girls in the [1963] church bombing in Birmingham, AL. . . . We connected because we are also sorors ... she is dynamic.

It is understandable that Pamela was influenced by Dr. King far beyond the academic connection. She was drawn to Dr. King because of her rich legacy and family history. Moreover, their being a part of the same African American sorority (hence the term *soror*) gave an additional personal connection. Unlike historically White sororities and fraternities, which focus primarily on membership during one's college careers, historically Black Greek letter organizations (BGLOs) have lifelong memberships, with an emphasis on participation and service long *after* college. The majority of national Black Greek organizations were founded in the early 1900s as a way to galvanize Black college students for networking, sisterhood and brotherhood, and an emphasis on community service both on college campuses and beyond. It is expected that the more seasoned alumni and college graduates look out for and mentor younger professionals entering their same field, most often fields in which African Americans are underrepresented.

This specific example of Black Greek life demonstrates a much larger aspect of the African American community that is ever-present. It represents fictive kinship, a lifelong commitment for which "family" extends beyond bloodlines and marriage (Martin and Martin 1985). "Play-cousins" are no different than real cousins and "aunts" may be actual relatives or best friends with one's mother. Geneva Smitherman (2000) might call this a representation of the sacred-secular, for in this relationship, there is no distinction between sacred matters and secular matters within the academic space. Drawing on an African worldview, Smitherman defines the sacred style as "rural and Southern ... the style of the Black preacher and that associated with the Black church tradition . . . [which] tend[s] to be highly informal" (64). Meanwhile, the secular style is "urban and Northern. . . . It tends to be . . . more emotionally restrained than the sacred style" (64). Taken together, this kinship of Greek life mimics other aspects of the African American community, as seen through Smitherman's sacred-secular framework, through its integration of Southern connectedness and the restrained professional persona needed in academia.

To be clear, this is not to say white mentors cannot establish close (or even closer) connections than mentors of color, for that is simply not true. Victor Villanueva (1993) points out in his autobiographical text *Bootstraps: From an American Academic of Color* that it was not his African American public school teachers who connected with him and his other classmates of color most easily, for those teachers were a bit distant and standoffish (see also Jackson and Jackson, forthcoming). Rather, it was the white teacher, Mr. D., who connected because he showed genuine concern and was part of the community.

> Color isn't always race when it comes to teachers. It's an attitude, more of an understanding of where we live than where we're from. . . . A teacher would have to go a long way to understand and convey an understanding of all those where-froms. But a teacher could have looked around and known the where-at. Few did, even among those who were racially of color. There were two African American teachers. . . . They weren't oreos or going about "incognegro." I can't imagine anyone saying they were trying to pass. They were Black. But there was also something like what Signithia Fordham calls a *racelessness* to them. "Mr. Musique" . . . a music appreciation teacher . . . dressed in shark-skin suits, starched white shirts with collar pins, thin ties, his hair in a process, horned-rim glasses. . . . He was an interesting character. He cared. But he was far from the block now. "Artsy-fartsy," we'd say, not one of us, not like Mr. D. who never pretended to talk in Black English or even to assert that he understood the ghetto. Mr. Musique cared, but remained aloof somehow. [For a disruptive student] Mr. D. forgoes the pink slip to the principal, meets the disrupter downstairs, in the gym, twelve-ounce gloves, the matter settled. He has a broad definition of art. He knows the world—and he understands the block, el bloque, what kids today call "the hood." Mr. D. was as close to color as any teacher I had known in school. (1–2)

So, the effectiveness of one as a mentor does not depend on race alone. Attitude, compassion, and genuine interest go much further. However, cultural connections, such as community group affiliations or those fictive kinships, often allow mentees to feel comfortable more easily than they do in formal academic communities.

As Cecilia Put It

My most valuable mentors are Black. One is a former chairperson . . . and . . . the only Black woman PhD in an HBCU English department. . . . Her political savvy taught me a lot about navigating the politics of the academy as a Black woman . . . she taught me that asserting myself, my ideas and my qualifications was a necessary skill if I had any intentions of staying in academia. She taught me not to wait for an available opportunity, but instead to make space for myself. She taught me to center myself—my interests, my research agenda, my teaching—in all of my other work and to make it work for me.

The other Black mentor . . . my "peer," in that she also directed a writing center at a sister institution, but she was several paces beyond me in her career . . . [is] my sounding board. I can tell her almost anything about what's happening at work. If she doesn't have advice (which is rare) she always has the confidence boost that I need to believe that I can figure it out and make a good choice. She is the person who encourages me to go after professional opportunities that seem out of reach and she uses her network to connect me to people who can help me.

Both [were] Black and women and . . . married with children. To be a woman and Black is rare enough in the academy, but to do so with a partner and children is extremely rare. For these two people, who are facing arguably the most stressful situations compared to [other mentors], to pour the most into me is incredible and I think it speaks to how important it is to have mentors who are like you and who have their own commitments to mentorship.

LaKela Explains

I believe that my African American and white advisors were all genuinely interested in my progress. I felt that I could depend on them to honor their commitments to me as agreed. Yet, the advice and extent of the advice differed between the two groups. My African American mentors were unafraid to discuss how race played a factor in my success. When I gave presentations, they advised me about our representation as an HBCU. On the other hand, I cannot recall instances where I discussed race or inequity with my white advisors beyond the course material.

My white advisors guided me as other students, rarely or never mentioning my race. For instance, as a graduate assistant, I attended school full-time and had multiple part-time jobs to support myself. While my various professors were aware of this, a few of my white advisors or instructors discouraged me from taking on these . . . [while my] African American mentors/instructors were more understanding of my obligations. . . . I think the collective understanding among my African American mentors is that as a community, sometimes, we must take on multiple roles and responsibilities in order to be afforded some of the same opportunities as other races . . . [which] may not be enough to remain competitive and sustain our positions in academia and society in general.

While I appreciate the role of all my mentors and advisors, I am more at ease when I confide personally and professionally in my African American mentors because of their ability to empathize with my accomplishments and challenges.

Kendra Relates Her Experiences

I acknowledge many in my village and their roles, and there were many times when my mentors, regardless of race or discipline, echoed the same or similar lessons in regards to my academic approach. . . . Some notable differences were that most of my African American mentors allotted more time and space for how I was experiencing the academy as a woman of color.

My advisor, Dr. Kristie Fleckenstein, was sensitive to my experiences and honest about her limitations and her different approach as a white woman. And I respected her for that, as well as her understanding of my need for both. By the end of the dissertation process, however, my advisor sent some of the most important and personal votes of confidence via email at a time when I was most fragile. She eventually encouraged phone calls, which were helpful. . . . It was refreshing to have an advisor who was willing to adjust to my sensitivities as needed, especially since I knew I was adjusting to her approach to foster a healthy relationship. I found that my advisor provided extensive written feedback with face-to-face conversations as a supplement.

[Phone calls] had been the initial approach with my mentors of color. [These Black women] wanted to hear my voice. . . . When I didn't pass their "tests," they scheduled face-to-face meetings. I found that many of my African American mentors would provide equal amounts of discussion and written feedback.

Dr. Faye Spencer-Maor is one who I credit with my awakening to nerddom/scholarly pursuits in rhet/comp. Before meeting her, my goals were simple: earn my bachelor's degree, get a good job, and live a decent life. And there was nothing wrong with those aspirations. What I learned from her is that I secretly desired more.

Dr. Veronica Yon, former Director of the Writing Resource Center, is the reason I have the depth of experiences in writing center studies. . . . She provided opportunities for me to travel, develop programs, and train staff—and eventually complete my dissertation in her Center. In other words, she not only saw something in me; she also cultivated it.

Dr. Rhea Lathan has been the ultimate cheerleader, prayer-partner, and other-mother. Not many people can say that they have had people who have taken their students' completion as their divine calling, but I had that in her. She sacrificed more than I know to make sure I crossed the finish line on her watch.

There are others that I cannot even begin to name because I don't know them. I consider many of the custodial staff, especially those who worked the night shift, as mentors. They encouraged me when I was in the graduate lounge past 3 a.m. because I didn't have a computer or the internet or either one. We laughed. We talked about life's challenges and promised to pray for one another. They . . . were equally entitled to celebrating my achievements as my family members. They kept me grounded and in touch with my purpose for all of the sacrifices.

As was the case for Pamela, both LaKela and Kendra identify differences in the means and contexts of communication between their White mentors and their Black mentors. Pamela and Kendra, in particular, note how their mentors of color were quick to pick up the phone or schedule face-to-face meetings to check in and ensure progress and success, while their white mentors more often used email as the primary form of communication, even during critical times. Moreover, all three women emphasize the personal nature of the mentoring relationship, noting especially how their mentors of color (who are primarily women), gave them room to explore through open discussion how to navigate academic life as women of color.

Cecilia Explains

> My Black mentors were/are much more personal with me. They inquire about and offer support to me both professionally and personally. They are less formal in their interactions. So for example, my Black mentors are usually the people that I call and text initially with when stuff goes down. They are my go to people when I'm in the thick of it. Then, when I have it somewhat together, I approach my other mentors to layer on their advice and insight. [Once] I've worked through the situation, I debrief with my Black mentors. Their mentoring is more of a relationship than it is a professional obligation. They don't "turn off" during holiday, breaks, etc. I still feel like I can reach out to them if I really need to. I also think I could reach out to other mentors in "off season" times, but it would feel like more of an imposition and I'd feel like I needed to apologize.

And so, possibly it is this last sentiment, the permission to discuss life as an academic woman of color without doing so much "extra" work, that often is missing in interactions between mentors of the majority and mentees of color.

Hope Says

> My advisor [was] a white woman. . . . [I had no mentors of color.] This was part of the problem in my PhD journey. . . . A lot of what I missed or didn't have during my graduate school experiences, I share with my students. . . . I believe the way I was and wasn't taught impacted that more. . . . As such, I do my best to show . . . both undergraduate and especially current gradu-

ate students . . . how much I am connected with their success and failures. . . . I wasn't taught professional development as a graduate student, so I taught it to my tutors. I become their "othermother" by "keepin' it real." I treat them as if they were my children through genuine nurturing.

Hope recognized the significant absence of a mentor of color and decided to ensure that her African American mentees never experienced that lack, for "without [African American] voices, our concerns become mute" (hooks 1994, 105).

Pamela takes her role of mentoring her Black students seriously, as well. She explains:

> I am proud to say that I have mentored several writing consultants. Most of them I taught in a writing course. To date, I still mentor two former writing consultants who are now directors of a university writing center. We keep in contact and I still encourage them to enter a doctoral program. One young lady recently got married, and has started a family. In addition, the other young lady is a third year Law student at UCLA. . . . She got a full ride to Winston-Salem State University and UCLA. She is a top scholar and writer and was offered a professional job as a Law researcher in Los Angeles. I make sure my students/mentees get great exposure to our professional societies. Also another mentee is entering Duke University's doctoral program in the fall.

And even Cecilia, who is now midway through her PhD career, also already sees her responsibility to help those behind her.

> I now see it as my obligation to pass on what has been given to me and to do it specifically for Black students. I try to make myself visible and available to all students, but particularly to Black students. I also try to connect with them both inside and outside the classroom. In my experience, some Black students have had experiences with school that suggest that teachers—all of them—embody whiteness uncritically and therefore cannot relate to other cultural experiences besides their own. I try to teach with a critical eye toward race and class so that my students see me value our shared culture (and other cultures) in the classroom. I suspect that this enables a kind of risk-taking in their approach to me (or responsiveness when I approach them) that doesn't happen with other professors who are not of color.
>
> The way that I have been mentored had a significant impact on the way that I directed my writing center. I directed a writing center at an HBCU . . . and mentorship was built into the way that I administered the writing center's program. I prioritized the professional development and leadership opportunities I could offer my consultants (tutors). I used my network to support these priorities. I included them in scholarly and professional work to show them that I had confidence in them and to [enhance] their qualifications and credentials. For example, when I did both formative and summative evaluations of the consultants, I always discussed my observations in individual conferences with them. This gave me

the opportunity to find out more about their goals and find ways to make their writing center work valuable to them. Then, I'd make sure that in my annual review of their resumes that they were maximizing the work they did for me in the writing center in support of their goals. I wrote countless letters of recommendation in support of them. Many of them are still in touch to this day and I attribute the kinds of relationships I was able to build with them to the model of mentorship I received.

In truth, because there are so few African American PhDs in any academic field, finding one in a particular discipline at any institution can be rather difficult, if not impossible. The National Center for Education Statistics reported that in fall 2013, only 6 percent of college faculty were Black (2015, table 1). Thus it often is necessary for students to go outside their institutions to connect with a mentor of color who resembles them. Fortunately, in 2018, the internet and social media can make support just a click away. Hope cites an organization called DIVAS, which stands for Distinguished Intellectual Virtuous Academic Sistas, as a space where she received informal mentoring and support. Founded in 2009, DIVAS's mission is to

> empower Black women in the academy by providing mentoring as well as academic and research support to enhance scholarship and community involvement. DIVAS are committed to civic engagement. We believe that service to one's community is an essential characteristic of social uplift. The DIVAS collective has allowed Black women doctoral students and new professionals to "stand in the gap" and become the "othermother" (Guiffrida 2005) for Black women during their PhD process. (DIVAS n.d.)

In addition, there are Facebook groups and other online spaces, along with symposia and conferences, that exist specifically for academic women of color (see Alvarez, Brito, Salazar, and Aguilar 2016). Karen's external source of support was from what she lovingly refers to as her "Sister Circle." When she was a graduate student at Wayne State University in Detroit, Michigan, she was selected to receive a fellowship sponsored by the Michigan Department of Education for MA and PhD students of color, the King-Chavez-Parks Future Faculty Fellowship. The state of Illinois sponsored a similar type of fellowship; and each year, they hosted an interdisciplinary joint conference where fellowship recipients not only presented research but also attended professional development sessions including how to survive thesis and dissertation processes, how to conduct a successful job search, how to obtain tenure, and more.

During her first attendance at this conference, Karen was blessed to meet one of her sorors (sorority sisters), Regina Dixon-Reeves, who was a few years closer to completing her doctoral degree and willing to share her survival strategies with her; in fact, Dixon-Reeves's research is on mentoring (and cited at the beginning of this article). The following year, Karen met five additional Black women who became her sisters on the road to obtaining higher degrees. They shared stories of preparing for exams, working with committee members, dating, marriage, and everything in between. Being a part of this fellowship program and in the Sister Circle literally filled Karen's soul and recharged her in an indescribable way, letting her know she was not alone in her struggle and that she, too, could do this "thing" called a PhD program. Research on retention affirms Karen's experiences, noting that there must be a good student-institution fit in order for a student to commit to graduating from that school (Griswold 2003). Students must feel invested in the institution, like they belong, as that makes them more likely to want to matriculate fully to graduation (Andres and Carpenter 1997). The doctoral fellowship program allowed Karen (and the other fellows) to feel like she "fit" into academia, that there was a space for her and people like her. Granted, the focus of much retention literature is on undergraduate students. Yet, we posit that for students of color at advanced levels, experiencing a connection to the institution is even more critical.

As we close this piece, we realize we have only scratched the surface of the experiences of Black women in academia. When we look at tenure, only 3 to 7 percent of tenure-track and full professors are Black (depending upon specific rank), and only 16 percent are non-White (National Center for Education Statistics 2015, table 1). We must do better. In order to have a more diverse pool of faculty to serve as mentors, we must first matriculate current Black female graduate students and recruit new ones. According to S. Rasheem, Ali-Sha Alleman, Dawnsha Mushonga, Darlene Anderson, and Halaevalu F. Ofahengaue Vakalahi (2018), there are several ways to go about doing this.

In terms of policy, Rasheem et al. (2018) suggest that "institutional policies can be deliberate and intentional about allotting funding and resources for efforts toward mentoring, recruiting, retaining, and graduating Black women graduate students, particularly at the doctorate level" (65). This could mean providing funds for conference attendance so Black women are afforded networking opportunities that enhance their experiences, as well as additional professional development resources that enable them to find informal networks. In terms of education, more pedagogies that center and make visible Black women's contributions to research, scholarship, and higher education are needed at the graduate level. In addition, institutions can establish mentoring programs specifically for Black women and other minoritized cultural groups, ones culturally sensitive to the needs of their population. We can look to HBCUs, and more specifically historically Black women's colleges such as Spelman College (Georgia) and Bennett College (North Carolina), as examples of institutions that have successfully created curricula and pedagogies geared toward the celebration and achievement of Black women.

Research has shown that mentoring networks based on fictive kinship "produced more emotional support for students with same-ethnic and same-gender relationships than cross-gender and cross-race pairing" (Fletcher and Mullen quoted in Rasheem et al. 2018, 53). As is evident in Dr. Hope Jackson's experiences (explained above), most Black female graduate students do not have mentors who look like they do; moreover, most White faculty do not have the "multicultural competence to mentor graduate students of color" (53). Thus, many Black women who have found informal mentors have done so on their own or in organic ways. However, institutions should make deliberate efforts to enable mentoring for all Black women. We should not leave it to chance for Black women to find mentors willing to fight for them; institutions should invest money, resources, and people towards helping Black women graduate students achieve both professional and personal success.

ACKNOWLEDGMENTS

We appreciate the editors, especially Shannon Madden and Michele Eodice, for their support of this work and for including voices in their collection that traditionally have been silenced in academia. Many thanks to the peer reviewers who gave us meaningful feedback to strengthen each draft of our work. Lastly, we acknowledge the many African American women scholars who have come before us and paved the way so we may stand in our truths and give them a voice.

REFERENCES

Alvarez, Nancy, Francia N. Brito, Cristina Salazar, and Karina Aguilar. 2016. "Agency, Liberation, and Intersectionality among Latina Scholars: Narratives from a Cross-Institutional Writing Collective." *Praxis: A Writing Center Journal* 14 (1): 9–14.

Andres, Lesley, and Susan Carpenter. 1997. "Today's Higher Education Students: Issues of Admission, Retention, Transfer, and Attrition in Relation to Changing Student Demographics." *Centre for Policy Studies in Education, University of British Columbia.* (December): 1–58.

Collins, Patricia Hill. 2008. *Black Feminist Thought.* New York: Routledge.

DIVAS (Distinguished Intellectual Virtuous Academic Sistas). n.d. Accessed July 25, 2016. https://sites.google.com/site/drdivas/.

Dixon-Reeves, Regina. 2000. "The Power of Mentoring." Paper presented at the IMGIP/ICEOP–KCP Joint Fellows Conference, Northbrook, IL, November 7–9.

Dixon-Reeves, Regina. 2003. "Mentoring as a Precursor to Incorporation: An Assessment of the Mentoring Experiences of Recently Minted Ph.D.s." *Journal of Black Studies* 34 (1): 12–27.

Fiegener, Mark K., and Steven L. Proudfoot. 2013. *Baccalaureate Origins of U.S.-Trained S&E Doctorate Recipients.* Re-Seed. https://web.northeastern.edu/reseed/2013/10/baccalaureate-origins-of-u-s-trained-se-doctorate-recipients/.

Fletcher, Sarah J. and Carol A. Mullen, eds. 2012. *The SAGE Handbook of Mentoring and Coaching in Education.* Los Angeles: SAGE.

Griswold, Gary. 2003. "Writing Centers: The Student Retention Connection." *Academic Exchange Quarterly* 7 (4): 277–282.

hooks, bell. 1994. *Teaching to Transgress: Education as the Practice of Freedom.* New York: Routledge.

Inzer, Lonnie D., and C. B. Crawford. 2005. "A Review of Formal and Informal Mentoring: Processes, Problems, and Design." *Journal of Leadership Education* 4 (1): 31–50.

Jackson, Karen Keaton, Hope Jackson, and Dawn N. Hicks Tafari. 2019. "We Belong in the Discussion: Including HBCUs in Conversations About Race and Writing." *College Composition and Communication* 71 (2): 184–214.

Jones, Ida. 2008. "Coming of the Race: Kelly Miller and Two Historically Black Colleges and Universities in the Niagara Movement Era." *Afro-Americans in New York Life and History* 32 (2): 51–64.

Ladson-Billings, Gloria. 2005. *Beyond the Big House: African American Educators on Teacher Education.* New York: Teachers College Press.

Madden, Shannon, and Michele Eodice, eds. 2016. "Access and Equity in Graduate Writing Support." Special issue, *Praxis: A Writing Center Journal* 14 (1). http://www.praxisuwc.com/141-final.

Martin, Joanne and Elmer Martin. 1985. *The Helping Tradition in the Black Family and Community.* Washington, DC: National Association of Social Workers.

Modern Language Association. 2010. *Data on Humanities Doctorate Recipients and Faculty Members by Race and Ethnicity.* MLA Office of Research. https://www.mla.org/content/download/2834/79690/data_on_humanities_2010.pdf.

National Center for Education Statistics. 2015. "Characteristics of Postsecondary Faculty." Figure 2.

Rasheem, S., Ali-Sha Alleman, Dawnsha Mushonga, Darlene Anderson, and Halaevalu F. Ofahengaue Vakalahi. 2018. "Mentor-Shape: Exploring the Mentoring Relationships of Black Women in Doctoral Programs." *Mentoring and Tutoring: Partnership in Learning* 26 (1): 50–69.

Reddick, Richard. 2006. "The Gift that Keeps on Giving: Historically Black College and University-Educated Scholars and Their Mentoring at Predominately White Institutions." *Journal of Educational Foundations* 20 (5): 61–84.

Robinson, Cynthia Cole, and Clary Hardy. 2010. *Tedious Journey: Autoethnography by Women of Color in Academe.* New York: Peter Lang.

Santamaria, J. O. 2003. "Mentoring Develops High-Potential Employees." *Asia Africa Intelligence Wire.*

Schrubbe, Katherine F. 2004. "Mentorship: A Critical Component for Professional Growth and Academic Success." *Journal of Dental Education* 68 (3): 324–328.

Smitherman, Geneva. 2000. *Talkin That Talk: Language, Culture and Education in African America.* New York: Routledge.

Toldson, Ivory A. 2018. "Why Historically Black Colleges and Universities Are Successful with Graduating Black Baccalaureate Students Who Subsequently Earn Doctorates in STEM." *Journal of Negro Education* 87 (2): 95–98.

Villanueva, Victor. 1993. *Bootstraps: From an American Academic of Color.* Urbana, IL: NCTE.

PART 2

Bridges and Borders

6
GRADUATE WRITING IN COMMUNITIES
Critical Notes on Access and Success

Alexandria Lockett

This collection explores the issue of *supporting graduate student writers* from two intersecting perspectives that constitute each part of the book: (1) the lived experiences of graduate students from historically marginalized groups and (2) research about strategies for "success." Part 1: Voices narratives vividly illustrate the problem of isolation as a consequence of intensive research and writing tasks required at the graduate level. Loneliness, of course, typically characterizes the graduate school experience. However, it is felt more intensely by students representing demographic groups whose historical exclusion from institutions of power continues to systematically oppress them.

Part 1 authors represent Black, Latinx, multilingual, and international students and mentors. Their distinctive experiences converged when they reflected on how writing affected their sense of belonging in the academy. They identify as "in-between," "other," and "isolated," while struggling to figure out how to "succeed." In fact, nearly all the part 1 authors contend that their graduate student status is an anomalous position. On one hand, their higher educational attainment earned them graduate school admission, marking them with a status of potential privilege and power. However, social advancement through graduate studies pressures historically underrepresented students to serve as gatekeepers for colonialism, especially as their language and communication fall short of their instructors' expectations. Indeed, Kirsten T. Edwards in chapter 2 analyzes how she was never meant to occupy the graduate student identity or the positions of authority that come thereafter. She testifies,

> I, as a Black, female, administrator, and scholar, do not simply function to my White male student as a class above the poor, useless, servants, and maintenance/facility workers he encounters daily. By virtue of my

professional position in the institution, I also function as a personal authority to him. Therefore, in the same epistemological space, I represent to my student both a higher ranking colonizer and a subhuman colonized.

Drawing on her discomfort, she dubs graduate students in her position "academic in-betweeners." She boldly argues that "the experience of the in-between space says loud and clear, 'Something ain't right!' When our 'colonizing agent' students look into our faces confused, disgusted, confrontational, it is not because we should not be here. It is because we should not stand there." Both Beth Godbee and Edwards contextualize their own experiences bearing witness to or personally experiencing the traumatic effects of white supremacist patriarchal communication and spatial norms. Their chapters inform Jennifer Friend, Jennifer Salvo, Michelle Paquette, and Elizabeth Brown's work, whose work is featured in Part 3: Approaches. As these authors show, equity ought to serve as one of the goals that influences the design and implementation of long-term graduate writing initiatives.

Finding community, then, is central to the chapters in part 1. For example, part 1 authors reflect on how they confronted extreme alienation by writing in communities and/or serving writing communities. Thus, writing centers (WCs) play a role in both parts 1 and 3 of the collection as sites of research and practice. Godbee concludes her chapter by recommending more research about feminist co-mentoring in writing centers after she observes Black feminist ways of talking—storytelling and testifying as methods of validating lived experiences connect a Black WC tutor to her Black woman client. The authors of the chapters by Richard Sévère and Maurice Wilson; Wonderful Faison and Anna K. (Willow) Treviño; and Karen Keaton Jackson, Hope Jackson, Kendra Mitchell, Pamela Simmons, Cecilia Shelton, and LaKela Atkinson all testify to having intentionally sought out writing centers as places where they could seek and provide strategies, as both writing consultants and writers themselves. More specifically, these authors claim their sociolinguistic competence by laboring in institutional learning spaces designed to support language and literacy.

Part 3 further elaborates on the value of writing centers because they offer the potential for community in various ways. They offer space, tutorial assistance, and campus-wide programming about graduate writing conventions. Furthermore, WCs might play a liaison role between disciplines and administrative units, which can lead to formalized institutional support organized through peer- and faculty-led writing groups (Zanzucchi and Fenstermaker; Rodrigo and Romberger), workshop series (Zanzucchi and Fenstermaker), dissertation boot camps

(Cayley; Russell-Pinson and Jafarian), and faculty development efforts (Bommarito; Friend, Salvo, Paquette, and Brown).

Furthermore, many part 3 authors advocate participating in writing groups. Rochelle Rodrigo and Julia Romberger provide numerous applications of writing groups. In particular, the authors suggest cultivating student-centered writing groups that focus on the generative aspects of invention. This chapter expands the notion of support beyond the technical sense of satisfying desires of faculty and mentors or fulfilling program requirements. The authors suggest writing groups should serve as intellectual spaces where the challenging work of idea development happens. Overall, both Parts 1 and 3 of this collection showcase the equitable knowledge-making potential of graduate writing communities.

Moreover, peer reviewing is a resource for graduate student writers that corresponds to two major writing communities described in part 1: writing groups and writing centers. As previously mentioned, institutional diversity is a factor that affects writing support—as pointed out by Faison and Treviño, as well as the HBCU faculty mentors featured in chapter 5. These authors affirm that working in HBCU writing centers enables them to mentor students effectively.

Overall, the rich experiences of part 1 authors clarify the fundamental problem of graduate writing: how do emerging professionals navigate spaces where their knowledge production is systematically obstructed, especially when they attempt to assert the power to construct and operate in language-learning spaces in the institution? In response, I agree with Zanzucchi and Fenstermaker that it is crucial to provide robust, flexible support for graduate writers. These chapters also offer an opportunity to evaluate and document models designed to serve all students, and students from historically marginalized populations, in particular.

Access to support for graduate writers depends on locating the places where graduate writing is learned and how graduate students identify themselves *as writers*. Part 3 authors acknowledge that strategies for "success" occur in multidimensional contexts that call for nuanced understandings of what these writers need. Lisa Russell-Pinson and Haadi Jafarian present a list of multiple actions that, for example, dissertation writers need to take in order to resist procrastination. These directives, such as having explicit conversations with mentors about writing expectations, reaching out to others for support, and starting or joining dissertation writing groups could stimulate better communication with faculty and provide structure for graduate writing communities.

This list offers a great start, and Russell-Pinson and Jafarian are well aware that procrastination is hardly the result of students being lazy or clueless. As their analysis of procrastination suggests, it is also often a consequence of racism and linguistic imperialism—interrelated forces that reduce motivation as a traumatic effect. Thus, examining the lived experiences of some of our part 1 authors raises questions about the kind of environment and/or scope of community necessary for ensuring graduate students' ability to strengthen their writing. Perhaps the readers who empathize with the personal experiences presented in Godbee's and Edwards's chapters will draw on these questions to shift their perspective about writing challenges from an experience of incompetence to an experience of practicing a new literacy with relative codes. By contrast, did Sévère and Wilson feel as though they could ask instructors these kinds of questions?

As a multilingual Black male who grew up in a Haitian household, Sévère reflects on how his experience attending an HBCU made him "unapologetically Black," and Wilson does not question his intellectual ability to improve his graduate writing. Instead, he blames poor mentoring and pedagogical gaps for his inability to acquire literacies for graduate writing.

> I had hoped to receive some information to explain how I might address my academic weaknesses, or how to more appropriately integrate my ideas into academic speak and in such a way demonstrate my status more appropriately as an emerging scholar instead of just a weak academic. In other words, my professor missed an opportunity not only to teach but also to mentor and groom me (assuming he was interested in doing so) for the discourse community of which I was now a part.

Of course, the problem of learning doctoral-level writing conventions is addressed in Bommarito's chapter, "Research Writing as an Adaptive Challenge: A Study with Implications for Supervisory Feedback Practices." Bommarito might say Wilson faced an "adaptive challenge" because his professor (like Professor Maddox) neglected to address what he perceived to be "academic weakness" outside the paper as written. To be sure, the faculty advisor could have explicitly described disciplinary writing conventions, or explained the kinds of moves various audiences expect from writing. Sévère and Wilson indicate that this was the advice they needed. Chapters 12, 13, and 14 confirm the necessity for a range of interlocking institutional networks responsible for supporting graduate writing, and chapters 3, 4, and 5 discuss how mentoring is more available at HBCUs and HSIs. Therefore, Sévère and Wilson expected better mentoring, whereas Professor Maddox's students in Bommarito's chapter may not know how to access the kind of faculty attention that would strengthen their writing. In either case, community graduate writing initiatives may shift student dependence on faculty feedback, as Shannon Madden points out in the introduction.

In general, graduate writing support means students have increased access to the social resources designed to acclimate them more fully to the kinds of knowledge making that must be advanced in the academy. Towards this end, we must recognize that learning disciplinary writing conventions isn't just a matter of being told explicitly what to do (see Bommarito) or being motivated by faculty approval to resist procrastination that is consequential to the trauma of graduate education (see Godbee). These concerns bring us back to Madden's introduction, which considers how to best support these students given that the concept and practice of *support* must be theorized in ways that expose and critique the supposedly neutral objective of "student success."

We acknowledge that this collection will likely be read by some students, faculty, and/or administrators who define success as a simple matter of completing a degree program or securing employment. Although these outcomes should be part of the assessment criteria for graduate support initiatives, part 1 authors are careful to draw our attention to the issues that attend writing support when it is offered within an educational stratum that has not historically recognized certain members as participating scholars. Thus, we should evaluate success as integral to support (e.g., writing in communities) because it means overcoming isolation and showing up—for oneself and for others.

ACKNOWLEDGMENTS

First, I want to thank my mother, Brenda J. Lockett, because she did not need a college degree to teach me how to cultivate the confidence necessary to demand a better world for Black women. Next, I am also grateful for the late Florida Cornelius, my grandmother, and my aunts Cynthia Johnson and Wanda Golston, for challenging me to grow a critical consciousness. To my father, a veteran, whose sacrifices made my access to higher education all the more possible. I appreciate Seth A. Evans, who always reads and edits all my work to ensure it is creatively perspicuous and with manageable liability. Next, I'm indebted to my coeditors—Michele Eodice, Shannon Madden, and Kirsten T. Edwards—who generously offered me feedback on my writing and the unique opportunity to collaborate on this project. I would also like to thank the scholars and mentors who inspired me to clarify and resist racialized discourses of success. These persons include Ann Hoover, Linda Seidel, Cole Woodcox, John Ishiyama, Bertha Thomas, Patrick

Lobert, Betty McLane-Iles, Chris Carter, Susan Kates, Catherine John, Richard Doyle, Jacqueline Jones Royster, Keith Gilyard, Jon Olsen, Cheryl Glenn, Lynette Kvasny, Jeffrey Nealon, Debbie Hawhee, Mya Poe, Asao Inoue, Iris Ruiz, James Sanchez, Anna Sicari, Harry Denny, Matthew Vetter, Jenn Fishman, Alexis Hart, and Rebecca Babcock. Finally, I appreciate the intellectual guidance from my James Weldon Johnson Institute (JWJI) family—Andrea Gillespie, Kali-Ahset Amen Strayhorn, and Michelle Gordon in particular, among several other remarkable scholars.

7
MI TESTIMONIO
Crossing Borders in the Academy

Amanda E. Cuellar

I open this piece with a short *testimonio* in the hope that my experience bridges the frameworks, reflections, and narratives included in part 1 of this anthology to the strategies offered in part 3 to help graduate student writers navigate the structural, pedagogical, and personal challenges we face in the academy. *Testimonio* is a powerful methodology popularized by Latin Americans to give voice to those who are usually marginalized or erased from dominant society. This form of sharing personal and community experiences offers a way to inscribe "lived realities" that might otherwise get lost (Latina Feminist Group 2001, 2).

Mi testimonio is about being a Spanglish-speaking Chicana in a PhD program at a predominantly white institution (PWI) in the Midwest. In the PWI, my minority status is pronounced in more ways than one. I am not phenotypically white. I've also been told that my cadence when speaking is "unique." I interpret this to mean that my struggle to maintain the expected level of academic discourse is obvious. I think in my first language—Spanglish. My fluency in nondominant discourses, such as Spanglish, border Spanish, and working-class English, create moments of tension with the academic discourses I find difficult to master and, admittedly, resist using (Gee 1989). Oftentimes, as I speak, I pause in specific places where I normally would use a Spanish word or phrase. The pause gives me time to code switch. A few times I've mentioned to my colleagues that one of my greatest fears is losing my nondominant discourse, and I am met with puzzled looks. I assume these looks mean I am supposed to strive to achieve fluency in academic English. I should see this fluency as a marker of membership in an academic community. The problem my colleagues do not understand is that gaining fluency in my nondominant discourse will drive me further away from my home community. These characteristics mark my Otherness in my academic institution. I wonder about the conscious and unconscious expectations that inform my professors' reactions to (and constructions of) my Otherness.

I never felt like a failed writer at the Hispanic-serving institution (HSI) I graduated from in West Texas. But at this stage, or *especially* at this stage, of writing my dissertation, I am made to feel my writing never meets adequate standards of graduate student work. In my first graduate seminar at the PWI, my professor told the class that if we had not yet found our "academic writing style," eventually everything would just "click." Instead of blaming the problematic expectations some of my professors had for their graduate students and a system that sets writers up for failure, I shouldered the blame by thinking academic writing just never "clicked" for me. I wondered why my professors had such a difficult time expressing their expectations for the writing standards I am supposed to meet. I have often been told by my professors that I need to "find my voice." The comments written directly on my chapters, seminar papers, and drafts mostly center on grammatical errors and sentence construction. I revise the chapters according to the comments I receive, trying harder to establish a stronger "voice" and correct the grammatical errors pointed out to me. Once, I was told I should avoid being "convoluted." When I receive feedback like this, what I hear is that my way of being, a Spanglish-speaking Chicana, is "convoluted."

My lived experiences of growing up on the border in West Texas between the United States and Mexico were never as painful as the ones I was constantly facing in my doctoral program. During these last five years, I have been enduring "*la herida abrieta*," or the open wound, Gloria Anzaldúa (2012) attributes to the "border culture" of a Third Space (25). The PWI is a Third Space where my ways of knowing and ways of being disrupt constructions of accepted discourses in graduate seminars and expected skills in graduate student writing. In other words, as Kirsten T. Edwards mentions in her afterword to this collection, the sociopolitical framework of the academy seeks to indoctrinate minoritized graduate students to "[comport] to whiteness and normative masculinity." These are the borders doctoral students of color are pressured to cross if they are to be "successful" scholars in the academy.

Similar to the narratives shared by Wonderful Faison and Anna K. (Willow) Treviño in part 1, *mi testimonio* offers a way for me to better discern and work through the structural challenges I have endured as a Chicana graduate student and writer. I consider my doctoral experiences at the PWI through the lens of "*una atravesada*" (Anzaldúa 2012, 25). Specifically, I recognize that *atravesando*, or "crossing," academic borders has revealed painful truths about graduate studies. In particular,

I question why the writing process became such an insurmountable obstacle I constantly face. Offering ambiguous advice like "eventually everything will just 'click'" or "you're struggling to 'find your academic voice'" is not helpful. Actually, these types of comments further impede my progress because I am left to figure out on my own how to make my writing "click" or discover what exactly an "academic voice" entails. In these instances, the borders between my professors and me are so wide it is difficult, oftentimes nearly impossible, to cross them. Usually, I feel I am the one who constantly must do the *atravesando*.

I also realize that for a long time, I lacked a supportive writing community. While I tried meeting with cohort members, making myself available for workshops and finding other kinds of writing groups, I always felt disconnected from other writers. Although the graduate students I met or temporarily worked with during these events mostly expressed similar reactions to the demands of writing substantive projects and meeting the challenges of the dissertation, I still felt like an outsider. Intense feelings of inadequacy and disconnection prevented me from building any form of academic kinship—a concept I would later learn is valued by some academic communities. More than likely, my status as a Spanglish-speaking Chicana impacts my relationships with other colleagues. I am never completely sure. Nevertheless, I lack a true sense of belonging.

During the summer of 2018, I was invited to join the Calmecac Collective (the CC). This group "emerged as a radical tactic of survival and resistance for graduate students and junior faculty against the backdrop of Texas A&M University for building intentional community with one another, centering [their] own cultures, families, and ancestors" (Calmecac Collective 2013, 299). Having moved on to faculty positions outside Texas A&M, the CC reunited during El Mundo Zurdo Conference in 2018 and invited other junior scholars to participate with them in the conference. As original members of the CC reminisced over experiences they shared during their graduate studies, I quickly realized the powerful support system they had created to help them survive the academy. I felt fortunate to have been invited to the group because the CC showed me I was not the problem. The members exposed the toxicity of their graduate school experiences. Many of them expressed similar sentiments to mine, such as feeling like outsiders, like they didn't belong, and strong disconnections in their department.

When I expressed my gratitude to everyone for letting me join the group, the founder of the CC told me they "take very seriously the idea of academic kin" and I was now in kinship with everyone in the group.

The importance they placed on building an academic community helped me realize my own experience at my university was unbearable at times because I had not found a community of my own. I also realized I needed to build my own community of academic kin with scholars who would be willing to be in kinship with me. In discussing the idea of critical kinship, Daniel Heath Justice (2018) posits these questions: How do we learn to be human? How do we behave as good relatives? How do we become good ancestors? How do we learn to live together? (28). Drawing on Justice's guiding questions, I endeavored to create the community I was desperately lacking and find scholars committed to the idea of academic kinship. To do so, I would need to search beyond the borders of my PWI.

Creating a community based on academic kinship is difficult. The doctoral students in the dissertation stage in my department had found strategies that were working for them. By this point, we had been indoctrinated to believe learning is not a communal process but an individual one (Burciaga and Tavares 2006). A couple of my mentors noticed my growing disappointment with my graduate school experience. I was frank with two of my gatekeepers about my lack of motivation. I openly told them I didn't believe I could tolerate the hostile environment of academia much longer. Instead of receiving the encouragement I expected, both asked me to share my expectations of what I had believed graduate school was going to be. One of my gatekeepers even told me this was just the way the academy worked.

Fortunately, one of my mentors who was no longer at my PWI came to my rescue. She suggested we start meeting virtually for writing sessions during the summer. After a couple of these online sessions, she invited one of her doctoral students to write with us. When summer ended, my mentor's student and I continued our online meetings. Mostly, we support each other by keeping a consistent writing schedule, but just as important, we share our stories about our experiences in the academy. Through sharing *testimonio*, we recognize that the hostility we have faced as doctoral students of color is the result of the way the academy is structured (see Edwards, chap. 2). Both of us have similar stories to share about the way our diversity disrupts the normativity of the structures of our universities. Our experiences expose the systemic injustices students of color are forced to face and are required to tolerate if they are expected to adequately meet the measurements of success the academy imposes on minoritized students. In our virtual writing space, my partner and I have started to foster our own version of academic kinship.

Writing this *testimonio* is difficult because I am reminded of the painful experiences I have faced during graduate school. Reflecting on some of my professors' advice makes me angry to some degree because I feel I should have been supported by more sympathetic faculty. But I have come to understand faculty are not entirely to blame. My PWI is structured to operate in this way, and the culture of the university does not reward faculty who devise different strategies for doctoral students of color to navigate the system. In part 3 of this collection, Jasmine Kar Tang and Noro Andriamanalina argue that the lack of support PWIs offer to doctoral writers of color is a "systemic problem that cannot be resolved with individual acts of resilience." I absolutely agree. However, I also know first-hand that these individual acts of resilience keep doctoral students of color afloat during their time in the academy. Groups like the CC and invitations by my mentor to join an online writing community have been essential to my survival in graduate school. Important, these strategies all afford doctoral students space to share their truths and tell their stories. I also agree with Tang and Andriamanalina that our stories are powerful enough to change the system. Collections like this one show we have been unabashedly telling our stories. The problem is that the academy has not been listening. Now we need administrators, faculty, and other allies, advocates, and accomplices (Green 2016) to help us implement the structural changes that better reflect and support our diverse experiences.

ACKNOWLEDGMENTS

I am grateful for the opportunity to contribute to this valuable collection. Many thanks to Shannon Madden for the guidance and encouragement. A special acknowledgement goes out to the Calmecac Collective, especially Gabi Ríos and Qwo-Li Driskill, who have warmly welcomed me into their academic community. Finally, I thank my sis, Clarissa Walker, who inspires me daily to keep moving forward.

REFERENCES

Anzaldúa, Gloria. 2012. *Borderlands/La Frontera: The New Mestiza*. 4th ed. San Francisco: Aunt Lute Books.

Burciaga, Rebecca, and Ana Tavares. 2006. "Our Pedagogy of Sisterhood: A *Testimonio*." In *Chicana/Latina Education in Everyday Life: Feminista Perspectives on Pedagogy and Epistemology*, edited by Dolores Delgado Bernal, C. Alejandra Elenes, and Francisca E. Godinez, 133–142. Albany: SUNY Press.

Calmecac Collective. 2013. "The Calmecac Collective, Or, How to Survive the Academic Industrial Complex Through Radical Indigenous Practice." In *El Mundo Zurdo 3: Selected Works from the 2012 Meeting of the Society for the Study of Gloria Anzaldúa*, edited by Larissa M. Mercado-López, Sonia Saldívar-Hull, and Antonia Castañeda, 299–318. San Francisco: Aunt Lute Books.

Gee, James P. 1989. "Literacy, Discourse, and Linguistics: Introduction." *Journal of Education* 171 (1): 5–17.

Green, Neisha-Anne S. 2016. "The Re-Education of Neisha-Anne S. Green: A Close Look at the Damaging Effects of 'A Standard Approach,' the Benefits of Code-Meshing, and the Role Allies Play in this Work." *Praxis: A Writing Center Journal* 14 (1): 72–82.

Justice, Daniel Heath. 2018. *Why Indigenous Literatures Matter*. Waterloo, ON: Wilfrid Laurier University Press.

Latina Feminist Group. 2001. *Telling to Live: Latina Feminist Testimonios*. Durham, NC: Duke University Press.

PART 3

Approaches

8
"I CUT OFF MY HAND AND GAVE IT TO YOU, AND YOU GAVE IT BACK TO ME WITH THREE FINGERS"
The Disembodiment of Indigenous Writers and Writers of Color in U.S. Doctoral Programs

Jasmine Kar Tang and Noro Andriamanalina

TWO NOTICINGS

We read about a 30 percent dropout rate of doctoral students (Sowell, Zhang, and Redd 2008). We witness the consequences of being in graduate school, such as emotional exhaustion (Hunter and Devine 2016) and high emotional labor (Nutov and Hazzan 2011). Within the US nation-state, we hear about the particular challenges faced in graduate school by multilingual folks (Phillips 2013; Simpson, Caplan, Cox, and Phillips 2016), by international students (Phelps 2016; Phillips 2014), and by students of color (Linder, Harris, Allen, and Hubain 2015).[1] We learn of the "Black tax" that accompanies the experiences of African American dissertators (Burrows 2016) and about a "dehumanizing narrative" that persists through the training of Black and Latinx doctoral students who find themselves wondering, "Am I going crazy?!" (Gildersleeve, Croom, and Vasquez 2011). We also come across tales of triumph and of perseverance that accompany a person of color's journey through doctoral education (e.g., Epps-Robertson 2016).

We are often flooded with messages about practicing self-care, self-compassion. We learn about the benefits of mindfulness and of the fallacy of the mind/body split. "Let go," Brene Brown (2010) teaches through her self-help books. We hear about the need to tune into the body. As members of a university community, we might try out sleep pods at student unions or drop in for free yoga classes at the student health center. We receive emails about stress-management webinars or pet-therapy days toward the end of each semester. Student workers stand in high-traffic areas, handing out flyers on combating anxiety, and university wellness programs feature mindfulness coaching sessions over the phone.

DOI: 10.7330/9781607329589.c008

In both these cases (of studies concerning graduate students of color, of our colleges' attention to mental health), it is always the *singular* body that must be tended to, nurtured, and supported, featuring *singular* acts of caretaking, self-care, reaching out, and resilience. In this chapter, we ask, What happens when we put these two noticings in conversation with one another? In short, *What does it mean to be an Indigenous person and/or a person of color who is writing a dissertation in the U.S. nation-state?* The process of dissertating is clearly high stakes since "at the graduate level, writing is the dominant way in which knowledge is presented and assessed" (Brooks-Gillies, Garcia, Kim, Manthey, and Smith 2015). Writing does not exist in isolation, for it is deeply woven in how one experiences graduate school.

When we consider the high-pressure, high-stakes nature of the dissertation in combination with the racialized experiences of US doctoral writers of color, what forms of support are there for these student-writer communities? In order to learn from those graduate students themselves, we facilitated focus groups with over thirty doctoral writers from Indigenous communities and communities of color across a range of disciplines.[2] From that data, we took a particularly close look at writers' observations and reflections on the feedback they receive from dissertation advisors or committee members. We found that two forms of feedback doctoral students receive from their professors—one of shame and the other of praise—are a function of liberal multiculturalist ideologies that subsume or individualize racial/ethnic difference. This chapter explores how the process of writing the dissertation can become another heightened site in which racialization and racism surface in the lives of people of color. We argue that a lack of support for Indigenous doctoral writers and doctoral writers of color at PWIs in the U.S. nation-state is a systemic problem that cannot be resolved by individual acts of resilience. In the following, we frame and ground this claim in Rasha Diab's (2016) *critique against/critique for* framework, supported by the observations of research participants. In turn we take a close look at writers' reflections on the feedback they receive from those who hold institutional power over them, and we assert that this feedback maintains a form of disciplinary gatekeeping and disembodiment that are connected to US racial formation (Omi and Winant 1994).

A NOTE ON METHOD/OLOGY: CRITIQUES *AGAINST* AND *FOR* EMBODIMENT

Diab's (2016) critique against/critique for dialectic proves especially useful in how to mount a productive critique of a system: "'We cannot talk about justice in the absence of talk about injustice. Likewise, we cannot talk about freedom or peace without talking about the dynamics of domination and oppression'" (quoted in Godbee, Ozias, and Tang 2015, 73). Thus, we must identify what's wrong with the system (*critique against*), and we must also figure out what to do to make it better (*critique for*): What is the problem, and what can we do to improve ourselves and the institutions and systems we are invested in? This chapter mostly *critiques against* renderings of the body as singular, individual entities. We *critique for* embodiment as it exists in a system. As Beth Godbee, Moira Ozias, and Jasmine Kar Tang (2015) note, we might view embodiment as simultaneously existing across three spheres:

> (1) the personal sphere (how we relate within our own bodies); (2) the relational sphere (how our bodies relate with other bodies); and (3) the systemic sphere (how our bodies together represent and relate with/in institutional structures and *larger body stories*). Drawing attention to the body across these three spheres helps us counter the damage done when the intellect or institution is divorced from the body or when certain bodies are made invisible in our educational spaces. (62; emphasis added)

While more and more institutions of higher education introduce programming that centers mindfulness and the body, too often are these manifestations stuck in "the personal sphere (how we relate within our own bodies)" (62). And while one might read these self-help programs as a *structural* response, we contend that for Indigenous doctoral writers and doctoral writers of color, these programs primarily help people on an *individual* level; it is left entirely to the student—not the department or the graduate school—to cope with structural racism. In other words, we must think more about "larger body stories": where and how do these singular bodies fit inside a system? Relatedly, nestled in this critique about embodiment is a *critique against* liberal multiculturalist narratives of individual resilience. For too long has academic success relied on a bootstraps model of achievement. We already know that students of color demonstrate resilience on their academic journeys (Cleveland 2004; González 2007; Green and Scott 2003; Withorn 1986), but we need to find structural ways to *do less harm*. We call for a *critique for* structural and institutional means of supporting and valuing Indigenous writers and writers of color in doctoral programs. We call for a *critique for* larger body stories—for stories, places, and structures that center the body as it is situated in a system.

We draw from focus groups at our institution (a large Research 1 university) involving thirty-two doctoral students from Native communities and communities of color representing disciplines in the engineering and natural sciences, health sciences, humanities, and social sciences.[3] We talked to students at varying stages of their graduate programs, though most had already advanced to candidacy and were "all but dissertation" (ABD). Group interviews were recorded and transcribed, and summaries were distributed to research participants for their review (Krueger and Casey 2015). The recruitment process for our research involved using an existing listserv for graduate students of color who are US citizens or permanent residents at our university. We recruited participants based in part on matters of scope (over eight hundred students fit these categories at our institution) and on logistics (there is a university program that specifically serves this student constituency).

We as coauthors write from our own embodied histories as multilingual cisgender women of color who received our doctoral degrees (and currently are employed) at the same US Research 1 institution as our research participants. Jasmine is U.S.-born, Thai Chinese American, and Noro is a native of Madagascar. As "vulnerable observers" (Behar 1996, cited in Wenger, Martorana, Hoerman-Elliot, Godbee, Wojcik, and Musgrove 2017, 130), we believe our partnership across race, ethnicity, language, and country of birth—as well as our deep familiarity with local context—place us in a strong position to mount a critique of graduate education in our institutional setting, with hopes that administrators as well as staff and faculty members can see the applicability of this argument to their respective institutions.

In what follows, we discuss what we call *critiques against* shame and *against* praise that together mount an argument or a *critique for* the institutional and disciplinary recognition and valuing of Indigenous writers and writers of color in graduate programs. While we argue elsewhere about the need for institutional spaces and programs for graduate students of color (Tang and Andriamanalina 2016), our focus here is to think about the interconnectedness of writing, research, and US racial formation as seen in a form of racialized disciplinary gatekeeping that occurs when a writer receives feedback from someone who has power over them (e.g., an advisor).[4] In the following sections, we argue that two forms of feedback doctoral students receive from their professors—of shame and of praise—are part of the same multiculturalist monster, reflecting a racialized tension that speaks to a systemic problem at the heart of graduate education and the teaching of writing.

"CHANGE YOUR STORY": A CRITIQUE AGAINST SEVERING AND SHAME

In this section, we consider one particular manifestation of racialized disciplining that appears in feedback participants told us about: the suggestion to the writer to "change their story" or change the language they use in the writing. We read this feedback as an insistence that writers should sever their racial, ethnic, and, at times, language backgrounds from their writing. Having to "divorce my writing from my personal," as a writer expressed, implicitly conveys to the writer that their experiential knowledge (of a community they are both part of and are studying) weakens their research. For us, asking a writer to sever these personal and community ties from their writing is a shaming move. One writer of color from a positivistic field in the social sciences spoke of the "humiliation" they felt in class after sharing their writing: the writer was arguing that their field needed to address its own racism, so in the essay, the writer briefly featured a personal story. In a peer response feedback session in class, the writer's colleagues questioned the relevance of the personal narrative to the argument, casting into doubt the overall legitimacy of the essay. We recognize that the role of a researcher's positionality is a methodological tension long discussed by feminist and ethnic studies scholars (e.g., DeVault 1999; Visweswaran 1994), but we must acknowledge its racialized dimensions and the power hierarchies involved: the student came to know the critique through their own embodied experience, as illustrated through the story in the paper. Still, after being shamed in class for bringing in their experience, the writer ultimately decided to omit the story from the dissertation so their work would be seen as more legitimate and legible by their peers and by their professor.

We connect this story of public shaming to another that involved a writer in the health sciences: after choosing a research topic related to their racial and ethnic identities, the writer was told that while their work was "passionate," they needed to draw less from their lived experience in their research. At this moment in the focus group, we remember another participant from the social sciences nodding and sharing that they had heard the same thing. Both students were bothered by the patronizing and dismissive undertones of being called "passionate." Of course, these encounters are tied up in disciplinary writing expectations; some disciplines in the humanities and other interdisciplinary fields (e.g., American studies) might encourage the incorporation of personal stories, whereas more positivistic disciplines do not, raising larger questions about whether western notions of empiricism have room for nonmainstream epistemologies. Still, writers from disciplines in the humanities report that their fields do not necessarily embrace experiential knowledge, either: "I'm told that I should divorce my writing, my research, from my personal. Then, what I do is that I write really objectively and very scientifically, but that's not who I am."

Indeed, research participants from across the disciplines emphasize that a particular "intellectual violence" occurs in such moments when someone is told to divorce their writing from their personal. As an example, one of our research participants turned away from studying their own communities, fearing the work would be perceived as too personal and therefore not rigorous: "At another point of my life, I would have loved to do research on communities I'm tied to or from my own personal background, but I didn't do that." They added, "And white students actually have that privilege of not having to choose a particular racial group or whatever to research." This student, who is from the social sciences, felt that racial privilege can be associated with one's choice of research topic. They strategically chose a research site unrelated to their own family histories.

This intellectual violence may extend into an "erasure" of identity and embodied history, speaking to Dolores Delgado Bernal's (2002) research on how the knowledge production of students of color draws from "critical raced-gendered epistemologies"; for example, for some Chicanas, this might include using "pedagogies of the home" to navigate US academic and disciplinary discourses and practices (Delgado Bernal 2001). When these epistemologies are denied, a tension or an erasure emerges, as one writer's reflections illuminate for us:

> I feel like there's a lot of tension between writing and identity.... When I tie research back to writing, it's an erasure of your identity. It's under this argument that "it's because research can't be biased. So you need to separate yourself from your research and your writing. It's not that we want to erase your identity." But through this process of disciplining yourself through writing, you become whitewashed. And it's a very contentious relationship that I'm trying to work out.

For this student (a social scientist), the act of being disciplined as a writer is not only racialized but also assimilative. While this student feels that an "erasure of your identity" is an outcome of graduate training, they continue to explore this uneasy relationship as a way to manage their education and professional development. Relatedly, in a health sciences discipline, a writer shared the following:

> I honestly believe that a white student (whether male or female) would not be told to "change your story," to "change your lived experience and how you would tell it because you would make other people feel

uncomfortable." And I've been told that three times in three months. So that's really hard for me because I can't change who I am.

It is hard to miss the blame-the-victim mentality in what the writer was told ("you would make other people feel uncomfortable"), and for this to be said repeatedly speaks to a larger systemic issue. In response to such feedback, we also heard participants insist that "our lenses have worth," which was a recurring idea across multiple focus groups. As another health sciences student said, "It's just that I have a very different lens, and sometimes I feel like it's almost like 'change your lens.'" The "change your story" or "change your lens" feedback our research participants receive is a classic move of disciplining the student writer to assimilate to a traditional mode of academic/disciplinary writing, an arguable refusal to embrace critical raced-gendered epistemologies.

This directive to sever and shame nonmainstream epistemologies also surfaces in feedback concerning language and word choice, reflecting a deficit view of multilingualism that recenters monolingualism as normative. We have found that students who engage with multilingual Indigenous communities and/or communities of color in their research may experience the editing (at best) or censorship (at worst) of language, in which they are disciplined for bringing the languages of their research participants and communities into the writing. Doctoral writers of color report that at times they feel pressured to make revisions (e.g., deletions) that are connected to their linguistic identities in ways also tied to their racial and ethnic group memberships. For example, observing professors' need to control students' writing, one writer from a positivistic discipline fought to capitalize a non-standardized-English word in order to maintain the trust of the Native community they were researching (and with which they had a personal connection):

> I had to fight for that because . . . this is where I am, so it's the local, the geographical context. It's a cultural context . . . I asked a lot of trust on behalf of people, the tribes around here, for their advice. So, [using a Native word in the writing] was a way of honoring that . . . [of] retaining *our* cultural voice. And I think that's something that's really hard.

For this writer, language use was connected to research ethics and integrity. In another instance, a science student felt conflicted by coming from and then researching a community underrepresented in academia. They did not want to "pass up that opportunity" to voice community concerns, and they wanted to use language and terminology more representative of the community being studied. However, told to only use English words in the writing, the student wondered aloud to us, "But how much do you give?

And how much do you suppress? Are you selling yourself short or your community short when you are doing that?" For this writer, producing English-only writing would amount to an incomplete analysis and would also not adequately represent or speak to the community being studied.

Thus, when writers in our focus groups discussed using languages other than English in their research, they connected this writerly move to the importance of respecting the communities they serve and research. In short, feedback from faculty can be quite consequential. Many of our study participants who conduct community-engaged research talked about having a strong sense of responsibility in academic and community settings given the fact that universities historically have a fraught relationship with local communities, especially those that are historically marginalized (Smith 2012). The feedback writers receive can reinforce the university/community dichotomy, in which disciplinary "ivory tower" gatekeeping occurs at the expense of historically underrepresented communities. Writers report that they struggle with how to position themselves within their respective communities, aware they are seen as representing the university and needing to gain the trust of research participants (and community members) in order to be an effective researcher. Simultaneously, students may see themselves as needing to represent their communities to the university, too, as they advocate for their communities within the need to maintain existing relationships in both settings. In this way, we point to our *critique against* shaming and severing: by discouraging students from featuring a community's epistemological and linguistic assets, faculty risk creating further schisms in an already fragile relationship. In such cases, it is the student who bears the burden and has the most to lose. Experiencing fear of being rejected by the community or the university (or both), those who are not able to reconcile this university/community dichotomy can have a hard time making progress with their writing. Thus, the feedback they receive around language use and around the incorporation of personal stories can be a highly racialized form of disciplining, mixed in with questions of ethics and respect for the historically marginalized communities they may be studying.

"THIS IS YOUR AUTHENTIC VOICE": A CRITIQUE AGAINST PRAISE

If the critique is that faculty are demanding the separation of a person's racial/ethnic identities from their research, then we might conclude that faculty should make more of an effort to encourage writers to incorporate their embodied histories. In this section, we want to complicate such acts of encouragement and praise, however, and connect them to race and racialization. Thus, while our discussion thus far has looked at feedback that may, for some, be obvious forms of disciplining (i.e., "change your story"), we now turn our attention to the limitations and problematics of the inclusion of voices, revealing a framework of *letting in*, not quite one of equitable practice.

Selecting a topic for dissertation research is a source of anxiety for many students (Fitzpatrick, Secrist, and Wright 1998; Lei 2009), and for some doctoral writers of color, even the seemingly positive feedback they receive from white faculty members about their research choices can be highly racialized; perceptions of what students "should" research are tied to their racial interpellation. For example, we came across students who feel pressured to research and write about their own racial and/or ethnic communities. We think here of a research participant who noted how "a kind of fetishism" or "exoticism" of people of color occurs in which such people are "pushed" to write about their racial or ethnic identities: the writer asked, "If that's not the work I'm taking up, why does someone want to force that on me?" Some immigrant writers further shared with us how they are encouraged to study their country of birth because of their presumed familiarity with its history. While this particular observation seems to mainly involve country of birth, we are struck by the fact that this issue emerged in response to a question about racial and ethnic identity, demonstrating to us what the participant perceived as the intersection of race and nationhood. In sum, although these examples recognize a student's experiential knowledge, they can also simultaneously send the message that the student could not be an expert on other nation-states or research areas not directly associated with their particular social locations or embodied histories.

Relatedly, a particular form of fetishism can take place in which faculty arguably overcompensate for the whiteness of the discipline (or of themselves) by generically praising writing that is not only personal but also invokes the writer's identity as an Indigenous person and/or person of color. A student from a social science discipline observed:

> I've gotten a lot of support in terms of thinking about writing about race and being a biracial person and all of those sorts of experiences that are tied in with that. But almost like so much support it kind of weirds me out sometimes. . . . People are kind of saying, "This is what about you has value. . . . This is your authentic voice, and you ought to be writing like this and doing work on this," and things along those lines.

While faculty may mean well, these acts of arguably excessive praise can make students feel as though the only way they can make a substantial contribution to their respective disciplines is to write about their experiences as racialized subjects. Here, praise becomes less an act of affirmation than an act of Othering, perhaps attesting to the speaker's/faculty's discomfort or fascination with the writer's lived experience. While one might say praise is always a characteristic of disciplinary gatekeeping, we want to take this further and consider how praise can invoke "helping" narratives that infantilize Indigenous graduate students and graduate students of color. That is, the speaker (a faculty member) assumes and maintains power, enacting white savior narratives historically tied up in US racial formation. We might also consider the possibility that the white faculty member's overcompensation (and subsequent excessive praise) is in anticipation of their own white fragility, "a state in which even a minimum amount of racial stress becomes intolerable, triggering a range of defensive moves" (DiAngelo 2011, 57). Marilyn Frye's (1992) work on whiteliness can also help us unpack this exchange. Reflecting on her social locations as a white person, she notes:

> I learned that I, and "we [as white people]," knew right from wrong and had the responsibility to see to it right was done; that there were others who did not know what is right and wrong and should be advised, instructed, helped and directed by us [as white people]. I was taught that *because* one knows what is right, it is morally appropriate to have and exercise what I now would call race privilege and class privilege. (153)

In the research participant's experience above, the faculty advises, instructs, helps, and directs the student on their writing, exercising control through a do-good mindset ("You ought to be writing like this"). Praise can also be a whitely move, one that asserts, "We know best, and we know what is best for others" (Levin and Tang 2013). In the context of our study, praise can become an exercise of racial privilege on the part of the white advisor/faculty member.

Further, feedback in the form of praise can function as an act of Derridean hospitality (2000) and of fetishism: a superficial valuing and conditional welcoming of the person of color and their singular voice—their singular body. Thus, we want to trouble words of praise and encouragement and suggest they can be forms of racialized fetishism, expressions of Othering. While praise may come from good intentions, the feedback "this is your authentic voice" is a liberal multiculturalist response to our research participant, a writer of color. That is, the incorporation of the person of color's "authentic voice" becomes a liberal project in which the white authority figure still maintains control, letting in the racialized subject through this act of hospitality. The lived experiences of the writer of color appear to be valued, though they are contained to a singular voice. This is a racialized power move: when praise becomes fetishistic, it involves a fascination with bodies of color on the grounds of inclusion in which the host maintains control of the space over the guest. In the feedback "*This* is your authentic voice," the speaker is the faculty member; that is, the student is not claiming racial or ethnic authenticity. The professor infers it. The advisor/faculty member maintains control of the discipline and control of the student.

It is too easy to read praise as a singular, well-intentioned act. We emphasize that acts of shaming *and* praising are in relationship with one another as forms of feedback that are twinned manifestations of liberal multiculturalist ideologies. In short, when we view praise and shame together, we might more clearly see the limitations of praise.

"IT HAS MADE ME A BETTER RESEARCHER": SIDESTEPPING THE RESILIENCE TRAP

While the previous sections concern the racialized disciplinary gatekeeping of writing, what do we do with this information? How do we as teachers and administrators respond when we realize what we are doing could be causing anxiety and distress in students? In this section, we focus on how resilience on the part of graduate writers is both a way for students of color to survive *and* a way for institutions to absolve themselves of responsibility. Let's begin with the comments of a research participant:

> I experience a lot of hostility and racism in the classroom . . . [a]nd from that experience, I learned a lot in how *not* to be. And making sure that when I'm conducting my research with members of a marginalized population . . . that I don't replicate the same type of abuses that I've endured here [at the university]. And it has actually made me a stronger writer. . . . Instead of just inserting yourself in a community and extracting knowledge, another way of doing things is, knowing a community for a certain amount of years, asking what you can do for the community and continue to work with the community while they're providing you with information and even after. . . . My experiences as a person of color being here and having endured a lot of violence have made me a more aware person, and I think it has made me a better researcher.

While we are struck by the writer's word choices ("hostility," "racism," "abuses," and "violence") to describe their experiences, it is hard to not also notice their resilience and sense of resolve. Well documented by scholars of doctoral education (e.g., González 2007), resilience is critical, as Indigenous students and students of color continue to enact resourceful ways to maintain voice and agency in their writing: as a writer from the humanities reflected, "I recognize that the university has a long history that is problematic. And I also know that I chose to participate in it. . . . I know that I have to be strategic in how I write in order to get a PhD, to get tenure, to get a job. And then really say what I want to say." This reflection is clearly a testament to our research participant's resilience. As researchers, we are tempted to fall into this multiculturalist trap in which we again resort to the singular body, one of boot-strappy self-care in which the individual digs their way out on their own. To be clear, we are not dismissing the power of individual resilience, nor do we wish to characterize Indigenous people and people of color as having no agency. We suggest a both/and approach, though: active self-care, self-advocacy, and attention to the singular body are important, as is active care enacted by the *institution.*

We are concerned. Based on the reflections of the writers who participated in our study, we are concerned about how such devaluing feedback and hostile learning environments can sediment in the body: Over time, what are the effects of such comments and experiences on writers—especially doctoral writers of color who find themselves managing institutional, racialized power hierarchies in the midst of high-stakes writing and research projects? And in the case of the writer above who talked about waiting until tenure to "really say what I want to say," what are the costs of this delayed gratification for scholars of color? Our research confirms what we see every day at our institution: as they challenge existing frameworks with their projects and ways of knowing, Indigenous students and students of color bring tremendous value to higher education, and while it is clear these doctoral writers are resilient and resourceful, institutions must do a better job supporting their writing since the thesis is seen as evidence of one's success. Thus, we cannot leave success in the hands of individual articulations of resilience.

CONCLUSION: MORE LARGER BODY STORIES

Finally, we also think of the advice writers receive when they get feedback or when their work gets rejected for publication: "Don't take it personally," they are told. While emerging scholars are often coached in this way, we wonder, How could it *not* get personal, especially for doctoral writers of color who may develop their dissertation topics from their own embodied histories? In the hope of centering "larger body stories"—of situating the body in the system (Godbee, Ozias, and Tang

2015, 62), we might be more open to writers of color who want to bring their whole, embodied selves to their work. As one writer in the humanities said, "It also seems like a lot of senior faculty at some point forgot how challenging it is. Because they just hand it [a draft] back to you, right?" The writer then made a comment that continues to linger with us as researchers: "You know, I cut off my hand and gave it to you, and you gave it back to me with three fingers." We wonder, What would happen if the embodied dimensions of doctoral writing were more explicitly recognized, named, and acted upon in both personal relationships (e.g., advisor and advisee) *and* programmatic ways (e.g., in graduate programs and in faculty professional development)?

Our work is incomplete. We have identified several *critiques against*. We need more *critiques for*. As Diab (2016) explains, "The need for both modes of critique emanates from their different affordances: the critique against is mainly deconstructive, whereas the critique for is revisionary and reconstructive" (12). We need to know what more can be done: we must identify existing models of what works and what is sustainable—and we must dream up new models. For example, if we acknowledge the limitations of traditional models of mentoring (which are hierarchical, can potentially rely on old-boy networks, and can facilitate unproductive and unhealthy host/guest dynamics, therefore facilitating the problematics of praise), could we learn from research on co-mentoring? (Godbee and Novotny 2013). In his discussion of the Black tax, Cedric Burrows (2016) also calls for co-mentoring groups among peers, but what are the possibilities of co-mentoring between a dissertator and their advisor? In other words, what could a co-mentoring model of advising look like? And taking a wider view, What would be larger, broader, and *sustainable* ways to structure support on a departmental level while acknowledging that faculty of color are often the ones responsibilized to take up this work? (Gutierrez y Muhs, Niemann, Gonzáles, and Harris 2012). As James Porter, Patricia Sullivan, Stuart Blythe, Jeffrey T. Grabill, and Libby Miles (2000) note, "'Though institutions are certainly powerful, they are not monoliths; they are rhetorically constructed human designs (whose power is reinforced by buildings, laws, traditions, and knowledge-making practices) and so are changeable. In other words, we made 'em, we can fix 'em. Institutions R Us'" (quoted in Diab, Ferrel, Godbee, and Simpkins 2013, 13). As administrators and scholars, where are the places we can improve? Much remains to be explored, and we hope our colleagues will tune in to the radical pedagogies and potential of larger body stories as ways to build structural support *without flattening and universalizing the experiences and embodied histories of Indigenous writers and doctoral writers of color.* It is time we see how the act of disciplinary gatekeeping is racialized in systemic ways.

ACKNOWLEDGMENTS

We would like to thank the University of Minnesota–Twin Cities Graduate School Diversity Office, the Interdisciplinary Studies of Writing program of the Center for Writing, and the Office for Equity and Diversity for funding this research. We also thank Dan Emery, Darren Tse Lee, Katie Levin, and Patricia Jones Whyte for their invaluable feedback and support; Charlotte Karem Albrecht, Juliana Hu Pegues, and Tom Sarmiento for helping us think through the politics and ethics of terminology; and the reviewers and editors for their feedback and for this opportunity to share our work. Finally, we especially want to acknowledge the individuals who participated in this study. Inspired by their commitment to broadening access to and participation in the academy, we are indebted to each of them.

NOTES

1. By *person of color*, we are referring to individuals who identify as members of African American, Black, American Indian, Asian American, Pacific Islander, and/or Latinx communities. (We employ the term Latinx—as Macarena Gómez-Barris and Licia Fiol-Matta [2014], Lilia Monzó [2016], and others have done—so all genders are included.) Also, it is important to note the absence of people of Middle Eastern and North African descent—including Arab Americans and Iranian Americans—in our formulation of the term *people of color* and in our pool of research participants. This glaring omission is one result of institutional limitations: our university (and the listserv from which we recruited participants) does not have a category that allows for the inclusion of people of Middle Eastern and North African descent as people of color, unless they also identify as and "check" one or more of the following on their university paperwork: American Indian, Asian/Pacific Islander, Black, or Hispanic.
2. It is important to note that since our argument is concerned with the racialization of self-identifying members of the communities discussed in the first endnote, we use the term *people of color* to include Indigenous peoples. However, we recognize how this usage is fraught and contested within Native communities and in American Indian studies (e.g., Reese 2011; Wilkins and Stark 2011). In the move to include Indigenous communities under the umbrella term *people of color*, we risk subsuming them and denying the importance of tribal sovereignty as an underlying distinction Indigenous peoples have from those who are not Indigenous. Still, as researchers, we wish to acknowledge both the racialization *and* sovereignty of Indigenous communities. Further, despite having to repeatedly use long phrases such as *Indigenous doctoral writers* and *doctoral writers of color* to more completely describe the communities we are studying, we are decidedly not employing any acronyms (e.g., *IPOC* for *Indigenous [people] and people of color*) that can have the effect of being

dismissive or performative, failing to represent a fuller, systemic acknowledgment of Indigenous peoples "as citizens of sovereign nations" (Reese 2011). And still, we are aware this essay falls short of such a systemic acknowledgment, as our study does not, for example, place questions of tribal sovereignty in conversation with the teaching of writing or with graduate education. As a result, we go in and out of explicitly coupling *Indigenous people* with *people of color* and its variations (e.g., at times, we may use the umbrella term *doctoral writers of color* only, and at other times, we use *doctoral writers of color* and *Indigenous doctoral writers* to describe research participants). Finally, as this piece goes to print, we are also thinking deeply about the increasing use of the terms "Black, Indigenous, People of Color [BIPOC]" and "Indigenous, Black, People of Color [IBPOC]." Our discussion about terminology remains incomplete and unresolved. Both troubled and humbled by this lack of resolution, we wrestle with discomfort and tension regarding the implications of our decisions as writers amidst our commitment to racial justice and to dismantling the logics of white supremacy and settler colonialism.

3. The IRB number is 1410E54662. Also, while we interviewed individuals from numerous disciplines, we limit our disciplinary descriptions of research participants to more general categories (e.g., humanities or social sciences). Though we lose disciplinary specificity in such a move, we do so to further protect our research participants' identities.

4. In this chapter, we follow Mari Matsuda's (1991) lead, using the gender-neutral, singular *they/them/their* when discussing and/or quoting individual research participants. Furthermore, at the risk of enacting cisnormative writing practices and appropriating the word choice used by individuals who actually identify as *they*, we also use *they* to protect research participants' identities (regardless of what, if any, pronouns they use).

REFERENCES

Behar, Ruth. 1996. *The Vulnerable Observer: Anthropology That Breaks Your Heart.* Boston: Beacon Press.

Brooks-Gillies, Marilee, Elena G. Garcia, Soo Hyon Kim, Katie Manthey, and Trixie Smith. 2015. "Graduate Writing Across the Disciplines, Introduction." In "Graduate Writing Across the Disciplines," edited by Marilee Brooks-Gillies, Elena G. Garcia, Soo Hyon Kim, Katie Manthey, and Trixie Smith. Special issue, *Across the Disciplines* 12. http://wac.colostate.edu/atd/graduate_wac/intro.cfm.

Brown, Brene. 2010. *The Gifts of Imperfection: Let Go of Who You Think You're Supposed to Be and Embrace Who You Are.* Center City, MN: Hazelden.

Burrows, Cedric D. 2016. "Writing While Black: The Black Tax on African American Graduate Writers." *Praxis: A Writing Center Journal* 14 (1): 15–20. http://www.praxisuwc.com/burrows-141/.

Cleveland, Darrell, ed. 2004. *A Long Way to Go: Conversations about Race by African American Faculty and Graduate Students.* New York: Peter Lang.

Delgado Bernal, Dolores. 2001. "Learning and Living Pedagogies of the Home: The Mestiza Consciousness of Chicana Students." *International Journal of Qualitative Studies in Education* 14 (1): 623–639.

Delgado Bernal, Dolores. 2002. "Critical Race Theory, Latino Critical Theory, and Critical Raced-Gendered Epistemologies: Recognizing Students of Color as Holders and Creators of Knowledge." *Qualitative Inquiry* 8 (1): 105–126.

Derrida, Jacques. 2000. "Hospitality." *Angelaki: Journal of Theoretical Humanities* 5 (3): 3–18.

DeVault, Marjorie L. 1999. *Liberating Method: Feminism and Social Research.* Philadelphia: Temple University Press.

Diab, Rasha. 2016. *Shades of Sulh: The Rhetorics of Arab-Islamic Reconciliation.* Pittsburgh: University of Pittsburgh Press.

Diab, Rasha, Thomas Ferrel, Beth Godbee, and Neil Simpkins. 2013. "Making Commitments to Racial Justice Actionable." *Across the Disciplines* 10 (3): 1–16. https://wac.colostate.edu/docs/atd/race/diabetal.pdf.

DiAngelo, Robin. 2011. "White Fragility." *International Journal of Critical Pedagogy* 3 (3): 54–70.

Epps-Robertson, Candace. 2016. "Writing with Your Family at the Kitchen Table: Balancing Home and Academic Communities." *Praxis: A Writing Center Journal* 14 (1): 44–49. http://www.praxisuwc.com/eppsrobertson-141.

Fitzpatrick, Jacqueline, Jan Secrist, and Debra J. Wright. 1998. *Secrets for a Successful Dissertation.* Thousand Oaks, CA: SAGE.

Frye, Marilyn. 1992. *Willful Virgin: Essays in Feminism, 1976–1992.* Freedom, CA: Crossing.

Gildersleeve, Ryan Evely, Natasha N. Croom, and Philip L. Vasquez. 2011. "'Am I Going Crazy?!': A Critical Race Analysis of Doctoral Education." *Equity & Excellence in Education* 44 (1): 93–114.

Godbee, Beth, and Julia C. Novotny. 2013. "Asserting the Right to Belong: Feminist Co-Mentoring among Graduate Student Women." *Feminist Teacher* 23 (2): 177–195.

Godbee, Beth, Moira Ozias, and Jasmine Kar Tang. 2015. "Body + Power + Justice: Movement-Based Workshops for Critical Tutor Education." *Writing Center Journal* 34 (2): 61–112.

Gómez-Barris, Macarena, and Licia Fiol-Matta. 2014. "Introduction: Las Américas Quarterly." *American Quarterly* 66 (3): 493–504.

González, Juan Carlos. 2007. "Surviving the Doctorate and Thriving as Faculty: Latina Junior Faculty Reflecting on their Doctoral Studies Experiences." *Equity & Excellence in Education* 40 (4): 291–300.

Green, Anna L., and LeKita V. Scott, eds. 2003. *Journey to the PhD: How to Navigate the Process as African Americans.* Sterling, VA: Stylus.

Gutiérrez y Muhs, Gabriella, Yolanda Flores Niemann, Carmen G. Gonzáles, and Angela P. Harris, eds. 2012. *Presumed Incompetent: The Intersections of Race and Class for Women in Academia.* Logan: Utah State University Press.

Hunter, Karen H., and Kay Devine. 2016. "Doctoral Students' Emotional Exhaustion and Intentions to Leave Academia." *International Journal of Doctoral Studies* 11: 35–61.

Krueger, Richard A., and Mary Anne Casey. 2015. *Focus Groups: A Practical Guide for Applied Research.* 5th ed. Thousand Oaks, CA: SAGE.

Lei, Simon A. 2009. "Strategies for Finding and Selecting an Ideal Thesis or Dissertation Topic: A Review of Literature." *College Student Journal* 43 (4): 1324–1332.

Levin, Katie, and Jasmine Kar Tang. 2013. "(Anti)Racism, 'Community,' and the Problem of Praise in Staff Development: A Roundtable Discussion." Presentation at the International Writing Centers Association Collaborative @ CCCC, University of Nevada, Las Vegas, NV, March 13.

Linder, Chris, Jessica C. Harris, Evette L. Allen, and Bryan Hubain. 2015. "Building Inclusive Pedagogy: Recommendations from a National Study of Students of Color in Higher Education and Student Affairs Graduate Programs." *Equity & Excellence in Education* 48 (2): 178–194.

Matsuda, Mari. 1991. "Voices of America: Accent, Antidiscrimination Law, and a Jurisprudence for the Last Reconstruction." *Yale Law Journal* 100 (5): 1329–1407.

Monzó, Lilia D. 2016. "'They Don't Know Anything!': Latinx Immigrant Students Appropriating the Oppressor's Voice." *Anthropology & Education Quarterly* 47 (2): 148–166.

Nutov, Liora, and Orit Hazzan. 2011. "Feeling the Doctorate: Is Doctoral Research that Studies the Emotional Labor of Doctoral Students Possible?" *International Journal of Doctoral Studies* 6: 19–32.

Omi, Michael, and Howard Winant. 1994. *Racial Formation in the United States: From the 1960s to the 1990s*. 2nd ed. New York: Routledge.

Phelps, Jennifer M. 2016. "International Doctoral Students' Navigations of Identity and Belonging in a Globalizing University." *International Journal of Doctoral Studies* 11: 1–14.

Phillips, Talinn. 2013. "Tutor Training and Services for Multilingual Graduate Writers: A Reconsideration." *Praxis: A Writing Center Journal*, 10 (2). http://www.praxisuwc.com/phillips-102.

Phillips, Talinn. 2014. "Developing Resources for Success: A Case Study of a Multilingual Graduate Writer." In *WAC and Second-Language Writers: Research towards Linguistically and Culturally Inclusive Programs and Practices*, edited by Terry Myers Zawacki and Michelle Cox, 69–91. Fort Collins, CO: WAC Clearinghouse and Parlor. http://wac.colostate.edu/books/l2/wac.pdf.

Porter, James E., Patricia Sullivan, Stuart Blythe, Jeffrey T. Grabill, and Libby Miles. 2000. "Institutional Critique: A Rhetorical Methodology for Change." *College Composition and Communication* 51 (4): 610–642.

Reese, Debbie. 2011. "American Indians Are Not 'People of Color.'" *ASCD Express*, 6 (15). http://www.ascd.org/ascd-express/vol6/615-newvoices.aspx.

Simpson, Steve, Nigel A. Caplan, Michelle Cox, and Talinn Phillips, eds. 2016. *Supporting Graduate Students Writers: Research, Curriculum, and Program Design*. Ann Arbor: University of Michigan Press.

Smith, Linda Tuhiwai. 2012. *Decolonizing Methodologies: Research and Indigenous Peoples*. 2nd ed., London: Zed Books.

Sowell, Robert, Ting Zhang, and Kenneth Redd. 2008. *PhD Completion and Attrition: Analysis of Baseline Program Data from the PhD Completion Project*. Washington, DC: Council of Graduate Schools.

Tang, Jasmine Kar, and Noro Andriamanalina. 2016. "'Rhonda Left Early to Go to Black Lives Matter': Programmatic Support for Graduate Writers of Color." *Writing Program Administration* 39 (2): 10–15.

Visweswaran, Kamala. 1994. *Fictions of Feminist Ethnography*. Minneapolis: University of Minnesota Press.

Wenger, Christy, Christina Martorana, Jacquelyn E. Hoerman-Elliot, Beth Godbee, Adrianne Wojcik, and Laurence Musgrove. 2017. "Connecting." *Journal of the Assembly for Expanded Perspectives on Learning* 22. http://trace.tennessee.edu/jaepl/vol22/iss1/14.

Wilkins, David E., and Heidi Kiiwetinepinesiik Stark. 2011. *American Indian Politics and the American Political System*. 3rd ed. Lanham, MD: Rowman & Littlefield.

Withorn, Ann. 1986. "Dual Citizenship: [An Interview with] Women of Color in Graduate School." *Women's Studies Quarterly* 25 (1): 132–138.

9
RESEARCH WRITING AS AN ADAPTIVE CHALLENGE
A Study with Implications for Supervisory Feedback Practices

Daniel V. Bommarito

INTRODUCTION

A text produced by a doctoral writer, particularly a text intended for publication, plays host to a complex drama. A key figure in this drama is of course the writer, whose development is often described in terms of an evolving disciplinary identity. Along this development arc, doctoral writers shift from being knowledge consumers to producers (Lovitts 2008) as they learn to use a field's specialized discourse (Casanave 2002) and position their voices among the voices of other scholars (Paré, Starke-Meyerring, and McAlpine 2011). This process is complicated by the fact that it is layered over other forms of professional and personal life. Doctoral writers navigate conflicts that can arise from competing demands of institutional policies, dissertation committee members, employment, and the job market (Lundell and Beach 2003), as well as their social and family life (Casanave 2016). Such conflicts can be especially pronounced for second-language writers, who are likely to encounter linguistic and cultural barriers that can impede full participation in the intellectual life of a target disciplinary community (Morita 2004; Seloni 2012). As Christine Casanave (2002) puts it, learning to write at the doctoral level invokes "the messy and unsettling nature of the very serious, identity-transforming academic literacy games in the enculturation process" (141).

Many writing problems that arise during this messy and unsettling development process can usefully be classified as "adaptive" challenges (Flower 2016, 308). According to Linda Flower, adaptive challenges are problems too complex for a community's existing knowledge to provide a viable solution. In such cases, because a community's available knowledge is inadequate, solutions must come from individuals who undergo a substantive change in understanding, beliefs, values, or behaviors. Flower contrasts adaptive challenges with "technical" problems, which

DOI: 10.7330/9781607329589.c009

are the kinds of problems a community encounters regularly and thus has developed a conventional, routinized response for (308). Solutions to technical problems involve coordinating existing know-how in order to find the right course of action. While technical problems call for external fixes, adaptive challenges call for internal reorientations.

A shortcoming of doctoral-level writing support is that adaptive challenges—the kinds of problems that call for substantive transformations—are treated as if they were technical problems requiring a conventional fix. This type of category mistake is addressed, albeit in different terms, in critiques of pedagogies that reduce writing to a universal, mechanical skill. For instance, Barbara Kamler and Pat Thomson (2006) argue that advice commonly offered to doctoral writers tends to "reduce writing to a set of arbitrary rules and matters of etiquette" and to assume "that the problems and their solutions are fairly straightforward, easy to identify and resolve" (7). The failure of such advice is that it overlooks the adaptive work writers must undertake as they become contributors to the disciplinary dialogue. Similarly, Mary Jane Curry (2016) critiques what she calls a "skills approach" to teaching writing because it assumes academic literacy is "an individual writer's ability to control discrete elements of language, specifically, the grammatical/mechanical/rhetorical conventions of standard English (whether American, British, Australian, etc.)" (82). As these critiques suggest, mischaracterizing adaptive challenges as technical problems can have the adverse effect of oversimplifying the written text, the writing process, and the ways writing operates in the world.

The primary purpose of this chapter is to examine doctoral research writing as an adaptive challenge. By looking closely at feedback sessions of a faculty mentor collaborating with two doctoral writers, this study provides a clearer understanding of how commentary on a piece of writing is linked to the challenges writers face *in situ*, challenges that run far deeper than the surface level of a written text. A second purpose of this chapter is to consider the usefulness of distinguishing between adaptive challenges and technical problems when it comes to providing commentary on writing. After analyzing the ways adaptive challenges emerge in the context of writing, this chapter concludes with a discussion of implications for dissertation advisors providing supervisory feedback on writing.

THE STUDY

The present study examines feedback sessions of a faculty mentor and two doctoral students as they collaboratively draft a research article.

This study emerges out of a larger study investigating collaborative research as a form of doctoral mentoring (Bommarito 2016). In the larger study, an experienced mentor collaborated with five novice doctoral researchers on a research project based in their local writing program. The collaborative project was unique because it doubled as a mentoring opportunity for students and an authentic study that leveraged the students' unique linguistic knowledge. Specifically, a key design feature of the collaborative project was the doctoral students' knowledge of Mandarin Chinese, which was used to interview Chinese-speaking undergraduate students enrolled in US college writing classes. Through cross-language interviews, the collaborative team hoped to learn about the experiences of Chinese-speaking students new to writing education in the United States. Toward that end, the team developed data-collection instruments, collected and analyzed data, and began (although never finished) drafting a research report based on their findings. During the drafting process, the team met monthly to discuss overall progress and to review the written draft, while the mentor provided feedback.

The study reported here focuses on two of the monthly meetings in which the faculty mentor provided commentary on a draft of the results section of the research report. The feedback sessions took place in January and February of 2014. The participants I include in this study are the faculty mentor, Professor Maddox (pseudonym), and two third-year doctoral students, Daisy and Chloe (pseudonyms), who were responsible for drafting the results section of the research report. Professor Maddox was a full professor of English, specializing in rhetoric and composition and in applied linguistics. Daisy and Chloe were both working toward a PhD in rhetoric and composition, with interests in second-language writing. As a participant-observer, I took field notes during the two feedback sessions and audio recorded the interactions, which were later transcribed. I collected written drafts, which were the focus of discussion during the two team meetings. Additionally, to learn more about the students' perspectives, I conducted interviews with Daisy and Chloe during their drafting process.

To identify adaptive challenges, I analyzed the feedback sessions in concert with interviews with the doctoral students. As a target construct of inquiry, adaptive challenges were defined using two criteria. First, an adaptive challenge had to be a writing-related issue commented on by Maddox during the feedback sessions. Second, the challenge had to be discussed, directly or indirectly, by the doctoral student writers during my interviews with them. Thus, the adaptive challenges identified in this study were a co-construction of the faculty mentor's commentary and the doctoral students' negotiation of that commentary.

To analyze the data from feedback sessions, I first divided each transcript by topic. I then focused attention specifically on the faculty mentor's commentary, which was broken up into individual comments and coded according to the writing issue discussed. In the initial analysis, the comments fell into three broad categories: grammar and mechanics, usage and style, and social-rhetorical practices. Occasionally, a comment was embedded within another comment, in which case I coded each separately, as two distinct comments. Next, I used these data to guide my reading of interview data with the doctoral students, which followed an emergent inductive approach. After multiple passes through the interview transcripts, I identified themes that correlated with the faculty mentor's commentary. Because neither of the doctoral students commented on any issues in the "grammar and mechanics" and "usage and style" categories, I focused attention exclusively on the "social-rhetorical practices" category. In the results section below, I highlight instances in which the faculty mentor's comments corresponded in some way with the doctoral students' descriptions of their experiences while drafting.

FINDINGS

After analyzing the faculty mentor's commentary alongside doctoral student interviews, I identified four adaptive challenges: inventing and advancing claims, aligning claims with data, translating and integrating cross-language data, and providing appropriate contextual information. In the case of each challenge, the faculty mentor raised concerns based on his reading of the written text, which were then negotiated by the doctoral students in various ways during the drafting process. Below, I describe each adaptive challenge by alternating between the perspectives of the faculty mentor and the doctoral students.

Adaptive Challenge 1: Inventing and Advancing Claims

Faculty Advisor's Commentary
A major focus of the mentor's feedback was the practice of inventing and advancing claims. Often, Maddox's commentary pointed out that no claims were discernible in a particular section of the draft. The issue became so pronounced during the two feedback sessions that Maddox went so far as to describe the nature of a claim and offer strategies for developing one.

Most commonly, Maddox commented when he did not find a claim where he expected. In such cases, Maddox voiced his concern in ways such as the following:

> MADDOX: So what's the focus of this section? What are you trying to establish? What's the argument? . . . Tell me about this whole section. What's the main point?
>
> MADDOX: So before you start mentioning the numbers, say what you're going to say. And the reason for delaying the number is because before I know the exact numbers, which is a supporting detail, I want to know what the claim is. So state the claim first.
>
> MADDOX: You start with the summary: "This is what I'm going to say, here's a claim, the big claim." Then you break it down into each building block. You need to at least say what this section is about. You can't just expect readers to follow your argument along.

At other times, claims in the text seemed to be implied rather than stated explicitly, and Maddox alerted the writers to this oversight. For example, Maddox often commented when he felt the writers did not sufficiently distinguish between elaborations of a claim and new claims altogether.

> MADDOX: Now that's a different reason . . . but, as it's written—"another student said that"—you know, that sounds like you are adding another example of how not being able to get into a top-tier is an issue. But that's not what you're doing here. So start a new paragraph, and then state the generalization: "This is what seems to be happening."
>
> MADDOX: In the first paragraph . . . *gaokao* [a standardized test administered in China] is mentioned as a factor, but there is no mention of what about it. . . . So you need to foreground the claim and what it is that you're saying about the nature of *gaokao*. That becomes really important.

After recognizing the writers were having trouble rendering claims, Maddox stopped simply noting where claims should be placed and provided practical instruction. In one instance, Maddox suggested the writers set aside the data altogether and focus more on stating the claims and showing their relationships. Here, Maddox draws on a more colloquial metaphor of "telling the story" to get his point across:

> I think at this point you should start focusing on telling the story, the narrative of what seems to be going on, and then not be driven so much by the data set. You can even set the data aside, and then start writing, "this is what's happening," and tell the story. And then, after you tell the story, you break it into each claim or each generalization is a paragraph, and then you start plugging in examples to support it.

Repeated attempts by the mentor to elicit claims from the doctoral students suggest that inventing and articulating claims may have been more than a technical problem.

Students' Corresponding Negotiations

In interviews with me, the doctoral writers' descriptions of their experiences suggested that addressing the mentor's commentary required the writers come to terms with their understanding of academic argument. Furthermore, Daisy indicated she had to confront background knowledge about the nature of academic argument and suggested the need to reconcile her emerging scholarly practice with her teaching practice.

Daisy and Chloe recognized they had to modify their understanding of scholarly argument, but it was also clear they did not fully understand the mentor's expectations. The unclear expectations resulted in a trial-and-error process in which the doctoral writers formulated claims and anxiously awaited guiding feedback. For example, Daisy noted that, prior to the feedback sessions with Maddox, she and Chloe believed they had articulated a suitable argument—"previously I thought we already had the argument"—but after a feedback session she reassessed her understanding: "I think we didn't, like, this I think we didn't really explain in depth what is the argument at the beginning." In preparing for the next meeting, although more confident she had fulfilled Maddox's expectations, Daisy recognized there was still a chance she and Chloe would not hit the target: "Hopefully we're right this time."

Daisy also indicated that addressing Maddox's comments required confronting her prior rhetorical knowledge and the way that knowledge related to her current teaching practices. Maddox consistently called for claims to be stated at the beginning of each section of the research article, but Daisy said she was unfamiliar with such a practice, indicating her writing was informed by a rhetorical style in which arguments slowly unfold over the course of an entire text and add up to an argument. Describing a portion of the draft she composed, Daisy said,

> I think this is more a, like, in general, like, a Confucius way of writing and indicating things that you're kind of, like, so you say something at the beginning but not very in depth, but you're using this like the evidence, like the data, to kind of make support, support a argument. But what Maddox is saying well you need to explain fully, OK, what is the problem, what is the issue, and then, after that, you're using your evidence to support that argument.

This conflict of rhetorical approaches appeared to extend into Daisy's employment as a college writing teacher. Specifically, Daisy indicated a conflict between what she was learning through her scholarly writing and what she was teaching in her college writing courses. In our interview, she described her attempts to accede to Maddox's suggestions: "I think what I'm doing is exactly probably sometimes what I told my Chinese students not to do, but I do it anyways." Daisy reference to her teaching suggests a relationship between her emerging scholarly self and her teacherly self, and the reference also suggests those selves are somehow in tension.

Adaptive Challenge 2: Aligning Claims with Data

   Faculty Advisor's Commentary

A large portion of Maddox's comments addressed the way the students used data to support claims. Often, the mentor's comments alerted the doctoral students to the kinds of information that counted as evidence. Other comments focused on the way the data were explicitly connected to the claim for readers. The following comments show how Maddox read looking for the way data were being used as evidence:

> MADDOX: OK, so you've paraphrased what the student said, so where is the quote that actually says it? That's how you use a quote. You need to, once you state your interpretation or paraphrase of what the student said in plain English, what you do is you restate it within student's words, so that your interpretation is backed up by a direct quote. And if you don't have that quote, your claim is just a made-up story without any credibility.
>
> MADDOX: Unless you quote, you are not presenting evidence. In other words, the readers will have to take your word for it.
>
> MADDOX: That's how the readers are reading. As they read each claim, they're looking for "Did students really say that? Where? How?" Right? And if there are sentences that don't make sense, unless the students themselves said it and you are representing it, the reader's thinking is, "Maybe you're making things up."

In addition to pointing out the need to include data altogether, other comments by Maddox focused on the way the writers explained the relationship between the data and the claim. That is to say, even when the evidence *was* present, the writers needed to explain how the evidence aligned with other elements in the text. Examples of Maddox's comments include the following:

> MADDOX: Introduce the quote. Provide as much information as possible so that the readers know what this quote is going to do. You need to explain what the quote is going to do before you present it. Don't let the reader interpret it; this isn't journalism. In news articles, you just say, "This person said," and then readers make the connections. In

academic articles, give the interpretation and then you provide the evidence.

MADDOX: OK, well first you need to introduce the source before going into the quote. Don't let it stand by itself.

In each case, Maddox's comments are pushing the students to make explicit connections for readers, to describe precisely how data served as evidence in the context of the team's written argument.

Students' Corresponding Negotiations

Aligning claims and data posed a significant challenge for Chloe, who had to grapple with her own conflicting understandings about how to use interview data as a researcher and a writer. One challenge Chloe described during our interview was analyzing data in ways not intended by the initial design of the study. This challenge arose because the collaborative team decided to shift the focus of their research questions due to practical constraints during participant recruitment. Shifting the focus of the research questions led to a conceptual difficulty for Chloe, who had trouble disentangling the original research questions from the new ones. In our interview, Chloe indicated that the team's shift in focus led to difficulties.

> But a difficult part is this, and I kind of feel like that's because the way we designed our interview questions. . . . So our purposes and focuses were changed, and this is where I'm kind of stuck. So this is probably still kind of struggling.

For Chloe, this struggle involved learning how to pose new questions to data that were collected under a different purpose. In order to address Maddox's comments about aligning data with claims, Chloe had to come to terms with her own evolving understanding of the study's purpose, which remained unsettled even as the team drafted the research report.

Chloe also struggled to develop claims warranted by the evidence available. Analyzing the data using new research questions led Chloe to separate the interview data in unexpected ways, leaving many sentences "disconnected," as she said. These disconnected sentences put Chloe in the difficult position of establishing claims based on indirect evidence rather than direct evidence. As her comments below indicate, Chloe grappled with how best to establish claims that, while true, did not have robust support in the data. She said,

> It's easier because I can say well there are 18 of 23 students who said this, so I can make some sort of a generalization. But in this section, maybe one student said this, another said that, one student said this, so I can't really

> base this [claim] on a few individual students who said this, even though I think what they said is true.... So I feel like I don't have enough evidence. I feel more confident explaining things based on students' [words], like most of the students said this or that, so I feel like I'm not putting my own words into it.

Chloe was unsure whether the data available warranted establishing a claim, and she was also unsure of the extent to which she could rely on her own authority—that is, "putting [her] own words into it." As her comments show, Chloe felt more confident relying on the authority of the voices of the interview subjects than on her own.

Adaptive Challenge 3: Translating and Integrating Cross-Language Data

Faculty Advisor's Commentary

The challenge of aligning data with claims was further complicated by the cross-language nature of the interview data the team had collected. Maddox's comments frequently addressed the way translations were conducted and integrated into the draft. Since the audience for the research report would likely not speak Chinese, the writers had to ensure their translations captured meanings rather than preserved unique linguistic features. Maddox's comments, then, often addressed the way Daisy and Chloe conducted meaning-based translations. The following comments are representative of Maddox's concerns regarding translation:

> MADDOX: The English translation has to make sense without reference to the Chinese text. It doesn't have to be a direct translation as long as the interpretation is reasonable.
>
> MADDOX: When you present the data in translation, you do it as accurately as possible. But what you do is you explain what they seem to be saying, or what they are functionally saying, in your generalization.... Even though they are not saying exactly the same thing, your generalization cannot contradict what the students are actually saying.

Comments such as these put Daisy and Chloe in a position of authority since they were specifically brought onto the project to leverage their linguistic expertise. At the same time, as liaisons between the interview subjects and future readers of the research report, they had to rely on their own authority as scholars to determine what counted as reasonable translation.

Students' Corresponding Negotiations

To address Maddox's comments, the doctoral students had to negotiate conceptual conflicts underlying the practice of translation, as well as the practical challenge of integrating cross-language data into the text. Chloe, for instance, struggled with the very practice of doing meaning-based translations in context, a task she indicated not having encountered before. Chloe described the challenge as a conflict between, on one hand, the need to preserve the integrity of language captured in interviews and, on the other hand, the need to make that language recognizable to a disciplinary audience. Chloe described this conflict in detail.

> So actually when I was writing this, at the beginning I thought it would be easier because it's in Chinese. But I feel like it's harder now because students use Chinese to describe their experience. And those are so different from the language we use among teachers describing student experience. We [teachers] use different terms, or we have specific terminologies for that. . . . I felt like, should I maintain their ways of expression, or should I change it to the way that other people would be able to understand? I feel like no one really taught me that.

Chloe's description of the conflict suggests it is a rhetorical one. The description also evokes the definition of an adaptive challenge insofar as she indicates not having encountered the problem before. Later in the same interview, Chloe amplifies the uniqueness of the issue when she mentions feeling a responsibility to be able to resolve the issue: "I want to ask Maddox, but I can't really ask him every single one. It should be my expertise, or actually I'm kind of insider, but that's a process I haven't really had experience with about how to solve those problems."

A concurrent challenge was determining how to integrate the cross-language data into the written draft. Because cross-language studies are uncommon in rhetoric and composition and writing studies (the disciplinary identities of the target audience), it was likely the doctoral writers would have to rely on their own ingenuity in developing a strategy for integrating translations alongside transliterations. Both Daisy and Chloe indicated they turned to published studies in search of models for managing data but found no suitable models existed.

> CHLOE: [It's] so hard. That's why I go to other books trying to see the books investigating Chinese students specifically and how they, but as far as I notice, most of the interviews were conducted in English. So none that I can find is . . . so that's the thing.
>
> DAISY: We're trying to look at some papers that also have interview data, and then we're kind of trying to learn from them how we can integrate the data into our paper. But unfortunately, the papers that we found is all, um, like they quote the big dialog, like sometimes they will quote even with like ten or fifteen sentences in a big dialog[, which is not what we're doing in our paper].

Both students encountered challenges that did not admit a conventional response. After discovering no suitable solution already circulating, Chloe and Daisy learned they would have to develop their own.

Adaptive Challenge 4: Providing Appropriate Contextual Information
Faculty Advisor's Commentary

Many of the mentor's comments addressed the need to contextualize elements of the written text. Maddox alerted the doctoral students to areas of the draft that called for additional background information or clarification. These comments pushed the writers to attend to issues of audience and genre—that is, to attend to how much information to include and where to put it.

Some of Maddox's comments recommended the writers create a broader context for readers to interpret the claims being made. For example, in the portion of the written draft discussing the students' transition from China to the United States, Maddox suggested the doctoral writers include background information about the nature of that transition before discussing the data. During the team meeting, Maddox said,

> It might be helpful somewhere . . . maybe in the Method section or discussing the population . . . to include some information about the education system and the background. Or it could be at the beginning of this section [the results section], in order to help the reader to understand what it means to transition from China to the US. It's important for readers to understand what the educational system looks like, right? So give an overview before going into the details.

In this case, Maddox suggests readers would benefit from a more thorough description of the transition the student subjects are encountering so readers can interpret the findings more substantively.

In another comment, Maddox recommends the writers provide additional information to contextualize a particular finding. In the following comment, Maddox points out that, although the information is not immediately relevant, it will be of interest to readers and should therefore be added. Maddox says,

> That seems like an important contextual information factor. It's not directly related to it, but since the audience is interested in how this experience contrasts with first-year composition experience, it would be good to include that information. . . . Maybe this is a good opportunity to add a comment. And that's an important point to make. So whenever you have an opportunity like that, you need to add supplemental information so that what the students said is fully contextualized and the significance is conveyed to the readers. That's the work of qualitative interpretation.

The suggestion Maddox makes here is nicely captured by a comment he offers later in the same meeting: "You mention the information when it's relevant." Of course, following this rule assumes writers know what counts as relevant to a certain group of readers.

Many of Maddox's comments in this category addressed smaller issues, involving a word or two for clarification. The following examples reflect this microscale contextual information:

> MADDOX: "Afterwards," after what? What does this "afterwards" refer to? . . . OK, that relationship and the time reference is not very clear.
>
> MADDOX: "Several participants reported that English language teachers spent." *Their* English teachers?
>
> MADDOX: "Just under a third of the students . . ." Students in this study or in general?
>
> DAISY: In this study.
>
> MADDOX: OK, that needs to be specified.

Whether the contextual information needed was broad or narrow, the doctoral writers had to have a clear sense of their audience and genre in order to place an appropriate amount of emphasis.

Students' Corresponding Negotiations

Contextualizing information in the written draft was a challenge particularly for Chloe. One reason was that her prior genre learning seemed to conflict with what Maddox was recommending on the current draft. A second reason was that Chloe did not seem to know the audience well enough to determine just how much background information she could assume her readers would bring with them.

In our interview, Chloe indicated that Maddox's comments seemed at odds with the comments she received from him while working on another project. In that other project, which was a research article she was completing in fulfillment of requirements for advancing to doctoral candidacy, Chloe ran into a question of where in the draft to place the demographic information of the study participants. In that earlier project, Maddox recommended she include the demographic information in the methods section. In the current project, however, Maddox was suggesting that some demographic information be included in the results section (this suggestion fell under Maddox's general rule: "You mention the information when it's relevant"). As a result of this seemingly conflicting information, Chloe felt a sense of cognitive dissonance. She said,

> But I remember in my own portfolio papers, I also gave students' background information, but Maddox told me I should be put those information in the results [section] because that's not maybe the research questions. It just tells you more about the participants. So I asked Daisy, "Do you feel can we put the results from the survey in the results section or in the methods section?" So that's where . . . and she said, well I don't know. Maybe we should ask Maddox, or I should still try my best to find information. I don't know, that's the conversation we just had yesterday. I'm not sure what to do.

Here, Chloe is attempting to draw on her prior genre knowledge to make sense of this new writing problem, but she is having trouble seeing the difference between the two situations. To address Maddox's comments about providing appropriate contextual information, she needed to learn the subtle elements that rendered the two situations unique.

A second source of difficulty for Chloe had to do with the amount of information she could presume her readers would bring with them. For example, one aspect of Chloe's draft involved describing the interview subjects' transitions from China to the United States, but Chloe wondered how much information could be considered common knowledge and how much needed to be described in detail. In our interview, Chloe described this difficulty in detail.

> So for example, here I'm still trying to explain what students said because they are comparing the difference between FYC [in the United States] and their experience in China. So student mentioned, "Well, it's because it's test preparation oriented [in China]." And it's kind of general common knowledge, I should say, but only one or two students specified because it's all exam oriented. So I feel like it's common knowledge, but in our study there are only two students mentioned that. And it's like can I really say that? . . . So it's like how am I going to present the data and results here? Can I rely more on common knowledge, something like that?

To describe the difference between educational experiences in the United States and China, Chloe noted she would have to rely on some shared knowledge with readers, but she was unsure of the extent of that shared knowledge. Addressing Maddox's calls to provide appropriate contextual information was, for Chloe, a complicated matter likely requiring more familiarity with the intended audience.

DISCUSSION AND IMPLICATIONS

This study set out to examine doctoral research writing as an adaptive challenge by looking closely at feedback sessions of a faculty mentor

Encouraging students to **invent and advance claims** prompted them to:
- negotiate diverging rhetorical approaches to academic argument
- confront contradictions between scholarly practices and teaching practices
- engage in a trial-and-error process to determine what counted as an argument

Encouraging students to **align claims with data** prompted them to:
- learn what counted as evidence in the context of a qualitative, interview-based study
- manage and repurpose qualitative data in unintended ways
- practice proportioning claims based on available evidence

Encouraging students to **translate and integrate cross-language data** prompted them to:
- distinguish between meaning-based and literal translations
- practice developing meaning-based translations, preserving original intent while rendering that intent accessible to disciplinary readers
- develop an internal framework for integrating cross-language quotations into a research article

Encouraging students to **provide appropriate contextual information** prompted them to:
- negotiate seemingly contradictory knowledge about genre conventions based on prior writing experiences
- actively question the extent to which certain knowledge is shared with the audience

Figure 9.1. Adaptive challenges: faculty commentary and subsequent negotiations by doctoral student writers

and two doctoral writers. The findings reveal, from the mentor's perspective, that the doctoral writers needed improvement in their ability to invent and advance claims, to align claims with evidence, to develop and integrate meaning-based translations in the written text, and to provide contextual information for readers. In many ways, these areas for improvement reflect the central intellectual work of doctoral researchers, who are trained to use evidence to advance claims useful to a particular community of scholars.

The results also reveal, from the students' perspective, that the writing issues at stake involved far more than learning to control surface features of the text. For each issue raised by the faculty mentor, the writers had to develop suitable responses, not by relying on existing know-how but by reorienting their own understandings, values, or behaviors. In some cases, the reorienting involved learning what a disciplinary audience might count as evidence or a successful argument; in other cases, it was a matter of contending with competing rhetorical traditions or conflicting understandings of genre conventions. In any case, the findings make clear that exhorting writers to perform a writing-related task does not necessarily induce acquisition in the way we might expect were these issues technical problems. Figure 9.1 captures the diverse actions taken up by the students in response to the faculty mentor's commentary.

Research on doctoral feedback suggests writers learn best through personalized, one-with-one feedback (Caffarella and Barnett 2000;

Rogers, Zawacki, and Baker 2016). However, research also suggests that feedback from faculty mentors can be especially difficult to interpret (Paré 2011; Rogers, Zawacki, and Baker 2016). To address the difficulty of interpretation, Anthony Paré (2011) recommends that faculty supervisors develop an awareness of the unique and often implicit knowledge-building practices that shape written discourse in a particular field and, in turn, develop a more precise "linguistic and rhetorical vocabulary" for communicating those expectations to students (66). Similarly, Paul Rogers, Sarah Zawacki, and Sarah Baker (2016) find that "one of the most frequent student complaints about advisors or committee members [has] to do with the vague or abstract advice they [give]" (65). Students, they find, appreciate instruction that is explicit and that links written products directly to expectations reflected in program guidelines (74).

However, these researchers are also quick to point out that explicitness is a "necessary but insufficient condition for learning in doctoral education" (Rogers, Zawacki, and Baker 74). Because of the complex and highly situated nature of writing, there is no guarantee any singular articulation of expectations for writing will ensure clarity and uptake on the part of students. The study reported in this chapter supports this claim. Specifically, the findings above suggest that, while clarity and explicitness are indeed important, no amount of either will adequately account for all the issues likely to arise. Even under the best conditions, writers are likely to confront some form of transformative negotiation due to the adaptive nature of many writing problems. The present study contributes to research on supervisory feedback by revealing in detail why, for the two doctoral student participants, it is the case that explicitness and precision are insufficient for ensuring the acquisition of writing knowledge. From the students' perspective, the problems arising during writing, although cued by the mentor's commentary, could not be reduced exclusively to the mentor's characterizations of them.

This point is worth stating in more general terms. Problems in writing tend to be identified by the way they appear on the surface of the textual product—as an issue of organization, say, or of style or grammar. But this kind of identification often reveals only half the story, a story typically told from the perspective of the reader without reference to the experience of the writer. As scholars in composition studies have argued for decades (Bartholomae 1980; Horner 1992; Williams 1981), errors in writing do not exist outside the lived experience of socially situated interlocutors; errors are social inventions, produced by encounters between readers and writers. A related concern, then, is the degree to which the identification and labeling of an error is open to negotiation.

Often, the identification and labeling is the purview of the privileged party in the interaction. How writing problems are defined can betray an asymmetry between the writer and reader.

It can be instructive to interpret the findings above with this asymmetry in mind. The findings suggest the writer's experience should be taken into account when identifying the nature of a writing-related issue. Defining the writing problem as, for example, an inability to advance claims clearly is necessarily partial and incomplete. Just as true is that the problem is a matter of negotiating competing rhetorical traditions of argumentation or that the problem is one of ensuring integrity across various aspects of one's professional duties. Neither the account from the faculty mentor's perspective nor the one from the students' perspective is entirely complete. Acknowledging the writers' experience, in conjunction with the mentor's own perception, is a step toward a richer account of the problem space.

The present study has implications for supervisors across the disciplines who engage closely with student texts. First, supervisors stand to benefit from recognizing the distinction between technical and adaptive problems since the distinction will suggest different forms of response. A decision point for supervisors might be to determine whether the issue at stake is simply a gap in the writer's knowledge, and therefore a technical problem, or a more substantive issue stemming from a deeper source of conflict. If technical, a suitable solution might reside in a writing handbook or program rubric, and the role of the supervisor may be to point students to those resources or to provide the information themselves.

But supervisors may run into trouble if they assume all writing problems to be of this type. In many cases, the problem will reflect deeper issues of identity development, intellectual growth, or a writer's level of familiarity with a field's nuanced knowledge-making practices. A second implication, then, is the importance of recognizing the need to inquire more deeply into contested aspects of writing and to invite students into the process of problem definition. One strategy to support this effort is posing questions, to the text and to the writer, that help draw out additional information about the writing experience and rhetorical situation, thus opening up the possibility for a richer description of the scene. Figure 9.2 lists a series of heuristic questions supervisors, regardless of disciplinary affiliation, might use to facilitate fruitful discussions with writers. Based in part on findings from this study, the questions listed below aim to direct attention to aspects of the writing process that might get short shrift in typical conversations about writing but are nevertheless likely to have significant impact on the written product.

Questions considering links between present and prior experience:
- How is this writing task similar to or different from tasks you've encountered before?
- What links, if any, exist between the current writing task and other aspects of your professional life? Are there conflicts that have affected your approach to the current writing task?

Questions aimed at detecting and diagnosing a writer's discomfort:
- What problems are you encountering? How are those problems aligning with the feedback you are receiving on your writing?
- When do you feel most uncomfortable when you are writing? How are those moments of discomfort reflected in the written text?
- Has this writing task proceeded according to plan since you've begun? What unexpected circumstances have affected the project, and in what ways have you had to improvise?
- What logistical aspects of the writing process are affecting your writing performance?
- What aspects of the genre have felt unfamiliar or limiting to you? In what ways might you push back against certain generic constraints?
- What is your overall purpose in this writing task? What academic community are you aiming to contribute to? What stance are you adopting as a writer?

Questions considering a writer's possible next steps:
- How might you prioritize the writing issues you are experiencing in terms of importance or most in need of attention? What are some options for possible next steps?
- Does your plan for next steps involve a "workaround" (i.e., maintaining the original purpose but finding a new approach) or a "workanew" (i.e., revising the project's purpose altogether)?

Figure 9.2. Prompts supervisors can use to facilitate discussions with doctoral writers

This chapter opens with a metaphor of doctoral writing as a complex drama. In closing, I call back to the metaphor to argue that supervisors play an important supporting role. Specifically, supervisors are in a position to resist the asymmetry that commonly characterizes the way writing is interpreted and assessed, a process that can marginalize the voices of students. To be sure, such an asymmetry is harmful if it limits a student's capacity to make visible the challenges they encounter. Recognizing that many writing problems are adaptive rather than technical and that any description of a problem benefits from the inclusion of multiple voices, supervisors are well positioned to provide feedback that is not only explicit and precise but also collaboratively composed.

ACKNOWLEDGMENTS

I would like to express gratitude to the participants in this study, who so generously shared their time and thoughtful attention, as well as to the anonymous reviewers for their insightful and constructive feedback on early drafts of this chapter. Additionally, I am grateful for the constructive conversations surrounding this project shared with members of my working group at the 2016 Consortium on Graduate Communication

Summer Institute, including Shannon Madden, Louise Wetherbee Phelps, Lisa Russell-Pinson, and David E. E. Sloane.

REFERENCES

Bommarito, Daniel V. 2016. "Collaborative Research Writing as Mentoring in a US English Doctoral Program." *Journal of Writing Research* 8 (2): 267–299.

Bartholomae, David. 1980. "The Study of Error." *College Composition and Communication* 31 (3): 253–269.

Caffarella, Rosemary S., and Bruce G. Barnett. 2000. "Teaching Doctoral Students to Become Scholarly Writers: The Importance of Giving and Receiving Critiques." *Studies in Higher Education* 25 (1): 39–52.

Casanave, Christine Pearson. 2002. *Writing Games: Multicultural Case Studies of Academic Literacy Practices in Higher Education*. Mahwah, NJ: Erlbaum.

Casanave, Christine Pearson. 2016. "What Advisors Need to Know about the Invisible 'Real-Life' Struggles of Doctoral Dissertation Writers." In *Supporting Graduate Student Writers: Research, Curriculum, & Program Design*, edited by Steve Simpson, Nigel A. Caplan, Michelle Cox, and Talinn Phillips, 97–116. Ann Arbor: University of Michigan Press.

Curry, Mary Jane. 2016. "More Than Language: Graduate Student Writing as 'Disciplinary Becoming.'" In *Supporting Graduate Student Writers: Research, Curriculum, & Program Design*, edited by Steve Simpson, Nigel A. Caplan, Michelle Cox, and Talinn Phillips, 78–98. Ann Arbor: University of Michigan Press.

Flower, Linda. 2016. "Difference-Driven Inquiry: A Working Theory of Local Public Deliberation." *Rhetoric Society Quarterly* 46 (4): 308–330.

Horner, Bruce. 1992. "Rethinking the 'Sociality' of Error: Teaching Editing as Negotiation." *Rhetoric Review* 11 (1): 172–199.

Kamler, Barbara, and Pat Thomson. 2006. *Helping Doctoral Students Write: Pedagogies for Supervision*. London: Routledge.

Lovitts, Barbara. 2008. "The Transition to Independent Research: Who Makes It, Who Doesn't, and Why." *Journal of Higher Education* 79 (3): 296–325.

Lundell, Dana Britt, and Richard Beach. 2003. "Dissertation Writers' Negotiations with Competing Activity Systems." In *Writing Selves/Writing Societies*, edited by Charles Bazerman and David R. Russell, 483–514. Fort Collins, CO: WAC Clearinghouse.

Morita, Naoko. 2004. "Negotiating Participation and Identity in Second Language Academic Communities." *TESOL Quarterly* 80 (4): 573–603.

Paré, Anthony. 2011. "Speaking of Writing: Supervisory Feedback and the Dissertation." In *Doctoral Education: Research-Based Strategies for Doctoral Students, Supervisors, and Administrators*, edited by Lynn McAlpine and Cheryl Amundsen, 59–74. London: Springer.

Paré, Anthony, Doreen Starke-Meyerring, and Lynn McAlpine. 2011. "Knowledge and Identity Work in the Supervision of Doctoral Student Writing: Shaping Rhetorical Subjects." In *Writing in Knowledge Societies*, edited by Doreen Starke-Meyerring, Anthony Paré, Natasha Artemeva, Miriam Horne, and Larissa Yousoubova, 215–236. Fort Collins, CO: WAC Clearinghouse.

Rogers, Paul, Terry Myers Zawacki, and Sarah E. Baker. 2016. "Uncovering Challenges and Pedagogical Complications in Dissertation Writing and Supervisory Practices: A Multimethod Study of Doctoral Students and Advisors." In *Supporting Graduate Student Writers: Research, Curriculum, & Program Design*, edited by Steve Simpson, Nigel A. Caplan, Michelle Cox, and Talinn Phillips, 52–77. Ann Arbor: University of Michigan Press.

Seloni, Lisya. 2012. "Academic Literacy Socialization of First Year Doctoral Students in US: A Micro-Ethnographic Perspective." *English for Specific Purposes* 31 (1): 47–59.

Williams, Joseph M. 1981. "The Phenomenology of Error." *College Composition and Communication* 32 (2): 152–168.

10
FROM AVOIDANCE TO ACTION
Helping Dissertation Writers Manage Procrastination

Lisa Russell-Pinson and Haadi Jafarian

> *[In preparing to write a dissertation,] heart work cannot be neglected . . . what connections and relationships to family and friends will sustain students during this period of stresses and strains, and how can energy and time be allocated to these relationships without jeopardizing work on the dissertation project? How can students build and sustain belief and confidence in themselves during a lengthy experience that can leave them feeling intimidated, depressed, confused, and defeated? The dissertation journey is an emotional as well as an intellectual one.*
> —Christine Pearson Casanave

INTRODUCTION

Writing specialists are typically well adept at assisting doctoral students in understanding and effectively using the building blocks of academic writing (e.g., clarity, audience awareness, argumentation, organization, and composing strategies) to produce successful texts in their disciplines (Russell-Pinson and Harris 2019). However, as Christine Pearson Casanave (2014) clearly describes in the epigraph to this chapter, the emotions involved in producing doctoral-level texts, especially the dissertation, are central to this endeavor, too (Aitchison et al. 2012; Casanave 2016, 2019; Marais, Shankland, Haag, Fiault, and Juniper 2018; Pauley 2004; Russell-Pinson and Harris 2019). Lawrence Blum (2010) echoes the importance of attending to the emotions of dissertation writers. In his clinical psychology practice, he has worked with numerous all-but-dissertation (ABD) students, and from this work concludes, "The dissertation requirement for a PhD candidate . . . inevitably has many psychological meanings; it can become a battleground of numerous emotional and developmental conflicts" (74). As such, psychological obstacles to writing can impede or even prevent doctoral degree completion (Maul,

DOI: 10.7330/9781607329589.c010

Berman, and Ames 2018; Pauley 2004; Straforini 2015). Due to systemic barriers and implicit bias, these difficulties can be even more pronounced in students from underrepresented groups (Hinsdale 2015). Despite the recognition that doctoral candidates benefit from attending to and addressing their emotional needs during the dissertation process, these needs have traditionally been marginalized by institutions (Aitchison and Mowbray 2013) and long ignored by the most popular dissertation "self-help" books on the market (Blum 2010; Straforini 2015).

With the notable exception of the growing body of literature on the manifold benefits of doctoral writing groups (e.g., Aitchison and Guerin 2014), little has been written about how writing professionals can directly assist doctoral students encountering psychological difficulties during the dissertation phase. This lack is understandable to some degree because there may be the expectation that doing so would require writing specialists to have specific education and training in counseling or psychology. However, writing specialists do not need mental health expertise to help students deal with some of the thorny issues in the dissertation process. Rather, writing professionals can further develop an increased awareness of how emotion can affect dissertation writing through learning about what such issues entail and how they may manifest themselves in doctoral candidates; they can also expand their repertoire of approaches in helping students grapple with such challenges in the dissertation stage (Carter and Cook 2014; Casanave 2016; Russell-Pinson and Harris 2019). Attending to student emotions during the dissertation phase could lead to not only improved rates of and time to completion (Ames, Berman, and Casteel 2018; Maul, Berman, and Ames 2018) but also to the beginning of understanding—from faculty and students alike—that such barriers can and must be addressed to ensure student well-being and success in the dissertation process and beyond (Graduate Assembly 2014).

Accordingly, we focus on a psychological issue that tends to affect many advanced academic writers: procrastination, or "the delay of the initiation or completion of a goal to the point of discomfort" (Krause and Freund 2016, 422). While a host of other challenges facing dissertation writers, including anxiety, stress, isolation, shifts in identity, tensions between student and advisor, financial problems, perfectionism, difficult relationships, and work/life balance, have been described in literature (e.g., Aitchison et al. 2012; Ames, Berman, and Casteel 2018; Badenhorst 2010; Blum 2010; Casanave 2014, 2016, 2019; Cohen 2011; Dinkins and Sorrell 2014; Inman and Silverstein 2003; Lambert 2014; Lenz 1997; Ma 2019; Marais et al. 2018; Pauley 2004; Russell-Pinson and

Harris 2019; Straforini 2015; Sosin and Thomas 2014; Wynne, Guo, and Wang 2014), our work with dissertation writers indicates procrastination often results from one or more of these challenges.

On the surface, attending to an effect (e.g., procrastination) rather than a cause (e.g., financial difficulties) may appear to be an insufficient approach to make a substantial change. However, assisting writers with many of the personal challenges noted above is beyond the scope of what writing specialists can professionally and ethically accomplish. For example, if, during writing consultations, dissertation writers disclose they are having financial difficulties, writing specialists knowledgeable about and well connected to both campus and community services may be able to refer writers to relevant resources for financial assistance. However, not all writers feel comfortable revealing such personal information, especially without prompting, and for those who do, writing specialists are unable to directly provide such students with the monetary support (e.g., loans, scholarships, assistantships, fellowships) that could truly make a difference to their plights. Nonetheless, writing specialists can and should help students recognize and mitigate detrimental writing habits, including those arising from personal challenges; accordingly, addressing procrastination is one way writing specialists can move these students forward with their dissertation writing.

Our discussion begins by reviewing the literature on procrastination, especially as it relates to advanced academic writers. Then, we present two vignettes featuring academic writers struggling with procrastination in the dissertation process; these short sketches describe doctoral students who represent composites of students we have worked with or known over the years. Each vignette is followed by ways those who work with dissertation writers can assist such students with the underlying causes of their procrastination, even if recognizing that a referral to the university's counseling center may be the best course of action. In the conclusion, we provide some further suggestions for working with dissertation students who procrastinate.

PROCRASTINATION AND ADVANCED ACADEMIC WRITERS

In order to complete their dissertations, doctoral-level writers must exert "an extraordinary amount of personal responsibility, commitment, time, cognitive effort, and motivation" while engaging in "a high-stakes, complex academic task that is often very different from anything that has been done before" (Kelley and Salisbury-Glennon 2016, 88; see also Dinkins and Sorrell 2014; Jalongo and Saracho 2016; Pauley 2004). This demanding backdrop can induce procrastination in dissertation writers. As Carol Straforini (2015) explains,

> The dissertation can make procrastinators out of nonprocrastinators and drive chronic procrastinators to despair: it can feel completely overwhelming. It must be an original contribution to the field. It is far too big a project to do at the last minute. The relevant time unit for completion is not weeks or months but years. It has no set beginning or end. There is no precise moment when one must start and no exact deadline for when one must finish. Faculty do not always regularly monitor its progress. Given these factors, what more fertile ground for procrastination? (298)

Procrastination is popularly attributed to laziness, a lack of willpower, or an inability to manage one's time effectively. However, researchers examining procrastination note the complexity of the behavior, which typically stems from cognitive, social-cultural, and/or emotional roots. For example, Martha Kelley and Jijll Salisbury-Glennon (2016) examined the role of self-regulation, "an active process in which learners analyze tasks, set goals and then attempt to monitor and regulate their cognition, motivation and behavior in support of these goals" (89), among dissertation writers and found an inverse relationship between levels of self-regulated learning and time to dissertation completion (Jalongo and Saracho 2016; also see Wolters, Won, and Hussain 2017 for a full discussion of academic time management); in other words, the ABD students in their study who exhibited low levels of self-regulated learning experienced longer times to dissertation completion. Sometimes doctoral candidates from sociocultural backgrounds traditionally underrepresented in graduate-level programs may experience "work inhibitions" related to the dissertation and be "stuck because of fears of leaving important others behind" (Straforini 2015, 304). Dissertation students can also experience intense emotional challenges rooted in past experiences, current circumstances, and/or future anxieties that can grind their progress to a halt. One difficulty many writers confront in the dissertation writing process is a problematic relationship with their advisors (Casanave 2014, 2016; Hwang, Bennett, and Beauchemin 2014; Paltridge and Woodrow 2012; Russell-Pinson and Harris 2019; Simpson 2016; Straforini 2015; Wang and Li 2011). As Straforini (2015) notes, "Countless students struggle desperately with their advisors, at times staging a kind of strike for better working conditions, slowing down or stopping progress" on their dissertations in the process (301).

In her review of the literature on procrastination and its relationship to advanced academic writing, Cecile Badenhorst (2010) concludes that procrastination is due to a need to

- protect writers from critical feedback or negative outcomes, as might be the case when someone puts off submitting a conference proposal for fear of harsh peer reviews;
- [a]void tasks that are
  * [c]ognitively difficult, such as when a student does not understand how to effectively synthesize and critique the literature in order to make a convincing and relevant argument;
  * [l]oathsome, such as when a student finds editing their writing an odious task yet knows submitting an unpolished text is unacceptable;
  * [i]mposed by someone else, such as when an advisor requires the incorporation of a theory into the dissertation the student does not find directly relevant to the dissertation topic. (65–66)

Badenhorst (2010) also notes that even academic writers who normally do not procrastinate may find themselves doing just that during the dissertation stage due to (1) the enormity of the project and the corresponding lack of "appropriate guidelines, feedback mechanisms or support," and/or (2) the high-stakes nature of the dissertation and the possibility that the writers might "be found unworthy" (71, 72).

In addition to the heavy cost to the students' time to degree completion, procrastination has been shown to lead to an increase in health problems and sleep disorders, a rise in stress and guilt, and a decrease in subjective well-being among college students (Krause and Freund 2016; Marais et al. 2018). Thus, writers who procrastinate often find this practice can have wide-reaching negative effects on many aspects of their lives.

VIGNETTES OF DISSERTATION WRITERS' EXPERIENCES

Since some of the causes of procrastination can be challenging to identify, below are two vignettes that portray procrastination in doctoral students. As mentioned above, the student described in each vignette represents a composite of several doctoral writers; consequently, pseudonyms have been used throughout this section, and all the specific details of the situations have been changed to protect the students' identities.

In the creation of these vignettes, the coauthors have drawn on their respective professional experiences in working with dissertation writers from various language, cultural, and disciplinary backgrounds. The first author, Lisa Russell-Pinson, is an applied linguist who currently serves as assistant teaching professor of writing at the University of North Carolina at Charlotte (UNC Charlotte). As a writing specialist housed in the graduate school at the university, Lisa teaches credit-bearing writing courses to native-speaking and EAL master's and doctoral students from multiple disciplines, develops and delivers writing-based initiatives for graduate students, works with graduate faculty on writing-related issues, and supports dissertation writers; this dissertation support includes providing individual dissertation-writing consultations, facilitating dissertation-writing retreats, and, in conjunction with Lynne Harris, a clinical psychologist at the university, leading counseling-focused dissertation initiatives. The second author, Haadi Jafarian, was once a doctoral student in one of Lisa's writing classes at UNC Charlotte and, under her supervision, later served as the inaugural doctoral writing fellow at the university; in this capacity, Haadi conducted writing-based workshops for graduate students and worked one on one with doctoral-level writers from a range of disciplines. Currently, Haadi is assistant professor of computer science at the University of Colorado at Denver, where he teaches cybersecurity and supervises the research and writing of the graduate students in his lab. The authors' diverse disciplinary and professional backgrounds complement each other and have helped them better understand the multifaceted challenges students can experience in the dissertation process. Some of these challenges are reflected in the vignettes below.

Diana's Story

Diana, a doctoral candidate in a social science discipline, is a very strong academic writer. Despite having received no instruction in graduate-level writing, she has a clear understanding of audience needs and genre expectations. As evidence of this, she has published two research articles in top-tier journals with her advisor and one book review as sole author; she has also presented papers at several national conferences in her field.

Diana's advisor, Dr. Morris, refers to her as "the superstar" because Diana entered the program as the most promising doctoral student in her cohort and has continuously excelled in her studies since: she finished her coursework ahead of schedule while maintaining a straight-A average, passed her comprehensive exam with distinction, and received multiple awards for her scholarship and teaching. Diana also defended her dissertation proposal without any difficulty. Unlike most of the students in her cohort, Diana had taken the option to write a brief study overview for her dissertation proposal, not the usual first three chapters that typify such proposals in her department, so she could get this milestone behind her and begin her data collection sooner. Since Diana had been such a strong student, Dr. Morris encouraged her to follow this route. However, now that she has collected and analyzed her data, Diana has found herself stalled on writing her dissertation. Although she has some text to draw upon from her dissertation proposal and the copious notes she took in the field, she finds it is not enough to move forward.

Instead of writing, Diana reluctantly finds herself spending hours online planning vacations she cannot afford to take, looking up old friends and acquaintances to see what they are doing, and having periodic "obsessions" with learning all she can about a particular movie or song that has piqued her interest. Because she has made so little progress with her writing, Diana rarely goes to campus out of fear she will see someone from her department, especially Dr. Morris, who may ask her how her dissertation is going. Diana says she is committed to finishing her doctorate but cannot determine how to make herself progress with writing her dissertation.

Commentary

Diana's situation is common among many of the dissertation students we assist. High-achieving and bright students like Diana often struggle with procrastination stemming from maladaptive perfectionism because such students "need to write faultlessly from the beginning, and will delay until they can, which never happens" (Badenhorst 2010, 72; Jalongo and Saracho 2016). For advanced academic writers, maladaptive perfectionism seems to develop from two main sources: the tendency to "set rigid standards and evaluate themselves harshly" and the assumption that "everyone else writes flawlessly the first time" (Badenhorst 2010, 71–72; Montgomery, Gregg, Somers, Pernice-Duca, Hoffman, and Beeghly 2017; Rice, Neimeyer, and Taylor 2011). These conditions often lead to an exclusive focus on a finished piece of writing, with little recognition of or attention to the arduous process required to create it. As a result, maladaptive perfectionistic writers "erroneously think that 'good' writers blithely churn out articles and books and that they must be 'bad' writers because they struggle" (Jalongo and Saracho 2016, 19). Furthermore, these writers often respond negatively to criticism of their writing and thus "may become even more reluctant to send it out for review" (Lambert 2014, 59). Their misperception of how strong writing is actually produced—through repeated revisions and continuous constructive feedback—makes them "inefficient in their use of time and energy, and their fear of failure keeps them stuck" (Badenhorst 2010, 76).

High-achieving students such as Diana likely have few or no true experiences with "failure" with respect to their academic performance. This lack of experience can be problematic, though, because making mistakes and learning how to overcome them helps individuals to develop a repertoire of strategies to draw from, to respond to a range of setbacks productively, and to be more confident they can problem solve. When "gifted" students are also maladaptive perfectionists, encountering a new academic task like a dissertation—for which performance standards are often amorphous and stakes are very high (Ames et al. 2018; Jalongo and Saracho 2016)—can make these students uneasy, so much so that they continue to avoid the task until they feel they can be successful, a time that may never come. Part of this fear of failure is related to their inability to cope with any academic adversity because it is so unfamiliar to them; they view themselves as an accumulation of their academic achievements, and any academic-related difficulty, which may in reality be merely a mishap, can seem like a catastrophe to them (Russell-Pinson and Harris 2019). Thus, they try to protect their sense of self by not engaging in the task at hand. Another aspect of the fear of failure is worrying about letting others down (Badenhorst 2010). For example, Diana's advisor, Dr. Morris, calls her a "superstar" and has praised her academic abilities throughout her doctoral program. She feels that if she shows a vulnerability, including asking for help, Dr. Morris will think she is academically incompetent and lose confidence in her. Since she cannot risk this possibility, she procrastinates more.

To help counter the rigid standards maladaptive perfectionistic students often set for themselves, it is important to demystify both the product and process for dissertation writers. For example, many students who seek our help on their dissertations have never seen an actual dissertation before. These students seem to have the sense that while the content, format, and features of journal articles can differ greatly according to discipline, dissertations are monolithic, perhaps because they fulfill a degree requirement and most doctoral students must write one. We think part of this impression is shaped by graduate schools, which tend to have formatting guidelines that promote a "one-size-fits-all" mentality. Also, many departments neglect to give students any guidance on dissertation requirements, expecting doctoral writers instead to "figure it out." However, the dissertation in the abstract does little to help doctoral writers who suffer from maladaptive perfectionism because without appropriate models of texts, the dissertation remains idealized, setting writers up for continued disappointment in trying to reach an unattainable goal.

Additionally, bright and high-achieving students like Diana may or may not have strong planning skills. By planning skills, we refer to the managing of the dissertation project, which requires the constant juggling of ever-changing priorities related to simultaneously conducting research, dealing with committee members, keeping up with administrative issues, and perhaps most important, writing (Russell-Pinson and Harris 2019). If students do possess strong planning skills, it is often a more or less straightforward task to help them apply these skills to the new context of managing a dissertation project. However, if they do not have these skills, the task is far more challenging. Some students like Diana never learned how to plan effectively, and because they are gifted students and excellent writers, they learned to compensate for a lack of planning skills on large writing projects, like master's theses, by binge writing. As Badenhorst (2010) notes, though, "The problem with [binge writing] is that it is debilitating and not sustainable for real productivity" (73). Also, a dissertation is even larger and more complex than a thesis, and the enormity and newness of this type of project sometimes leave students unable to break down the process into manageable tasks, hence leading to a standstill in writing progress. This cessation in progress can feed into maladaptive perfectionists' sense that when they resume work on their dissertations, the writing must be perfect, resulting in a downward spiral of more anxiety and more procrastination.

Jakub's Story

Jakub, an international student from Eastern Europe, began his doctoral program in a STEM discipline approximately three years ago. He progressed through his doctoral program in a timely manner, finishing both his coursework and qualifying exam on schedule; he has also gained significant practical experience by working on several NSF projects as a research assistant. On these projects, Jakub is a part of a team led by his advisor, Dr. Ivanov, with whom he has coauthored several research articles.

In Jakub's doctoral program, dissertations consist of three interrelated but distinct problem statements, which must be first approved by the advisor, so Jakub has been meeting with Dr. Ivanov to identify the specific problems he must address in his dissertation. These meetings leave Jakub feeling frustrated because he and Dr. Ivanov disagree on which research problems should be a part of Jakub's dissertation.

While Jakub admits his advisor is very knowledgeable, he also believes Dr. Ivanov overemphasizes his own ideas and discounts those of Jakub, often criticizing them harshly and considering them too incremental or impractical. At the same time, Jakub does not appreciate the research problems proposed by Dr. Ivanov because he finds them irrelevant to his background and specific research interests, thus making him reluctant to pursue them.

This situation has led to increasing tension between Jakub and Dr. Ivanov and to a virtual standstill in Jakub's work on his dissertation. Although Jakub goes to the university every weekday, he finds himself demotivated to write and avoiding weekly meetings with his advisor to instead attend professional development workshops or audit-optional classes. This protracted process continues to be a source of enormous anxiety for Jakub, as he feels confused about how to proceed; he wonders whether he should change advisors, and if he does, whether his circumstances will change.

Commentary

Difficulties with advisors are common for many dissertation writers (Bazrafkan, Shokrpour, Yousefi, and Yamani 2016; Casanave 2014; Dinkins and Sorrell 2014; Paltridge and Woodrow 2012; Russell-Pinson and Harris 2019; Straforini 2015). Moreover, even the most harmonious relationships between advisors and advisees are not always ideal because although "the advisor means to be supportive and the student wants to be open to new ideas and criticism, the differing personalities and expectations may create conflicts" (Dinkins and Sorrell 2014, 114). Thus, for a less than ideal pairing, problems can abound. As Straforini describes (2015), "The relationship between the two often becomes a central arena for enacting old wishes and unmet needs. . . . Real and imagined virtues or flaws of both candidates and their advisors can become greatly intensified in the experience of the relationship" (301).

Jakub's relationship with his advisor is fraught with conflict stemming from Jakub's perception that Dr. Ivanov disrespects his ideas, and, by extension, Jakub himself. They are rarely able to agree on any aspect of Jakub's dissertation research, which has led to angry words and bruised egos. Jakub's situation is further complicated by the cultural differences between him and his advisor. While both come from the same geographical region, their native countries have historically had political differences, which may have further exacerbated negative feelings between Jakub and Dr. Ivanov. Lisa Russell-Pinson and M. Lynne Harris (2019) write that such cultural differences "may evoke fear of times when students must collaborate with their advisors and lead to avoiding required meetings" and consequently halting text production, as has happened with Jakub.

In certain situations when the advisee-advisor relationship is intractable and results in misery for both parties, changing advisors could be a solution. Doing so may allow the dissertation writer to find an advisor whose research interests and approaches are more closely aligned with those of the writer so progress can resume. It may also help the writer if the new advisor is compatible with respect to not only research focus but also personality and culture. However, other factors must be taken into consideration. First, this solution must be considered only when all other avenues have been exhausted, as this change could have severe and long-lasting repercussions for both advisee and advisor. Making this transition must also be done in accordance with the regulations of the dissertation writer's academic program and policies of the university; otherwise, it may entangle the writer in procedural or legal challenges that may become a new source of anxiety and discouragement.

While on the surface Jakub's situation presents solely as an interpersonal conflict with his advisor, ongoing conversations with Jakub have revealed another factor contributing to his lack of progress: he is resistant to conducting research or engaging with ideas and theories unfamiliar to him. This type of inflexibility can result in a stalemate in which the writer does not make any progress (Badenhorst 2010). Related to not wanting to move beyond their comfort zones, dissertation writers may develop a fear of criticism linked to their insecurity in revealing gaps in knowledge or skills. This fear may cause some dissertation writers to overgeneralize negative feedback on writing and, instead of applying the feedback only to the text, they extend the criticism to their worth as researchers and writers (Russell-Pinson and Harris 2019). Jakub is prone to this type of misinterpretation of feedback not only from his advisor but also from us and others assisting him with his dissertation writing. He often becomes prickly when feedback veers from praise to constructive criticism, a situation that can be frustrating for all involved since he regularly seeks writing assistance.

DISCUSSION

In this section, we draw on the commentaries above to suggest ways two groups—dissertation advisors and writing specialists—can assist students like Diana and Jakub. We also make recommendations that may be useful to doctoral-level writers with tendencies to procrastinate.

Graduate Faculty and Dissertation Advisors

Dissertation chairs play key roles in helping maladaptive perfectionistic doctoral candidates like Diana. In our experience, when maladaptive perfectionists have not been producing text for some time, they are often reluctant to contact their advisors until they can accompany a meeting request with a dissertation document attachment. This situation then contributes to perfectionists' fear of failure and unreal expectations of how good a piece of writing must be before it is submitted, furthering the delay in communication. Thus, advisors should *initiate contact*, either face to face or through video conferencing, with advisees from whom they have not recently heard. During the first meeting, dissertation advisors should reassure high-performing students like Diana that they are capable of completing this degree requirement and remind them of some of their accomplishments during their graduate school careers, such as the completion of their coursework and proposal defense, as evidence of their abilities to succeed in the dissertation process. If applicable, chairs can *share their own experiences* with procrastination and maladaptive perfectionism as a way to make students more at ease during their discussions of these difficult issues; they may also offer to *connect doctoral candidates with former students* who also struggled with these issues as a way to decrease the sense of isolation and shame the dissertation writers may be experiencing. Such connections can be particularly important for underrepresented students, who may benefit from being in touch with mentors from similar backgrounds. For the dissertation writers we assist, breaking their sense of isolation can be a starting point for successfully addressing procrastinative behaviors.

Furthermore, advisors can *require regular meetings with their advisees*, ones for which the students themselves set the agenda. This practice will reinforce the need for students to remain in regular contact with advisors, thereby ensuring that dissertation writers continue to have frequent interactions with their advisors and more opportunities to receive support from them. Importantly, regular student-led meetings remind advisors and students alike that writers have agency in the dissertation process; these meetings also can increase accountability and decrease isolation for writers.

When clashes over the content of a dissertation arise between dissertation advisors and advisees, as happened with Jakub and Dr. Ivanov, it can be helpful for advisors to *ask writers to present their arguments for inclusion or exclusion of material in writing*. Requiring writers to clearly articulate their own rationales and refute those of their advisors in writing will allow them to more carefully consider the nuances in both their and their advisors' positions. Parts of these writings could subsequently be revised and then included in the dissertation as a justification for choices made during the research process, such as the use of a particular conceptual framework, methodology, or type of analysis. This practice can also jump-start stalled writers' progress. If advisors and advisees are still unable to resolve their disagreements, advisors can *enlist someone trusted by both the advisor and advisee* (e.g., program chair or committee member) to serve as a mediator in disputes. Having a more objective party weigh in on conflicts can be an effective approach to resolving disputes related to the content of the dissertation, such as which research questions are worthy of being addressed in a dissertation study, and consequently spark progress.

Additionally, advisors should remind dissertation writers all of the university is committed to student success. Because students may need more dissertation help than their advisors can provide, advisors should *refer students to free, campus-based services* that can support them throughout the dissertation process. Examples of such services include writing centers, support programs offering methodological and statistics assistance, and perhaps most important, student counseling centers. Students like Diana who struggle with maladaptive perfectionism, as well as those like Jakub who deal with interpersonal difficulties, stand to benefit greatly from receiving counseling services. These services can help students to become aware of the underlying sources of their difficulties and to develop strategies to challenge unproductive thoughts and behaviors.

In an effort to help students overcome unrealistic expectations, advisors should *make available well-regarded dissertations and successful dissertation proposals*, the latter of which are often difficult to locate. This sharing should also be accompanied by explicit, ongoing dialogues to help dissertation writers understand advisors' expectations in terms of organization, language, and style. Reviewing successful proposals and dissertations can also help writers understand the depth and scope of research required for acceptable dissertations in their doctoral programs and spur discussions of how the research to be undertaken by the advisee meets departmental and disciplinary standards.

Perhaps the most important support dissertation chairs can give their supervisees, however, is to take the time to *provide appropriate feedback on their dissertation drafts*. By appropriate feedback, we refer to the extensive comments that take into account at least

- the accuracy of the content,
- the soundness of the arguments and evidence,
- the suitability of the methodology and data-analysis process,
- the clarity of the writing, including organization, and
- the appropriateness of the language and style for the intended audience.

Criticism should be constructive so dissertation writers know advisors are supportive of their work. Advisors should also include positive comments about the submitted work; such encouraging remarks can lessen fear of failure and may increase the uptake of criticism among writers. Finally, feedback should be clearly worded so writers understand what steps they need to take to improve drafts.

Writing Professionals

When dissertation writers seek support from writing professionals, we should *ask them questions about their writing practices*. A simple question such as, "What brings you here today?" may elicit a flood of relevant information, perhaps more than enough to understand how to help the student. However, while some writers unburden themselves easily, others may respond to this question with something akin to "I'm stuck," "I don't know where to start," or "I don't know what's wrong" with no additional comment; those students can benefit from being asked additional, more pointed questions, such as,

- What is your dissertation topic? What do you enjoy about studying it? What is challenging about studying it?
- Could you tell me a bit about yourself as a writer in your doctoral program? What parts of writing in your discipline do you enjoy/not enjoy? Why?
- Could you describe your writing work habits, including the location(s), time(s) of day, process, and so forth? Do you have any writing rituals that are helpful? What do you do that does not promote success in your writing process?
- Who has been giving you support during the dissertation process? How has that support been shown? What other kind of support would you like to receive? By whom?
- Have you looked at the recent dissertations coming out of your department and written under your advisor to clarify what is expected? What have you learned from these texts?
- Have you spoken with other students ahead of you in the dissertation process to learn about the "ins and outs" of what is required in your department? What advice have they given you?

While the students' answers to these questions may not pinpoint the underlying causes of the students' difficulties in moving forward with their dissertations, they do begin a dialogue that can lead to a better understanding of the students' research motivations, attitudes towards writing, writing habits, support system(s), and connectedness to the practices of their disciplinary homes, information that may help get at the root of their difficulties. Also, these and other such questions can be the first step in helping students to recognize they have agency in their writing processes, which, in itself, may aid them in becoming a bit less "stuck."

When working with students whose answers indicate maladaptive perfectionistic tendencies, writing specialists should first *normalize the dissertation*. We recommend that students like Diana look at the last three to five years' worth of dissertations written under the direction of their dissertation chairs to learn about the depth and scope of what is expected in the content; these models can also help writers understand that the writing in these dissertations needs only to be "good enough" and is never "perfect." Once students take the time to examine these dissertations, either with or without our guidance, they usually realize they have the knowledge and skills to write one, too. Therefore, this normalization can help maladaptive perfectionistic students to begin identifying their own unreasonable expectations vis-à-vis the dissertation, a first step in a long endeavor to address maladaptive perfectionism and resulting procrastination. For students like Jakub, examining recent dissertations directed by their advisors allows them to more fully appreciate the types of research required for dissertation-length studies in their departments. Such examinations should be accompanied by the assurance that a dissertation is solely a degree requirement and the means towards the end of completing a doctoral degree. Reframing writers' expectations that the dissertation must define the course of their future research can help reduce the pressure that can lead to procrastination.

Writing professionals should also work with dissertation writers to *normalize the dissertation process*. We often ask dissertation students to reach out to others in their departments who are ahead in the process to get advice and even to commiserate. At times, though, maladaptive perfectionistic students may be more comfortable with those from other departments because they often feel less competition and embarrassment discussing these issues with students they do not know personally. Thus, writing specialists can *keep a list of doctoral candidates and recent doctoral graduates from different departments* who are willing to speak to others at earlier stages in the process since these candidates and graduates can be safer resources of dissertation-related support and encouragement. Writing specialists can also *review the dynamic nature of the writing process in general* with students; such explanations can remind them drafts of dissertation chapters are written and rewritten multiple times to be improved through a number of channels, including committee members' feedback, the writers' own deepening understanding of the dissertation topic, and their growing familiarity with the genre. Some students, especially those for whom English is a second/additional language, may be unaware of the recursive process required to produce strong scholarly writing, so explicitly discussing this iterative approach with doctoral students may help dispel the notion that early drafts must be of publishable quality, thereby lessening the possibility of delay in composing.

When working with writers who have made little recent progress on their dissertations, we *ask stalled writers to compose text* during our sessions. To get them started, we ask them to choose from a menu of options to engage with their topics or their feelings about the dissertation. These strategies, inspired by Badenhorst (2010), include

- listing reasons they chose their research topic,
- freewriting about their research,
- diagramming the content of the problematic chapter or section,
- composing a letter to a friend describing their research,
- drafting a plan for completing a problematic chapter or section,
- making a timeline of their academic accomplishments,
- brainstorming about the writing difficulties they have been having, and
- writing a paragraph exploring their feelings about their dissertation process.

During our sessions, some students find it useful to work on one or more of these strategies in five- to ten-minute blocks of time, which gives them multiple opportunities to practice starting and lessens the possibility they will be overwhelmed by the task at hand. Composing text during writing consultations allows writers to take immediate action, talk through any difficulties they might have in beginning or resuming a piece of writing, and perhaps most important, learn some techniques that can help them break the procrastination cycle.

For students like Jakub who actively seek assistance from writing professionals but sometimes have difficulty accepting feedback during writing support sessions, we have enacted two practices to facilitate our work with them. First, sometimes writers have preferences for a certain person from whom to receive a specific type of writing support. For example, a dissertation writer may value feedback from one writing consultant when seeking improvements to the overall clarity of a draft; however, the same writer might prefer working with a different consultant when seeking input on discipline-specific writing practices. Thus, prior to booking an appointment, we *ask writers to carefully consider the type of feedback they want* so they can arrange a time to work with the person who they feel can provide them with the most appropriate feedback. Having them specifically articulate the kind of writing help they seek also makes them feel more in control of the situation, improves odds that the writing support session will be successful, and reduces the likelihood of frustration among all involved. Also, at the beginning of each session, we *remind writers we are working with, not against, them* in order to improve their writing, and a necessary step to improving writing is receiving and responding to constructive criticism. We continue by asking writers to tell us what they have done well in the text so far and what they feel still needs improvement; then we look at each part of the text identified as strong and weak. This practice gives us an opportunity to offer praise—even if it is only praise for continuing to engage with a difficult piece of writing through another revision of it—at the outset of the session and more closely examine the parts of the text they themselves have already criticized. In our experience, writers such as Jakub are more likely to listen to feedback if they initiate and are included in the critique. Collectively, these practices for working with writers who are reluctant to accept critical feedback have been essential in helping them move forward on their dissertations.

At the end of our sessions with dissertation writers, we *ask them to develop an action plan for revision* based on our discussions. Specifically, we encourage dissertation writers to create this action plan using SMART (specific, measurable, attainable, realistic, time-oriented) goals. These small, concrete, and manageable tasks can be particularly useful for writers who become overwhelmed with complex, high-stakes, and sometimes emotion-laden writing projects, such as dissertations, and become a catalyst for progress.

Finally, when students need more aid in managing their procrastinative behavior than we can provide, we *refer them to the university's counseling center for additional support* because work habits and attitudes developed over a lifetime are hard to change with a simple intervention. Between our work with them and the guidance received from the counseling center, most students are able to take the necessary steps needed to effectively plan and follow through on a dissertation project.

Dissertation Writers

Dissertation writers should *have explicit conversations with advisors about specific writing requirements and expectations* for the dissertation. While such discussions should begin ideally before choosing an advisor and continue throughout the dissertation process, they can be useful even if initiated at later stages. Understanding these requirements and expectations can help assuage writers' fear of failure by more clearly identifying what they must do to be successful in the process. Since advisors may not be skilled at talking about writing, students should *prepare a list of questions* to ask their supervisors. Questions could include,

- Could you send me some model dissertation proposals/dissertations, ones that you consider to be exemplary?
- Why do you consider these documents to be strong? How is the content strong? In which ways is the writing strong?
- What practices do successful dissertation writers engage in?
- What practices should be avoided in the dissertation process?

Writers should also *be proactive in the dissertation process*. This could take a number of forms: for example, if advisors do not require them, advisees should *initiate regular meetings to discuss their progress*. Doing so can ensure writers have more accountability and more support in the dissertation process. Regular meetings can work against the avoidance behavior maladaptive perfectionistic writers tend to exhibit while also increasing these writers' confidence in the process by seeing their progress over time; frequent meetings can also help writers who have difficulty with criticism receive continuous input throughout the process, thus lessening the possibility of substantial negative feedback. In addition, dissertation writers should *reach out to others for support*. Students can gain much support from family members and friends during the dissertation process, but they may not always be the best sources of help for students trying to manage procrastinative tendencies in the dissertation process. Rather, students dealing with procrastination in a mild form may benefit from consulting writing specialists who regularly work with dissertation writers; these professionals can often help procrastinative students employ writing-based practices to make progress on their dissertations. When procrastination becomes crippling, though, students should seek assistance from the university's counseling center or other psychological services.

We also recommend doctoral students *start or join dissertation groups*. As mentioned above, dissertation groups are becoming more common on campuses, and with good reason: they can mitigate the isolation so many dissertation writers experience and offer social support and accountability. Participants in these groups can help each other troubleshoot difficulties by sharing strategies for managing the process and associated emotions more effectively. For procrastinators, dissertation groups can provide an ongoing opportunity to discuss challenges and learn effective strategies from others who may struggle with similar issues.

CONCLUSION

Because emotional issues can negatively impact writers' abilities to produce text, it is important for all stakeholders in the dissertation process to help doctoral-level writers manage these issues in productive and healthy ways. Below we present several ideas writing specialists can consider incorporating in their own practice to assist dissertation writers and the faculty who work with them.

Collaborate with Doctoral Programs

Establishing strong relationships with doctoral programs is a must for writing specialists who work regularly with dissertation writers. These connections help writing professionals better understand the local needs of dissertation writers in departments across campus. They also provide opportunities for doctoral faculty to learn what writing centers and other writing-focused support services can offer the university community. Once ties have been established, doctoral faculty and writing professionals can work together on a number of initiatives to support prospective and current dissertation writers. For instance, panel discussions, cofacilitated by a doctoral faculty member and a writing specialist—and featuring current and former dissertation writers—can provide frank discussions of emotional challenges in the writing process and practical strategies for managing such difficulties. Furthermore, faculty can invite writing specialists to doctoral classes to present on issues such as procrastination that can hamper the writing process. An illustration of this is the collaboration between Lisa and Phyllis Post, a doctoral faculty member in the Department of Counseling at UNC Charlotte. Because several of Phyllis's advisees had benefited from the dissertation support services offered through the university's graduate school, Phyllis now invites Lisa to her dissertation proposal writing classes each semester to discuss challenges in the dissertation process. Lisa's presentation includes strategies for identifying and managing unproductive writing behaviors. As a result of these presentations, there has been an increase in the number of students from Phyllis's department requesting dissertation support. We believe part of the reason for the rise in these requests is due to the buy-in of the importance of explicitly addressing these issues in the dissertation process by Phyllis, who is a respected mentor in her department.

Another avenue for collaboration between writing professionals and doctoral faculty is in helping dissertation advisors work more effectively with their advisees, including attending to their emotional needs more directly. For example, Lisa has been working on a number of dissertation-related initiatives with faculty in the College of Education at UNC Charlotte. At the invitation of several doctoral program directors in the college, Lisa has participated in monthly faculty meetings to discuss dissertation-related concerns, including ways to provide appropriate feedback and support to dissertation writers. She was also asked to review the dissertation writing support classes offered in the college, an opportunity that allowed her to provide information about the emotions involved in high-stakes writing to the courses. Finally, Lisa has been working directly with several faculty members in the college to provide them with specific strategies to support doctoral students who are nearing the end of their timelines but are not close to finishing their dissertations.

Collaborate with Student Service Providers

Partnering with campus-based providers can also enrich the services offered to dissertation writers. To illustrate such a partnership, we describe an ongoing collaboration between Lisa and Lynne Harris, a clinical psychologist housed in UNC Charlotte's Center for Counseling and Psychological Services. For the past four years, Lisa and Lynne have developed and delivered several dissertation-based initiatives that unite their respective areas of expertise in academic writing and psychology. For example, they designed and implemented one program that supports students through the dissertation process by attending to both their psychological and writing needs; the program ran one day a month for one and one-half years, and participants reported that combining writing and psychological support in one space was a key part of the initiative's success.

Building upon what they learned from this initiative, Lisa and Lynne also created psychoeducational support groups focused on helping doctoral candidates gain skills and strategies needed to meet the psychological and writing challenges inherent in the dissertation process (Russell-Pinson and Harris 2019). The support groups drew on the literature in psychology, higher education, writing studies, and linguistics, and the curriculum blended social support with direct instruction. The curriculum used a cognitive behavioral therapy approach and focused on helping students build skills in the following areas, all of which can stave off procrastination:

- setting and reaching dissertation goals
- managing writing-induced stress, including dealing with maladaptive perfectionism and receiving critical feedback
- being proactive in the dissertation process
- addressing dissertation-based anxiety
- developing and maintaining positive relationships with their advisors and others

The participants in the support groups, many of whom suffered from procrastination stemming from emotional causes, found the approach and materials beneficial and reported that the skills emphasized in the groups helped them move forward in their own dissertation processes. Based on their experiences in cofacilitating the support groups, Lisa and Lynne furthered their collaboration by developing a credit-bearing course for dissertation writers, which they currently co-teach.

Learn from Current Doctoral Students.
It is often easy for those of us who earned our doctorates a decade (or more) ago to forget the day-to-day struggles of those writing their dissertations, so speaking regularly with current dissertation writers can help writing professionals better understand these students' needs. For example, Haadi is a recent doctoral graduate; during his PhD studies, he sought Lisa's assistance on a regular basis. In this context, he frequently initiated conversations with her about the challenges and triumphs in his own dissertation process. These open-ended discussions deepened Lisa's understanding of the dissertation process and reminded her of the multifaceted problems and solutions that can be present in a single student's experience.

Even if writing professionals are blessed with clear memories of their own ABD experiences, circumstances change. For example, Lisa was ABD before the advent of social media, so the constant siren call of Facebook, Twitter, Instagram, and other services was not luring her away from her dissertation writing. However, during his own dissertation process, Haadi had to manage these distractions, in addition to the expectation that he always be accessible and responsive to his advisor and lab mates via text messaging. Thus, Haadi has taught Lisa about a number of tools available to thwart digital distractions; he has also introduced her to electronic resources to assist with project management. Learning about these resources from Haadi has enabled Lisa to share them with other dissertation writers who can also benefit from them.

REFLECTIONS

> Dum differtur vita transcurrit *(when we postpone, life passes).*
> —Seneca the Younger

While delaying work on some projects may not necessarily result in negative consequences, doctoral students who postpone writing their dissertations can suffer serious repercussions. For this reason, we urge dissertation writers to reflect on their own difficulties with writing procrastination and to be proactive in seeking support to overcome this unproductive behavior. Likewise, we urge those who support dissertation writers, including faculty and writing specialists, to be proactive in recognizing and addressing procrastination when working with these doctoral students. Only through such concerted efforts can procrastination among dissertation writers begin to be combated and conquered.

ACKNOWLEDGMENTS

We would like to thank the anonymous reviewers of this volume for their insights on our chapter, which helped us sharpen our thinking and writing. We also appreciate the support Shannon Madden and Michele Eodice provided throughout each revision of this chapter. Finally, we are very grateful to the many writers who have shared their experiences in the dissertation process with us; their candor about their own struggles with procrastination has deepened our understanding of this behavior and challenged us to expand our ways of working with writers who procrastinate.

REFERENCES

Aitchison, Claire, Janice Catterall, Pauline Ross, and Shelley Burgin. 2012. "'Tough Love and Tears': Learning Doctoral Writing in the Sciences." *Higher Education Research & Development* 31 (4): 435–447.

Aitchison, Claire, and Cally Guerin. 2014. *Writing Groups for Doctoral Education and Beyond: Innovations in Theory and Practice.* Abingdon: Routledge.

Aitchison, Claire, and Susan Mowbray. 2013. "Doctoral Women: Managing Emotions, Managing Doctoral Studies." *Teaching in Higher Education* 18 (8): 859–870.

Ames, Cathrine, Ronald Berman, and Alex Casteel. 2018. "A Preliminary Examination of Doctoral Student Retention Factors in Private Online Workspaces." *International Journal of Doctoral Studies* 13: 79–107.

Badenhorst, Cecile. 2010. *Productive Writing: Becoming a Prolific Academic Writer.* Pretoria: Van Schaik.

Bazrafkan, Leila, Nasrin Shokrpour, Alireza Yousefi, and Nikoo Yamani. 2016. "Management of Stress and Anxiety Among PhD Students During Thesis Writing: A Qualitative Study." *Health Care Manager* 35 (3): 231–240.

Blum, Lawrence D. 2010. "The 'All-But-the-Dissertation' Student and the Psychology of the Doctoral Dissertation." *Journal of College Student Psychotherapy* 24 (2): 74–85.

Carter, Susan, and Catherine Cook. 2014. "Motivation: Collaboration between Counseling and Academic Advising." In *Developing Generic Support for Doctoral Students: Practice and Pedagogy*, edited by Susan Carter and Deborah Laurs. New York: Routledge.

Casanave, Christine Pearson. 2014. *Before the Dissertation: A Textual Mentor for Doctoral Students at Early Stages of a Research Project.* Ann Arbor: University of Michigan Press.

Casanave, Christine Pearson. 2016. "What Advisors Need to Know about the Invisible 'Real-Life' Struggles of Doctoral Dissertation Writers." In *Supporting Graduate Student Writers: Research, Curriculum, and Program Design*, edited by Steve Simpson, Nigel A. Caplan, Michelle Cox, and Talinn Phillips, 97–116. Ann Arbor: University of Michigan Press.

Casanave, Christine Pearson. 2019. "Performing Expertise in Doctoral Dissertations: Thoughts on a Fundamental Dilemma Facing Doctoral Students and their Supervisors." *Journal of Second Language Writing* 43: 57–62.

Cohen, Shannon Munro. 2011. "Doctoral Persistence and Doctoral Program Completion Among Nurses." *Nursing Forum* 46 (2): 64–70.

Dinkins, Christine Sorrell, and Jeanne Merkle Sorrell. 2016. *Our Dissertations, Ourselves: Shared Stories of Women's Dissertation Journeys.* New York: Palgrave Macmillan.

Graduate Assembly. 2014. *Graduate Student Happiness and Well-Being Report.* http://ga.berkeley.edu/wp-content/uploads/2015/04/wellbeingreport_2014.pdf.

Hinsdale, Mary Jo. 2015. *Mutuality, Mystery, and Mentorship in Higher Education.* Rotterdam: Sense.

Hwang, Bong, Robert Bennett, and James Beauchemin. 2014. "International Students' Utilization of Counseling Services." *College Student Journal* 48 (3): 347–354.

Inman, Arpana G., and Michael E. Silverstein. 2003. "Dissertation Support Group: To Dissertate or Not Is the Question." *Journal of College Student Psychotherapy* 17 (3): 59–69.

Jalongo, Mary Renck, and Olivia N. Saracho. 2016. *Writing for Publication: Transitions and Tools that Support Scholars' Success.* New York: Springer.

Kelley, Martha J. M., and Jill D. Salisbury-Glennon. 2016. "The Role of Self-regulation in Doctoral Students' Status of All but Dissertation (ABD)." *Innovative Higher Education* 41 (1): 87–100.

Krause, Kathrin, and Alexandra M. Freund. 2016. "It's in the Means: Process Focus Helps against Procrastination in the Academic Context." *Motivation and Emotion* 40 (3): 422–437.

Lambert, Nathaniel M. 2014. *Publish and Prosper: A Strategy Guide for Students and Researchers.* New York: Routledge.

Lenz, Kathryn S. 1997. "Nontraditional-Aged Women and the Dissertation: A Case Study Approach." *New Directions for Higher Education* 99: 65–74.

Ma, Lai Ping Florence. 2019. "Academic Writing Support through Individual Consultations: EAL Doctoral Student Experiences and Evaluation." *Journal of Second Language Writing* 43: 72–79.

Marais, Gabriel A. B., Rebecca Shankland, Pascale Haag, Robin Fiault, and Bridget Juniper. 2018. "A Survey and a Positive Psychology Intervention on French PhD Student Well-being." *International Journal of Doctoral Studies* 3: 109–138.

Maul, June, Ronald Berman, and Cathrine Ames. 2018. "Exploring the Psychological Benefits of Using an Emerging Video Technology to Coach and Retain Doctoral Learners." *International Journal of Doctoral Studies* 13: 49–78.

Montgomery, Sonja, David H. Gregg, Cheryl L. Somers, Francesca Pernice-Duca, Alan Hoffman, and Marjorie Beeghly. 2017. "Intrapersonal Variables Associated with Academic Adjustment in United States College Students." *Current Psychology* 38 (1): 40–49.

Paltridge, Brian, and Linda Woodrow. 2012. "Thesis and Dissertation Writing: Moving Beyond the Text." In *Academic Writing in a Second or Foreign Language: Issues and Challenges Facing ESL/EFL Academic Writers in Higher Education Contexts*, edited by Ramona Tang, 88–104. London: Continuum Books.

Pauley, David. 2004. "Group Therapy for Dissertation-Writers: The Right Modality for a Struggling Population." *Journal of College Student Psychotherapy* 18 (4): 25–43.

Rice, Kenneth G., Greg J. Neimeyer, and Jennifer M. Taylor. 2011. "Efficacy of Coherence Therapy in the Treatment of Procrastination and Perfectionism." *Counseling Outcome Research and Evaluation* 2 (2): 126–136.

Russell-Pinson, Lisa, and M. Lynne Harris. 2019. "Anguish and Anxiety, Stress and Strain: Attending to Writers' Stress in the Dissertation Process." Special issue, *Journal of Second Language Writing* 43: 63–71.

Simpson, Steve. 2016. Conclusion to *Supporting Graduate Student Writers: Research, Curriculum, and Program Design*, edited by Steve Simpson, Nigel A. Caplan, Michelle Cox, and Talinn Phillips, 286–297. Ann Arbor: University of Michigan Press.

Sosin, Lisa S., and John Thomas. 2014. "Managing Stress and Burnout." In *Navigating the Doctoral Journey: A Handbook of Strategies for Success*, edited by Amanda J. Rockinson-Szapkiw and Lucinda S. Spaulding. Lanham, MD: Rowman & Littlefield.

Straforini, Carol Morrison. 2015. "Dissertation as Life Chapter: Managing Emotions, Relationships, and Time." *Journal of College Student Psychotherapy* 29 (4): 296–313.

Wang, Ting, and Linda Y. Li. 2011. "'Tell Me What To Do' vs. 'Guide Me Through It': Feedback Experiences of International Doctoral Students." *Active Learning in Higher Education* 12 (2): 101–112.

Wolters, Christopher A., Sungjun Won, and Maryam Hussain. 2017. "Examining the Relations of Time Management and Procrastination within a Model of Self-Regulated Learning." *Metacognition and Learning* 12 (3): 381–399.

Wynne, Craig, Yuh-Jen Guo, and Shu-Ching Wang. 2014. "Writing Anxiety Groups: A Creative Approach for Graduate Students." *Journal of Creativity in Mental Health* 9 (3): 366–379.

11
DISSERTATION BOOT CAMPS
Developing Self-Efficacy and Building Community

Rachael Cayley

INTRODUCTION

Over the last ten years, interest in writing boot camps for graduate students has been increasing. While there is a great deal of anecdotal enthusiasm for such boot camps, we are still in the early stages of understanding their value for graduate writers. Dissertation boot camps are generally thought to have originated at the University of Pennsylvania in 2005 (Mastroieni and Cheung 2011). In 2013, Sohui Lee and Chris Golde wrote about their experience launching a dissertation boot camp at Stanford in 2008; their analysis makes a useful distinction between a model that emphasizes writing product and one that emphasizes writing process. In the former, students are provided space, time, and accountability; the emphasis is often on meeting quantitative goals. In the latter, students are given space, time, and accountability, as well as the opportunity to learn more about the academic writing process and more about themselves as writers (Lee and Golde 2013). This process-oriented approach has proved influential, even as facilitators adapt it to suit the needs of their participants (Blake, Bracewell, and Stivers 2015; Powers 2014). The basic idea of creating a dissertation boot camp that emphasizes writing process is supported by a body of research that focuses on the complexity of becoming an academic writer and the particular challenges of dissertation writing (Aitchison and Lee 2006; Badenhorst and Guerin 2016; Caffarella and Barnett 2000; Cotterall 2011; Kamler and Thomson 2006; Micciche and Carr 2011; Paré, Starke-Meyerring, and McAlpine 2009; Rose and McClafferty 2001; Thomson and Kamler 2017).

In recent years, some work has been done to try to find evidence of the effectiveness of boot camps (Simpson 2013). Working on process-oriented boot camps, Gretchen Busl, Kara Donnelly, and Matthew Capdevielle (2015) have claimed that such boot camps can lead to "incremental but meaningful improvements in the beliefs and

DOI: 10.7330/9781607329589.c011

behaviours of graduate student writers." As part of a broader investigation in the life sciences, David Feldon, Soojeong Jeong, James Peugh, Josipa Roksa, Cathy Maahs-Fladung, Alok Shenoy, and Michael Oliva (2017) found that the use of boot camps and summer bridging projects showed no observable benefits in skill development, scholarly productivity, or academic socialization over time; these researchers did not look at the effects of boot camps on the actual writing of graduate students. The challenges in determining the impact of boot camps on the writing process are significant since to do so would require eliminating the wide range of variables that determine the graduate writing process. One way to respond to that difficulty is to pay close attention to self-reflective feedback from writers. That is, given the methodological challenges in determining whether writing boot camps have a measurable impact, I would like to stress the importance of listening to what writers themselves observe about their lived experience as writers in relation to these camps. In what follows, I focus on the reflections a group of graduate writers offered about their experience of a process-oriented boot camp by looking at questionnaire responses from four iterations of a dissertation boot camp. These questionnaires asked students to reflect on a range of topics related to their boot-camp experience, including writing time, group discussions, and writing instruction. Overall, these responses offer insights into the implications of having dedicated time to write with others in an atmosphere of growth; taken together, these questionnaire responses suggest boot camps may support graduate writers by encouraging a sense of self-efficacy and an awareness of the need for community.

QUESTIONNAIRES

The dissertation boot camps[1] in question were run between 2014 and 2016 at the University of Toronto, a large Canadian university with approximately eighteen thousand graduate students. These boot camps are offered by a center that supports graduate academic communication as a part of the School of Graduate Studies. Each boot camp is open to twenty doctoral writers, all of whom must be finished with coursework, data collection, and qualifying exams and fully engaged with the dissertation writing process. The boot camp runs from 9:00 a.m. until 4:00 p.m. for three consecutive days. Each morning starts with a one-hour presentation on some aspect of the writing process. On the first day, we discuss prewriting strategies such as using writing as a form of thinking and using various forms of outlining. On the second day, we examine productivity challenges; in this session, we speak broadly about the inherent tensions in a using a productivity framework for academic labor while also talking more concretely about strategies for managing complex work demands as a graduate student. On the final day, we turn our attention to the importance of revision and the way different aspects of a text demand different revision strategies. Once the formal presentation is complete each day, we have a two-hour writing block. After a one-hour lunch break, we then write for another hour before stopping for a group discussion. That discussion is a time for reflection on the boot camp itself, as well as a chance to ask questions about dissertation writing challenges. We resume writing at 3:00 p.m. for a final one-hour writing block. Students are welcome to continue writing past 4:00 if they wish; similarly, students are welcome to start writing prior to our morning discussion block. While everyone is required to write during writing blocks, participants are told they are welcome to write during the morning lectures or afternoon discussions if doing so would better serve their needs; most choose to follow the group schedule, but everyone has the flexibility to respect their own writing momentum.

The four iterations of the boot camp being discussed here had seventy-three participants from twenty-two disciplines; of those seventy-three, twelve were from the physical and life sciences and sixty-one were from the humanities and social sciences. After each boot camp was complete, each participant was emailed a voluntary questionnaire. From the possible seventy-three responses, I received forty-five questionnaires, which were then stored anonymously. This questionnaire was not designed to evaluate whether the boot camp itself was well executed; participants were given a separate anonymous evaluation form with which to assess the boot camp. Instead, the questionnaire was designed to encourage participants to reflect on what the experience meant for their ongoing writing process; while I was, of course, eager to read these responses, I also saw the process of reflection in the days following the boot camp as a crucial part of the overall process for them as writers. Since over a third did not respond, I am constrained from suggesting the following reflections apply to the entire group. However, they do allow me to comment on significant commonalities among the forty-five respondents. While there could be differences among the four sets of responses that correspond to the different dynamics of each boot camp, particularly as pertains to group discussion, I am going to treat the forty-five questionnaires as one set of responses for the purposes of this paper. Since I ran each boot camp, and since each camp was organized in the same fashion, the responses work as a single set of reactions to a particular writing experience.

QUESTIONNAIRE RESPONSES: REFLECTIONS ON FACILITATED WRITING

These boot camps are organized around a model of facilitated writing that combines three elements: opportunities to experiment with set periods of uninterrupted writing time; interaction with peers about writing; and writing instruction. In practice, this organization meant participants could take advantage of intensive writing sessions interspersed with opportunities for group discussion and formal writing instruction. Students were able to benefit from writing instruction while also having the opportunity to implement writing advice and tackle the isolation so many graduate writers encounter. Since this model explicitly relies on this combination of uninterrupted writing time, peer interaction, and writing instruction, I used those three categories when soliciting their responses.

As the following table shows, respondents were asked to reflect on the helpfulness of uninterrupted writing time, group discussion, writing in a group, and presentations on writing. The responses were not formally coded: a positive response was simply equated with a characterization of helpful (or a comparable adjective).[2] This informal approach was justified by the fact that I am more interested in their individual reflections than in establishing broad trends. The overall trends are given, but they are not being used to establish the value of these aspects of the boot camp; my interest here is in the way participants reflect on the boot camp as part of their broader lived experience as academic writers. In what follows, I provide participant responses that reflect common themes; given the personal nature of these reflections, each one represents a personal experience that also fits into a broader shared experience.

Dissertation Boot Camp Questionnaire Responses

Please reflect on how helpful the **uninterrupted writing time** was.
- **All 45 respondents** rated the uninterrupted writing time positively, with positivity being equated with a characterization as helpful (or a comparable adjective).

Please reflect on how helpful the **group discussions** were.
- **40 (of 45) respondents** rated the group discussions positively, with positivity being equated with a characterization as helpful (or a comparable adjective).
- **5 respondents** found the group discussions less helpful because topics were too familiar or too personal or because treatment of topics was too extensive.

How did you find the experience of **writing in a group**?
- **43 (of 45) respondents** rated writing in a group positively, with positivity being equated with a characterization as helpful (or a comparable adjective).
- **2 respondents** found the experience of writing in a group either irrelevant or distracting.

Please reflect on how helpful the **presentations on writing** were.
- **40 (of 45) respondents** rated the presentations on writing positively, with positivity being equated with a characterization of helpful (or a comparable adjective).
- **5 respondents** found the presentations on writing less helpful because topics were too familiar or the treatment of the topics was too extensive.

Note: Of 73 participants over four iterations of the dissertation boot camp, **45** responded to the questionnaire.

Uninterrupted Writing Time

At the simplest level, boot-camp participants enroll for the chance to have someone else ensure they devote significant time to writing. If nothing more, they should leave having written more than they otherwise would have. However, writing according to my preset schedule was a chance not just to write more but also for them to learn more about their own optimal writing practices. In order to elicit those sorts of reflections, I used two different prompts:

- Please reflect on how helpful the uninterrupted writing time was.
- What did you learn about yourself as a writer during the boot camp?

Unsurprisingly, everyone (n=45) rated the uninterrupted writing time positively. Since this was the one thing they all wanted and expected when they enrolled, this reaction is predictable. Of more interest are their further comments regarding how and why this dedicated writing time was so important. Overall, participants focused on three aspects of this uninterrupted writing time: the value of time constraints, the role of distractions, and the benefits of peer support.

Value of Time Constraints

Without a doubt, the most powerful concrete awareness that emerged from these questionnaire responses was the value of approaching writing with a finite time frame in mind.

> Having time dedicated to writing with no distractions was really important. But it was also equally important for me to realize how much I could achieve in a few uninterrupted hours. I had previously felt I needed full days, and only an hour or two was plenty productive.
>
> I couldn't believe how much I got accomplished and from that I learned a lot about what to expect from myself and the time I should allot to writing.
>
> The writing times were extremely productive. I couldn't believe how much I could accomplish in such a short writing period.

These participants, like many others, expressed great surprise that more writing time was not invariably better. My goal was not to pressure them into writing more in less time but rather to alert them to the hazards of believing writing can only happen in long stretches of time. I wanted them to see how much they could get done in shorter blocks of time of the sort we often find ourselves with, and I also wanted them to hear how paradoxically challenging long periods of writing can be for many writers. The prospect of writing for a full day often has two implications: on the one hand, we may feel anxious at the thought that we might fail to accomplish goals commensurate with that expanse of time; on the other hand, we may be able to justify too many interim periods of distraction. If we have all day, writing can feel less urgent. If this pattern of time use becomes habitual, it can mean the worst of both worlds: lots of time invested with little accomplished. Trying shorter and more regulated writing blocks showed many participants a different way to organize their scarce writing time.

Role of Distractions

A second common theme concerned the role of distractions and, more important, the way uninterrupted writing time showed participants how much interruption there may be in their usual writing time.

> I didn't realize how much of my everyday writing is interrupted until I actually went to boot camp and had to eliminate distractions. I didn't know how much of an effect it was having on my productivity.
>
> When left to my own devices there are just way too many easy excuses to put it off another hour, another day. Forced writing time was such a gift.
>
> This was immensely helpful because it is very difficult for me to impose these constraints by myself. I tend to start researching, answer emails, and perform other tasks during my writing time.
>
> This was very valuable. It helped me to understand my tendencies to interrupt my own writing.
>
> Very helpful, especially in light of discussions/lectures about preparing for writing and productivity (i.e., paying attention to goals and distractions—and working to refocus when distracted).

The key here is that participants were making concrete observations about distractions, becoming aware of their specific patterns of time use.

The ability to avoid those distractions was frequently attributed to the effect of externalized discipline.

> I found this to be very helpful. Even if I didn't "feel like writing," I had to so I actually wrote.
>
> The best part for me was that I couldn't stop writing when I reached the end of a paragraph or a sticky point in my thinking (as I might be inclined to do when writing by myself).
>
> Normally in writing, when I get "stuck," I move away from the work—with an aim to clear my mind. What I realized in this camp is that

> this is a strategy of procrastination. I need to sit with the difficult ideas and writing through them.
>
> This was, hands down, the most helpful part: the structured, uninterrupted, mandatory writing time. I can't imagine that this would have been as effective, however, without the discussion on writing in general—and I found it really helpful to focus our breaks around a conversation about writing.

This final comment suggests the importance of marrying protected writing time with reflections on writing; one of the key themes in my first-day presentation is the importance of staying with our writing when it gets hard and recognizing the procrastination patterns that often correspond to hitting those inevitable "sticky points." A commitment to writing through those difficulties increases our chances of coming to terms with the problem while also maintaining our writing productivity.

Benefits of Peer Support

Finally, the benefit of peer support was frequently mentioned in the context of uninterrupted writing time.

> This was the best part of boot camp for me. Having a room of "friendly strangers" was exactly the environment I needed to focus and feel like there was a community at the same time.
>
> Supremely important—arguably the most important part of the process. It was surprisingly rewarding and satisfactory to be working on this solitary endeavor in a room full of people also working on solitary endeavors. The frame and expectations were enough to keep me conscious of how I was spending each moment of the writing time.
>
> I found this component of the program very valuable. Upon registering for this course I was unsure if I would be able to focus in a group setting as I generally require silence when writing, but the experience of being in a room where everyone else was writing increased my productivity. This was a terrific surprise.
>
> This was the best part of boot camp for me: having a quiet and also motivating space to write and keep writing—accountability to not get distracted and turn to something else, and also a sense that the whole room was working towards a goal.

Not only did many find peer support to be the "best part"; for many, that realization was surprising. As is explored further in this chapter, the experiment of writing in a group often showed participants a new way to think about the role of sociability and accountability in our writing lives.

Writing Identity

Overall, the participants' appreciation for uninterrupted writing led to further insights related to time management, distraction, and accountability.

By having to write in the way mandated by the boot camp structure, students both met their short-term goal of getting writing done and gained self-awareness through being asked to adopt unfamiliar writing patterns. To help them solidify these insights, they were asked to reflect on what they had learned about themselves as writers. Many responses touched upon the idea, discussed above, that they could get more done in less time that they expected.

> The boot camp changed my expectations of myself: previously, I'd assumed that the most I could write in a day was about 1,000 words, and that it would take me all day to produce that. After the boot camp, I realized that I could write about 1,000 words in two hours—and that even if I didn't hit that word target, I could do most of the writing that I'd previously assumed was my "limit" within two hours of focused work.
>
> I learned that I can be a productive writer in a shorter period that I had thought I needed. I really like how each day was structured during the boot camp—2 hours of writing the morning, and two hours in the afternoon with breaks in between. I will try to set up this schedule at home.
>
> That I can write in small segments, and can be very productive during them too! It was good to see an entire paper come out in about 12 hours of work, without them being 12 consecutive hours where I then needed to recover from a writing hangover.

Since this notion can be counterintuitive—less time spent, more words written—writers may need to experience it for themselves. Having the opportunity to hear this principle and then immediately experiment with it increased the chance that they might see its relevance to their own writing practice.

In addition to this generally applicable insight about the benefits of finite writing times, participants also gave more personal insights. I quote a greater number of these responses since each one represents a unique reflection on a particular writing experience.

> That I am better with structure and specific goals. I learned that I don't love my own writing but that with better editing skills and approaches I am more likely to want to edit and reread what I've done.
>
> I like to write, so I resist writing poorly. I need to be more content to get thoughts on a page that are messy and awkwardly phrased—then go back and clean it up later.
>
> That I'm more social than I'd thought. As I contemplate getting back to work I find myself conjuring the bootcamp productive space, what that felt like—the sense of purpose, knowhow, and a kind of loosely-defined community—and feel motivated by that.
>
> That like push-ups writing is hard, and it is likely to be hard every time, but that is okay. For me the name boot camp helped me to link tactics I use in fitness boot camps to my writing practice, which is beyond helpful to me

as a writer. I tend to think that at some point writing would just get easier, yet I know that physical activity is always challenging. Making the comparisons between these two activities—physical and mental—was something that will continue to be formative from now on.

That I respond well to external pressure; that I work best in short bursts; that I don't have to "clear the decks" before starting to work; that I can write even without a firm outline or sense of what I'm going to say. I hope it will give me the confidence to write every day, for at least short periods, and not to listen so much to my self-doubt. I am hoping to make writing a habit rather than an occasional, stress- and deadline-induced occurrence!

It also made me realize that the other work I take on is, in some ways, a kind of procrastination. After this boot camp I thought to myself that I should quit a great deal of the other jobs I have that take me away from my dissertation.

I learned that the more I romanticize writing and productivity, the more difficult it is for me. The best thing I learned was to reserve time for my writing each day and get something written. Don't harp on it or be cruel to yourself about how it can improve because it is simply a first draft and it will improve. Boot camp taught me that the only way to work through writing problems is to actually write. Get something down, leave breadcrumbs for yourself to go back to. Take a walk if you need to—but writing is not optional.

The most interesting and helpful thing I realized is that my ability to write solid pages for my dissertation is remarkably consistent regardless of my mood, energy level, sense of flow, etc.

It has been helpful to show me that there are still ways I can experiment with productivity. Being part of a boot camp gave me the freedom to try a new structure.

While these reflections each represent a unique personality and set of writing circumstances, they are united in showing the benefit of altering your writing routine in a systematic way to allow new insights to emerge. Since I was making all the scheduling decisions for these three days, the participants were able to see what actually worked for them rather than assuming their habitual practice—however unsatisfactory—was the only possibility.

Peer Interaction

In these reflections on the writing process, we are starting to see that the role of other writers is a significant part of the boot camp experience. To learn more about their experience writing with others, I used two prompts:

- Please reflect on how helpful the group discussions were.
- How did you find the experience of writing among a group of other writers?

These two aspects of interaction are obviously distinct, so I discuss them in turn. The group discussion, elicited a largely positive response: most people (n=40) rated them positively. Before looking at these responses, it should be noted that participant reactions to group discussions—and to my formal presentations, which I discuss below—could be related to two things, both of which are difficult to capture here. By treating all forty-five participants as one group, I have lost the ability to see how specific group dynamics may have affected these responses; while that level of analysis might have been fruitful, it would also have required a significant degree of speculation about interpersonal dynamics. At a more practical level, responses about interruptions to writing time involve the contingent question about when participants wanted to be interrupted. Nonwriting time is essential in a boot camp, but there is no way of ensuring it falls at the right time for everyone. Some participants said they liked the afternoon discussion sessions in part because they needed a break, while others said they had wanted to keep writing. Similarly, some liked the morning presentations on writing as a way to warm up, while others wanted to get straight to writing. All of which is to say it is impossible to schedule the day in a way that works optimally for everyone; the participants are all making a trade-off between personal control and the potential benefits of externalized discipline. As much as possible, I encourage participants to write according to their own preferred rhythms; however, their reactions to group discussion and instructional breaks may still reflect their personalities and preferences.

Group Discussion

The positivity about group discussion times largely focused on the perspective gained from hearing about other writers' experiences and struggles. Evidently, hearing about the challenges faced by others was particularly potent.

> The validation of other people in other disciplines was surprisingly useful to my own mental health and desire to keep going with the dissertation.
>
> It is the whole misery loves company thing—I have been quite isolated from my department and it is nice to talk to other students about their experiences, share resources and feel connected again—this helps to give me the confidence to continue.
>
> Sharing a room with fellow dissertation writers was great: at some moments, I found it helpful to be reminded that all of these other people are also struggling with their dissertations; at others, I found it motivating to see so many other people moving forward—and their progress made me feel like I could move forward, too.

> I learned that many people struggle with their writing and that I am not alone so this took away a lot of the feelings of shame which I think can happen to many graduate students when you don't meet your own productivity goals.
>
> The sense of camaraderie and community of doing the boot camp together was very helpful. I found the communal aspect of boot camp not only to be helpful to my productivity during the boot camp but also helpful to my general mental health.

Similarly, learning about doctoral writing from a group of writers with widely divergent experiences also proved beneficial.

> Was helpful to actually reflect on writing and get the opinions of others. A lot of aspects that I didn't think might affect productivity were brought to light based on reflections that boot camp prompted.
>
> It's always helpful to hear about other people's struggles and success. It's not only validating but can give you some ideas for tweaking your own process.
>
> I appreciated the more informal style, and the opportunity to have open discussion with other students—this was a nice blend of expert advice and peer support. Groups provide all sorts of benefits—the shared agonies, challenges and encouragement that can only be offered by someone facing the same daunting task. Coming to the group provided a structure and accountability that we all valued, and a welcome change from the isolation so often experienced while writing.
>
> This created a community, which was beneficial. I liked hearing about other students' struggles, strategies and accomplishments. The whole thing never devolved into a pseudo-therapy session or self-help support group. The tone was just right—respectful, open, but focused on productivity.

Interestingly, it appeared some participants were more able to learn from others because the dynamic also included an honest sharing of challenges: the credibility of writing advice appeared to be enhanced by the acknowledgement of the persistent challenge of dissertation writing.

As mentioned above, five of the participants expressed some reservations about the discussion sessions.

> Some of the discussion topics weren't as relevant to me, though, as I am almost finished a full draft of the dissertation.
>
> Minimally helpful; it was nice to get a "socializing" break but I think the discussions lasted too long. [Writing in a group] was the best part! The silence, the "forced writing" kept me focused.
>
> At times, the personal reflections tended to stray and become a little too personal and therefore less relevant.
>
> I could have done without this. I found most people's problems either unrelated to the problem at hand, and advice from peers was a bit repetitive or I didn't agree with it. I loved [writing in a group]—the atmosphere

was very conducive to writing, as there was pressure from multiple angles: the authority figure in the room, peers who can see your screen, and guilt from myself. Simply witnessing other people writing made me feel like writing!

I found the afternoon sessions to disrupt my flow somewhat but did appreciate the opportunity to hear of the struggles others are facing. This made me feel less alone in the process of dissertation writing and had the added benefit of helping me see the strengths that I bring to my writing process.

We can see that discussions, while valuable to many, can also easily lose their relevance, especially if they are too extensive or too personal or if the material being discussed is too familiar.

Writing in a Group

While group discussions are always likely to leave some participants unsatisfied, the simple act of writing together in a group was rated highly: all but two respondents (n=43) rated it positively. As we saw in the discussion of uninterrupted writing time, most respondents enjoyed the accountability that came from writing in a group.

I found the environment very supportive. I felt I could stay focused but not that I was being evaluated or monitored by others in the group. The collective concentration was also very inspiring.

I found this created a very comfortable and inspiring environment for writing. When your own productivity/energy wanes, it's nice to look around the room and see other students writing well, and knowing that they too are working on their thesis. This helped to motivate me in a very gentle yet positive way.

It is helpful to see other people doing different versions of this hard project—I tend to feel like a very slow writer, so knowing that while some writing faster than me, others weren't, was very reassuring.

Surprisingly, I found the experience quietly supportive and motivating. I have avoided group writing sessions in the past, and this week has made me reconsider joining writing groups in my department/elsewhere on campus.

I found the social aspect to be motivating, but also not overwhelming, and I really liked the practice of writing with people who I knew were writing from very different disciplines and even at different states of their degree. It was relaxing in a sense to feel that we were all putting our heads down to write, but we didn't need to really discuss the content of our topics.

As these responses show, the group writing environment was largely seen as inspiring, motivating, and encouraging. At various points, respondents also remarked on being surprised by the motivating effect of writing in a collegial group; some credited this positive effect to the interdisciplinary dimension, which was seen to lessen the competitiveness that can, in some cases, hamper departmental community for graduate students. As mentioned above, not everyone was positive: one person said writing in a group made no appreciable difference and one person said the presence of others was distracting at times.

While I have separated writing in a group from group discussions, many respondents linked the two together.

> It made me more productive seeing everyone else working so hard. Hearing about the roadblocks that others face as well made me feel much better and that I'm not the only one having trouble.
>
> I didn't realize how important it would be to hear that other people also struggle with similar writing problems. Then you would give us advice to combat those problems so I went from not feeling alone to then feeling like I could overcome the writing obstacle we were discussing. Also being accountable to other people in the room was fabulous. Knowing that others weren't going to the Internet but were trying and writing made me focus more on my own work.
>
> Being in a group setting was energizing in that it addressed one of the challenges that I've often had with dissertation writing—solitude. It was also nice to know that there were other students on campus facing the same dissertation writing challenges.

I have included these responses that combine discussion and group writing because they emphasize that the different elements of boot camp can operate in concert to help support graduate writers. For some, writing together was enhanced by the opportunities for discussion: participants enjoyed writing in a group at least in part because the dynamics of the group discussions showed them the group was genuinely supportive.

Writing Instruction

The final element of the boot camp I wanted to understand concerned their reactions to the writing instruction component. In order to elicit those reflections, I used the following prompt:

- Please reflect on how helpful the presentations on writing were (pre-writing, productivity, revision).

Participants were generally happy with the time spent on writing instruction: all but five participants (n=40) rated it positively. Some of the positive responses mentioned particular topics such as metadiscourse, contribution and voice, and separating the writing process from the editing process.

> I also found the discussion about metadiscourse and voice as original contribution to be tremendously beneficial.
>
> Once we were told to clarify a writing goal for the day and had talked about the need for a "bad first draft" I began producing much more material. This writing had, surprisingly, more depth and focus than a great deal of my "edited" writing.
>
> If I can enact the strategy of not editing while I write I believe my writing will take me to new places and new ideas.
>
> The advice/information offered was super valuable. Some of it wasn't exactly new but said in a way that made me shift my thinking.
>
> This was all new to me, so I really appreciated these aspects. . . . I will likely consider going to more of the structured classes from the writing centre to get more of this content.
>
> Many of the tips/tricks and general guidelines for writing and editing were hugely useful for me.

The five people who expressed reservations found the time devoted to instruction too extensive or found the content too familiar.

> This was somewhat helpful, though most of it was a reminder for me and not new information.
>
> The topics that we discussed were interesting and helpful, but I felt anxious at the times that I wasn't getting to write.
>
> Honestly, sometimes I wrote through these, or let my mind wander. When I did pay attention, though, I recognized that many of the suggestions were helpful. . . . Some of the discussion topics weren't as relevant to me, though, as I am almost finished a full draft of the dissertation.

As with the group discussions, the timing of these elements made a difference: some wanted to start writing first thing without having my presentation happen first. There were no comments that suggested instructional time was not a good idea; the only hesitation seemed to come from those who were already familiar with the instructional materials being covered or who found the timing inappropriate for them.

For some writers, it appeared valuable to have instruction adjacent to time for writing. These writers seemed to appreciate writing instruction precisely because they were then able to apply those constructs or techniques.

> I appreciated that these were not discussions/lectures in isolation from the practice.
>
> I really appreciated this part of the boot camp. The morning discussions felt like a writing warm-up (without doing any actual writing). Even though the topics were general I felt as though I was being eased into the writing process and that was helpful.
>
> I like that the discussions felt like a break but that they also kept me thinking about writing—they definitely added to the immersive boot camp feeling of the whole process!

> The discussions were engaging and insightful. On a broader level, they were a nice way to help us maintain focus on the writing while also giving us a "break" from the actual writing.
>
> I really like the morning discussion on writing. It gets me to think about writing and sets me into a writing mood for the two-hour writing time. The strategies we discussed are quite helpful as well.
>
> These sessions helped to orient and prepare myself for the writing time in the morning. The strategies about how to get into the writing process were very helpful.

The connections made by participants among different elements of the boot camp reflect, in my view, the value of the way boot camps can combine protected writing time, peer interaction, and writing instruction. We have seen that peer learning is supported by authentic group interactions and that writing instruction is particularly valuable when there is an opportunity to experiment with new ideas.

Limitations

There are clear limitations to my analysis of these questionnaire responses. We have already seen that the lack of subdivision of the forty-five respondents into four distinct boot camps limits my ability to analyze group dynamics. Another source of limitation can be identified in the nature of the survey questions. Participants were asked to comment on how they experienced the existing elements ("How helpful was x?") rather than a more open-ended question that might have elicited reflections on ways the boot camp could have been different. Finally, since the boot camp offers a rare opportunity for writing time and writing support in an atmosphere of care, participants are likely to focus on positive reactions to the experience. However, if we treat the responses less as evaluation and more as reflection, I think we can still use them to learn more about the writing experiences of doctoral students.

SELF-EFFICACY AND COMMUNITY

As we consider these reflections on protected writing time, peer interaction, and writing instruction, we can see two overarching themes emerge: self-efficacy and community. These reflections suggest that a sense of self-efficacy as a writer can come from the practical experience of writing. Rather than simply hearing what they ought to be doing differently, students were given the opportunity to learn things about themselves as writers: that they are capable of writing a great deal in a short time; that they can be at their desk first thing in the morning; that writing breaks are essential and do not have to devolve into procrastination; that struggling as a writer is a common byproduct of the inherent challenge of that undertaking rather than a sign of our inadequacy; and that writing amongst others can be a source of support and accountability. These insights seem consistent with writing advice we are all accustomed to hearing, but hearing advice—however sound it may be—does not necessarily lead us to action. In fact, writers often dismiss possible solutions to their very real problems as implausible or wrong for them without trying them out. Writing together, in an atmosphere of both discipline and openness, while being exposed to new ideas about writing, may allow them to see what they can accomplish. In other words, the boot camp may lead to self-efficacy via self-awareness. If we force our way through all our writing projects, drawing our motivation primarily from immediate pressure, we may end up with a defended dissertation or the requisite number of publications but not necessarily with the self-awareness that allows us to understand and refine our writing process. Developing an explicit identity as a writer can be a sustainable way to tackle the ongoing demands of an academic writing practice (Beal 2014; Mewburn 2011; Thomson and Kamler 2016).

The second theme that emerged from the questionnaire responses is that a writing community could be a valuable goal for graduate writers. This view can be seen in the scholarly investigations into thesis writing groups (Aitchison 2009; Ferguson 2009; Maher, Seaton, McMullen, Fitzgerald, Otsuji, and Lee 2008; Phillips 2012). In the boot camp context, writing in a group and talking about the writing experience is a way to replace isolation and even shame with motivation. When we are caught up in feeling negative about ourselves and our writing process, the productivity of others can feel like a reproach; when we shift the dynamic towards honesty and humility, the productivity of others can feel like an inspiration. One participant used the phrase "misery loves company." In general, that expression signals an excess of negativity: miserable people getting together to talk about how miserable they are and taking some comfort from the knowledge that others are equally miserable. But because the boot camp involves an opportunity to contemplate why writing can be so difficult and to learn strategies for counteracting those challenges, as well as time to put these ideas into practice, the sharing of "misery" appears to become something more useful. In particular, the boot camp highlights the possibility of creating a writing community, a place in which shared experience undergirds accountability. By experimenting with an approach to writing that diverges from their usual practice, graduate writers can discover the value of a discussion-based writing community.

This suggestion that graduate writers could benefit from a sense of self-efficacy as writers and from involvement in a community of writers is based on the assumption that this constituency is in need of writing support. Graduate writers, however, are often treated as though they already ought to know how to write or as though they will learn to write as a natural by-product of their development as researchers. In other words, while the idea that academic writing is a complex activity replete with technical, emotional, and intellectual challenges is commonplace among those who work with such writers (Cameron, Nairn, and Higgins 2009; Starke-Meyerring, Paré, Sun, and Nazih El-Bezre 2014; Thomson and Kamler 2016), graduate writers themselves still often feel as though they are expected to possess skills that have not been consistently nurtured at an institutional level. Paying attention to the reflections these writers offer about themselves can help us demonstrate that graduate writers are actually in need of explicit attention to writing as an integral part of their academic training. The key here is to understand graduate writers as having meaningful lived experience *as writers*, experience that may be underemphasized by supervisors and students alike. The responses quoted here suggest the potential of this sort of boot camp to support the emergence of more confident and self-aware academic writers. An approach to writing support that emphasizes reflection on lived experience as a writer has the potential to help any graduate writer and most particularly those who feel least comfortably housed within the strictures of academia. If, for reasons of gender, ability, race, class, or linguistic background, a graduate writer feels a general sense of precarity vis-à-vis academia, the complex demands of becoming an academic writer are naturally more acute. A dissertation boot camp can be a valuable component of a broader program to support all graduate writers. More specifically, a boot camp that emphasizes a reflective writing community can be effective in countering persistent notions of individualized success and failure in graduate school. By making writing reflection a part of the writing process for graduate students, a boot camp can reveal that writing struggles are widespread and frequently grounded in complex systemic challenges.

Putting writing support in place to increase the chance that all graduate students thrive is a laudable goal, but it does require an understanding of what optimal writing support looks like (Simpson, Caplan, Cox, and Phillips 2016). In this paper, I have argued that a model of writing facilitation provided in a boot camp setting is one way to build self-efficacy and community; that is, students may see an improvement in their writing process because of the self-efficacy and sense of community that derive from protected writing time, group interaction, and writing instruction. Despite the limitations outlined above, hearing the way boot camp participants were able to frame their experience writing in a boot camp setting may be helpful to those designing graduate writing support initiatives of their own. Such initiatives are a crucial response to our growing awareness of the challenges of long completion times or outright attrition during the dissertation writing phase. The voices of boot camp participants themselves are a valuable contribution to the important conversation about how to provide meaningful writing support to graduate students. In the future, we may see research that can tease apart the complex factors that lead to writing efficacy in a way that will allow us to see the specific role played by opportunities for intensive group writing. At present, I am suggesting we can gain valuable insights by working with reflective responses from graduate writers themselves, responses that suggest graduate writers can benefit from a structured environment in which to learn about themselves as writers, to interact with a community of supportive peers, and to receive formal instruction about the academic writing process.

ACKNOWLEDGMENTS

I would like to thank the peer reviewers for their helpful comments on this chapter and the book editors for their enthusiastic commitment to this project. Running dissertation boot camps over the last four years has been inspiring. I'm so grateful to all the participants for their engagement; in particular, I'd like to thank those who took the time to respond to the questionnaires quoted in this chapter. When we introduced dissertation boot camps at the University of Toronto, we also introduced research article boot camps, which are run by my colleague Peter Grav. We worked closely in designing these writing camps, and I'm grateful to Peter for all his insights into graduate writing pedagogy. Last, I'd like to thank Talinn Phillips, Lisa Russell-Pinson, Sandra L. Tarabochia, and Megan Titus for helpful and enjoyable conversations about this chapter.

NOTES

1. Some may, of course, have reservations about using the term *boot camp* for these exercises in communal writing and support. I chose to do so for two reasons. When I offered my first boot camp in 2014, I felt the term *dissertation boot camp* was well-enough established to be able to withstand any militaristic echoes; I opted to stick with a name I thought would be recognizable to doctoral writers looking for an opportunity for intensive group writing. And while my boot camps have no

resemblance to the coercive-style discipline of a military boot camp or the vocal boosterism of a fitness boot camp, I have found the name resonant in its open acknowledgment of the fact that writers may be seeking external motivation. Writing a dissertation is hard; offering a dissertation boot camp acknowledges those challenges and normalizes the desire for the externalized discipline of a supportive writing community.

2. Throughout, I treat a positive rating as equivalent to a characterization of the aspect of the boot camp as helpful (or a comparable adjective).

REFERENCES

Aitchison, Claire. 2009. "Writing Groups for Doctoral Education." *Studies in Higher Education* 34 (8): 905–916.

Aitchison, Claire, and Alison Lee. 2006. "Research Writing: Problems and Pedagogies." *Teaching in Higher Education* 11 (3): 265–278.

Badenhorst, Cecile, and Cally Guerin, eds. 2016. *Research Literacies and Writing Pedagogies for Masters and Doctoral Writers*. Leiden: Brill.

Beal, Heather K. Olson. 2014. "Authorial Identity A Graduate Student Odyssey." *Writing & Pedagogy* 6 (1): 31–58.

Blake, Brandy, Joy Bracewell, and Clint Stivers. 2015. "'Just Write?' . . . Not Quite: Writing 'Procedure' for STEM-Focused Dissertation Boot Camps." *Writing Lab Newsletter* 39 (9–10): 13–17.

Busl, Gretchen, Kara Lee Donnelly, and Matthew Capdevielle. 2015. "Camping in the Disciplines: Assessing the Effect of Writing Camps on Graduate Student Writers." In *Graduate Writing Across the Disciplines*, edited by Marilee Brooks-Gillies, Elena G. Garcia, Soo Hyon Kim, Katie Manthey, and Trixie Smith. Special issue, *Across the Disciplines* 12.

Caffarella, Rosemary S., and Bruce G. Barnett. 2000. "Teaching Doctoral Students to Become Scholarly Writers: The Importance of Giving and Receiving Critiques." *Studies in Higher Education* 25 (1): 39–52.

Cameron, Jenny, Karen Nairn, and Jane Higgins. 2009. "Demystifying Academic Writing: Reflections on Emotions, Know-How and Academic Identity." *Journal of Geography in Higher Education* 33 (2): 269–284.

Cotterall, Sara. 2011. "Doctoral Students Writing: Where's the Pedagogy?" *Teaching in Higher Education* 16 (4): 413–425.

Feldon, David F., Soojeong Jeong, James Peugh, Josipa Roksa, Cathy Maahs-Fladung, Alok Shenoy, and Michael Oliva. 2017. "Null Effects of Boot Camps and Short-Format Training for PhD Students in Life Sciences." *Proceedings of the National Academy of Sciences of the United States of America* 114 (37): 9854–9858.

Ferguson, Therese. 2009. "The 'Write' Skills and More: A Thesis Writing Group for Doctoral Students." *Journal of Geography in Higher Education* 33 (2): 285–297.

Huerta, Margarita, Patricia Goodson, Mina Beigi, and Dominique Chlup. 2016. "Graduate Students as Academic Writers: Writing Anxiety, Self-Efficacy and Emotional Intelligence." *Higher Education Research & Development* 36 (4): 716–729.

Kamler, Barbara, and Pat Thomson. 2006. *Helping Doctoral Students Write: Pedagogies for Supervision*. London: Routledge.

Lee, Sohui, and Chris Golde. 2013. "Completing the Dissertation and Beyond: Writing Centers and Dissertation Boot Camps." *Writing Lab Newsletter* 37 (7–8): 1–5.

Maher, Damian, Leonie Seaton, Cathi McMullen, Terry Fitzgerald, Emi Otsuji, and Alison Lee. 2008. "'Becoming and Being Writers': The Experiences of Doctoral Students in Writing Groups." *Studies in Continuing Education* 30 (3): 263–275.

Mastroieni, Anita, and DeAnna Cheung. 2011. "The Few, the Proud, the Finished: Dissertation Boot Camp as a Model for Doctoral Student Support." *NASPA: Excellence in Practice: A Knowledge Communities Publication*, 4–9. https://www.naspa.org/images/uploads/main/2011-NASPA-KC-Fall-Publication.pdf.

Mewburn, Inger. 2011. "Troubling Talk: Assembling the PhD Candidate." *Studies in Continuing Education* 33 (3): 321–332.

Micciche, Laura R., and Allison D. Carr. 2011. "Toward Graduate-Level Writing Instruction." *College Composition and Communication* 62 (3): 477–501.

Paré, Anthony, Doreen Starke-Meyerring, and Lynn McAlpine. 2009. "The Dissertation as Multi-Genre: Many Readers, Many Readings." In *Genre in a Changing World*, edited by Charles Bazerman, Adair Bonini, and Dbora Figueirido, 179–193. Fort Collins, CO: WAC Clearinghouse and Parlor.

Phillips, Talinn. 2012. "Graduate Writing Groups: Shaping Writing and Writers from Student to Scholar." *Praxis: A Writing Center Journal* 10 (1).

Powers, Elizabeth. 2014. "Dissercamp: Dissertation Boot Camp 'Lite.'" *Writing Lab Newsletter* 38 (5–6): 14.

Rose, Mike, and Karen A. McClafferty. 2001. "A Call for the Teaching of Writing in Graduate Education." *Educational Researcher* 30 (2): 27–33.

Simpson, Steve. 2013. "Building for Sustainability: Dissertation Boot Camps as a Nexus of Graduate Writing Support." *Praxis: A Writing Center Journal* 10 (2).

Simpson, Steve, Nigel A. Caplan, Michelle Cox, and Talinn Phillips, eds. 2016. *Supporting Graduate Writers: Research, Curriculum, and Program Design*. Ann Arbor: University of Michigan Press.

Starke-Meyerring, Doreen, Anthony Paré, King Yan Sun, and Nazih El-Bezre. 2014. "Probing Normalized Institutional Discourses about Writing: The Case of the Doctoral Thesis." *Journal of Academic Language and Learning* 8 (2): A13–27.

Thomson, Pat, and Barbara Kamler. 2016. *Detox Your Writing: Strategies for Doctoral Writers*. London: Routledge.

12
NOT JUST NUTS AND BOLTS
Building a Peer Review Framework for Academic Socialization

Anne Zanzucchi and Amy Fenstermaker

INTRODUCTION

Akin to many universities, our graduate program offers a nuts-and-bolts professionalization workshop series about how to be academically successful, with the degree program represented as a sequence of milestones—from seminar to dissertation. These nuts and bolts are essential to navigating a program structure and part of the fundamental procedural knowledge of the academy; however, developing as an independent scholar involves a complex and iterative social process that "in practice always involves the whole person" (Wenger 1998, 47; see also Tang and Andriamanalina, chap. 8 in this collection). This holistic social process begins with an advisor, who can be a powerful mentor for guiding field-specific communication strategies; paradoxically, however, faculty advisors who are most knowledgeable in a given field are often unpracticed in making conventions and common practices explicit to graduate students (Walker, Golde, Jones, Bueschel, and Hutchings 2008). In addition, graduate student academic needs are heterogeneous; they come with varying levels of preparation to engage in field-specific genres, conventions, and discourses (Casanave and Li 2008; see also Bommarito, chap. 9 in this collection). This heterogeneity of experience and preparation is no small matter, as graduate students must write to make their knowledge available to specialists and generalists, with publication as an increasing imperative for postgraduate employment (Lee and Aitchison 2008). Such academic acculturation issues contribute to high attrition rates of 50 percent on average; as emphasized in this collection's introduction, these rates are even higher for underrepresented graduate students whose persistence is markedly affected by academic integration opportunities, or a lack thereof (see, for example, Vaquera 2008). As a matter of equity, supplemental mentoring strategies are becoming more widely recognized as essential to

DOI: 10.7330/9781607329589.c012

graduate education and academic success (Walker et al. 2008; Aitchison 2014). Overall, given the importance of writing to graduate students' careers, their varying levels of preparation, and high attrition rates, we must develop a flexible and inclusive framework of mentoring, beyond just nuts-and-bolts advice. In response to this high-priority need, we developed a peer review workshop series and subsequently a semester-length course to support graduate writing processes and academic community building—which we offer here as a supplemental mentoring approach to dissertation development.

Overall, limited academic socialization is a contributing factor to what is an all-too-common graduate experience of alienation and isolation. Universities and academic programs must learn from and be responsive to graduate student needs, voices, and experiences—such that there is an iterative, reflexive exchange facilitated by the academic opportunities and communities we foster. In general, supplemental graduate writing support has been experimental in practice and emergent as a scholarly field (Simpson, Caplan, Cox, and Philips 2016). Our reimagining of academic and supplemental support has anticipated traditional institutional patterns and experimented with innovative partnerships between writing specialists and graduate programs. University of California, Merced, is relatively new (founded in 2005) and has been a dynamic context for graduate education and academic support, particularly for diverse student populations.[1] While this diversity profile is distinctive, it is also in step with how higher education's demographics are changing (Ennis, Rios-Vargas, and Albert 2011). What is often absent in these institutional profiles and demographic contexts is student voice, as emphasized in part 1 of this collection. Within our campus's distinctive profile, our project suggests that gendered expectations and disciplinary traditions do factor into access and persistence with supplemental support. In general, graduate students have limited academic literacy opportunities, particularly in STEM seminars, with a high overall need for supplemental practice.

Our peer review project supplemented students' advisory mentorship with a focus on supporting the cognitive and affective experiences associated with advanced academic writing. Through guided peer review of draft projects over time, the goals of both the workshop series and the course were to foster community around writing and model routine professional activities. In this way, learning became a participatory process in which work is individual and simultaneously socially determined (Lave and Wenger 1991); such opportunities for practice within academic communities are essential to progress and growth in learning and transforming the full range of academic writing norms. As a community-oriented learning activity, this guided peer review process engaged a full range of academic writing norms, from discourses to genres. These academic writing norms are actively engaged and negotiated through discussion among writers and peer reviewers regarding paper drafts. With a participatory approach to knowledge making, peer review communities can empower individual students, as well as engage discipline-specific understandings. By supporting inclusion within a robust framework for acquiring tacit knowledge about academic communication, peer review workshops have the potential to supplement traditional mentoring in powerful ways. Initial evidence, from student surveys, suggests these collaborative learning approaches mitigate the isolation characteristic of independent scholarship and foster equity in publishing outcomes.

THE IMPORTANCE AND POWER OF PEER REVIEW

For graduate students, participating in peer review and producing feedback contributes to the development of advanced writing skills, as this exchange constitutes the process by which expert knowledge—from fellowships to monographs—is produced, shared, and distributed. When we employ and model peer critique and collaboration in the teaching of writing, we socialize students to what we value in academia. However, acculturation is a complex activity involving a negotiation of prior experience and expectations. As Kenneth Bruffee (1993) notes, "Collaborative learning is a re-acculturation process that helps students become members of knowledge communities whose common property is different from the common property of the knowledge communities they already belong to" (3). Through this active negotiation of knowledge that occurs during peer feedback, graduate students are engaging an authentic process, as well as formulating an academic identity (Aitchinson 2014).

By focusing on a guided and peer-based forum for developing manuscripts, we created a social and academic space that supplemented the traditional apprentice model of dissertation development, which the introduction to this collection and Shannon Madden's 2018 Consortium on Graduate Communication keynote emphasize can be problematic and even oppressive. Further, consistent with a call for graduate student academic support to move from tactical solutions to systematic and situated strategies (Walker et al. 2008; Simpson, Caplan, Cox, and Phillips 2016), our comprehensive framework project expands mentorship and feedback loops to include informed peers. Peer review spaces create a participatory approach to knowledge making intended to empower individual students, as well as foster discipline-specific unity (Gardner 2008). As a result, sustained engagement with peer review models the knowledge-making process of writing through dialogue, critique, and response as "we construct and maintain knowledge not by examining the world but by negotiating with one another in communities of knowledgeable peers" (Bruffee 1993, 9). With this attention to co-creation of knowledge, collaborative learning was fundamental to the workshop and/or course experience, with peer and instructor feedback focused on the complexities and structures of knowledge production (Gordon 2006; Hass 2012). The dialogic and critical thinking processes of an ongoing peer review group present opportunities for "cognitive apprenticeship" (Maher 2014), with productivity as a potential outcome.

Our primary emphasis here is to explore how peer review facilitates academic socialization, particularly developing the ability to review projects as the basis for preparing publications. Fundamentally, giving feedback involves learning about writing conventions and revision (Lundstrom and Baker 2009). Because the peer feedback groups included a mixture of disciplines, graduate students were engaged in both learning the conventions of their disciplines and encountering those of other fields (Badenhorst, Moloney, Rosales, Dyer, and Linu 2015; Starke-Meyerring 2011). A feedback process also engages the social and cultural nature of genres and conventions, which is a crucial conceptual transition for advanced students (Brooks-Gillies, Garcia, Kim, Manthey, and Smith 2015; Micciche and Carr 2011). Often these genres and conventions go unexplained, as professors may assume they are transparent or that graduate students have previous preparation. The role of a writing specialist in a supplemental writing opportunity, such as a peer review-focused workshop or course, is to prompt conversation that gets writers to make tacit knowledge explicit—or even to encourage more seasoned graduate students to share their explicit knowledge with those less seasoned. Arguably, peer review is a powerful professional activity that can be leveraged as an authentic practice with development and refinement over time—particularly by providing feedback to a variety of writers.

Our project was initiated in stages, beginning with a noncredit workshop series (2011–2013) and continuing as a credit-bearing academic writing course (2014–2016). To participate in the workshop series, writers had to be working on a project for which they had an initial draft; nearly all the projects were technical papers, with variations like grant proposals and white papers (depending on field of study or publication plan). This prerequisite of a draft project tended to attract more doctoral candidacy-level students than entry-level graduate students; over time, we modified the call to encourage incoming graduate students to consider work from undergraduate or previous laboratory contexts (an approach that became popular and increased early participation). Identifying a reasonable baseline for participation was an important element in maintaining access goals and ensuring equity—particularly in a context in which graduate student preparation is highly variable. Peer review groups tended to be a combination of novice to advanced graduate writers within common intellectual areas, which led to formative discussions about progress to degree, professional and academic goals, and informal coping strategies.

In describing and tracing the development of the workshop series and course, we used student surveys to develop weekly schedules and specific goals for project development. Program activities included (1) identifying a desired academic style and structure based on existing literature, (2) providing substantial feedback to peers, attending to both local and global considerations, (3) judging and incorporating relevant feedback to improve drafts, and (4) submitting drafted writing for professional review. Shortly after participating in the series, a majority of students reported in the postproject survey (see appendix 12.B) a short-term plan to submit their project to intended venues and audiences beyond dissertation committees. While our project was not explicitly concerned with productivity, students reported having accelerated project completion and gaining some confidence about submitting projects to publishing venues. This pathway is particularly significant given that STEM graduate students were least likely to be assigned writing in their early coursework.

WHAT DID WE LEARN FROM THE STUDENT SURVEY DATA AND FACULTY INTERVIEWS?

A significant portion of the university's graduate population participated in our peer review programs. When the first version of this program was initiated, the university's total graduate population was around 350, and we have since doubled in total enrollment. Over the course of these projects, we tracked completion rates to determine persistence levels. About 15 percent of the total graduate population completed the noncredit workshops or the credit-bearing course, and 40 percent of those who participated in the workshops or course had advanced to candidacy (when they participated).[2]

We gathered periodic survey data in both the workshop series and course, with narrative responses and quantitative patterns. A pre- and postsurvey was administered in all iterations of this graduate writing support project, in part to identify preparation and also to summarize outcomes and ongoing needs (for the preproject survey, see appendix 12.A; for the postproject survey, see appendix 12.B). With our peer review project's focus on the social context and processes behind knowledge production and genre conventions, survey protocol was an important means to identify common goals and field-specific resources.

From surveys at the beginning of term, we learned from graduate students that little or no writing was assigned in entry-level graduate STEM courses at our campus. This finding is consistent with national graduate curriculum studies, which emphasize humanities students are more likely to write, and write in a variety of genres during seminars, whereas STEM students infrequently engage in writing as a seminar activity or outcome (Cooper and Bikowski 2007). Across disciplines, these variations in number of writing activities could impact preparation, academic acculturation, and engagement, which are elaborated in our project's persistence and retention data. It is worth underscoring, then, that graduate student writing preparation and behaviors are heterogeneous and often influenced by a disciplinary culture around writing.

These survey results provided a basis for outreach to faculty program leaders to discuss reading and writing opportunities in seminars; this outreach, which was conducted in the form of interviews, was part of a broader strategy to diversify and situate writing support within graduate program curricula. Our aim was to encourage faculty program leads, from across eight disciplines, to consider a comprehensive mix of reading and writing opportunities in graduate seminars with supplemental support activities, which necessitates an active partnership between writing specialists and graduate faculty. Several developments followed these discussions. As one example, many graduate programs require graduate students to attend guest-speaker events; a simple enhancement was to require a short reflection to summarize content and analyze the presentation style. These subtle updates to reflective and summative writing opportunities were particularly significant in STEM fields in which academic literacy activities tend to be infrequent.

These structured conversations with graduate faculty leaders proved to be crucial in developing and sustaining this project, particularly because they created space for needed dialogue between writing experts and STEM faculty. These interviews emphasized the question, What do you want your graduate students to know about writing? The goal of the question was to avoid a deficit focus on student writers and favor a constructive response around writing experiences and academic priorities (Badenhorst et al. 2015). Perhaps not surprisingly, the common response from faculty was a desire for students to "tell a research story" with their writing, which emphasizes awareness of audience, field-specific conventions, and genre parameters (Swales and Feak 2012). Overall, these structured conversations with faculty formed an informal and ongoing partnership with graduate groups, with an active negotiation about advanced reading and writing needs that not only shaped our project but also incrementally enhanced our graduate culture.

The following two sections describe the design and learning experiences in our workshop series and course formats, outlining significant experiences and outcomes.

NONCREDIT WORKSHOP SERIES

The following completion rates and survey data illustrate the benefits and challenges of the workshop design and informed a subsequent credit-bearing course proposal.

Entry and Completion Rates

Since this workshop series was noncredit and voluntary, we were interested in completion rates. Predominantly, entry enrollment was from STEM fields, with 80 percent of workshop participants representing science and engineering graduate programs. The 50 percent completion rate, when disaggregated, reveals variation by broad disciplines with engineering (25%), natural sciences (40%), and social sciences, humanities, and arts (78%).[3] Overall, then, STEM graduate students were most likely to participate but also least likely to complete the workshop series.

Nonnative-speaker-of-English (NNSE) and native-English-speaker (NES) participation was equal, with 50 percent self-identified NNSE and 50 percent NES. Both groups persisted equally well, and the curriculum was designed to benefit both language backgrounds. Equal interest was expressed by NNSE and NES students in language topics, with comparable interests in developing a writing process and engaging genre conventions. Generally, both groups reported in pre- and postsurveys the priority of developing an academic style and engaging in technical editing practices. Our syllabus design similarly reflected this emphasis on the norms and contexts for genres, with practice in writing and peer review processes.

Participant gender distribution was 50/50; however, it is notable that 85 percent of those who completed the workshop series were female. One possible explanation for this gender difference in persistence is discipline specific, as most of the female applicants were in social sciences and humanities disciplines and received consistent faculty support for participating in a noncredit writing workshop. Another possibility is that women are socialized to value group dynamics, such that the individual benefit of working in a group may have been initially more self-evident to this cohort than otherwise (Austin and Wulff 2004; Gardner 2008; Ongiti 2008). It may be gender socialization favors female persistence in collaborative opportunities, with further investigation needed.

Powerful Influences

These persistence patterns were subtly and yet powerfully influenced by faculty mentors. Over time and with experience, we found it was important to support graduate students in an active engagement with faculty advisors on expectations about writing development goals. Supportive faculty mentors tended to be seeking remediation such that a graduate student could quickly "fix" their writing and publish on short timelines. This pattern corresponds with Daniel Bommarito's claim in chapter 9 of this collection that graduate writing support may often focus on technical issues rather than adaptive challenges associated with the messy and unsettling process of developing a disciplinary identity. We noticed in our workshop series and course that faculty advisors tended to emphasize technical issues for nonnative speakers of English; this focus on technical issues had a noticeable deficit logic and narrow perspective on benefits to supplemental writing support (Casanave 2002; Curry 2016). A small subset of faculty advisors actively opposed graduate student participation in the workshop series, as activities apart from the laboratory were perceived as detracting from limited research time. Our communication strategies included early consultations with graduate student applicants, common talking points about supplemental writing support, a syllabus for circulation to graduate advisors, staff specialists, postdoctoral scholars and potential graduate applicants, and on occasion meeting briefly with faculty advisors as follow-up to make a personal connection and listen.

Continued Needs and Ongoing Benefits

At the start of the series, all participants completed an entry survey (see appendix 12.A). When asked what aspects of research writing were of highest priority for development, a majority of responses were (1) composing an introduction, (2) describing an approach (methodology) within the existing literature, and (3) employing a professional/academic voice or style. These responses were similar in the exit survey; however, those exit surveys also emphasized proofreading and editing as a high priority. Our survey data also echo the findings of an in-depth institutional doctoral survey and interviews by Paul Rogers, Terry Zawacki, and Sarah Baker (2016), in which students describe the sections of articles that are most difficult to write: (1) findings/analysis, (2) proposal, (3) discussion, (4) review of literature, (5) and description of approach and/or theories framing the study (58). While our survey categories are related but not directly aligned, it is worth noting that "describing an approach" in our survey fits with multiple areas in the Rogers, Zawacki, and Baker study. What we found in our survey was that students also prioritized academic style and editing; one possible reason for this priority was that our workshop instructors were TESOL certified, with an additional language specialist who routinely visited and offered special sessions. Overall, these elements and our survey data emphasize common rhetorical moves of academic writing, or what Swales (1990) refers to as "creating a research space." Tacit knowledge of this structure, as part of critical engagement with concepts, is a significant part of becoming an advanced academic writer.

Notably, in the presemester survey for the workshop series, in which graduate students documented time spent on literacy and collaborative activities, they consistently reported having very little experience with collaboration or peer review. Peer review experience was self-reported as very limited, with only 10 percent having engaged in a peer-based feedback loop within the past year, whether inside or outside a course. The myth of writing as a solitary activity seems to be a persistent one (Maher, Seaton, McMullen, Fitzgerald, Otsuji, and Lee 2008), such that the collaborative and social activity of the academy must be incentivized and modeled. Further, we have opportunity to not just combat isolation but also to address an academic trajectory—as graduate student writers are often in a process of learning the discourse conventions of their disciplines (Badenhorst et al. 2015; Starke-Meyerring 2011).

In the pre-semester survey, graduate students' summaries of frequency and time spent in dialogue with faculty dissertation advisors were mixed. About 60 percent reported having asked a faculty advisor to review drafts at least once annually. In a traditional apprentice model, one would expect a semester-by-semester basis for project management dialogue and draft review, so these data seem a bit surprising.

Apart from infrequent faculty-advisee contact, traditional "apprenticeship" models in academia may also limit intellectual scope and isolate graduate students from a larger community of potential peer and faculty mentors (Walker et al. 2008); this pattern is intensified if a student is nontraditional or underrepresented (Dorn and Papalewis 1997; Vaquera 2008). Given the high potential for intellectual isolation in graduate education, a sequenced, holistic plan to support advanced writing is imperative.

To give voice and thematic concepts to academic acculturation topics, we found narrative feedback from surveys to be informative and rich. The following are some emphases from this open commentary:

Planning and Progress. This process of collective learning (in particular, by providing feedback about each other's writing) and narrative feedback tended to value specific elements—including group work and reflective practice: "The [peer review] process made me delve into the paper I was writing more deeply. This allowed for progress to be made much faster than if I was not in the workshop. It also provided a step by step guide in putting down my ideas on a challenging topic." This student is noting the cognitive and affective aspects of gaining efficiency and familiarity with the writing process, with a mixture of fluency and confidence about addressing difficulties.

Collective Planning and Group Dynamics. Graduate students encountered and practiced what effective peer feedback is and how to give it, with anticipation of continued practice. The importance of the group work dynamics was emphasized: "The most important thing that I learned was how to go about editing work for others and how to work as a group. I feel the group dynamic was very important." Part of group dynamics is the language of negotiation (rather than directives and commands) in which group members engage in open dialogue with peers by responding with questions and suggestions. Part of the editing process noted here is based on a negotiation in explaining rhetorical choices and justifying approaches to an audience (Phillips 2012).

Facilitator Role and Expertise. A focus on building an adaptive and supportive environment was important to collaboration goals. As one respondent noted, the role of the instructor was "to lead discussions, provide feedback, and encourage participation." In a multidisciplinary writing group, facilitated by a writing instructor, academic communication strategies and goals need to be linked to models and considered through group response. Expertise, then, was distributed, with the facilitator asking questions like "How would your discipline do that?" and "What are we seeing in representative literature from our fields?" Such strategies helped reveal hidden conventions graduate students are struggling to learn and exposed subtle communication conventions across fields—encouraging students to view themselves as evolving practitioners.

Tacit knowledge of academia and discipline-specific communications is part of collaborative practice. Of particular importance is building networks and community around scholarly communication. Writing groups, with a peer review emphasis, heighten access to what appears to be the most shockingly underutilized of academic resources—other graduate students and faculty advisors (Simpson 2012). Comprehensive and effective graduate writing support programs address academic-acculturation needs and create pathways to encourage faculty and peer input on writing.

CREATING NEW FORMATS, FROM WORKSHOP SERIES TO SEMINAR COURSE

Our summer workshop series functioned much like writing center laboratories or noncredit courses. In some ways, the workshop series also served as a "rough draft" to developing a credit-bearing course, particularly for entry-level graduate writers. Participants in the noncredit workshop noted the amount of work required, and a common refrain in the survey comments mentioned how a credit-bearing course would recognize effort and resolve time investments. Further, a course might be more easily justified to a faculty mentor than supplemental support. Students who had fully participated in the workshop series all noted the value of developing credit-bearing course options as well, which motivated us to work with the School of Natural Sciences on a two-credit (eventually full-credit) graduate-level academic writing course. For our campus, a course-based approach had broad faculty and administrative support; however, it is not the only pathway to providing this kind of institutional recognition for writing support. Other models that create "credit" for workload might include a certificate resulting from a workshop series or learning community. Certificates are increasingly an incentive and reward for alternative projects in graduate education, conferring a new kind of prestige to academic support and professionalization activities. For our campus, however, a course-based model provided a balanced and sustainable option for broad graduate student involvement.

Planning and Course Design

Similar to the workshop series, the course design[4] featured drafted projects including a writing notebook, which involved documenting weekly reflections on science writing topics, an introduction to an anticipated research report, a background and significance statement, research summary presentations, and a short genre-specific final project. That final project could be a research statement, section of a technical report, fellowship letter of intent, or poster. Documenting weekly reflections on field-specific communication topics as notebook entries also established low-stakes practice with summary, analysis, and reflection. These notebook exercises were a distinctive feature of the course; it is worth emphasizing, then, the importance of written reflection as a kind of a rhetorical exercise that persuades others about academic identity and associated values (Newkirk 1997)—leaving open a creative opportunity for analysis and dialogue. In the course, notebook entries on readings and topics were part of group work activities and further bolstered the intellectual rationale and activity-based learning around collaboration.

Expansion points in the course, versus the workshop series, included more assigned readings from peer-reviewed journals for students to analyze as models of style and genre. In addition, the course materials included readings about publishing paradigms, with a librarian partnership for database introductions and dialogue about open-access publishing opportunities. Given students' various preparation levels, sustained contact with an instructional librarian supported database and file management, information literacy, scope of topic, and referencing tools. Emerging trends in academic research could be featured through partnerships with the library, providing a broader context and support for future faculty and professional goals.

Overall, the goal with the course design was to emphasize "research story" elements and related institutional or academic resources, with students having opportunity to analyze academic communications and propose field-specific projects. We found that engaging in regular reflections and drafting in short genre forms provided insight into immediate and future writing contexts. Campus survey data had already indicated graduate students were seeking sustained feedback on their writing. The course design, then, emphasized routine and sequenced short assignments to encourage practice and collaboration.

Opportunities

Our enrollment trends for the course were similar to the workshop series, with an equal distribution of NNSE and NES enrolled in the course. Most of the students enrolled during their second or third year, with a first draft of an anticipated publication prepared. Female and male students were also 50/50. Persistence was high and steady, with nearly no attrition from start to finish. Overall with the credit-bearing course, persistence was even and stable, with nearly 100 percent persistence and passing-grade rates.

The course model provided a significant opportunity for practice of academic skills and field-specific concepts, with an emphasis on drafting and review processes, analytical reading practices, and style activities. In the course, there was also opportunity to assign readings on related and common academic acculturation topics, including collaborative theory, peer review history and practice, and open-access publishing policies. At the conclusion of the course, the top three actual outcomes best supported by the current course design were nearly the same as the priorities the workshop participants had expressed in their entry surveys: (1) composing an introduction, (2) employing a scientific voice or style, and (3) editing and proofreading their own work. These priorities were similar to the ones in the workshop series pattern but with an even greater emphasis on language study. A majority of students also identified writing abstracts and annotations as a significant activity. Most student participants had written informal reading notes but had not yet practiced formal annotations for a bibliography; the process of learning to write condensed critical reading notes was a significant prewriting activity that engaged summary and analysis skills.

MOVING FORWARD

As graduate populations continue to diversify nationally, graduate education urgently needs a paradigm shift. Systematic writing support provides access to academic acculturation, which could be an important part of equity efforts in graduate education. Our approach was to focus on peer review, as it is both a high-impact feedback process and a professionalization opportunity. We found that within traditional apprenticeship structures, graduate students usually have few opportunities to review peers' writing or they may engage feedback processes with limited input from faculty advisors. However, such review activities are crucial to learning to engage academic discourse, genre conventions, and integrative thinking. Through such activities, graduate students and faculty can be the primary resource for writing support—as advanced writing constitutes and is constituted by the professional norms of an academic community.

The sustainability of writing support involves an interdisciplinary partnership between writing specialists and graduate-level disciplines at our institutions. Disrupting some boundaries between disciplines can be quite productive. Our faculty interview protocol, for example, was conducted not just to document data about writing activities and expectations; we also initiated a significant and ongoing conversation about graduate education with other faculty leaders, with some influence on the frequency and amount of writing and reading assigned in STEM courses. Ultimately, writing activities must be encouraged both inside and outside seminars to encourage practice and mentorship.

Supplemental writing support is part of what has been called an "interdisciplinary contact zone," where expertise can be represented, negotiated, and shared (Monty 2016). How space is configured matters towards fostering this integrative teaching-and-learning context, particularly to facilitate "a common interest that might connect and advance a variety of pedagogical and extracurricular experiments" (Hall 2011, 45). In the spirit of reimagining space arrangements to encourage interdisciplinary dialogue, we are developing a process for STEM faculty to reserve writing center space for office hours (what is being called "Massively Open Office Hours"). With instructional librarians, we have also offered consultation time with faculty to offer feedback on assignments for graduate seminars in an effort to encourage academic socialization—particularly in STEM fields with likely gaps in this curriculum.

Graduate students themselves are the most important and missing resource in access to writing support. Peer review facilitates socialization and can be leveraged in many formats to encourage academic acculturation and community around writing. Graduate students have diverse writing support needs, particularly students from historically underrepresented groups in STEM fields. Learning communities are a flexible format, provide sustained engagement with feedback and process, and set a necessary foundation to support the persistence, retention, and success of all graduate students on their own terms.

ACKNOWLEDGMENTS

This graduate peer review project was supported by the Fund for the Improvement of Post-Secondary Education grant, from a special opportunity call for Hispanic-serving institutions. We are appreciative of our graduate student participants who were part of providing feedback on this initiative and our faculty and specialist involvement with Derek Merrill, Paul Gibbons, and Belinda Braunstein. The reviewers of this book chapter took care and provided insight to inspire significant thinking and revision; we are grateful to them for their intellectual generosity and thoughtful commentary. Finally, we thank the book collection editors for taking the time to provide online writing forums and to share related research and bring authors together in continued dialogue and thinking about equity within graduate education. We learned a great deal from this process and value the communal editorial philosophy.

NOTES

1. Our graduate population is nearly three times the national postbaccalaureate Hispanic representation, with 16 percent Hispanic locally and 6 percent Hispanic as national average (National Center for Education Statistics 2010). Also, our campus is among the few research universities nationally to be Hispanic-serving (Hispanic Association of Colleges & Universities 2013). UCM is one of five research universities within 238 total Hispanic-serving institutions.
2. At a certain scale, it is worth considering the indirect effects of support projects, too, with the emergence of study and writing groups—independent of formal interventions. Support of informal collaboration can be crucial to sustaining some practices, including small efforts like "writing cafes" and other social events to maintain dialogue, promote resources, and foster community.
3. Our project had only two teams from the social sciences, humanities, and arts; those who participated had a high degree of mentor support, with faculty input parallel to the peer review process.
4. To access the course syllabus, see SNS 270: Academic Writing as part of the Consortium on Graduate Communication site at https://www.gradconsortium.org/resources/courses-and-syllabi/.

REFERENCES

Aitchison, Claire. 2014. "Learning from Multiple Voices: Feedback and Authority in Doctoral Writing Groups." In *Writing Groups for Doctoral Education and Beyond: Innovations in Practice and Theory*, edited by Claire Aitchison and Cally Guerin, 51–64. New York: Routledge.

Austin, Ann, and Donald Wulff. 2004. *Paths to the Professoriate: Strategies for Enriching the Preparation of Future Faculty*. San Francisco: Jossey-Bass.

Badenhorst, Cecile, Cecilia Moloney, Janna Rosales, Jennifer Dyer, and Ru Linu. 2015. "Beyond Deficit: Graduate Student Research Writing Pedagogies." *Teaching in Higher Education* 20 (1): 1–11. doi: 10.1080/13562517.2014.945160.

Brooks-Gillies, Garcia Marilee, Kim Elena, Soo Hyon, Katie Manthey, and Trixie Smith. 2015. "Graduate Writing Across the Disciplines, Introduction." In *Graduate Writing Across the Disciplines*, edited by Marilee Brooks-Gillies, Elena Garcia, Soo Hyon Kim, Katie Manthey, and Trixie Smith. Special issue, *Across the Disciplines* 12. http://wac.colostate.edu/atd/graduate_wac/intro.cfm.

Bruffee, Kenneth A. 1993. *Collaborative Learning: Higher Education, Interdependence, and the Authority of Knowledge*. Baltimore: Johns Hopkins University Press.

Casanave, Christine Pearson. 2002. *Writing Games: Multicultural Case Studies of Academic Literacy Practices in Higher Education*. Mahwah, NJ: Lawrence Erlbaum.

Casanave, Christine Pearson, and Xiaoming Li, eds. 2008. *Learning the Literacy Practices of Graduate School: Insiders' Reflections on Academic Enculturation*. Ann Arbor: University of Michigan Press.

Cooper, Amy, and Daniel Bikowski. 2007. "Writing at the Graduate Level: What Tasks Do Professors Actually Require?" *Journal of English for Academic Purposes* 6 (3): 206–221.

Curry, Mary Jane. 2016. "More Than Language: Graduate Student Writing as 'Disciplinary Becoming.'" In *Supporting Graduate Student Writers: Research, Curriculum, and Program Design*, edited by Steve Simpson, Nigel A. Caplan, Michelle Cox, and Talinn Phillips, 78–98. Ann Arbor: University of Michigan Press.

Dorn, Shelly, and Rosemary Papalewis. 1997. "Improving Doctoral Student Retention." Paper presented at the annual meeting of the American Educational Research Association, Chicago, IL, March 24–28.

Ennis, Sharon, Merarys Rios-Vargas, and Nora Albert. 2011. *The Hispanic Population: 2010 Census*. US Census Bureau. http://www.census.gov/prod/cen2010/briefs/c2010br-04.pdf.

Gardner, Susan. 2008. "Fitting the Mold of Graduate School: A Qualitative Study of Socialization in Doctoral Education." *Innovative Higher Education* 33 (2): 125–138.

Gordon, Lewis. 2006. *Disciplinary Decadence: Living Thought in Trying Times*. New York: Routledge.

Hall, R. Mark. (2011). "Theory in/to Practice: Using Dialogic Reflection to Develop a Writing Center Community of Practice." *Writing Center Journal* 31 (1): 82–105.

Hass, Angela. 2012. "Race, Rhetoric and Technology: A Case Study of Decolonial Technical Communication Theory, Methodology, and Pedagogy." *Journal of Business and Technical Communication* 26 (3): 277–310.

Hispanic Association of Colleges and Universities. n.d. *Hispanic Serving Institute Directory*. Accessed July 2016. http://www.hacu.net/assnfe/companydirhiectory.asp.

Lave, Jean, and Etienne Wenger. 1991. *Situated Learning: Legitimate Peripheral Participation*. Cambridge: Cambridge University Press.

Lee, Alison, and Claire Aitchinson. 2008. "Writing for the Doctorate and Beyond." In *Changing Practices of Doctoral Education*, edited by David Boud and Alison Lee, 87–99. New York: Routledge.

Lundstrom, Kristi, and Wendy Baker. 2009. "To Give Is Better Than to Receive: The Benefits of Peer Review to the Reviewer's Own Writing." *Journal of Second Language Writing* 18: 30–43.

Madden, Shannon. 2018. "Pathways to Inclusion: Identity, Difference, and Institutional Innovation." Keynote at the Summer Institute of the Consortium on Graduate Communication, Ann Arbor, MI, June 10.

Maher, Damian, Leonie Seaton, Cathi McMullen, Terry Fitzgerald, Emi Otsuji, and Alison Lee. 2008. "'Becoming and Being Writers': the Experiences of Doctoral Students in Writing Groups." *Studies in Continuing Education* 30 (3): 263–275.

Maher, Michelle. 2014. "Transparent Transactions: When Doctoral Students and Their Supervisors Write Together." In *Writing Groups for Doctoral Education and Beyond: Innovations in Practice and Theory*, edited by Claire Aitchison and Cally Guerin, 82–93. New York: Routledge.

Micciche, Laura R., and Allison D. Carr. 2011. "Toward Graduate-Level Writing Instruction." *College Composition and Communication* 62 (3): 477–501.

Monty, Randall W. 2016. *The Writing Center as Cultural and Interdisciplinary Contact Zone*. New York: Palgrave Macmillan.

National Center for Education Statistics. n.d. "Fast Facts: Enrollment." Accessed October 2016. http://nces.ed.gov/fastfacts/display.asp?id=98.

Newkirk, Thomas. 1997. *The Performance of Self in Student Writing*. Portsmouth, NH: Heinemann.

Ongiti, Orpha. 2008. "The Impact of Policies and Practices on the Professional Socialization of Women in Doctor-Level Mathematical Sciences." PhD diss., State University of New York at Albany.

Phillips, Tallin. 2012. "Graduate Writing Groups: Shaping Writing and Writers from Student to Scholar." *Praxis: A Writing Center Journal* 10 (1). http://www.praxisuwc.com/phillips-101.

Rogers, Paul, Terry Meyers Zawacki, and Sarah Baker. "Uncovering Challenges and Pedagogical Complications in Dissertation Writing and Supervisory Practices: A Multimethod Study of Doctoral Students and Advisors." 2016. In *Supporting Graduate Student Writers: Research, Curriculum, and Program Design*, edited by Steve Simpson, Nigel Caplan, Michele Cox, and Tallin Philips, 52–77. Ann Arbor: University of Michigan Press.

Simpson, Steve. 2012. "The Problem of Graduate-Level Writing Support: Building a Cross-Campus Graduate Writing Initiative." *Writing Program Administration* 36 (1): 95–118.

Simpson, Steve, Nigel Caplan, Michele Cox, and Tallin Philips. 2016. *Supporting Graduate Student Writers: Research, Curriculum, and Program Design*. Ann Arbor: University of Michigan Press.

Starke-Meyerring, Doreen. 2011. "The Paradox of Writing in Doctoral Education: Student Experiences." In *Doctoral Education: Research-Based Strategies for Doctoral Students, Supervisors and Administrators*, edited by Lynn McAlpine and Cheryl Amundsen, 75–95. New York: Springer.

Swales, John. 1990. *Genre Analysis: English in Academic Writing and Research Settings*. Cambridge: Cambridge University Press.

Swales, John, and Christine Feak (2012). *Academic Writing for Graduate Students: Essential Tasks and Skills*. Ann Arbor: University of Michigan Press.

Vaquera, Gloria. 2008. "Testing Theories of Doctoral Student Persistence at a Hispanic Serving Institution." *Journal of College Student Retention: Research, Theory, and Practice* 9 (3): 283–305.

Walker, George, Chris Golde, Laura Jones, Andrea Conklin Bueschel, and Pat Hutchings. 2008. *The Formation of Scholars: Rethinking Doctoral Education*. San Francisco: Jossey-Bass.

Wenger, Etienne. 1998. *Communities of Practice: Learning, Meaning, and Identity*. Cambridge: Cambridge University Press.

APPENDIX 12.A

PREPROJECT SURVEY

Graduate School Level (please check all that apply):
[ ] Master's Program OR [ ] PhD Program [ ] Entry (Year 1)
[ ] Pre-PhD candidacy (prequalifier exam)
[ ] PhD Candidacy Graduate Program: _____

(1) What aspects of research writing do you need to develop? Please select the three of highest order of concern; conversely, draw a line through categories over which you feel mastery.

[ ] Interpreting grant calls or technical paper requirements

[ ] Composing an introduction

[ ] Describing an approach (or methodology) within the existing literature

[ ] Summarizing data

[ ] Proofreading/editing

[ ] Employing a professional/academic voice or style throughout the prose

[ ] Creating an abstract

The following questions are about the frequency with which you have engaged in professional development or writing activities. Please note that not at all = never; rarely = once in past few years; often = 1–2 times in past year; frequently 2+ times in past year

(2) How often have you participated in a peer review process in a graduate-level class?

Not at all / Rarely / Often / Frequently

(3) How often have you submitted an article or grant for consideration?

Not at all / Rarely / Often / Frequently

(4) How often do you attend professional conferences in your field?

Not at all / Rarely / Often / Frequently

(5) How often do you read professional journals in your field?

Not at all / Rarely / Often / Frequently

(6) How often have you contributed to a grant writing process?
Not at all / Rarely / Often / Frequently

(7) How often have you contributed to a manuscript writing process?
Not at all / Rarely / Often / Frequently

(8) How often do you ask a peer to review your writing?
Not at all / Rarely / Often / Frequently

(9) How often do you ask a faculty mentor to review your writing?
Not at all / Rarely / Often / Frequently

(10) In your prior experience, what has typically been most helpful to you with peer review feedback? Please provide specific examples.

(11) In your prior experience, what has typically been least helpful to you with peer review feedback? Please provide specific examples.

APPENDIX 12.B

POSTPROJECT SURVEY

Exit survey questions:
(1) Did you complete this course by attending a majority of workshop sessions and participating in our wiki site process? [Y/N]
(2) Which THREE aspects of research writing were best supported/developed in this series?

   [ ] Interpreting grant calls or technical paper requirements

   [ ] Composing an introduction

   [ ] Describing an approach (or methodology) within the existing literature

   [ ] Summarizing data

   [ ] Proofreading/editing

   [ ] Employing a professional/academic voice or style throughout prose

   [ ] Creating an abstract

(3) What has been the single most important skill you have learned from this workshop series/course?
(4) How would you describe the role of the instructor in your peer review process?
(5) How helpful was this peer review process towards the development of your current writing project?

   Very helpful / Helpful / Uncertain / Not helpful

(6) How interested would you be in repeating this workshop series?

   Very Interested / Interested / Uncertain / Not Interested

(7) What are your thoughts about this workshop series becoming a 2-unit semester-long course? Would that be useful and valuable to you and other graduate students?

NONCREDIT WORKSHOP SERIES, GRADUATE-LEVEL PEER REVIEW

Schedule and Intended Learning Outcomes (Summer 2012)
Course Description: Learning how to respond to peers' drafts has

several personal and professional benefits. Composition research demonstrates that students (at all levels) learn more about writing conventions and revision from giving feedback than from receiving feedback (Lundstrom and Baker, 2009). Beyond skill development, peer review is also consistent with current and future academic responsibilities for which one might serve as an external reviewer for grants or technical papers, provide feedback to a variety of audiences in teaching, or collaborate with colleagues. From this noncredit workshop series, you will be able to (1) identify a desired academic style and structure based on existing literature, (2) provide substantial feedback to peers, attending to both local and global considerations, (3) judge and incorporate relevant feedback to improve drafts, and (4) submit drafted writing for professional review.

Overview: The following schedule is intended to outline benchmarks for successful completion of this peer review workshop series. This schedule will adjust to reflect the needs of groups or scope of topics, so please regard this document as a roadmap that will evolve over time.

This project is grant funded, based on a Department of Education grant. If you have any questions about language or international student support, please contact the CRTE's English Language Institute Coordinator, Belinda Braunstein, at bbraunstein@ucmerced.edu or 228-4762; she is available to consult on activities and support as needed. Anne Zanzucchi, Associate Director of the Merritt Writing Program, is also available to respond to any general questions about writing curriculum or professional development opportunities; she can be reached at azanzucchi@ucmerced.edu or 228–4173.

Time Commitment: The design of this workshop series is to be equivalent to a two-unit course. Graduate student participants, then, are expected to dedicate at least four hours of preparation, peer review, and writing time to gain anticipated outcomes from this workshop series. This time allocation is for a drafted project, with an emphasis on developing it into a publishable form as a result of intensive feedback. If you choose to develop a project from its beginning, you will need to allocate additional time to compose a first draft.

Peer Review Responsibilities: Participants have several responsibilities that are outlined in the weekly schedule. You are expected (1) to attend weekly meetings with your peers and faculty member, (2) provide feedback to a partner's writing sample, and (3) review all group writing to prepare for weekly meetings.

Writing Projects: To successfully collaborate in a peer review format, participants should choose a writing sample that has a clear set of audience expectations, generic elements of a scientific research paper, and outcomes. To situate projects, we are suggesting a drafted project like a seminar paper, grant proposal, or technical paper.

Possible drafted work to revise and share with your peer review group might include completed dissertation chapters, grant proposals, seminar papers, technical papers, or articles. These current documents would be significantly revised and critiqued for publication, such as a seminar paper revised for a journal submission.

Open-session opportunities are built into the schedule to share other ongoing writing projects for feedback.* Because thesis and dissertation projects are specific to the expectations of a research faculty mentoring relationship, we will not formally include review of these projects. Please choose a writing project that is for external publication and review.

The research-writing process will be divided into predictable sections, including an abstract, introduction, methodology, results, and discussion/conclusion. The syllabus is organized around those stages of development, which are roughly parallel to technical papers, articles, and even conference presentations.

Project/Research Log: In addition to your weekly writing and peer review responsibilities, you will maintain a summary of key updates, questions, and learning processes. Entries should generally be 250–500 words and posted on our PBworks site two full days in advance of your weekly writing meetings.

Shared Worksite: Our collaborative workspace is PBworks, a free and privacy-enabled collaborative writing space. This site provides an infrastructure for archiving readings, drafts, and communications. In essence, PBworks provides a collaborative workspace that resembles a content management system. You will receive account information by email from your Merritt Writing Program faculty member.

Listed Readings: For participants to have a common understanding of foundational topics, some readings are listed for collective discussion at the beginning of the summer session. Your MWP faculty may suggest additional readings throughout the semester to support specific group dynamics.

Recommended Textbooks: These resources are comprehensive and recommendable writing guides.

Glasman-Deal, Hilary. (2010). *Science Research Writing for Non-Native Speakers of English.* London: Imperial College Press.

Hofmann, Angelika. (2009). *Scientific Writing and Communication: Papers, Proposals, and Presentations.* New York: Oxford University Press.

APPENDIX 12.B: POSTPROJECT SURVEY

Swales, John, and Christine Feak. (2004). *Academic Writing for Graduate Students, Second Edition: Essential Tasks and Skills* Ann Arbor: Michigan Series in English for Academic & Professional Purposes.

* We will primarily refer to Hofmann and can provide digital copies of chapters on PBworks under Resources.

SCHEDULE: The following schedule is intended to give us a shared sense of direction—however, it is also subject to change. <u>All postings are due two days in advance of weekly meeting to allow time for meaningful commentary.</u>

* We are currently scheduled to meet from * on * in KL 159 (Acorn Room).

Prior to Class

Activities	Preparation for Week 2
• Explore PBworks • Confirm fall semester writing project	(1) Writing Response 1: Summarize (1) what you anticipate contributing to the peer review process and (2) what you hope to learn from your peers and lead faculty (2) Email your rough draft (in whatever state!) to your lead instructor and upload to PBworks "Drafts" folder, under your name. (3) Select an article (possibly from your bibliography) that exemplifies "good" writing or benchmarks. Upload to "Drafts," too.

Week 1 of June 18

Week 1 Activities	Preparation for Week 2
• Complete survey • Confirm writing partners • Discuss useful feedback strategies • Review tech questions	(1) Research Log, Entry 1: Summarize (1) what you anticipate contributing to the peer review process and (2) what you hope to learn from your peers and lead faculty (2) Read Hofmann "The Abstract" (312–325) (3) Draft and post an abstract of your "good" writing example to "Drafts" folder in PBworks

Week 2 of June 25

Week 2 Activities	Preparation for Week 3
• Model feedback loop	(1) Research Log, Entry 2: Based on the posted example and class discussion, how would you define good academic writing? How does this example reflect your writing goals, particularly style and structure? (2) Review and comment on partner's posted abstract (3) Prepare and post Introduction in "Drafts" folder for peer review (4) Read Hofmann "The Introduction" (221–242) (5) Read your partner's introduction section and post a comment

Week of July 2 — Holiday Break

Week 3 of July 9

Week 3 Activities	Preparation for Week 4
• Review introductions function and purpose	(1) Research Log, Entry 3: Summarize the feedback you have received on your introduction (in class and online). Does the feedback connect to aspects of the reading? What feedback was most instructive and why? Next steps? What are your ongoing questions about this section? (2) Prepare and post to PBworks your Materials and Methods section (3) Read "Materials and Methods Section" (247–259)

Week 4 of July 16

Week 4 Activities	Preparation for Week 5
• Review materials and methods function and purpose	(1) Read your partner's methodology section and post a comment

Week 5 of July 23 — Materials and Methods, continued

Week 6 of July 30 — Results, Narrative

Week 7 of August 6 — Results, Figures and Graphs

Week 8 of August 13

Sending article or grant to agency, final considerations about audience expectations

Review PBworks writing portfolio, discuss progress

Complete final survey

13
PLAYING WITH THEORY IN GRADUATE WRITING GROUPS

Rochelle Rodrigo and Julia Romberger

INTRODUCTION

Much scholarship about supporting graduate student writers focuses on using writing groups (e.g., Aitchison and Lee 2006; Garcia, hee Eum, and Watt 2013; Parker 2009) and/or learning communities (e.g., Kiley 2009; McKenna 2016) to produce graduate-level writing. There is also often a focus on facilitating language learning for academic writing in English (e.g., Rafoth 2015; Swales and Feak 1994; Tardy 2009). A smaller segment focuses on graduate students' need to be aware of very discipline-specific genres (e.g., Delyser 2003; Sundstrom 2014). What we address here is a guided approach to a specific writing problem—how graduate students learn to use theory to develop methodologies for what is often interdisciplinary research one particular theory or method does not necessarily support. The use of theory has potential to be a stumbling block for students, as justifying theoretical backings for methodology is a complex task that needs much nuancing to work well. Therefore, more than a rhetorical analysis and application of a genre is needed for articulation. Theoretical framing in most dissertation work informs choices in methods and epistemological alignments within competing lines of argument in a field. Because of this, understanding how theory is to be integrated into the dissertation is a crucial first step affecting the entire scholarly approach. We argue that prompting graduate students to playfully work through theoretical concepts in low-stakes writing group environments provides scaffolding to both learning specific theories and learning how and why to use theory for their scholarship. We have seen guided writing-to-learn activities with feedback to more productive thinking about how theory operates in their work.

WRITING GROUPS AND COMMUNITIES OF PRACTICE

Writing groups have become a means of assisting graduate student writers to acclimate to the writing of new genres and supporting the practices needed to do so. Talinn Phillips (2012) argues for graduate student writing groups as a cogent strategy for graduate writers to learn about entering their community of practice based upon Jean Lave and Etienne Wenger's (1991) "legitimate peripheral participation," or learning to become part of a community of practice through doing work with others who are in a similar position. Learning to be a member of a community of practice by engaging in a variety of activities that provide exposure to discourse and documents ties to Elizabeth Wardle's (2009) observations about the need to learn genre in context from writers actively engaged with the genres. This learning is not always an easy process. As Hye Yeong Kim (2011) notes, international students in particular struggle to become part of the community of practice as scholars because of the sociocultural differences their diversity presents. Such "communities of practice may often be invisible for them because of their linguistic, sociocultural and historical differences." Additionally, "organizations of access in the educational system may not be in favor of international students" (283). As discussed in the introduction to this collection, it can be argued that problems encountered by first-generation college students are similar to ones encountered by international students. The authors believe that, at times, explicit instruction or guidance for such writing tasks during the course of peripheral participation can be beneficial and may be necessary when writers wrestle with understanding the often unshared invention work, the process of marshaling thoughts and existing studies in order to develop lines of argument and new information—work necessitated by the process of connecting theory to research questions and then turning theory(s) into methods for the dissertation. Invention work is of use to every graduate student writer regardless of sociocultural background, but this work is not susceptible to traditional rhetorical analysis that allows for engaging with genre conventions. The approach we detail, which relies more upon guided use of various invention[1] strategies, can be leveraged in a writing group that crosses disciplinary lines, where each writer may approach the actual integrating of the theory into their dissertation work slightly differently, depending upon disciplinary expectations.

The guided exercises we outline here were developed to foster a language of negotiation and feedback, also a critical piece of group cohesion (Phillips 2012, 2). Graduate student writers need to know they are all grappling with some aspect of the dissertation process, reinforcing the all-in-it-together nature of a writing group. These types of exercises also encourage mutual accountability (Wenger 1999, 81) and lead toward identity building as the person moves from the periphery to full membership (Phillips 2012, 1; Wenger 1999, 100), which can be extremely valuable to students who might not be from a more traditional graduate student population as they work to situate themselves in the academy. And yet this type of work is low stakes. There are no grades attached, failure is often as illuminating as success, and any accountability is to their fellow writing group members and the group facilitator.

Writing groups that have guidance in the form of some direct instruction are not unheard of. Generally, dissertation boot camps have been used to assist graduate student writers for some time. In "Camping in the Disciplines: Assessing the Effect of Writing Camps on Graduate Student Writers," Gretchen Busl, Kara Lee Donnelly, and Matthew Capdevielle (2015) report on a student who attended two separate dissertation boot camps, one of which had writing process instruction as integral part of the camp. Facilitation of this sort, should the writing group be associated with a writing center or part of a course, can be the site of not only discussion on writing process but also for exercises designed to help students interrogate and reflect upon the role of theory in their dissertation project. Such exercises, as we discuss here, are more targeted toward addressing this particular piece of the dissertating process, the use of theory, that many students struggle with rather than providing more general writing guidance about process. However, we believe that for the reasons we listed above, this piece of the dissertation process is critical because the decisions made within it have significant impact on the entire dissertation project.

LEARNING HOW TO USE THEORY

The lack of support for the work of integrating and using theory can be problematic, as this understanding is a key to becoming an independent scholar. Based on a qualitative study's results in which doctoral students near completion were interviewed, Susan Mowbray and Christine Halse (2010) theorized that "the purpose of the PhD [is] the acquisition of an interrelated suite of intellectual virtues" (662), specifically practical, cognitive, and technical (referring to research processes) skills. They concluded that "the acquisition of cognitive skills (the capacity to perceive and know) involved developing their knowledge and understanding and accumulating skills in generating and applying new knowledge, *theories* [emphasis added] and concepts" (660). Margaret Kiley's

(2009) research identified theory as one of several threshold concepts for doctoral-level researchers. More important, understanding "theory as underpinning research and being an outcome of research" (299) was a critical threshold concept. While discussing how and why films can function as scholarly, even theoretical, texts, John Jackson (2014) argues that both scholarship and theory are already artistic and require craftsmanship; in other words, invoking theory and writing theory are difficult and require intellectual engagement and finesse. Many other scholars also mention the challenge of theory while discussing the mentoring and support of graduate students (Kamler and Thomson 2014). Beyond the commonly discussed approaches of working collaboratively and/or in communities, Kiley's 2009 list of strategies designed to help doctoral students work through these threshold concepts, like theory, includes active pedagogies like concept maps and "little assignments on writing" (300). The transparent pedagogy strategies we discuss below are similar in nature and function to Kiley's. They make explicit various types of scholarly work that happen implicitly during the course of many academic projects.

Wardle's (2009) scholarship about "mutt genres" explains why it is difficult to prepare students for writing in the disciplines (WID) considering the variety of expectations required to enter into and move past legitimate peripheral participation in the discourse. Wardle reminds us that "recent findings about the nature of genre suggest that genres are context-specific and complex and cannot be meaningfully mimicked outside their naturally occurring rhetorical situations and exigencies" (767). She discusses how neither first-year composition instructors nor their undergraduate students are engaged within the rhetorical scenarios of other disciplines to better explicitly participate within a specific disciplinary genre. Instructors, mentors, and writing tutors working with graduate students, however, are in a better place to support writing-in-the-disciplines work because the graduate student is already engaged within specific disciplinary activities as part of their education, including opportunities for legitimate peripheral participation. They have been exposed to the common genres in use and discourse expectations even if they have not written within them quite yet. That does not mean these graduate students do not need support processing and then communicating their ideas within these conventions that are still relatively new to them, especially if they are dealing with issues of standard-English use within the academy or different cultural-discourse conventions. This is why a focus on various parts of the writing process within writing groups can be helpful.

A valuable intervention comes from a staple of writing-across-the-curriculum (WAC) pedagogy—low-stakes writing-to-learn activities. These are used to both incorporate more writing into a nonwriting focused course and scaffold the production of larger writing projects such as those graduate students engage with (Herrington 1981; International Network of WAC Programs and CCCC Executive Committee 2014; McLeod and Soven 2000). As they are learning the discourse conventions of their disciplines, graduate students working on large projects like dissertations or theses can benefit from guided use of writing-to-learn activities or invention activities such as those listed here and others mentioned in the writing-across-the-curriculum and writing-in-the-disciplines scholarship. If graduate students are struggling to enter into their community of practice, such activities from WID and WAC pedagogies, which often operate as invention work, can assist them in negotiating the discursive issues that arise. To facilitate this negotiation, writing groups that have invention and writing strategies built into them and are guided by facilitators can be useful.

The pedagogical approach that incorporates such invention strategies within a guided curriculum presented here we term *transparent learning*. We developed transparent-learning pedagogy for a class designed to tackle the issue of teaching how and why to use theory, a class we argue, given its approach and structure, was in fact a graduate writing group focused on invention and generative "sandbox" work. In the following, we discuss the pedagogical approach and theories that support it, the pedagogical practices, and student responses to the pedagogy. We conclude by arguing that adapting this structure for a humanities graduate student writing group can provide some useful scaffolding for integrating new understandings of theory and method into the development of the dissertation or thesis.

TRANSPARENT LEARNING

The transparent-learning strategy relies upon students developing the ability to see connections between theory and practice—praxis, bringing together theoretical and applied knowledges to create an informed practice. Our concept of transparent learning or, more properly, an open, safer space for students to make their learning processes visible, asks students individually to read and engage with an introduction to theoretical content (usually reading and taking notes) prior to synchronous class time; class meetings are spent discussing and working with/through the concepts. By requiring engagement with content prior to class and focusing on interacting with and using content within class, this approach is understood to be a flipped classroom. This flipped approach intentionally replicates the work students will do as independent scholars, reading and organizing their ideas outside a structured environment on their own, and hopefully encourages them to see the value in the long term of working with peers or peer writing groups for feedback and support on their various scholarly projects. Once in class, we not only used intentional learning activities that ask students to apply what they read, we explicitly ask students to take risks by working with tricky content and new materials and environments and then share the results with one another and us (and potentially the world). We ask that both faculty and students be transparent and open with one another about how and why they constructed meaning from the content and from their learning activities, and where they struggled both in conceptualizing the content and in applying it to projects. Seeing the struggles of the other graduate students, even those who may seem already well embedded in the community of practice, can assist students anxious about their own abilities to participate.

In other words, to help students learn and apply theory to create praxis, we challenge students to work through and collaborate on activities that allow them to generate their own understanding and learning. As opposed to a more top-down strategy of providing students with metacognitive frameworks to help them understand and learn complex concepts and theories, in transparent-learning activities we ask that students generate relationships with the content and prior knowledge and experience, as well as with the instructors and one another. This approach creates an emphasis on generative learning. Merlin Wittrock (1992) describes the generative-learning process as a relationship created among concepts, prior learning or experience, and new information, which is consonant with invention practices in the focus on creation of new knowledge as described by Janice Lauer (2004; see note 1) and is descriptive of the activities and approaches taken in transparent pedagogy.

Asking graduate students to develop and share their ideas as they grapple with complex concepts requires a safe environment. Kimberly Howard and Kindel Turner-Nash (2011) use the term "alimentar" to describe a graduate teaching and mentoring approach based in caring (30). *Alimentar* is a term that could easily be applied to a number of similar approaches, but the focus on safe environments is the same. Howard and Turner-Nash emphasize "supporting, fostering, nourishing, and nurturing" in the caring pedagogy (30). While describing graduate student communities most likely to foster deep learning and the crossing of threshold concepts, Sioux McKenna (2016) says the following criteria must be met:

1. develop supportive community,
2. encourage risk taking,
3. foster regular opportunities to articulate ideas, and
4. prompt "fortuitous encounters" with theories and concepts. (6–7)

Given the student-focused and safe nature of this pedagogical approach, we see it as something that can easily be repurposed within a graduate student writing group or a guided dissertation boot camp or used by faculty mentors. Activities were designed that stressed invention over polished work. Playing with theories, concepts, and application was supported even if through the process students learned they were trying to fit a square peg into a round hole. Sometimes theoretical and methodological applications fell apart for the students, in which case postmortems were conducted to assess the how and why and to better understand why other applications of theory might work instead. Failure bred understanding. In-class activities, several of which we share below, were presented as low-stakes assignments. Students were there; they had to participate. However, there were no negative implications for "wrong" answers. (Most of the time it was impossible for something to be blatantly wrong; more often there was a poor fit between the student's own research needs and frameworks and the theory.) The emphasis was on articulating possibilities that might then be shared and discussed through a variety of feedback mechanisms.

PEDAGOGICAL APPROACH AND EXAMPLE ACTIVITIES

In this section we discuss three transparent pedagogical strategies and the technologies that supported them. We believe these could be easily adapted for a graduate writing group where contending with the type of invention work we discuss previously is an issue. But certainly, this strategy need not be limited to just the type of invention work we mention above. Such approaches can be useful across aspects of the thesis- or dissertation-writing process.

Digital Note Taking

Writing reading notes, an activity that could take place outside of and supplement writing group work, permitted both exploration of content and connections to personal work. Students were required to submit multimodal reading notes on their blogs, all of which were linked to the course website. Students were asked to categorize and tag, explicitly mark the entries as part of their course materials, and point to specific concepts and content. Categorizing and tagging allowed students to build archives of their own and peers' engagement with the class readings for later use. Reading notes were required every week, and connections among class discussion, concepts, personal experiences, and course and personal outcomes were encouraged. The students were also required to link to other materials and supplement their reading notes with various media that could help them better conceptualize connections they were making to their projects. Students within the course found that reviewing others' reading notes could be reassuring (they were all in this together and had similar struggles), promoting group cohesion and providing them with diverse ideas and approaches.

Application and Sharing Activities
During class time, we generated a wide variety of activities connected to the readings that explicitly asked for connections to other theories and their projects. Each activity was designed to get students to engage with the theory in a nontraditional way. We asked them to design 3D representations of theoretical concepts for the kinesthetic and visual learners with both arts-and-crafts supplies and Chrome Builder—a digital Lego application. Jeanette Berman and Robyn Smyth (2015) claim using conceptual frameworks helps doctoral students better understand and articulate the new knowledge they are producing within their research. Student reaction was mixed but overall positive: "I struggled with [theory], and the Lego activity, but it ended up being really helpful to see people's representations of that. I definitely came out of that activity with a stronger theoretical understanding." Not all these guided strategies worked for all students, and it was clear there were preferences. The variety of approaches provided over the course of the semester exposed students to opportunities to use strategies that worked for them. And sometimes struggling with an approach was useful, too. As the writer above acknowledged, it was helpful to see what their peers were doing—this is why accountability to their peers and a safe environment are critical to making this guided experience work.

Additional activities included crafting hypertextually linked narratives of their learning in the class, timelines, and theory trees. The narratives acted as pieces that reflected upon what they were learning and how they were applying it while garnering feedback from their peers as they were constructing new knowledge. The timelines and theory trees provided two additional ways of seeing connections of both chronology and influence to the various theories used in class (and from elsewhere if students chose to include them). These types of invention approaches could work equally well for a literature review, in which students must make connections and understand the chronology of various scholarly works that inform their own research questions. Using visualization for invention work is not new. Martin Eppler (2006) lays out the advantages of four different types of graphic representations, including mind mapping and visual metaphors, in the course of learning, arguing that each approach has advantages when used in a complementary manner.

More specifically, such visualization strategies have been shown to help doctoral students while they are writing their dissertations. Based upon their study, Terry Barrett and Jennie Hussey (2015) share methods for how visualization strategies act "as a meta-cognitive tool that enables doctoral students to: depict their thinking, weave and map the different strands of a thesis together and highlight the significance of their concepts and arguments" (60). Specifically, they illustrate seven visualization methods encouraging "breakthroughs" in doctoral writing:

- An organizer of the links and threads of the thesis
- A trigger for discourse and peer feedback
- A vehicle for conceptual work
- A metaphor to express and share key concepts
- A trigger for professional development
- An aid for the viva [defense]
- Prompts for free-drawing and freewriting. (61)

Any one of these conceptualizing activities could benefit students in a writing group who are looking to make a variety of connections to enhance their own thinking or to engage with materials in a different way. The focus on articulating potential connections and their value and receiving feedback from peers provides students with alternate views and constructive questioning. This research bears out what we saw occurring in our students' coursework and later in their prospectus and dissertation writing.

Reflection Mind Maps

After each class, we required that students update individual mind maps they were keeping to document their networked learning. Students were asked to add at least three nodes and at least one connection to their course reflection mind maps. One student commented that the mind-map assignment "forced connections" and that it was "painful but useful and ultimately meaningful." This type of activity, forcing connections, also helped students envision the interrelationships among the various pieces of scholarship and their own learning.

The reflection mind maps were material examples of what Lynn McAlpine (2012) calls "intertextual networks," "historical, epistemological and methodological webs—among texts which 'spoke' to each other" (354). While discussing the importance of reading as a doctoral student, McAlpine claims "the goal in both reading and conversation is to create a network of key scholars and ideas pertinent to the thinking underlying the thesis, as well as academic thinking more broadly" (358). In visualizing the connections within the mind map, students were forced to consider connections more deeply and, perhaps, create connections that were not initially obvious but that had potential use value.

STUDENT RESPONSES

> *Transparency. I found it humbling, but in humility I found strength and courage to be open and vulnerable. The results were powerful and meaningful.*—Student response

For two separate sections of this course offering, we explicitly asked students to reflect on their learning. After grades were submitted, we asked students to complete IRB-approved consent forms to give us permission to share their responses. In both cases, a majority of the students agreed to participate in the qualitative study.[2]

Some students talked about how specific activities helped them engage with and better understand a specific theory. One student reflected,

> The Lego builder activity was very useful for me because I found it incredibly difficult at first and was actually completely stuck. I really didn't want to do it when we first did the activity and found myself panicking because I wasn't sure if I would be able to produce anything. Having to push beyond that initial feeling of discomfort and having to work through an idea in a new way, not only helped me deepen my understanding of the theory, but was a good lesson in empathy for the times I might be assigning activities that stretch my students like this and make them uncomfortable.

Others discussed how useful it was to make connections among the theories they were reading. Additional student comments include

- I enjoyed the theory tree that we did at the end. I found it helpful for capturing relationships between theories, something that, of course, the mind map did as well. I also found the 3D visualization a great way to get a grips on Castells. It did take me awhile because I had to thoroughly understand the chapter before figuring out how to conceptualize it, but I found it valuable and fun besides.

- I did not find any activities "very useful." However, those that asked for more uses of combinations of theories generally were deemed more useful than others.

A few more appreciated the transparent nature of the work and what they learned from working with others.

- I like being part of a learning community. I found blogging became more and more comfortable, and I came to like the fact that we were sharing our work in this way. I have also given my own blog link to a couple of colleagues that I thought might be interested in what I am doing in this course.
- Seeing how people used and approached the theories in their own case studies was enlightening because there were such different approaches.

However, no method is without its drawbacks, and the students were more than happy to share some of the negative aspects (especially the issue of never having enough time). In the survey administered after the class concluded, students were critical about specific assignments and learning-related issues. One of the biggest complaints students had about the precourse note-taking activity was the time it took. One student from the first course specifically commented,

> The amount of time it takes to be thorough. With some weeks having over a hundred pages of reading, it is difficult to encompass all the important things in the notes without writing the equivalent of a four page paper every week. Sometimes the visual format options get added superfluously just to be "visual" for the sake of being visual. Maybe that is more about me finding more relevant visuals, but it feels sometimes like just grabbing whatever content to meet the requirement. Mostly the notes are just a major task each week above the task of actually reading. Sometimes it feels like notes have to be done twice—once in the margins and in my notebook (old habits are hard to break) while reading then again for the blog.

A few students from the second cohort also commented on time. However, we were not alone in finding students might at first doubt and struggle with unfamiliar learning activities. Cecil Badenhorst, Cecilia Moloney, Janna Rosales, and Jennifer Dyer (2012, 2016) repeatedly found students might initially resist unfamiliar activities and, therefore, sometimes deem them not useful or too difficult.

Additionally, despite the fact that we were trying to make it a very low-stakes set of student-centric assignments, some graduate students put pressure on themselves that we didn't anticipate or encourage.

Having them publicly posted on a blog. Though this was a "sandbox" class where we could test out ideas, and though it's unlikely that many of my blog posts will be read, there is a difference between things posted in a class-only accessible environment versus posted on the web where anyone could access. There's an additional level of pressure for work shared in this way to be strong as a reflection of the writer to a potential outside audience. I just wish a lower stakes assignment like this didn't have that kind of pressure.

Although we were explicit about the how and why of the pedagogical choices, and students also acknowledged the benefit of time on task, everyone was brutally reminded of the time and dedication it takes to critically engage theoretical concepts and frameworks. Transparent pedagogy is an approach both risky and rewarding on multiple levels. Based on the qualitative data and experiences from the courses and activities described above, we feel such an approach helps produce praxis, thus encouraging a closing of the theory-practice divide.

CONCLUSION: APPLICATIONS

Our transparent pedagogical approach was developed in a graduate course that was ostensibly about theories of networks (which can make for easier visualizations); however, the rationale behind the development of the class stemmed from an observed issue with graduate student writing—the difficulty in articulating the use of theory in various scholarly projects, especially the dissertation. Faculty within our English-studies program realized students were not able to able to understand connections between theory and methods because they were not being provided the cognitive space in which to do the connective work; they were not being overtly told making such connections was something they needed to do. Rather, the expectations were implicit to the writing process. So, in many ways, this course operated as a formalized graduate writing group because students brought their research projects from technical writing, games studies, cultural studies, literature, writing center studies, and so on into the classroom and grappled together with "trying on" a variety of theoretical "fits" and methodological developments until coming up with particularized approaches that would inform their research questions. As the activities were sandbox activities, strategies aimed at producing invention work, with the parameters for success being individual engagement, allowing students to play with their ideas in what was essentially a formalized writing group, we believe they could readily be adopted by a writing group that has a facilitator and is organized around the writing process, as the fundamental nature of writing groups is transparent, invention focused, supportive, and generative, operating within a community of practice. The value of creating overt, guided access to the invention work behind scholarly decision-making, much like creating accessible websites, lies in the potential to create pedagogical practices beneficial for everyone—from traditional students to nontraditional adult learners to first-generation college students to international students.

NOTES

1. We argue that grappling with threshold concepts is invention work, and if this grappling is made explicit and placed within a community of practice where nearly everyone is doing similar work, it can better assist graduate students in their writing process. Invention, as Janice Lauer (2004) describes in her introduction to her work on the same, has historically been seen as strategic acts that provide the discourse with direction, multiple ideas, subject matter, arguments, insights or probable judgments, and understanding of the rhetorical situation. Such acts include initiating discourse, exploring alternatives, framing and testing judgments, interpreting texts, and analyzing audiences (3). Invention is a highly complex rhetorical concept, but fundamentally, it is various strategies employed to determine content, which at the graduate level include discerning theoretical applicability and value in chosen research questions. It also implies contending with questions regarding appropriate deployment of genre, which varies from discipline to discipline to different degrees, which complicates the learning of how to write in those disciplines.
2. This study was exempt from IRB Review.

ACKNOWLEDGMENTS

We would like to thank the reviewers and the editors for their fine guidance. And we would like to express gratitude to the students who participated in our Theories of Networks class in 2014 and 2016 for all their hard work and engagement in this challenging pedagogical approach. You are all awesome.

REFERENCES

Aitchison, Claire, and Alison Lee. 2006. "Research Writing: Problems and Pedagogies." *Teaching in Higher Education* 11 (3): 265–278.

Badenhorst, Cecile, Cecilia Moloney, Janna Rosales, and Jennifer Dyer. 2016. "Thinking Through Play: 'Visual' Approaches to Post/Graduate Research Writing." In *Research Literacies and Writing Pedagogies for Masters and Doctoral Writers*, edited by Cecile Badenhorst and Cally Guerin, 335–355. Leiden: Koninklijke Brill.

Barrett, Terry, and Jennie Hussey. 2015. "Overcoming Problems in Doctoral Writing through the Use of Visualisations: Telling our Stories." *Teaching in Higher Education* 20 (1): 48–63.

Berman, Jeanette, and Robyn Smyth. 2015. "Conceptual Frameworks in the Doctoral Research Process: A Pedagogical Model." *Innovations in Education and Teaching International* 52 (2):125–136.

Busl, Gretchen, Kara Lee Donnelly, and Matthew Capdevielle. 2015. "Camping in the Disciplines: Assessing the Effect of Writing Camps on Graduate Student Writers." In "Graduate Writing Across the Disciplines," edited by Marilee Brooks-Gillies, Elena G. Garcia, Soo Hyon Kim, Katie Manthey, and Trixie Smith. Special issue, *Across the Disciplines*. https://wac.colostate.edu/docs/atd/graduate/busletal2015.pdf.

Delyser, Dydia. 2003. "Teaching Graduate Students to Write: A Seminar for Thesis and Dissertation Writers." *Journal of Geography in Higher Education* 27 (2): 169–181.

Eppler, Martin J. 2006. "A Comparison between Concept Maps, Mind Maps, Conceptual Diagrams, and Visual Metaphors as Complementary Tools for Knowledge Construction and Sharing." *Information Visualization* 5 (3): 202–210.

Garcia, Elena, Seung hee Eum, and Lorna Watt. 2013. "Experiencing the Benefits of Difference within Multidisciplinary Graduate Writing Groups." In *Working with Faculty Writers*, edited by Anne Ellen Geller and Michele Eodice, 260–278. Logan: Utah State University Press.

Herrington, Anne J. 1981. "Writing to Learn: Writing across the Disciplines." *College English* 43 (4): 379–387.

Howard, Kimberly J., and Kindel Turner-Nash. 2011. "Alimentar: Theorizing Pedagogy, Curriculum, and Mentorship for Democratic Doctoral Education" *Equity & Excellence in Education* 44 (1): 22–39.

International Network of WAC Programs. 2014. "Statement of WAC Principles and Practices." WAC Clearinghouse. http://wac.colostate.edu/principles/statement.pdf.

Jackson, John L. 2014. "Theorizing Production/Producing Theory (Or, Why Filmmaking Really Could Count as Scholarship)." *Cultural Studies* 28 (4): 531–544.

Kamler, Barbara, and Pat Thomson. 2014. *Helping Doctoral Students Write: Pedagogies for Supervision*. 2nd ed. London: Routledge.

Kiley, Margaret. 2009. "Identifying Threshold Concepts and Proposing Strategies to Support Doctoral Candidates." *Innovations in Education and Teaching International* 46 (3): 293–304.

Kim, Hye Yeong. 2011. "International Graduate Students' Difficulties: Graduate Classes as a Community of Practices." *Teaching in Higher Education* 16 (3): 281–92.

Lave, Jean, and Etienne Wenger. 1991. *Situated Learning: Legitimate Peripheral Participation*. New York: Cambridge University Press.

Lauer, Janice M. 2004. *Invention in Rhetoric and Composition*. West Lafayette, IN: Parlor.

McAlpine, Lynn. 2012. "Shining a Light on Doctoral Reading: Implications for Doctoral Identities and Pedagogies." *Innovations in Education and Teaching International* 49 (4): 351–361.

McKenna, Sioux. 2016. "Crossing Conceptual Thresholds in Doctoral Communities." *Innovations in Education and Teaching International* 54 (5): 458–466. doi: 10.1080/14703297.2016.1155471.

McLeod, Susan H., and Margot Soven, eds. 2000. *Writing Across the Curriculum: A Guide to Developing Programs*. Fort Collins, CO: WAC Clearinghouse. Originally published in 1992 by SAGE.

Mowbray, Susan, and Christine Halse. 2010. "The Purpose of the PhD: Theorising the Skills Acquired by Students." *Higher Education Research & Development* 29 (6): 653–664.

Parker, Rachel. 2009. "A Learning Community Approach to Doctoral Education in the Social Sciences." *Teaching in Higher Education* 14 (1): 43–54.

Phillips, Talinn. 2012. "Graduate Student Writing Groups: Shaping Writing and Writers from Student to Scholar." *Praxis: A Writing Center Journal* 10 (1).

Rafoth, Ben. 2015. *Multilingual Writers and Writing Centers*. Logan: Utah State University Press.

Sundstrom, Christine Jensen. 2014. "The Graduate Writing Program at the University of Kansas: An Inter-Disciplinary, Rhetorical Genre-Based Approach to Developing Professional Identities." *Composition Forum* 29. compositionforum.com/issue/29/kansas.php.

Swales, John M., and Christine B. Feak. 1994. *Academic Writing for Graduate Students: Essential Tasks and Skills: A Course for Nonnative Speakers of English.* Ann Arbor: University of Michigan Press.

Tardy, Christine M. 2009. *Building Genre Knowledge.* West Lafayette, IN: Parlor.

Wardle, Elizabeth. 2009. "'Mutt Genres' and the Goal of FYC: Can We Help Students Write the Genres of the University?" *College Composition and Communication* 60 (4): 765–789.

Wenger, Etienne. 1999. *Communities of Practice: Learning, Meaning, and Identity.* 1st pbk. ed. Cambridge: Cambridge University Press.

Wittrock, Merlin. C. 1992. "Generative Learning Processes of the Brain." *Educational Psychologist* 27 (4): 531–541.

14

PLANNING, IMPLEMENTING, AND EVALUATING A CAMPUS-WIDE GRADUATE WRITING INITIATIVE AT AN URBAN MIDWESTERN UNIVERSITY

Jennifer Friend, Jennifer Salvo,
Michelle M. Paquette, Elizabeth Brown

INTRODUCTION

It all started with a group of people who were passionate about increasing support for graduate students' writing at the University of Missouri–Kansas City. Several staff members from the School of Graduate Studies, along with representatives from the University Libraries and the director of the Writing Studio formed an ad hoc graduate writing advisory group that engaged in a two-year planning process for a campus-wide graduate writing initiative. The purpose of the advisory group was to investigate graduate student and faculty experiences and needs relative to graduate writing and to research effective graduate writing supports at other institutions. This chapter discusses the needs-assessment processes and results that informed the development of the campus-wide Graduate Writing Initiative (GWI), as well as the early-stage implementation of this program. The authors conclude this chapter by sharing their diverse perspectives related to their roles and experiences with the GWI through the lenses of faculty member, librarian, graduate student, and administrator.

SETTING

The setting for this GWI was the University of Missouri–Kansas City (UMKC), a public university in the midwestern United States located in the urban core of a large metropolitan area. The graduate programs at UMKC involve more than 3,600 graduate students, or one-third of the overall student population, with 354 graduate faculty members. The institution has a strong commitment to serving the surrounding urban

DOI: 10.7330/9781607329589.c014

community, with a mission that includes leadership and expansion in the health sciences and in the visual and performing arts, collaboration with the community to address urban issues and education, and the development of a professional workforce in a vibrant learning environment. There are fifty-eight master's programs, an interdisciplinary PhD program involving more than twenty-six disciplines, five stand-alone PhD programs in fields such as nursing, psychology, and business, and more than twenty graduate certificate programs currently offered at the university.

BIRTH OF THE GRADUATE WRITING INITIATIVE: A CAMPUS PARTNERSHIP

The need for graduate student writing support was first identified during informal campus conversations with administrators and staff in the School of Graduate Studies. The assistant dean in the School of Education advanced faculty concerns regarding graduate students' writing skills that ranged from adhering to discipline-specific formatting guidelines to addressing writing organization and crafting a thorough literature review. A graduate advisor in the physics department shared that there was insufficient graduate student writing support for advanced scientific and technical writing. There were also concerns about incidents of plagiarism that appeared to be caused by a lack of understanding about writing conventions such as quotation and citation formatting. All these concerns echo a common theme found across universities: a clear need for, yet evident lack of, graduate student writing support (Caplan and Cox 2016, 22–47; Simpson 2012, 96–97).

The university offered writing center support; however, with a focus on undergraduate students, its resources and implementation were insufficient to meet the complex needs of the graduate student population. In order to support graduate writing, the writing center would need to collaborate with other campus entities. Steve Simpson (2012) attributes the "problem" of graduate writing support among writing centers to overtaxation with the work to support undergraduate writing and hesitation to implement strong efforts to engage the graduate student population (95). This problem, he argues, can be solved through collaborations among student services and academic units (97), which can foster dialogue about graduate writing and bring about new collaborations (108). Indeed, the most common models for graduate writing programs are based on cross-campus partnerships, which—depending on the school—might include writing centers, graduate school deans' offices, writing-across-the-curriculum programs, libraries, teaching-and-learning centers, language centers, and other departments (Brady and Singh-Corcoran 2016, 3; Simpson 2012, 97).

The Graduate Writing Initiative (GWI) at UMKC began as such a partnership—in this case with representatives from the School of Graduate Studies, the Writing Studio, and the University Libraries. The University Libraries and the Writing Studio already had a working relationship, as the Writing Studio has a satellite location inside the main library. There were avenues of potential collaboration, however, that the University Libraries and the Writing Studio had not yet explored. Elise Ferer (2012), in a study of collaborations between libraries and writing centers, identified several common types of partnerships, including designing instructional tools and cofacilitating workshops (552). As Ferer highlights, library and writing center collaborations make sense because of their overlapping goals and the strong ties between research and writing (544). The School of Graduate Studies was a powerful addition to this collaboration: it provided a focus on graduate student needs, a direct communication pathway to graduate students and faculty, and additional resources.

Having assembled into a motivated team, this core group could thus begin to address these grassroots conversations with faculty and administrators and investigate the problem with graduate writing support at the university. The group's goal was to determine graduate student needs for writing support unique to the university and use that information to engage further with campus partners to find solutions.

PLANNING AND LAUNCHING THE GRADUATE WRITING INITIATIVE
Phase 1: Data Collection

To assess the goals of a graduate writing initiative at the university, an ad hoc graduate writing advisory group was convened by the dean of the School of Graduate Studies. The group was comprised of two librarians, the Writing Studio director, an administrator and staff member from the School of Graduate Studies, and the coordinator of Undergraduate Writing Assessment. The advisory group began by collecting data in the form of online surveys and focus group sessions with graduate students and faculty. The surveys were developed and piloted with a small group of students and faculty by the advisory group during the summer 2013 semester, and changes were made based upon their input. During the fall 2013 semester, the dean of the graduate school sent an email invitation to all graduate students and graduate-faculty members to respond to online surveys focused on graduate student writing resources and needs across all graduate degree programs. There were responses from 537 graduate students (14% of graduate students) and 142 faculty members (40% of graduate faculty, including both master's and doctoral advisors). The majority of the graduate student survey respondents were in the early stages of their degree programs, with 75 percent in their first year of coursework and only 13 percent who had completed their comprehensive examinations.

After the advisory group conducted a preliminary analysis of survey results, seven focus groups took place during the spring 2014 semester to further explore graduate students' writing needs and available resources across campus. The responses to questions in a focus group may yield richer data because of the synergy that occurs among the focus group participants (Kamberelis and Dimitriadis 2008, 397). Focus group participants were selected through an email to all graduate faculty to seek volunteers and recommendations for student participants. Each one-hour focus group session was led by one or two members of the advisory group, with focus group sizes ranging from one to six participants.

There were four faculty focus groups: three groups consisted of advisors of master's and doctoral students, and one group included graduate faculty who taught in graduate programs but did not serve on thesis or dissertation committees. Three student focus groups were formed, which included one group of graduate students in their first semester in their programs, one group of students whose thesis or dissertation proposals had been approved (and were in the final writing stages), and one group of international graduate students. The advisory-group members served as co-facilitators who strived for every participant's voice to be heard. Everyone was encouraged to share their responses to the questions so one or two individuals did not dominate the group. Responses to questions were captured using a digital recording device and were later transcribed and reviewed by the advisory group.

Sample items for each of the five major findings from the student and faculty surveys are provided in appendix 14.A with the percentages of responses for these questions. Overall, findings from the student surveys indicated that across all programs and levels, graduate students were most interested in online tutorials and designated writing spaces to support their writing, followed by evening, weekday, and weekend workshops, as well as summer courses. International students who responded to the survey were more interested in weekend retreats or weekend workshops than other types of writing support. School of Education master's, educational specialist, and doctoral students typically work full time in schools, and these respondents were most interested in online tutorials, a designated writing space, and evening workshops. Nursing master's and doctoral students were enrolled in online programs, and these students were most interested in online tutorials, virtual writing groups, and a summer writing course. Overall, weekend retreats and evening workshops were more popular than eight- or sixteen-week writing courses for which students would have to enroll and pay tuition.

Focus group discussions with graduate students demonstrated a high level of interest in creating designated writing spaces on campus for graduate students to work without distractions. International students and students who were in the writing phase of their degree programs were interested in the opportunity to join peer writing groups. Students in the beginning semester of their programs and international students were most interested in utilizing online tutorials and attending writing workshops to explore topics that included (1) citation formatting requirements (i.e., APA, MLA, Chicago, Turabian), (2) writing a literature review, (3) preventing plagiarism, (4) how to write a thesis or dissertation proposal, and (5) editing/proofreading to avoid common errors in writing.

Faculty surveys and focus groups yielded another perspective. Regarding the optimal time frame for graduate writing support, the majority of faculty believed this support would be most beneficial at the start of graduate work (67 percent); however, several noted it would be better spread throughout the degree. Overall, faculty most strongly endorsed support in the form of an eight-week course, a summer course, evening workshops, or online tutorials. Issues raised by multiple faculty included the need for writing support to take into account discipline-specific conventions and to offer specific support for students for whom English is not their native language. Faculty in both the advisor and nonadvisor groups were interested in faculty development related to teaching writing, technical tools, and sample rubrics to assess writing. Faculty also expressed an interest in the development of an orientation to writing support for both students and faculty that would provide an introduction to available resources online and on campus.

Phase 2: Planning and Implementation

The ad hoc advisory group used the results from the surveys and focus groups to create a summative report with prioritized recommendations for a campus-wide graduate writing initiative. The first recommendation was to form a graduate writing advisory committee with diverse

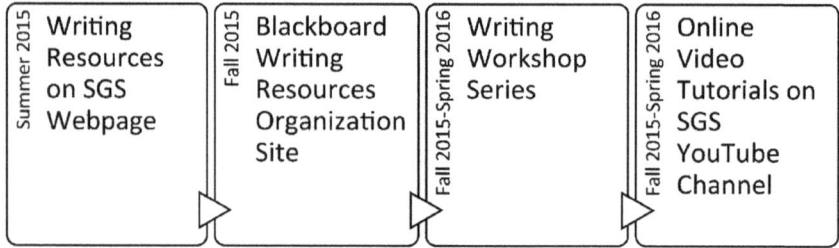

Figure 14.1. Year one of the Graduate Writing Initiative: Writing resources for graduate students

representation to plan, implement, and evaluate campus-wide activities associated with the GWI. The Graduate Writing Advisory Committee (GWAC) was assembled in spring 2015 and was comprised of diverse student and faculty representatives from a variety of graduate programs (e.g., nursing, business, education, physics), the School of Graduate Studies, University Libraries, the Writing Studio, Academic Assessment, Diversity and Inclusion, Services for Students with Disabilities, Online Education, and International Student Services. The GWAC began to roll out initiatives based on the advisory group report, with the goal of starting small and building on success. Four major resources were introduced in the first year: a "Graduate Writing Resources" web page, a Blackboard Writing Resources organization site, a series of online tutorials, and a series of writing workshops (fig. 14.1).

As a platform for the GWI, a "Graduate Writing Resources" web page was launched in the summer 2015 semester on the School of Graduate Studies website, with links to online and campus-based writing resources and development opportunities. Evaluation of the web page using Google Analytics showed this web page received approximately 150 page views per month, and 79 percent of these views were users who started with the writing page, then exited the SGS website. In addition to the web page, Blackboard, the university's content management system, was utilized to create an organization site titled Writing Resources for Graduate Students, in which all graduate students and graduate faculty members are automatically enrolled at the beginning of each semester (fig. 14.2). The site is collaboratively curated by GWAC members and continually updated with new content including links to writing resources and exemplars, video tutorials, content from writing workshops, library resources, and access to librarians. Blackboard Analytics provided data to examine usage of the site, which had more than two

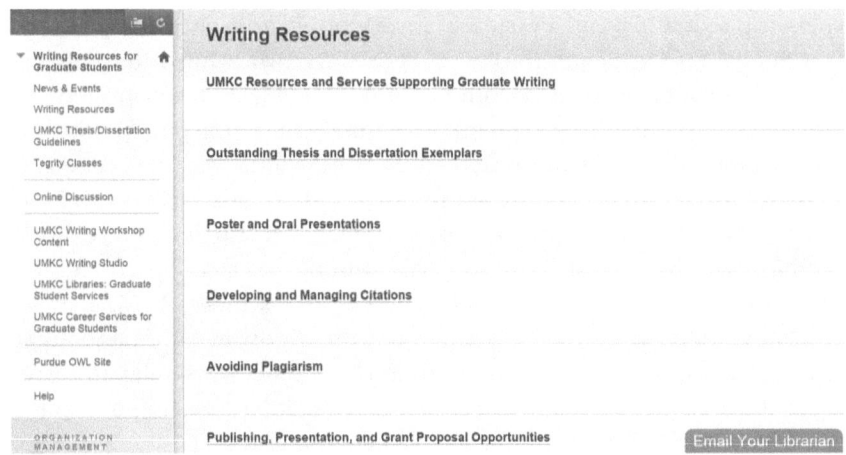

Figure 14.2. Blackboard organization for site Writing Resources for Graduate Students

thousand unique graduate student users and approximately one hundred graduate faculty users during the summer and fall 2015 semesters. Some of the most commonly accessed content included resources related to citation, attribution, and avoiding plagiarism, as well as Pivot research funding opportunities available for graduate student and faculty researchers.

Several online tutorials were created for the School of Graduate Studies' YouTube channel, accessible to the general public via the web. These tutorials included a series of short videos recorded by the dean of the School of Graduate Studies titled *Avoiding Plagiarism* and a two-part video series on thesis and dissertation formatting by the staff member in graduate studies who reviews these manuscripts as part of the university's format review prior to graduation. During the first three semesters of the GWI, the writing resource videos had more than 970 views, and future plans include adding to the library of short video tutorials.

One of the most highly requested resources by graduate students, a series of short writing workshops, most lasting one hour but some as long as three hours, was first implemented in the fall 2015 semester, with subsequent offerings of both repeat and new content in the following semesters. These workshops were facilitated on a volunteer basis by faculty members, librarians, writing specialists, and administrators and covered topics such as formatting theses and dissertations, writing for the humanities, writing for the sciences, proofreading tips and techniques, and grant writing. Each facilitator produced their own workshop materials, and a variety of instructional approaches were used. The School of Graduate Studies marketed the workshops to graduate students through email and other pathways such as flyers posted on campus and asking faculty members to make announcements during class sessions. Students interested in the workshops were not required to register ahead of time; the number of participants was not limited, and the GWAC made sure to reserve rooms and learning spaces with flexibility to adapt to a small or large number of participants. Long-term plans that will require additional resources include using these workshops as a jumping-off point for more rigorous short and long courses, as requested by graduate students and faculty, similar to those that have been developed in other successful graduate writing programs (Freeman 2016, 232; Starfield and Mort 2016, 243).

In the spring 2016 semester, the GWAC expanded opportunities for students to participate in workshops online through Blackboard Collaborate; the online availability of resources was an important consideration highlighted by many individuals in both the surveys and focus groups. In addition to synchronous online participation, most writing workshops were archived on the Blackboard Writing Resources organization site. Attendance at each of the 2015–2016 workshops varied depending on the topic; some workshops drew only a handful of students while one workshop drew approximately fifty students. It was typical, however, for eight to ten students to attend workshops in person, with approximately four students attending each synchronous online workshop. Students were asked to complete an evaluation form after each workshop, and the overall results on three Likert-scale questions demonstrated that students learned new information that was useful to them as graduate students. For example, 82 percent of workshop attendees in the first year of implementation responded to the evaluation question "Please rate your interest in attending future graduate student writing workshops" with a rating of "Highly Interested" or "Somewhat Interested." As one workshop facilitator and GWAC member stated,

> In their workshop evaluations, students remarked that they learned something new, that they were excited to try it out for themselves, and most frequently, they asked for more time and longer workshops so they could have more hands-on experiences with the instructor in the room.

Students' open-ended responses also shared a desire for more interaction between participants, opportunities to receive feedback on their writing, discipline-specific writing workshops, and additional writing workshop topics.

In 2016, the GWAC oversaw hiring a half-time graduate writing specialist, opening a new graduate writing space, and piloting graduate writing groups and write-ins. The new graduate writing specialist, with an MA in English and a strong writing center background, supported the graduate writing community through both facilitating programming and working directly with graduate students. The graduate writing specialist was funded through the SGS and reports to the Writing Studio director. She shared her first impressions of the GWI:

> Right away the commitment was clear—the hiring committee that interviewed me was diverse, with representation from the Writing Studio, School of Graduate Studies, Math, Physics, Career Services, and the student body. This diversity indicated the GWI's inclusion of all relevant voices in the conversation.

The graduate writing specialist took over as chairperson of the GWAC and has played a pivotal role in interfacing between it, the Writing Studio, the SGS, and other campus partners to continue to facilitate existing initiatives, as well as plan and implement new ones.

Two graduate workstations were opened in the spring 2016 semester. Because graduate workspaces were a high priority for the GWAC, steps were taken toward the implementation of this resource as soon as the advisory-group report was released; however, it took over a year until the official launch. The new workstations are housed within the Writing Studio and designated exclusively for graduate student use. They include desktop computers with dual monitor set-ups, printing capabilities, and specialized writing software. An online reservation system operates through the Writing Studio, and the usage of the workstations steadily increased during the second year of the GWI. The writing workstations have been described by students as providing a quiet and comfortable work environment.

A key program implemented by the graduate writing specialist in the second year of the GWI was writing groups. Research on writing groups and other graduate support systems demonstrates that organizing graduate students to help one another is one of the most important opportunities universities can offer (Simpson 2012, 111). In addition to supporting graduate students through writing skills development, there is a pronounced need to support their emotional health. Vincent Tinto (1993) suggests a correlation between the increasing isolation graduate students experience as they progress through doctoral programs and the waning of their persistence (231). Emily Klein, Megan Riordan, Amanda Schwartz, and Stacey Sotirhos (2009) assert that dissertation writers need support to overcome the isolation they experience and need to feel their faculty and their institution care about their success (130). This caring, the authors argue, is a crucial piece affecting student persistence. Dissertation writing groups can provide support and encouragement, foster community and identity building, and allow students to experience learning through discourse (Maher, Seaton, McMullen, Fitzgerald, Otsuji, and Lee 2008, 274). Graduate students who enter the thesis or dissertation writing stage of their careers may have not yet constructed an identity as a writer. A writing group can help expand a student's scholarly identity, both in the individual sense and in the revelation of a group identity (Maher et al. 2008, 274).

The GWI made an earlier attempt to organize writing groups via the Blackboard organization site in the fall 2015 semester. During this first trial, an online message board was created, where students could sign up for groups and self-organize. After following up with some of the small number of students who had signed up, the GWAC learned no groups had formed and concluded this outcome was likely due to the low number of participants, as well as a lack of structure. In a reflection on establishing doctoral writing groups, Damian Maher, Leonie Seaton, Cathi McMullen, Terry Fitzgerald, Emi Otsuji, and Alison Lee (2008) found that peer writing groups for doctoral students only formed after a faculty member sent out a call to students, and that students were hesitant to make a commitment when the groups still lacked protocols (266). This experience at UMKC further highlighted the importance of providing some structure for writing groups while still allowing members to determine their own goals and meeting times to meet their unique needs. Writing groups were thus piloted a second time in the summer of 2016 by the graduate writing specialist, this time with much better results. To increase awareness of the program, the dean of the School of Graduate Studies sent a direct invitation email to all graduate students, and within twenty-four hours there were thirty responses from interested students. The graduate writing specialist organized students into appropriate groups and attended initial and occasional follow-up meetings. The graduate writing specialist did not take charge of the groups but rather helped guide them by providing a loose structure and suggested guidelines such that the groups could develop their own goals and organization.

Of the six initial writing groups formed, the single online writing group did not gain traction, two were moderately successful, and three flourished, with members taking ownership of the group and its success. Writing groups organized during the following semester exhibited similar success rates. Some of the students who participated in writing groups shared positive feedback about their experiences:

- For me, the biggest "excuse" is not having a sizable amount of time. Just setting aside a couple of hours helps immensely!
- Do it! You get to decide the goals of your group, so commit to try it. You have nothing to lose. It has definitely added value to my graduate experience.
- It is helpful as a support, especially if your schedule involves a lot of unstructured writing time.
- Writing groups are very useful to learn more about your field, but also about yourself, if you are willing to share your work. . . . What might seem obvious to you in your research might not be to your reader(s) and this group allows you to see your work in perspective.

Moving forward, the graduate writing specialist is exploring ways to ensure both the highest success rate of groups and the sustainability of the program. She identified that the most time-consuming parts of the program were organizing the original groups and attending regular meetings. Thus, avenues for future exploration include developing more simple algorithms for group formation, as well as recruiting and coaching faculty or student leaders to take over the role of overseeing the groups.

Write-ins were also implemented during the second year of the GWI. These are day-long writing retreats, mainly held on Saturdays, that begin and end with some discussion of the writing process, available resources, and goal setting activities/reflections but are primarily focused on providing uninterrupted time and space for students to write. A writing tutor and librarian are available for consultations throughout the day. Advance registration is required to attend write-ins, which are limited to no more than twenty students due to space constraints and a limited budget for lunch and snacks. For prospective attendees exceeding the capped attendance, there is a wait list, and students are contacted when slots become available. To ensure attendance, students are asked to confirm their registration a few days before the event. Write-ins are one of the most popular GWI programs offered, often waitlisted and with repeat attendance. One master's student who attended several GWI activities stated, "I would say the most beneficial workshop for me has been the all-day write-ins, because I am forced to set goals for the day . . . and I have reached those goals within that day—that has given me a great sense of accomplishment." A work-study student who was hired to support the graduate writing specialist and attended the write-ins recalled, "Students came ready to write. The environment was very conducive . . . very calm, and there was a writing consultant and a librarian to help the graduate students with any question they had. All these resources in one place."

SELF-REFLECTIONS, DISCUSSION, AND RECOMMENDATIONS

The GWAC members bring diverse perspectives to the planning, implementing, and evaluation of GWI activities. The coauthors of this article engaged in self-reflection related to their roles and experiences with the GWI at UMKC using four guiding questions.

The first question was, *What motivated you to become involved with the GWI?* One research professor from the physics department was highly engaged with the GWI, serving as a member of the GWAC and facilitating a writing workshop each semester that focused on writing for the sciences. She shared the belief that

> one's productivity and success as a graduate student and subsequently as a professional scientist hinges on one's ability to write both effectively and productively. . . . My dedication to improving writing, combined with the clear lack of writing resources available to my students, motivated me to join the GWI.

In addition to the graduate students serving on the GWAC, the School of Graduate Studies created a half-time graduate student-assistant position with responsibilities that included communicating with graduate students and faculty through social media, emails, and the Blackboard organization site, in addition to supporting the logistics and evaluation process for the graduate writing workshops. The graduate student assistant shared the following reflection:

> As a graduate student I felt that I could bring a very important view to the table: the view of a graduate student. Because of the conversations that I have with my peers in my classes I have insight into what graduate students feel they themselves need to become better writers. I am in the classroom hearing what our instructors are teaching us about writing, so I can contribute that to the Graduate Writing Advisory Committee to help us to plan initiatives that would best serve the graduate student population.

One of the GWAC members served as the head of Graduate Student Services at the University Libraries, and she explained what brings her to this work.

> I have an interest in the process of graduate student research, information-seeking behavior, and information literacy. I also serve as the Head of Resource Sharing and manage interlibrary loan services at the university. Graduate students are the primary users of interlibrary loan, and it is a service graduate education cannot do without. I wanted to be involved with the Graduate Writing Initiative because I understand that the library plays a crucial role in graduate education and I wanted to be an advocate and contributing partner for graduate student success.

A second question asked, *What are some strengths and areas of need you have seen among graduate students relative to their writing?*

From the perspective of the university librarian, UMKC's graduate students are passionate about their fields of study and bring an enthusiasm to their research. "I most commonly see two significant needs among graduate students: (a) the need to broaden their use of scholarly research tools, particularly library databases and interlibrary loan, and (b) the need to learn how to effectively write a literature review."

The physics professor noted,

> One of the challenges to working with graduate students in the context of writing is the sheer diversity of their proficiency levels and areas of interest. Students with advanced skills may need some guidance on academic writing formats, as well as practice managing and structuring large writing projects and learning the traditions and vocabulary unique to their fields. Other students, however, struggle not only with these issues, but also more fundamental ones of grammar and establishing coherence, clarity, and flow. In a traditional graduate class setting, an instructor can progress from fundamental through advanced concepts with sufficient detail and breadth, ensuring that a majority of students can be brought up to the same level and walk away with a comprehensive understanding of the topic. However, a campus-wide GWI is generally limited to providing content in a more piece-meal fashion, and addressing the diversity of student interests and needs is much more difficult.

Indeed, a key challenge faced by the GWI at this university is to provide resources that support all students, across all skill levels and the various disciplines represented on campus, and to match students with the resources specific to their needs.

One special population of students, for example, is international students. Ting Wang and Linda Li (2008) observed that graduate faculty tend to provide feedback to these students that focuses on their English-language proficiency over the content of their writing, and that the students are often dissatisfied with this type of feedback (94). Many international graduate students struggle with writing confidence in a nonnative language, and there may be other cultural and educational background factors that affect their writing skills development (91). Wang and Li ultimately advocate for more understanding of international students' challenges and needs among faculty supervising thesis writers and for thesis supervisors to be clear and articulate in their expectations for theses (95). The GWI can take steps to better address the immediate needs of international students and to bridge the gap between them and their faculty advisors.

Not only do the needs of students differ dramatically from individual to individual, but the needs of a given individual differ over the course of their graduate career. Lucinda Covert-Vail and Scott Collard (2012) discuss the graduate student lifecycle as one that moves the graduate student from "reader and learner" to "job hunter" in a linear fashion by moving from foundational to complex tasks and building upon existing knowledge once it is acquired (9). All graduate students, however, may not develop or progress in a linear fashion and may meet certain milestones at differing paces or at different points in their graduate education. Kent Beeler (1991) describes a four-stage model with suggestions for when graduate students might exist in each stage based on an academic calendar, which may allow for more fluidity and individualized development along a graduate student lifecycle.

- Stage 1: Unconscious Incompetence—They do not know they do not know.
- Stage 2: Conscious Incompetence—They know they do not know.
- Stage 3: Unconscious Competence—They do not know they know.
- Stage 4: Conscious Competence—They know they know. (169)

Beeler's model highlights an additional challenge faced by the GWI: students in the earlier stages of their life cycle—one of the most important times for writing intervention, as highlighted by faculty surveys—may not be aware that they should be seeking help with their writing, and if aware, may not know what type of help they need.

One of the recommendations from the ad hoc group was to begin the GWI with the development of quality initiatives by starting small and building on success, as opposed to implementing too many activities in the first year. The third question asked was, *Reflecting on your experiences as a GWAC member, (1) what do you perceive as some of the most important activities that were achieved during the first year of the GWI?, and (2) in what ways could the GWAC have been more effective during the first year of the GWI?*

The establishment of the GWAC in and of itself was a significant accomplishment, providing a forum for campus collaboration and programming oversight that shares the work of the initiative with campus partners who contribute skills and momentum. Our first committee included a university librarian, who stated,

> As with any new committee, GWAC had growing pains as it attempted to pull together a group with adequate representation from campus units, which led to a significantly large committee. Some members were highly motivated and active contributors; others may have seen their inclusion as merely ceremonial or did not have a clear understanding of their role or

what they could contribute. As a result, attendance at committee meetings dwindled, leaving a core group of active members to do the work intended for a much larger group. The GWAC could have been more effective if we would have established a clear mission for the group, set expectations for committee members, and chosen members who expressed interest and motivation to actively contribute to the GWI.

To better make use of GWAC resources, the committee decided to more clearly delineate member roles and distinguish between advisory and core members. In this way, the GWAC could take advantage of the diverse voices and experts on campus while streamlining the work of a core group of members to drive new initiatives. In addition, the GWAC is continuously analyzing its composition to ensure all relevant parties across campus are represented.

Another success during the first year involved the development and facilitation of graduate student writing workshops. The graduate student assistant was responsible for supporting the writing workshop facilitators by promoting attendance through flyers and announcements and collecting and compiling evaluation data from the workshop participants. Reflecting on these experiences, the student shared the following:

> One of the bigger activities we started were the free-of-charge writing workshops that covered a number of different discipline areas from the humanities to the hard sciences. As I kept records of the attendance at each workshop I saw that many students were attending workshops that covered materials outside of their areas of study. I felt that students were starting to see the importance of interdisciplinarity. While all workshops had multiple attendees, if we could have provided better descriptions for each workshop, the attendance would have been much better. Now that we have had some of the workshops multiple times it will be easier to create the advertisements.

Despite graduate student survey responses indicating need for this initiative, there was low attendance at several of the writing workshops. Survey responses indicated that students need the support provided through GWI, but they are busy, which may contribute to low participation.

Most of the workshops were one hour in length, and the topics were intended to connect with the most common needs graduate students expressed through the initial surveys and focus groups and their interactions with campus faculty and support staff. The physics professor reflected on some of the challenges with preparing the content for writing workshop sessions that were open to all graduate students across diverse programs.

As a workshop facilitator, I faced the challenge of curating content that would prove the most helpful to the most students, in a short "crash course" format. My approach of tackling middle-to-high level writing topics that had proven useful to myself or my students was apparently effective in that student feedback was very positive; however, it is not clear whether the workshop truly helped students improve their writing in a tangible way. At the very least, my hope is that the content provided the students with some awareness of areas in which they may need improvement, as well as inspiration to devote more effort to the skill of writing.

The student evaluation surveys were collected by the graduate student assistant, who prepared a report to share with each workshop facilitator after the session. One workshop facilitator planned to make changes based on the student feedback.

> Given the students' requests for more experiential learning, I intend to plan future workshops with more hands-on time and more opportunities for individualized help. These may end up being longer workshops, but I want the students to leave feeling like they can do it on their own.

The final question for reflection was, *What do you believe are some of the next steps that should be addressed in the GWI?* It was apparent early in the implementation of the GWI that marketing and communicating the available resources to both graduate students and their graduate faculty advisors was an area of need. As the librarian stated,

> One of our biggest obstacles is marketing. We need a focused plan to market, through existing university communication channels, the GWI and its programming to maximize our reach to graduate students and their faculty. This needs to be a continual effort, as graduate student populations, particularly in Masters' programs, overturn quickly.

The physics professor echoed these sentiments.

> One of the greatest challenges faced by the GWI is marketing: making students aware of resources, establishing student buy-in (convincing them that using certain resources is worth their time), and matching students with the resources most appropriate for their specific needs. I promoted my own workshop heavily via personalized emails to colleagues across campus. This was very effective, as my workshop drew 3–4 times the attendance of others that same semester, which were promoted via mass emails and flyers. It is clear that targeted emails and word-of-mouth promotion can be very effective, but these are also some of the most time-consuming types of marketing efforts. One might argue, however, that perhaps a majority of GWI efforts should be spent on marketing during the early stages to ensure that the initiative gains needed momentum during this critical time.

The professor further indicated the GWAC must engage in "continual assessment of resources, and—importantly—establishing systems for archiving, evaluating, and acting upon the results of these assessments." In order to be most effective with the limited resources available for the GWI, the GWAC will need to conduct continual and consistent evaluation and assessment of the initiative and seek ongoing feedback from graduate students and faculty to identify student needs.

Emerging from an organic, grassroots effort, this initiative made vast strides over the course of two years of assessment and two years of planning and implementation, successfully recruiting an advisory committee with diverse representation, hiring a graduate writing specialist, and implementing a number of resources, including resource webpages, online tutorials, workshops, writing space, writing groups, and write-ins. We attribute the success of our program, particularly in a climate of scarce resources, to our slow and systematic approach, invested members, strategic partnerships, and diverse representation. By approaching the problem systematically and starting with a needs assessment followed by the gradual implementation of resources, the GWAC was able to build momentum, relationships, and credibility. The initial implementation of "low-hanging fruit," even if these did not address the most urgent concerns, helped ground the program and demonstrate tangible accomplishments; these early efforts and successes prompted support for hiring a graduate writing specialist, who was indispensable in taking the program to the next level. Passionate, engaged, and connected founding members contributed the sweat equity and political capital needed to launch this effort. Finally, by seeking out a diverse representation of voices, the GWAC was able not only to more thoroughly understand the needs of the entire campus and propose creative solutions but also to leverage these voices in marketing and networking, as well as to draw from this pool to recruit talent.

Looking to the future, the GWAC has identified some of the most pressing areas for further growth of the GWI: better addressing the diversity of students and their needs, as well as marketing resources effectively. To begin to address these issues, the GWAC plans to create a formal mission statement and long-term strategic plan that includes an emphasis on addressing student diversity. Toward increasing student participation, the GWAC will seek ways to help students see the initiative's relevance to their projects, to show them it is worth participating despite their busy schedules. One way to do this, which ties in with the development of a mission statement, is branding: developing a cohesive theme or metaphor for the GWI—for example, one that emphasizes project completion, developing scholarly identity, and fostering community—may make the GWI's usefulness more apparent and increase its overall visibility on campus.

ACKNOWLEDGMENTS

The authors would like to thank the coeditors of this collection for the opportunity to share the story of our graduate writing initiative. We also appreciate the feedback provided by the peer reviewers to inform the development of this chapter. We appreciate the collaboration with our UMKC colleagues Dean Denis M. Medeiros, School of Education Assistant Dean Renique Kersh, Writing Studio Director Thomas Ferrel, university librarian Fu Zhuo, School of Graduate Studies Senior Student Support Specialist Michelle Heiman, and Graduate Writing Specialist Kara Kynion. Finally, thank you to the graduate students, faculty, and staff colleagues who engaged in this work to build a graduate writing program at the University of Missouri–Kansas City.

REFERENCES

Beeler, Kent D. 1991. "Graduate Student Adjustment to Academic Life: A Four-Stage Framework." *NASPA Journal* 28 (2): 163–171.

Brady, Laura, and Nathalie Singh-Corcoran. 2016. "A Space for Change: Writing Center Partnerships to Support Graduate Writing." *WLN: A Journal of Writing Center Scholarship* 40 (5–6): 2–9.

Caplan, Nigel A., and Michelle Cox. 2016. "The State of Graduate Communication Support: Results of an International Survey." In *Supporting Graduate Student Writers: Research, Curriculum, and Program Design*, edited by Steve Simpson, Nigel A. Caplan, Michelle Cox, and Talinn Phillips, 22–47. Ann Arbor: University of Michigan Press.

Covert-Vail, Lucinda, and Scott Collard. 2012. *New Roles for New Times: Research Library Services for Graduate Students.* Association of Research Libraries. www.arl.org/storage/documents/publications/nrnt-grad-roles-20dec12.pdf.

Ferer, Elise. 2012. "Working Together: Library and Writing Center Collaboration." *Reference Services Review* 40 (4): 543–557.

Freeman, Jane. 2016. "Designing and Building a Graduate Communication Program at the University of Toronto." In *Supporting Graduate Student Writers: Research, Curriculum, and Program Design*, edited by Steve Simpson, Nigel A. Caplan, Michelle Cox, and Talinn Phillips, 222–238. Ann Arbor: University of Michigan Press.

Kamberelis, George, and Greg Dimitriadis. 2008. "Focus Groups: Strategic Articulations of Pedagogy, Politics, and Inquiry." In *Collecting and Interpreting Qualitative Materials.* 3rd ed. Norman K. Denzin and Yvonna Sessions Lincoln, 375–402. Thousand Oaks, CA: SAGE.

Klein, Emily J., Megan Riordan, Amanda Schwartz, and Stacey Sotirhos. 2009. "Dissertation Support Groups: Building a Community of Practice Using Noddings' Ethic of Care." *Learning Communities in Practice. Explorations of Educational Purpose* 4: 117–131.

Maher, Damian, Leonie Seaton, Cathi McMullen, Terry Fitzgerald, Emi Otsuji, and Alison Lee. 2008. "'Becoming and Being Writers': The Experiences of Doctoral Students in Writing Groups." *Studies in Continuing Education* 30 (3): 263–275.

Simpson, Steve. 2012. "The Problem of Graduate-Level Writing Support: Building a Cross-Campus Graduate Writing Initiative." *WPA: Writing Program Administration* 36 (1): 95–118.

Starfield, Sue, and Pamela Mort. 2016. "Written and Oral Communication Skills Support for PhD Students at the University of New South Wales." In *Supporting Graduate Student*

Writers: Research, Curriculum, and Program Design, edited by Steve Simpson, Nigel A. Caplan, Michelle Cox, and Talinn Phillips, 239–254. Ann Arbor: University of Michigan Press.

Tinto, Vincent. 1993. *Leaving College: Rethinking the Causes and Cures of Student Attrition.* 2nd ed. Chicago: University of Chicago Press.

Wang, Ting, and Linda Y. Li. 2008. "Understanding International Postgraduate Research Students' Challenges and Pedagogical Needs in Thesis Writing." *International Journal of Pedagogies and Learning* 4 (3): 88–96.

APPENDIX 14.A

GRADUATE STUDENT AND FACULTY SURVEY AND FOCUS GROUP RESULTS

Finding 1: Graduate students access some available writing resources more than others. (student survey)

Do you use the campus library resources?
Yes, from campus 59%
Yes, from home 75%
No, do not use/unsure 13%

Do you use the School of Graduate Studies thesis/dissertation workshops?
Yes, from campus 13%
Yes, from home 3%
No, do not use 72%

Do you use the Writing Studio resources?
Yes, from campus 16%
Yes, from home 4%
No, do not use 72%

What other resources do you use (write-in response)?
Online/internet 12%
Databases/guidebooks 4%
Friends/peers 4%
Librarians/other libraries 4%
Purdue OWL 4%
Professor/adviser/committee 3%

Finding 2: Graduate research and writing support varies by department. (faculty survey)

Does your department currently offer support for graduate research and/or writing?
Yes 48%
No 52%

What does your department offer?
Research course(s) 18%
Personal/one-on-one assistance 15%

Finding 3: Graduate students are interested in an initiative that would provide support for a variety of writing purposes. (student survey)

Have you completed professional writing or presentations?

Yes, presentation at conference 35%
Yes, multiauthor article 15%
Yes, single-author article 14%
Yes, grant proposal 13%
No, I have not yet completed any 51%

How could you benefit from a graduate writing initiative—what would you like to see? (write-in response)
Overall writing improvement 26%
Reviews/feedback/peer interactions 11%
Thesis/dissertation writing and formatting 10%
Grant writing 8%
Writing professionally 8%
Help prepare for publishing 6%
Specific support for international students 4%
Discipline-specific workshops 4%

Finding 4: Graduate faculty members are interested in an initiative that will help students with challenges they face in their graduate writing processes. (faculty survey)

What challenges do your students face in their graduate writing processes? (check all that apply)
Scheduling/time/work and life obligations 63%
Lack of writing confidence 49%
Lack of preparation 70%
Other challenges 32%
i.e., English as second language, lack of experience, lack of organization, writing skills need improvement

How could a campus-wide initiative support your department and its students? (write-in response)
Focus on strong writing skills 15%
Provide writing support and resources 11%
Help students write papers 9%
Provide a forum for sharing research and writing 7%

Finding 5: Graduate students are most likely to utilize online resources and to attend brief, focused programs that are free or inexpensive. (student survey)

How likely would you be to participate in each of the following initiatives? (top 5 based on responses)
1—online tutorials
2—designated writing space on campus
3—evening workshops
4—virtual writing groups
5—once-a-semester weekend retreats

An After(word)
ON THE FUTURE OF HIGHER EDUCATION

Kirsten T. Edwards

READING CIRCLES AND WRITING FREEDOM

This year I participated in an act of radical self-care and fugitivity (Roberts 2015). I started a reading circle for Black women graduate students. The reading circle began with a request from a Black woman graduate student in a different college from my own. She asked me if I would be willing to direct an independent study on race in higher education. She shared that no one in her department had expertise on race or critical perspectives. She was concerned she would not be able to write her dissertation and make the arguments she needed to make without this scholarly background. I also had the strong impression she was receiving pushback from the faculty in her college about the direction her work was taking.

At the time, I was an overworked, anxious, pretenured faculty member with little to no bandwidth (today I'm all the preceding but with tenure). I definitely did not have the time or energy to direct an independent study. I was also irritated with and resentful of the institution for *again* putting me in a position to have to clean up behind their laziness and ineptitude (Dancy, Edwards, and Davis 2018; Harley 2008). Here before me was a brilliant Black woman with strong critical inclinations who could not find the support she needed to write a substantive dissertation about race. In my mind I could hear my white and male senior colleagues telling me to limit my service and guard my time from students. And despite all the institutional rhetoric about "student support," I knew I would receive no reward for this labor.

Yet, here she stood in need of a lifeline. I knew I could not turn my back on her. So, I had to figure out a way to give this graduate student the love and support she needed without destroying myself in the process. This is where the reading circle was born. I figured if the academy was going to continue to structure itself in ways that required me to be its maidservant, I would continue to imagine revolutionary practices that attempted its destruction. I decided we would read critical perspectives on race in higher education in community with other Black women graduate students who undoubtedly needed scholarship that would validate their experiences. Also, I knew the collective aspect of the reading group would serve as a moment of marronage, a freedom space in a context of enslavement and colonization (Dancy, Edwards, and Davis 2018; Roberts 2015). We would read and discuss frankly the characteristics of the academy that would normally be disallowed in the formal curriculum. And we would speak! We would tell our stories freely and honestly in the ways the academy would never be willing to hear. Then after we told our stories, I would teach them how to write those stories for resistance.

The women who attend my reading circle are working within a sociopolitical framework that believes it is doing minoritized graduate students a favor for allowing them into the academy. Their payment for occupation is comportment to whiteness and normative masculinity. The reading circle reminds them that instead of payment they deserve reparations. Every other week we gather to read increasingly radical perspectives, offer our stories, and deny the dominant narrative intent on our silence.

EPISTEMIC AND EMBODIED INJUSTICE

Shannon Madden argues in the introduction to this collection (echoing Godbee, also in this collection) that the challenges minoritized graduate student writers face are fundamentally rooted in "epistemic injustice," the academy's commitment to de*nig(e)r*ating the ways of knowing and being in the world produced within marginalized communities. I intentionally use the term *denigrate* recognizing its etymology is to "make dark" or "to Blacken" (*Merriam-Webster*). By refusing to appreciate the epistemic positions of minoritized graduate writers, the academy reinforces notions of race and human hierarchy. It marks these students and scholars as dark/unen*light*ened and subsequently unworthy.

Academic marking happens at both the epistemic and embodied level. There are stories minoritized graduate writers attempt to tell, and there are stories the institution has already written onto their lives. When these narratives are in conflict, minoritized writers are the casualties. In her article "Beyond All Reason Indeed," Denise Baszile (2008) stories her experience as a Black woman professor teaching about race in predominantly white classrooms. She notes that despite her best efforts to introduce the subject matter as *objectively* as possible, to design curriculum that was *rigorous* and academic, the students continued to make assumptions about and then question her position on the topics. Her body was being "read as text" (252). Her Black, female body became part of the syllabus. Baszile's experiences reveal the vicious cycle of academic appeasement: the impossibility of adjustment and the presumption of incompetence that precedes and follows the bodies of minoritized faculty (Gutierrez y Muhs, Niemann, González, and Harris 2012). These tactics are only further entrenched during graduate study, a time when hypercritique and surveillance-like evaluation are excused under the rubric of advisement and disciplinary initiation.

THE POWER OF "SEXY" COUNTERNARRATIVES

Uncovering the implicit and explicit aims of academic practices that discipline counternarratives and marginalized epistemologies reveals the power of stories written by minoritized graduate writers. Stories expose and disrupt power. I am reminded of an article I wrote in 2014 (Edwards 2014). In this article, I narrated my experience as a pre-tenure Black woman scholar attempting to teach in an academic environment that had trained students and teachers to organize learning within white masculinist frames of hierarchy and power, an environment that had also relegated my scholarship to the arena of "sexy" and not substantive. It was through a revisiting of Freire's writings that I reflected on the need for dialogue and narration in the liberatory pedagogical process. To date, this article has been one of my most impactful pieces. It was published in a second- (possibly third-) tier journal, a journal that supports radical perspectives. I did not receive institutional rewards for the publication. In many ways the content and placement of the article incurred institutional rebuke. However, I have received countless emails, notes, and words of gratitude from Black women graduate students who, after searching for scholarship that would affirm their experiences, came across my article. My counternarrative—my bold, honest, fearful appeal—became the rescue they needed in the midst of a suffocating dominant narrative that felt intent on writing them out. This is the power of story! Counternarratives, narratives written from minoritized perspectives, challenge white masculinist assumptions about the fixity of objectivity and subjectivity, civility and disorder, appropriate and inappropriate, right and wrong, enlightened and endarkened (Collins 1990; Dillard 2000). This is what happens when critical scholars work to create educational environments that support graduate writers in telling their stories.

Throughout history and across various communities—particularly those that have struggled under oppression—there have been storytellers and strategizers; those of us who speak truth in the presence of the powerful, and those who use that truth as a road map to subvert systems of domination. In many ways this collection models these age-old resistant practices. These stories and strategies also serve another purpose. They are an invitation to the reader. We invite those who take seriously the propositions made in this text to mobilize with us and participate in the visionary labor of mapping liberation through writing praxis.

ENDARKENED FUTURES

I have a confession: I'm a bit obsessed with Afrofuturism. My love affair began over a decade ago with Octavia Butler's *Kindred*. Currently, my affections have been arrested by all things N. K. Jemisin. Beyond the genre's ability to tickle my imaginative senses with fantasy and otherworldliness, there is a real intellectual challenge I experience during my pleasure reading time. The Black women authors I have been most drawn to regularly imagine futures where Black people are free or working towards freedom amidst great injustice. These are not utopian societies. In fact, they are often quite dystopian and eerily familiar. The characters draw on magic, spirit, soul, body, culture, community—every real and imagined ability—to deal with terror and envision freedom. In the presence of great tragedy, there is always hope in these Black and Brown stories.

The more I read the genre, the more I recognize that my love for Afrofuturism is entangled with my ongoing preoccupation with the past, the ways oppressive practices and patterns generally assumed to have been left in history *magically* (do you hear the sarcasm in my voice??) reemerge in our contemporary lives. As an activist-scholar, a scholar committed to liberation, oppression's tenacious persistence can become overwhelming. The almost absolution of systemic injustice weighs heavy on my mind and heart. It is in those most weary moments that I escape for hope to the stories of Black women writers.

During a conversation with my coeditors, Michele asked me, "What do you think the future of higher education is if we don't pay attention to marginalized graduate student writers and their needs?" She directed this question towards me because I am the higher education researcher in the bunch. My immediate instinct was steeped in such realism that it bordered on cynical: "Academic plantations will continue to terrorize and exploit marginalized students as they have since the founding of Harvard College in 1636." Honestly, I believe there is no future for higher education. The academy will be left in bondage to its oppressive past and present. It is doomed to continue to weave in and out of patterns of domination and dehumanization.

Still, as Afrofuturism has taught me, there is always hope. Higher education probably will never listen. It was founded on a commitment to not listen (Dancy, Edwards, and Davis 2018; Edwards 2010). In truth, higher education as constituted today, requires a caste-based social order to survive. Despite its dominant narrative as an engine of social equality, it continues to participate in social reproduction. It is fundamentally rooted in a system of winners and losers. Nevertheless, instead of feeling defeated by this reality, I am compelled to question, What magic will minoritized graduate writers produce in response to this bleak present and unknown future? What kinds of educational futures will they imagine if we diligently create spaces and strategies committed to their freedom? I still have hope. My hope is not in the progression of higher education but in the tenacity, brilliance, and power of the stories I know minoritized graduate writers will continue to tell and the supportive strategies their fellow justice workers will continue to create.

REFERENCES

Baszile, Denise Taliaferro. 2008. "Beyond All Reason Indeed: The Pedagogical Promise of Critical Race Testimony." *Race Ethnicity and Education* 11 (3): 251–265.

Collins, Patricia Hill. 1990. *Black Feminist Thought: Knowledge, Consciousness, and the Politics of Empowerment.* Crows Nest, AU: Unwin Hyman.

Dancy, T. Elon, Kirsten T. Edwards, and James Earl Davis. 2018. "Historically White Universities and Plantation Politics: Anti-Blackness and Higher Education in the Black Lives Matter Era." *Urban Education* 53 (2): 176–195.

Dillard, Cynthia B. 2000. "The Substance of Things Hoped For, the Evidence of Things Not Seen: Examining an Endarkened Feminist Epistemology in Educational Research and Leadership." *International Journal of Qualitative Studies in Education* 13 (6): 661–681.

Edwards, Kirsten T. 2010. "Incidents in the Life of Kirsten T. Edwards: A Personal Examination of the Academic In-between Space." *Journal of Curriculum Theorizing* 26 (1): 113–128.

Edwards, Kirsten T. 2014. "Teach with Me: The Promise of a Raced Politic for Social Justice in College Classrooms." *Journal of Critical Thought and Praxis* 2 (2): 1–20.

Gutierrez y Muhs, Gabriella, Yolanda Flores Niemann, Carmen G. González, and Angela P. Harris, eds. 2012. *Presumed Incompetent: The Intersections of Race and Class for Women in Academia.* Logan: Utah State University Press.

Harley, Debra A. 2008. "Maids of Academe: African American Women Faculty at Predominately White Institutions." *Journal of African American Studies* 12 (1): 19–36.

Merriam-Webster, s.v. "denigrate." https://www.merriam-webster.com/dictionary/denigrate.

Roberts, Neil. 2015. *Freedom as Marronage.* Chicago: University of Chicago Press.

ABOUT THE CONTRIBUTORS

Noro Andriamanalina is at the University of Minnesota–Twin Cities as director of Academic and Professional Development for the graduate school. She oversees initiatives to support graduate students in establishing positive relationships with advisors, ensuring timely degree completion, and developing skills to prepare for multiple career options. She and Jasmine Kar Tang are co-principal investigators on research examining the writing experiences of Indigenous students and/or students of color in doctoral programs. She is also working on a project exploring factors that influence career paths of doctoral students across disciplines.

LaKela Atkinson earned her BA in English with summa cum laude distinction in 2007 and her MA in English in 2010 from North Carolina Central University (NCCU). While completing her graduate degree, Atkinson worked as a writing consultant in NCCU's Writing Studio, and after earning her master's degree in 2010, she worked as an English instructor at Louisburg College and a professional writing consultant at NCCU. In 2011, Atkinson transitioned full time to NCCU, where she served nearly six years as a professional writing consultant in the Writing and Speaking Studio. Atkinson has presented at several local and national writing conferences, including Southeastern Writing Center Association (SWCA) conferences. In 2012, she received the North Carolina Professional Tutor of the Year/Consultant of the Year Award for the first North Carolina Writing Center Network (NCWCN) and SWCA Statewide Conference. Currently, Atkinson is a second-year PhD student in East Carolina University's (ECU) English rhetoric, writing, and professional communication program. She has a passion for bridging the achievement gap in writing for African Americans and students of color.

Daniel V. Bommarito earned his PhD in rhetoric, composition, and linguistics from Arizona State University in 2015. He is currently an assistant professor at Bowling Green State University, where he teaches in the doctoral program in rhetoric and writing and directs the writing program. Dan researches writing theory and pedagogy at undergraduate and graduate levels, and his work has appeared in *Composition Studies*, *E-Learning and Digital Media*, and the *Journal of Writing Research*, as well as in edited collections.

Elizabeth Brown, MA, is the program coordinator of the infection prevention program and the system administrator of the patent safety reporting network at the University of Washington Medical Center in Seattle. Elizabeth's research includes hospital administration at large academic medical centers. She is currently designing and implementing a health sciences student-driven hand-hygiene monitoring program at the medical center.

Rachael Cayley is an associate professor (teaching stream) at the Graduate Centre for Academic Communication at the University of Toronto, where she teaches both academic writing and academic speaking to graduate students. Before joining the University of Toronto, she worked as an editor at Oxford University Press in Toronto. She has a PhD in philosophy from the New School for Social Research and a BA in political science from the University of British Columbia. Rachael blogs about academic writing for graduate students at *Explorations of Style*.

ABOUT THE CONTRIBUTORS

Amanda E. Cuellar is a native *fronteriza* from the El Paso/Juarez borderlands. She received both her BA and MA from the University of Texas at El Paso and taught high school English for six years before pursuing a PhD at the University of Oklahoma. Her academic interests include Chicana/o/x literature, border studies, and Mexican film and media. Her dissertation project, titled *Frameworks of Healing: The Process of Reconciliation and Transformation in Gloria Anzaldúa*, examines Anzaldúa's notion of *la frontera* in contemporary Chicana/o/x texts and media.

Kirsten T. Edwards is associate professor and associate department chair of Educational Leadership and Policy Studies, as well as core affiliate faculty for Women's and Gender Studies and the Center for Social Justice at the University of Oklahoma (OU) in Norman, Oklahoma. Her research merges philosophies of higher education, college curriculum, and pedagogy. More specifically, Dr. Edwards is interested in the ways sociocultural identity and context influence teaching and learning in postsecondary education.

Michele Eodice is emeritus director of the OU Writing Center at the University of Oklahoma. She now serves as the senior writing fellow in the Center for Faculty Excellence. She is also a codirector of The Meaningful Writing Project (meaningfulwritingproject .net) and coauthor of *The Everyday Writing Center: A Community of Practice*. With Shannon Madden, she coedited a 2016 special issue of *Praxis: A Writing Center Journal* on access and equity for graduate student writers.

Dr. Wonderful Faison is an assistant professor in the School of Arts and Sciences at Langston University. She is interested in the intersections among race, class, gender, and sexuality in the writing center. Specifically, she is interested in how writing center design affects historically marginalized populations. Currently, her work is centered on the use of Black language in the writing center, the use of and aiding people to use linguistic difference in academic writing, and tutor approaches to marking and addressing microaggressions in both writing and the writing center.

Amy Fenstermaker is a lecturer with continuing appointment in the Merritt Writing Program at UC Merced. Dr. Fenstermaker's teaching experience includes first-year writing, writing in the disciplines, and rhetorical theory courses, with scholarly interests in pedagogy, faculty development, transfer, and threshold concepts. She is currently conducting a classroom research project involving the use of threshold concepts in first-year writing courses.

Jennifer Friend is the dean of the College of Arts and Sciences and professor of education at Rockhurst University in Kansas City. Her twenty-six years of experience in education include faculty and administrative roles in educational leadership, graduate education, assessment, and academic affairs. She began her career in K-12 schools as a middle-grades principal and language-arts teacher. Dr. Friend's research focuses on educational leadership and issues of social justice in US public education. She is currently collaborating on an oral history and educational website project titled *Kansas City Speaks: Stories of School Desegregation*. She is the coauthor of the book *Great Expectations: What Kids Want from Our Urban Public Schools* and coeditor of the book *Principal 2.0: Technology and Educational Leadership*. Recent publications also have appeared in the open-access *International Journal of Learning, Teaching and Educational Research*, the *Journal of Urban Learning, Teaching, and Research*, and *Educational Studies*.

Beth Godbee is an educational consultant, entrepreneur, and public writer focused on everyday living for justice. In 2018, Beth left a faculty position after being promoted with tenure to associate professor of English (writing studies) at Marquette University. As an independent scholar, Beth continues to pursue research in matters of relational communication; social interaction; and racial, social, and environmental justice. Among her publications are articles in *Research in the Teaching of English*, the *Community Literacy Journal*, *Feminist Teacher*, *College English*, *The Writing Center Journal*, *Inside Higher Ed*, and *Praxis*. Beth's current projects include several pieces on microaggressions and trauma in higher education; her blog *Heart-Head-Hands.com* (feeling, thinking, and doing for justice); and a book project on epistemic justice.

Hope Jackson is a lecturer in the North Carolina A&T State University English Department. She teaches courses ranging from composition to African American Film and Culture, as well as Hip-Hop Discourse. Hope's research interests involve interpreting the complexity of storytelling and narrative discourse in rhetorical and literary genres. Her current projects include a pending journal article that critically examines the absence of HBCU voices in the composition field, as well as a forthcoming book project that presents a compelling narrative that examines the voices of residents from a North Carolina black beach community who sought refuge from a segregated society through community and recreational landownership. Select publications include the journal article "We are Family: I Got All My (HBCU) Sisters With Me" in the fall 2016 *Composition Studies* issue, along with book chapters entitled "Yes! Black Folks Can Tan Too!" in the *Critical Black Studies Reader* edited by Rochelle Brock, Dara Nix-Stevenson, and Paul Chamness Miller-Kuriyama, as well as "Unpacking Notions of Citizenship through James Baldwin's *Another Country*" in *Critical Insights: Civil Rights Literature, Past and Present* edited by Christopher Varlack. She received her PhD from UNC–Greensboro in cultural studies.

Karen Keaton Jackson is a native of Detroit, Michigan, and began her academic career at Hampton University in Virginia, earning a bachelor of science in English secondary education with summa cum laude distinction. She went on to receive her master's and PhD in English composition from Wayne State University in 2004. While pursuing her PhD, she was awarded a predoctoral fellowship at LeMoyne College in Syracuse, New York, where she taught undergraduate and graduate courses on multicultural literacy. Since arriving to North Carolina Central University in 2004 as an assistant professor, she has become the director of the Writing Studio, coordinates the campus-wide writing intensive program, and has served on the executive boards of the International Writing Centers Association, the Southeastern Writing Center Association, and the Council of Writing Program Administrators. In May 2015, she received a University of North Carolina Board of Governors Award for Teaching Excellence. In addition, she was a facilitator at the International Writing Centers Association (IWCA) Summer Institute in 2009, 2016, and 2018. She maintains an active research agenda on the interrelated notions of literacy, race, and identity in the writing classroom, and more recently she has focused on composition instruction and writing centers at HBCUs and on how writing center tutorials can impact student success.

Haadi Jafarian PhD is an assistant professor in the Department of Computer Science and Engineering at the University of Colorado at Denver. His area of expertise is security and privacy of cyber systems and infrastructures. Haadi also serves as the director of the Active Cyber and Infrastructure Defense (ACID) lab, where he supervises several PhD students.

Dr. **Alexandria Lockett** is an assistant professor of English at Spelman College, where she codirected the writing-intensive initiative (2016–2018) and organized the institution's first-ever Art+Feminism *Wikipedia* edit-a-thon (2017). She writes about the technological politics of race, surveillance, and inclusion in her forthcoming coauthored book *Race, Rhetoric, and Research Ethics* (WAC Clearinghouse), articles in *Composition Studies* and *Enculturation*, and chapters featured in *Out in the Center* (Utah State University Press), *Bad Ideas about*

Writing (West Virginia University Digital Publishing Institute), and the forthcoming collection *Black Perspectives on Writing Program Administration: From the Margins to the Center* (SWR Press). An extended biography is available via her portfolio at: www.alexandrialockett.com.

Shannon Madden holds a PhD in composition, rhetoric, and literacy from the University of Oklahoma. She has been an invited keynote speaker at multiple annual meetings of the *Consortium on Graduate Communication* as well as the inaugural *Writing through the Lifespan* conference. With her corecipient Sandra L. Tarabochia, she won the 2017 CCCC Emergent Researcher Grant from the National Council of Teachers of English. Her coedited and coauthored work on equitable and inclusive practices for student writers has been published in *Praxis: A Writing Center Journal* and *Kairos PraxisWiki*, presented at numerous national and international conferences, and awarded by Computers and Composition Digital Press.

Kendra L. Mitchell is a writing center specialist and instructor at Florida A&M University, where she earned her BA in English. She holds an MA and PhD from Florida State University. Some of her research interests include the intersections of language and identities throughout the African diaspora. Through her recent Fulbright guest lectureship in South Africa and her forthcoming publication, "'African American' Anglophone Caribbean Writers in an HBCU Writing Center," she explores these intersections.

Michelle M. Paquette is an associate research professor in the Department of Physics and Astronomy at the University of Missouri–Kansas City. She obtained her BSc in Chemistry from the University of Guelph, Ontario, Canada, in 2006, and her PhD in chemistry as an NSERC Canada Graduate Scholar and a P.E.O. Endowed Scholar from the University of Victoria, Canada, in 2010. Her first foray into professional writing occurred during graduate school, when she worked as a freelance copyeditor for the *European Journal of Inorganic Chemistry*. Foremost a researcher, she currently studies the basic and applied materials science and condensed matter physics of unusual thin-film electronic materials and has received a Defense Threat Reduction Agency Young Investigator Award (2014) and an Intel Outstanding Researcher Award (2015) for her work. She has coauthored more than twenty peer-reviewed articles, has been an active member of the UMKC Graduate Writing Advisory Committee since 2014, and additionally is the local coordinator for the American Chemical Society Project SEED program that facilitates research internships for financially disadvantaged high school students.

Rochelle (Shelley) Rodrigo is associate director of the writing program and Online Writing and associate professor in rhetoric, composition, and the teaching of English (RCTE) in the Department of English at the University of Arizona. She researches how "newer" technologies better facilitate communicative interactions, specifically teaching and learning. As well as coauthoring three editions of *The Wadsworth/Cengage Guide to Research*, Shelley also coedited *Rhetorically Rethinking Usability* (Hampton Press). Her scholarly work has appeared in *Computers and Composition*, *C&C Online*, *Technical Communication Quarterly*, *Teaching English in the Two-Year College*, *EDUCAUSE Quarterly*, the *Journal of Interactive Technology & Pedagogy*, and *Enculturation*, as well as various edited collections. In 2014 she was awarded Old Dominion University's annual Teaching with Technology Award and in 2012 the Digital Humanities High Powered Computing Fellowship.

Julia Romberger is the coordinator of the professional writing program, English Department Lab coordinator, and associate professor of professional writing in the Department of English at Old Dominion University. She researches the environment's impact upon writing practices and the labor conditions of faculty who do technology-related service for writing programs. Her work has appeared in *Computers and*

Composition, the *International Journal of the Image*, the edited collection *Pressures on Technical Communication Programs in a New Age of Austerity*, the *Proceedings of the Annual Simulation Symposium*, and the proceedings of the *INTED Conference*.

Lisa Russell-Pinson PhD is faculty associate for writing in the graduate school at the University of North Carolina at Charlotte, where she teaches academic writing to graduate students and oversees the university's dissertation support services. In addition to examining affective factors in high-stakes writing, Lisa's research interests include English for academic purposes, curriculum development, and written medical discourse.

Jennifer Salvo is the head of Resource Sharing and Graduate Student Services at the University of Missouri–Kansas City Libraries. In this role, she has significantly transformed the university's interlibrary loan service, which processes over forty thousand requests annually. She helped established the UMKC Graduate Writing Initiative, a campus-wide effort to improve and maintain the quality of graduate student writing by providing workshops, online research, and personalized help. In 2016, she was named Outstanding New Librarian by the Missouri Library Association, and she served as principal investigator for the Amigos Library Services Opportunity Award, a grant to create a digital and physical display of library resources to support student writing. In addition, she conducts research on library user behavior, interlibrary-loan use, and resource sharing practices, with emphasis on efficiencies and cost effectiveness. Her book chapter entitled "Interlibrary Loan and Serving Graduate Students," in *Transforming Libraries to Serve Graduate Students* edited by Crystal Renfro and Cheryl Stiles, is forthcoming from the Association of College & Research Libraries (ACRL) Publications.

Richard Sévère, a graduate of Florida A&M University and Purdue University, is an associate professor of English at Valparaiso University, where he teaches medieval literature and business/professional writing. In addition to his scholarly focus in Medieval romance and epic, he also has research interests in social justice in writing center theory and praxis. He is coeditor of the recent book *Out in the Center: Public Controversies and Private Struggles*.

Cecilia D. Shelton is a Black feminist technical rhetorician whose broad interests explore the intersections of cultural rhetorics, technical communication, and social movement/activist rhetorics. Her work also interrogates the tension between oppressive power structures and the transformative potential of writing classrooms and writing centers, both of which are sites of activism for her. She is a doctoral candidate at East Carolina University studying rhetoric, writing, and professional communication.

Pamela Strong Simmons earned a bachelor's degree in speech and theatre at Albany State University, a master's degree in English at Northwestern State University of Louisiana, and a PhD at Walden University. She is an associate professor of English at Winston-Salem State University, where she directs the writing in the major program and formerly directed the writing center. In 2009, she received the James E. Patterson Outstanding Teacher Award and earned a service award for the writing in the major program. Her professional service includes former regional director of the NC English Teachers Association; participation in the National Council of Teachers of English, where she was appointed to the Committee Against Racism and Bias in the Teaching of English; participation in the Council of Writing Program Administrators; cofounder of the North Carolina HBCU Writing Center Consortium; coadvisor of Sigma Tau Delta International English Honors Society; and a former NC Ready for Success Fellow.

Jasmine Kar Tang is at the University of Minnesota–Twin Cities as co-director of the Center for Writing, affiliate graduate faculty member in literacy and rhetorical studies, and assistant director of the Minnesota Writing Project. Her research interests involve critical race and ethnic studies, migration studies, and writing studies. She and Noro Andriamanalina are co-principal investigators on research examining the writing experiences of Indigenous students and students of color in U.S. doctoral programs.

Anna K. (Willow) Treviño is pursuing a PhD in composition, rhetoric, and literacy at the University of Oklahoma and is program assistant at the OU Writing Center. As a Xicana Tejana first-generation college student from a working-class background, her primary research interest is the intersection of the politics of education and identity and focuses on the dynamic relationships between the writing and literacy experiences of minoritized students and space (writing centers, first-year composition, and the First-Year Experience). She is committed to developing more just ways of teaching and interacting across communities.

Maurice Wilson, a graduate of Florida A&M University and the University of Illinois at Chicago, is an assistant director of pedagogy and training in the writing center at the University of Houston, where he also oversees the developmental writing program and teaches professional writing methods for PhD candidates in the College of Education. As a retired army officer, his research examines military and veteran writing experiences in academia. He also has research interests in the writing experiences for students in HBCUs.

Anne Zanzucchi is an associate teaching professor in writing studies at the University of California–Merced. With university teaching experience in first-year composition, science and technical writing, and pedagogy, Dr. Zanzucchi's scholarly interests are in classroom practice, faculty development, and academic planning. Her service and administrative record focuses on educational policy, with system-wide and campus leadership experience. Recent projects focus on writing assessment and access/equity factors in higher education.

INDEX

Ableism/disability, 10
Academic acculturation/enculturation/ socialization, 10, 16, 73, 75, 156, 199, 218–241
Accountability, 15, 18, 86, 185, 191, 192, 198, 204, 208, 209, 213, 244, 249
Across the Disciplines, special issue on "Graduate Writing Across the Disciplines," 10, 36, 73, 83, 87, 140, 221
Advisor (of dissertation committee), 13, 15, 17, 22, 23, 25(n3), 35, 36, 42, 47, 48, 52, 60, 111, 113, 115, 116, 117, 128, 140, 142, 148, 149, 151, 156–173, 175, 177, 178, 179, 181, 182, 183, 184, 185–187, 188, 191, 193, 194, 214, 218, 219, 225, 226, 228, 230, 258, 260, 261, 269, 272. *See also* chair; supervisor
Agency, 15, 16, 21, 37, 39, 44, 62, 65, 84, 101, 149, 150, 185, 188
Answerability, 18
Attrition, 4, 5, 10, 11, 13, 19, 215, 218, 219, 230. *See also* completion

Belonging, 11, 13, 14, 20, 21, 23, 35, 44, 53, 59, 64, 66, 67, 68, 70, 75, 76, 78, 81, 86, 111, 120, 125, 133
Black students, 4, 8, 11, 12, 13, 17, 40, 44, 45, 53, 55, 65, 73–91, 92–107, 118, 120, 121, 125, 139–155, 278–281
Black tax, 13, 37, 40, 83, 87, 139, 151
Body/Embodiment, 8, 11, 13, 44, 53, 56, 66, 97, 98, 99, 100, 101, 104, 105, 118, 139–155, 280, 281
Border culture, border crossing, borderlands, 22, 96, 131–136
Burrows, Cedric, 10, 12–13, 37, 40, 83, 84, 87, 139, 151

Campus partners/campus support, 17, 48, 192–197, 193–194, 219, 223, 224, 229, 230, 257–277. *See also* collaboration: across campus
Caplan, Nigel, 10, 73, 139, 214, 219, 220, 258
Care, 8, 15, 19, 63, 67, 104, 114, 140, 212, 266, 278, 281; self-care, 41, 139–140, 150, 278. *See also* love

Casanave, Christine Pearson, 4, 9, 83, 156, 174, 175, 177, 183, 218, 225
Chair (of dissertation committee), 13, 15, 17, 22, 23, 25(n3), 35, 36, 42, 47, 48, 52, 60, 111, 113, 115, 116, 117, 128, 140, 142, 148, 149, 151, 156–173, 175, 177, 178, 179, 181, 182, 183, 184, 185–187, 188, 191, 193, 194, 214, 218, 219, 225, 226, 228, 230, 258, 260, 261, 269, 272. *See also* advisor; supervisor
Class, 37, 42, 54–57, 62, 69, 75, 77, 80, 81, 93–95, 96, 98, 100, 102–105, 118, 125, 131, 214; classism, 21, 97, 99, 101, 148; role of higher education in reproducing, 54–57, 92
Collaboration, 15, 17, 23, 35, 73, 82, 88, 220, 226, 228, 229, 245, 258; collaboration across campus, 17, 48, 192–197, 193–194, 219, 223, 224, 229, 230, 257–277; collaboration across power differentials, 44, 158; collaborative learning, 86, 220, 221; collaborative mentorship, 17 (*see also* mentorship, feminist co-mentoring); collaborative writing partnerships, 36, 44–47, 86, 156–173
Collins, Patricia Hill, 45, 56, 58, 61, 111, 280
Colonizing, 7, 14, 16, 18, 54–59, 69, 126, 279
Community, 3–31, 35, 40, 42, 44, 47–49, 61, 63–70; community of practice, 8, 9, 23, 73, 88, 102, 243–256
Completion, 23, 116, 174, 175, 177, 178, 185, 215, 222, 224–225, 238, 244, 273. *See also* attrition
Consortium on Graduate Communication, 9, 220, 232
Cox, Michelle, 10, 25(n2), 73, 139, 214, 219, 220, 258
Crenshaw, Kimberlé, 35, 47
Critical race theory, 6, 11, 47, 52–72, 111, 144, 145

Decolonizing, 18, 54
Digital/online programs, 119, 134, 135, 232, 260–266, 273, 276

290 INDEX

Discipline (academic), disciplinary/disciplinarity, 5, 8–19, 35, 42, 46, 76, 77, 86, 88, 119, 126, 128, 129, 140, 142–149, 152, 156, 157, 165, 169, 171, 181, 186–188, 190, 203, 207, 209, 219–221, 223, 225–228, 230, 231, 242–246, 254(n1), 258, 261, 264, 269, 271, 277, 280

Discourse conventions, discourse norms, 9, 11, 13, 14, 44, 59, 61, 62, 73, 76–80, 82–88, 99, 101–103, 105, 128, 131, 132, 144, 156, 170, 218, 220, 226, 229, 243, 245, 246, 250, 254(n1), 266

Dissertation boot camp/completion camp, 23, 86, 126, 198–217, 244, 248

Dissertation (in passim), 11, 16, 17, 22, 23, 36, 38, 39, 41, 44, 45, 65, 66, 82, 83, 86, 87, 113, 116, 119, 126, 127, 132–134, 139–155, 156, 157, 174–197, 198–217, 218, 219, 220, 222, 226, 239, 242–256, 260, 261, 263, 265, 266, 276, 277, 278

Emerging scholars, 8, 9, 74, 77, 86, 102, 127, 128, 150, 161, 162

Emotion, 23, 36, 87, 88, 96, 104, 111, 114, 121, 139, 174–197, 214, 265; emotional labor, 104, 139; emotional support, 121, 174–197

Eodice, Michele, 6, 12, 16, 36, 88, 102, 109

Epistemology, 3, 5, 7, 11, 13, 14, 16, 17, 20, 38, 53, 56, 57, 126, 132, 143, 144–146, 150, 242, 251; epistemic justice/injustice, 13, 14, 16, 19, 35–51, 53, 144–146, 279, 280. *See also* ways of knowing

Faculty development, 8–9, 15–16, 18, 46, 48, 89, 121, 127, 135, 146–149, 151, 168–172, 185–187, 192–193, 225, 230–231, 247, 248, 253, 261, 269

Faculty diversity, 5, 10–11, 37, 38, 40, 53, 59–69, 89, 96, 98, 110–111, 119–121, 127, 133, 147, 151, 278, 280. *See also* faculty of color

Faculty of color, 5, 10–11, 37, 38, 40, 53, 59–69, 89, 96, 98, 110–111, 119–121, 127, 133, 147, 151, 278, 280. *See also* faculty diversity

Feak, Christine, 224, 240, 242

Feedback (on student writing), 14, 22, 37, 42, 48, 77, 85, 86, 88, 99, 116, 129, 132, 140, 142–152, 156–172, 178, 181, 184, 186–187, 189–191, 193, 194, 199, 220–222, 226–227, 229–231, 238–241, 242, 243, 247, 248, 250, 264, 269

Feminist/feminism, 17, 20, 36, 37, 44–49, 65, 66, 86–87, 126, 143; Black feminism, 45, 56, 58, 111, 281; Latinx feminism, 45, 131

Freire, 15, 56, 58, 59, 78, 93, 95, 280

Future, 16, 18, 24, 55, 58, 60, 164, 177, 188, 215, 229, 238, 273, 278–282; Afrofuturism, 281, 282

Gatekeepers/gatekeeping, 12, 21, 69, 125, 134, 140, 142, 146, 148, 149, 152

Gender, 5, 42, 53, 65, 70, 102, 108, 121, 142, 144, 145, 152, 153, 214, 219, 225

Genre, 11, 18, 166, 167–169, 172, 179, 189, 218, 220–224, 229, 230, 242, 243, 245, 253(n1); high stakes genres, 13; "mutt genres," 245

Grollman, Eric, 10, 37, 38, 42, 47

Hidden curriculum, 11, 38, 92–107, 227

Hispanic Serving Institutions, 20, 87, 93, 96, 132; research in, 218–234

Historically Black Colleges and Universities (HBCUs), 20, 21, 63, 73–91, 108–122, 127, 128

hooks, bell, 58, 63, 93, 95, 110, 111, 118

Identity, 6, 7, 12, 15, 17, 18, 22, 39, 42, 56, 63, 76, 83, 87, 88, 95–97, 102, 105, 125, 145, 175; cultural/ethnic/racial identity, 10, 12, 69, 83, 95, 97–98, 105, 143, 144, 146; epistemic justice and, 12, 39, 43, 44, 69; identity development, 171, 213, 244, 266; marginalized identity groups, 12, 16, 37, 56, 83; writer/researcher/scholarly/disciplinary identity, 17, 18, 19, 147, 156, 204–206, 213, 220, 225, 229, 266, 273; writing and, 11, 15, 17, 87, 144, 147

Impostorship, impostor syndrome/phenomenon, 13, 75, 76, 84

Inclusion, 3–6, 10, 15, 17, 20, 21, 23, 24, 54, 73, 76, 87, 92, 104, 109, 147, 149, 152(n1), 172, 219, 220, 265, 270

Indigenous students, 5, 7, 22, 54–55, 96, 140–142, 145, 149–151, 152(n2)

Interdisciplinarity, 23, 143, 209–210, 230, 231, 242, 271

International students, 9, 22, 101, 125, 128, 139, 145, 182–184, 224, 225, 243, 254, 260–261, 269

Intersectionality, 42, 43

Latinx students, 4, 22, 92–107, 125, 131–135, 139, 144, 152(n1)

Literacy practices, 12, 80, 81, 84, 95, 100, 126, 128, 156, 157, 219, 223, 226; information literacy, 229, 269; literacy myth, 81

Lived experience, 5, 6, 12, 15, 19, 21, 24, 46, 54, 56, 57, 61, 62, 70, 74, 103, 125, 126, 128, 132, 143, 144, 148, 170, 199, 201, 214
Love, 8, 15, 19, 63, 67, 104, 114, 140, 212, 266, 278, 281; pedagogy of love, 15, 19. *See also* care

Madden, Shannon, 11, 109, 129, 220, 279
Marginalization, 4, 5, 7, 10–13, 15, 16, 18–20, 24, 36–39, 41, 42, 54, 84, 86, 105, 125, 127, 131, 146, 149, 172, 175, 279, 280, 281
Mentorship, mentoring, 6, 7, 8, 11, 12, 14–25, 36, 37, 47, 65, 74, 75, 77, 79, 80–83, 86, 88, 108–122, 125, 127, 128, 134–135, 151, 157–172, 185, 193, 218–220, 225, 227, 228, 231, 245, 247–248; feminist co-mentoring, 20–21, 23, 36, 44–49, 86–87, 89, 126, 151
Metadiscourse, 210–211
Microaggressions, 10, 11, 36, 37, 42
Minority Serving Institutions (MSIs). *See* Hispanic Serving Institutions; Historically Black Colleges and Universities
Multilingual students. *See* international students

Native American students. *See* Indigenous students

Pedagogy, 10, 92, 96, 104, 105, 110, 111, 245–256; critical race pedagogy, 111; pedagogy of love, 15, 19
Phillips, Talinn, 10, 17, 73, 139, 213, 214, 220, 227, 243, 244
Postcolonial, 53, 54, 58, 59, 63, 69
Power, 17, 35, 38, 39, 41, 42, 43, 45, 62, 82, 84, 101, 125, 127, 143, 149, 151, 280; Black power, 44; empowerment, 15, 16, 17, 23, 45, 119, 220, 221, 281; power over, 44, 103, 106(n6), 140, 142, 148, 150; power with, 45, 47, 133
Praxis: A Writing Center Journal, special issue on "Access and Equity in Graduate Writing Support," 12–15, 37, 109
Predominantly/historically white institutions (PWIs/HWIs), 7, 12, 13, 17, 20–22, 53, 59, 63, 67, 73, 81, 94, 95–98, 100, 102–104, 106(n1), 131–132, 134–135, 140
Presumed Incompetent, 10, 13, 14, 37, 38, 44, 151, 280
Privilege, 5, 15, 16, 20, 22, 24, 38, 39, 42, 54, 56, 57, 59, 63, 66, 67, 75, 80, 82, 83, 84, 87, 94, 125, 144, 148, 170

Productivity, 11, 87, 182, 192, 199, 200, 202–206, 208–210, 213, 221, 222, 231, 268
Programs, programmatic approaches, 5, 9–10, 13, 20, 23, 48, 118, 120, 126, 139, 141, 151, 170, 186, 192–194, 198–217, 218–241, 242–256, 257–277
Psychology/psychological factors, 36, 68, 174–197. *See also* emotion
Publishing/publication, 189, 220, 222, 225, 229, 230, 238, 277

Racism, 11, 19, 21, 22, 56, 60, 83, 97, 99, 101, 104, 105, 128, 140, 141, 143, 149
Resilience, 47, 135, 140, 141, 149–150

Science, technology, engineering, and mathematics (STEM), 3, 182, 219, 222–224, 231
Self-efficacy, 23, 84, 86, 198–217
Simpson, Steve, 9, 10, 23, 73, 139, 177, 198, 214, 219, 220, 228, 258, 259, 265
Social justice, 58, 59, 64–66
Standard American English/Standard Written English, 12, 15, 22, 75, 80, 84, 95, 145, 157, 245
Student success, 4, 11, 18, 19, 23, 24, 41, 43, 46, 58, 73, 74, 76, 78, 80, 81, 85–88, 93–95, 97, 111, 112, 115, 117–118, 121, 125, 127, 129, 132, 134, 141, 150, 175, 181, 186, 187, 191, 208, 214, 218, 219, 231, 244, 253, 266, 268
Supervisor (of dissertation committee), 13, 15, 17, 22, 23, 25(n3), 35, 36, 42, 47, 48, 52, 60, 111, 113, 115, 116, 117, 128, 140, 142, 148, 149, 151, 156–173, 175, 177, 178, 179, 181, 182, 183, 184, 185–187, 188, 191, 193, 194, 214, 218, 219, 225, 226, 228, 230, 258, 260, 261, 269, 272. *See also* advisor; chair
Surviving/survival/survivance, 17, 112, 119, 133, 135, 149, 282; "survival-of-the-fittest" culture in academia, 11
Supporting Graduate Student Writers collection, 10, 73, 139, 214, 219, 220
Swales, John, 9, 11, 224, 226, 240, 242

Third space, 97, 98, 132
Time pressure, 68, 82, 108, 176, 177, 278; time to degree, 4, 19, 175, 177, 178, 182; writing time, 199, 201–207, 209, 211–212, 215, 238, 267
Tokenism, 10, 13, 96
Trauma, 11, 19, 20, 21, 35–51, 126, 128, 129

Ways of knowing, 3, 5, 7, 11, 13, 14, 16, 17, 20, 38, 53, 56, 57, 126, 132, 143, 144–146, 150, 242, 251. *See also* epistemology

Whiteness/whiteliness, 22, 66, 96, 98, 118, 132, 147, 148, 279; white fragility, 148

Writing Centers, 12, 15, 21, 35, 40, 45, 48, 75, 80, 82, 85–87, 92–107, 108, 109, 115, 116, 118–119, 126, 127, 186, 192, 228, 231, 244, 253, 258–259, 265

Writing Pedagogies for Masters and Doctoral Writers, 9, 73, 198

www.ingramcontent.com/pod-product-compliance
Lightning Source LLC
Chambersburg PA
CBHW060515080526
44586CB00012B/489